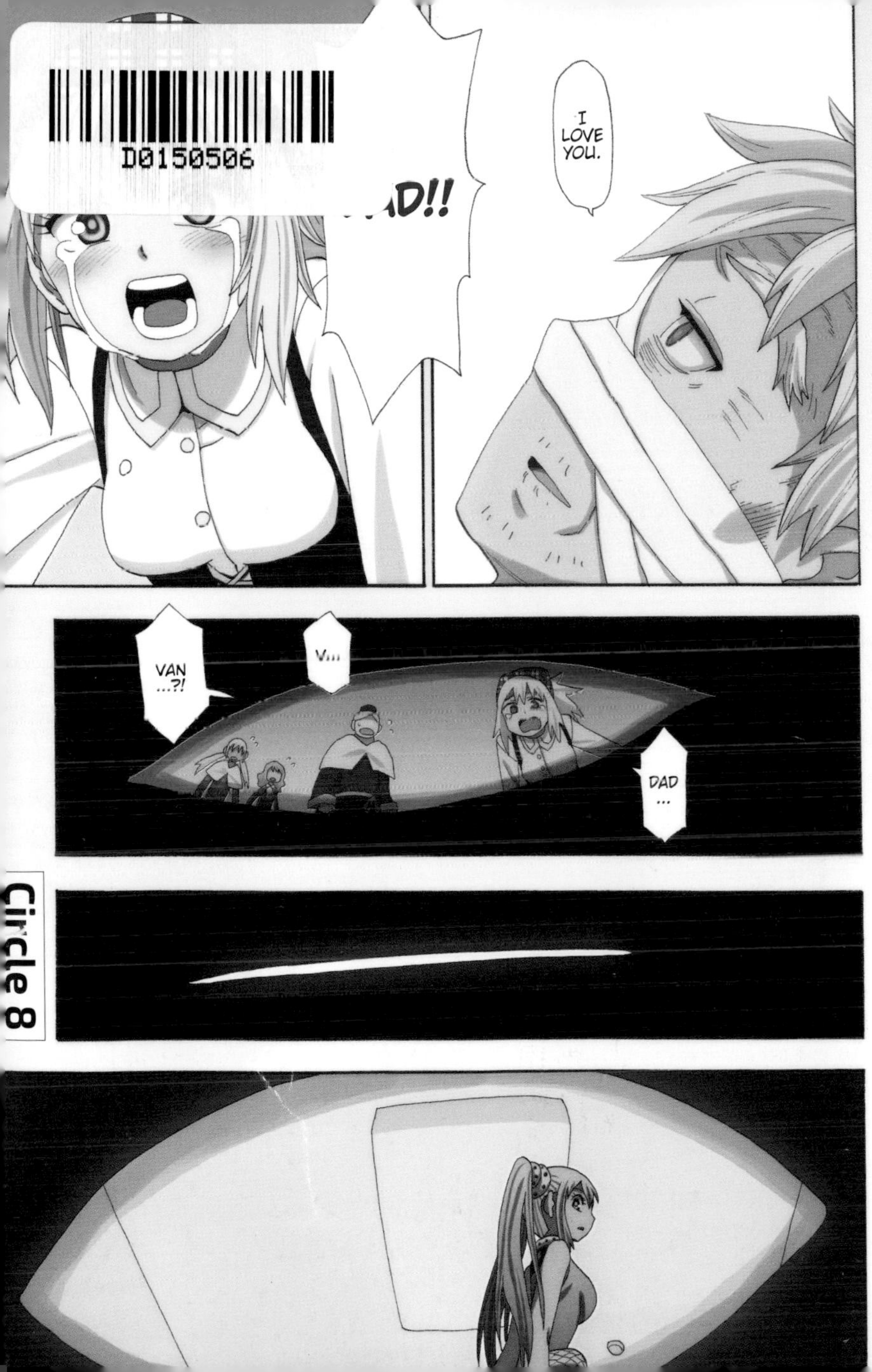
I LOVE YOU.
AD!!
DAD ...
V...
VAN ...?!

Circle 8

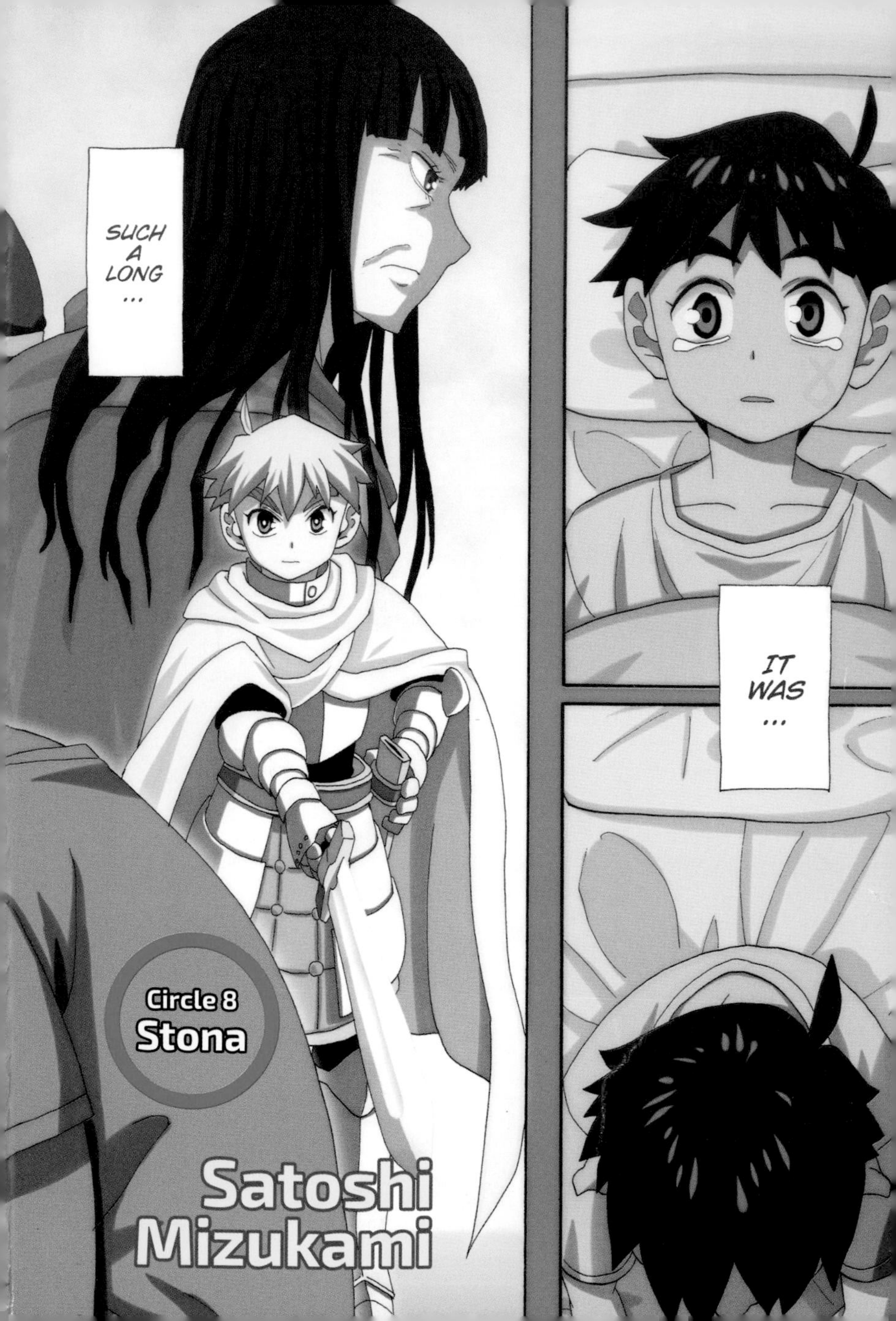
IT WAS ...
SUCH A LONG ...
Circle 8
Stona
Satoshi Mizukami

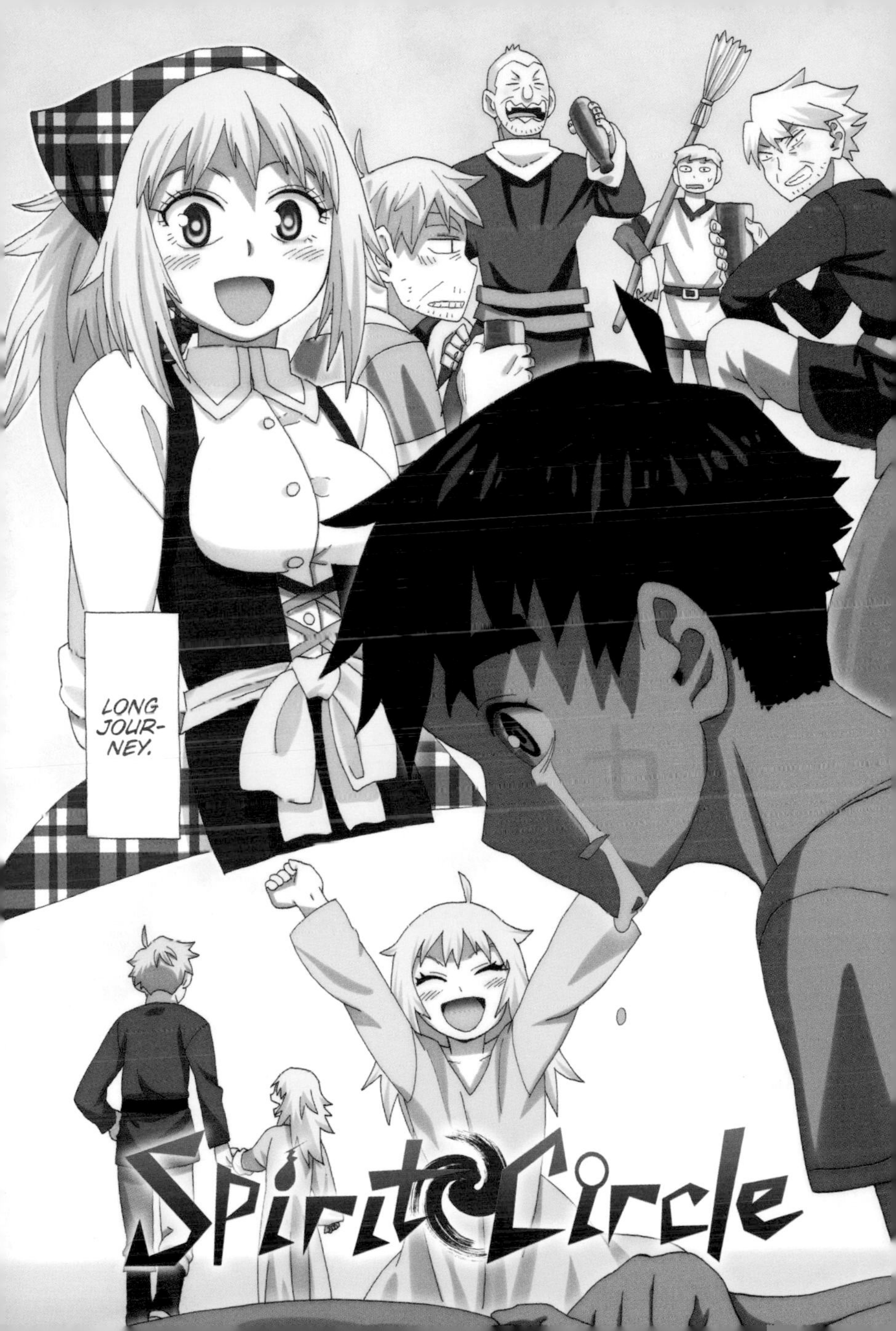
LONG JOURNEY.
Spirit Circle

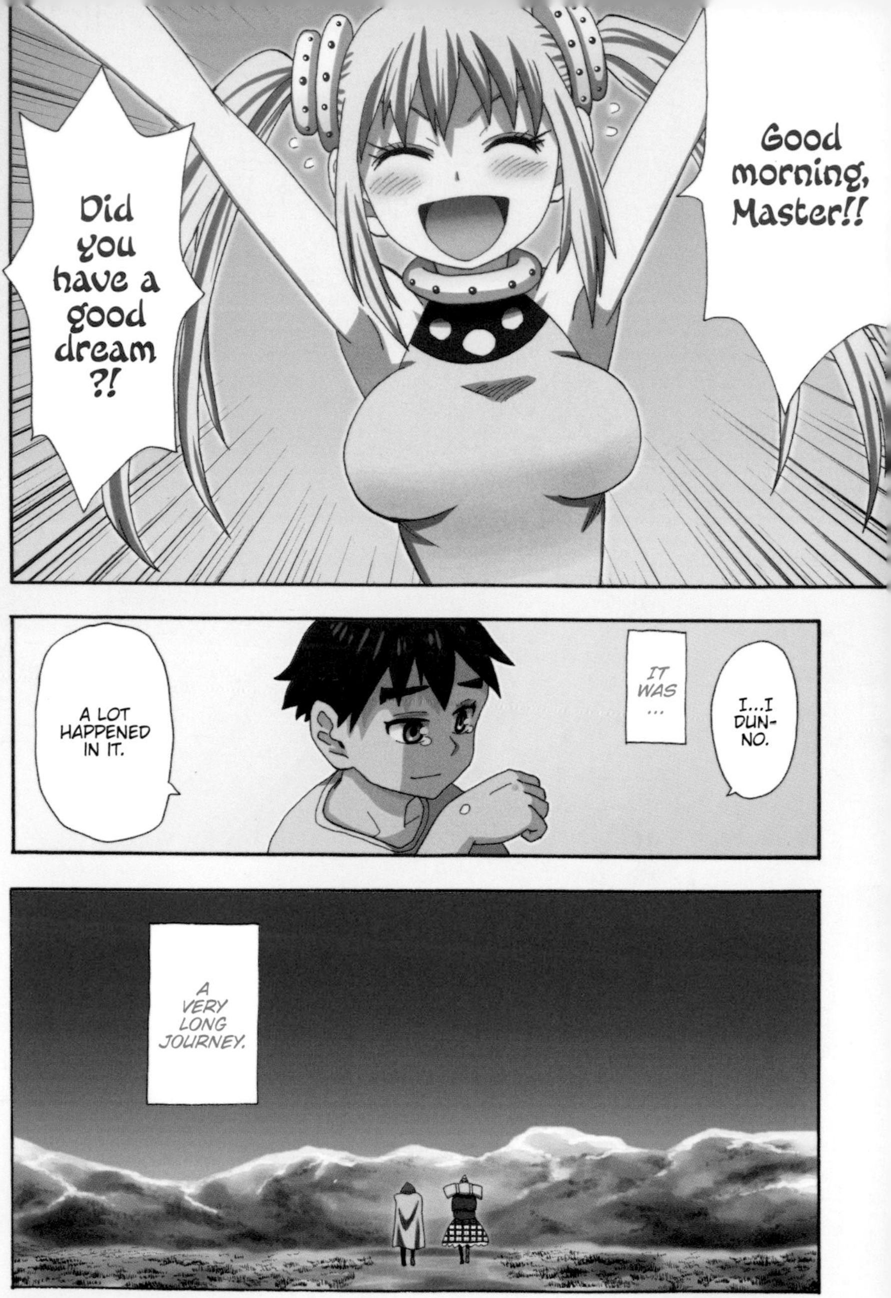
Good morning, Master!!
Did you have a good dream?!
I...I DUN-NO.
IT WAS...
A LOT HAPPENED IN IT.
A VERY LONG JOURNEY.

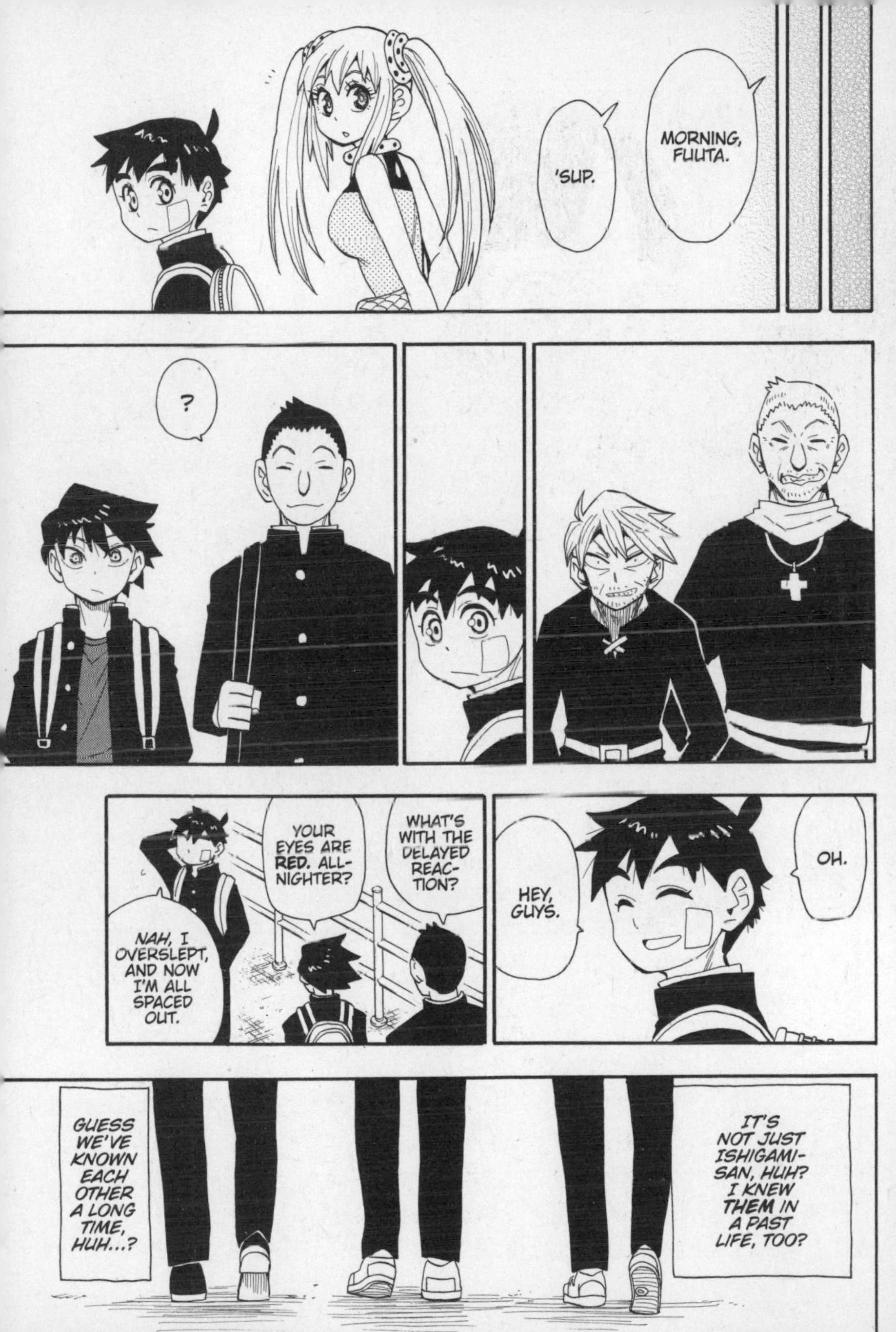
MORNING, FUUTA.
'SUP.
?
OH.
HEY, GUYS.
WHAT'S WITH THE DELAYED REACTION?
YOUR EYES ARE RED. ALL-NIGHTER?
NAH, I OVERSLEPT, AND NOW I'M ALL SPACED OUT.
IT'S NOT JUST ISHIGAMI-SAN, HUH? I KNEW THEM IN A PAST LIFE, TOO?
GUESS WE'VE KNOWN EACH OTHER A LONG TIME, HUH...?

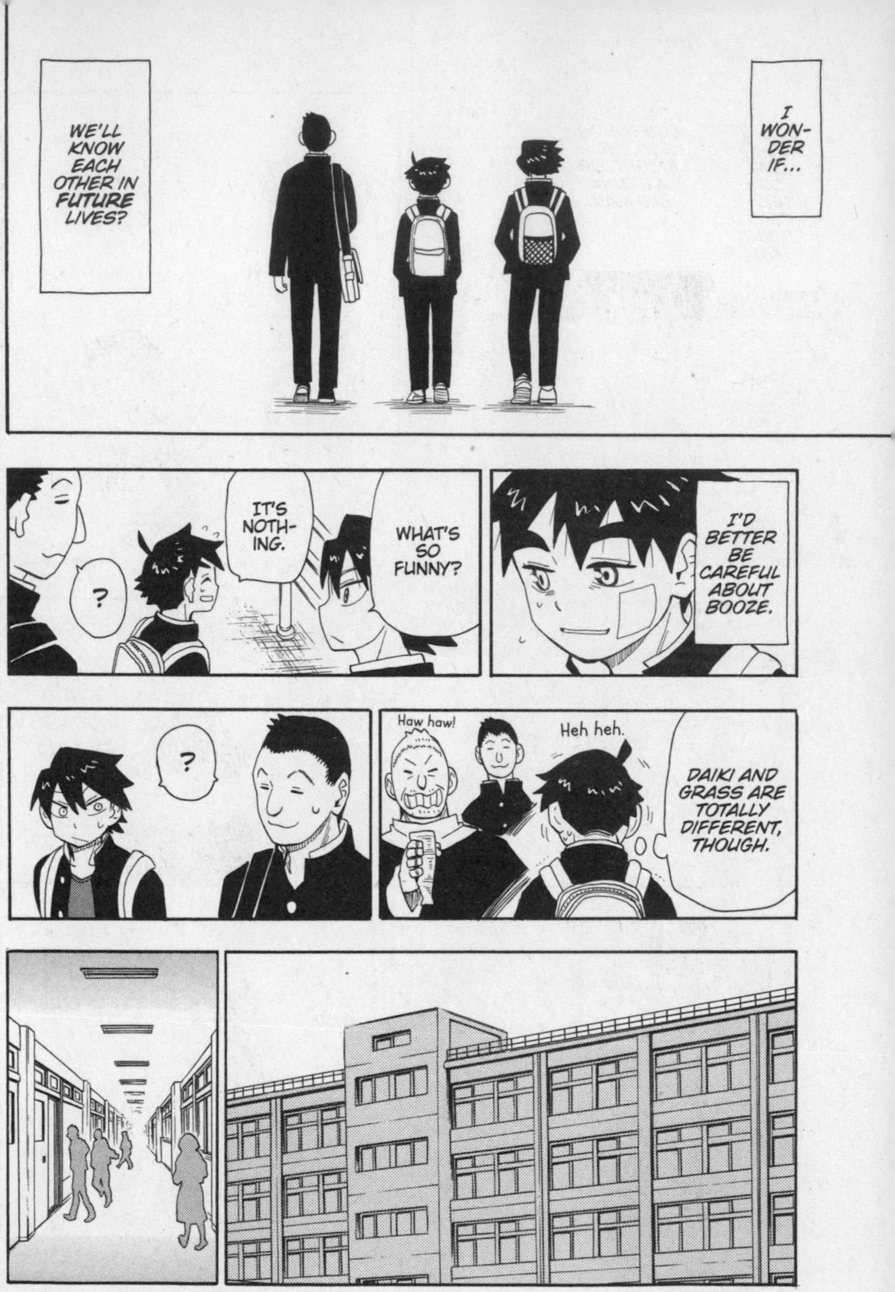
I WONDER IF...
WE'LL KNOW EACH OTHER IN FUTURE LIVES?
I'D BETTER BE CAREFUL ABOUT BOOZE.
WHAT'S SO FUNNY?
IT'S NOTHING.
?
DAIKI AND GRASS ARE TOTALLY DIFFERENT, THOUGH.
Heh heh.
Haw haw!
?

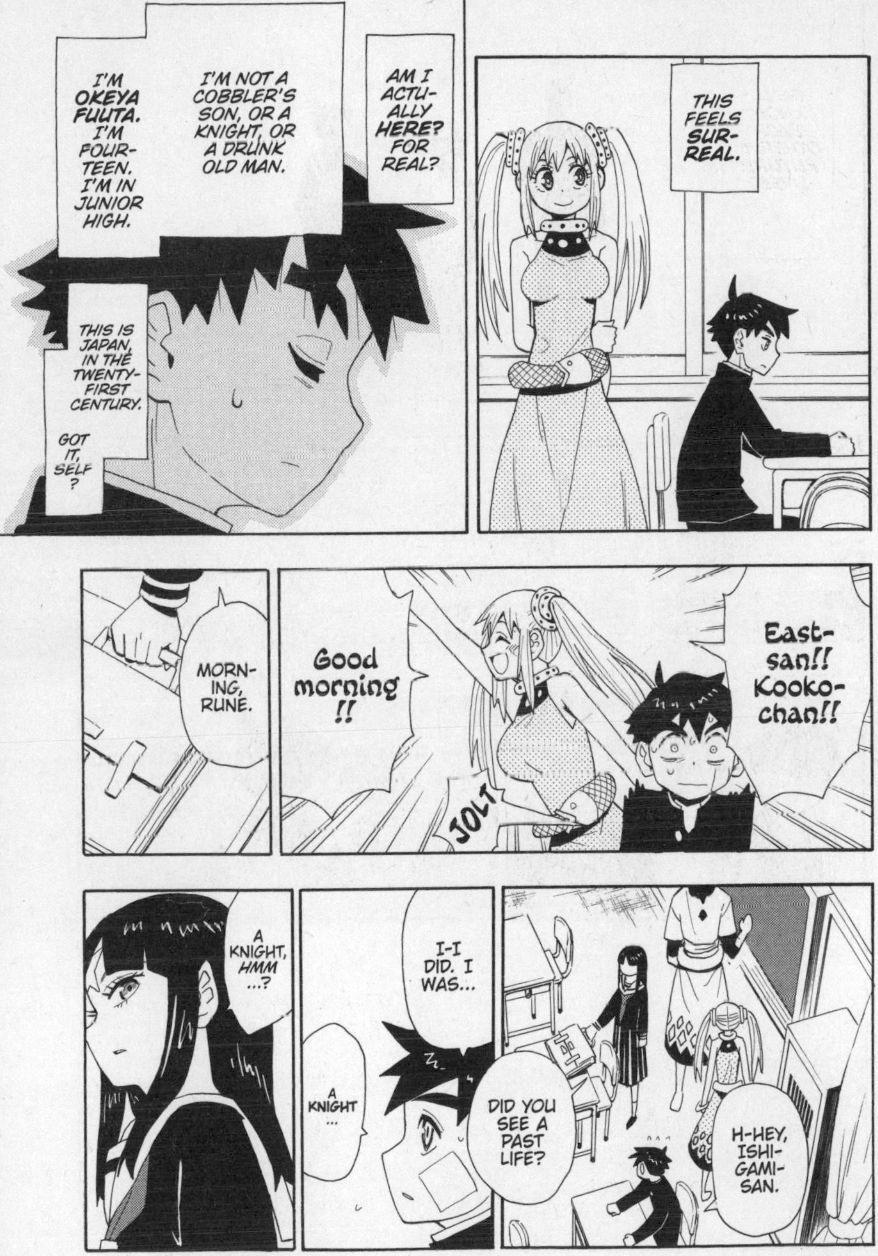
THIS FEELS SURREAL.
AM I ACTUALLY HERE? FOR REAL?
I'M NOT A COBBLER'S SON, OR A KNIGHT, OR A DRUNK OLD MAN.
I'M OKEYA FUUTA. I'M FOURTEEN. I'M IN JUNIOR HIGH.
THIS IS JAPAN, IN THE TWENTY-FIRST CENTURY.
GOT IT, SELF?
East-san!! Kooko-chan!!
Good morning!!
JOLT
MORNING, RUNE.
H-HEY, ISHIGAMI-SAN.
DID YOU SEE A PAST LIFE?
I-I DID. I WAS...
A KNIGHT...
A KNIGHT, HMM...?

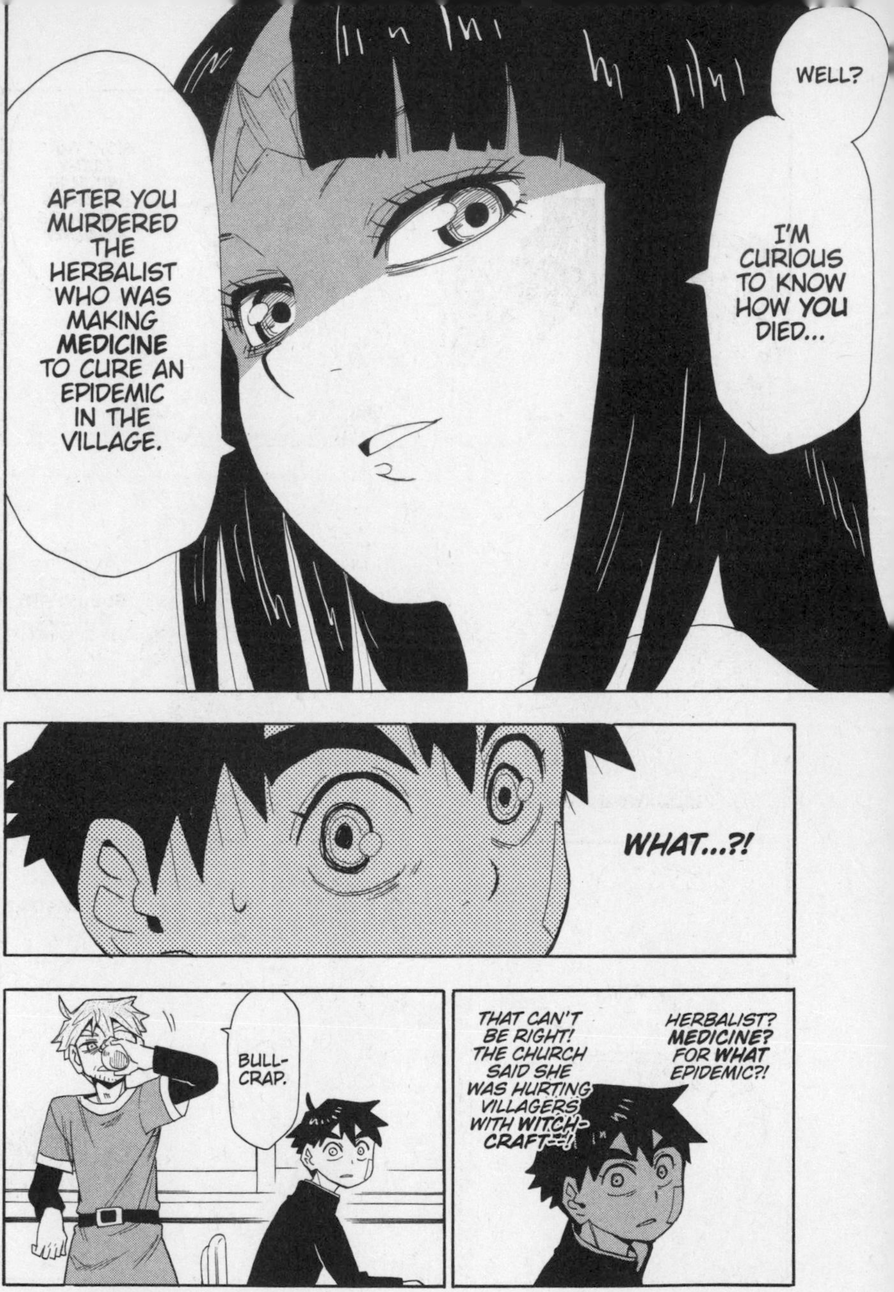
WELL?
I'M CURIOUS TO KNOW HOW YOU DIED...
AFTER YOU MURDERED THE HERBALIST WHO WAS MAKING MEDICINE TO CURE AN EPIDEMIC IN THE VILLAGE.
WHAT...?!
HERBALIST? MEDICINE? FOR WHAT EPIDEMIC?!
THAT CAN'T BE RIGHT! THE CHURCH SAID SHE WAS HURTING VILLAGERS WITH WITCH-CRAFT--!
BULL-CRAP.

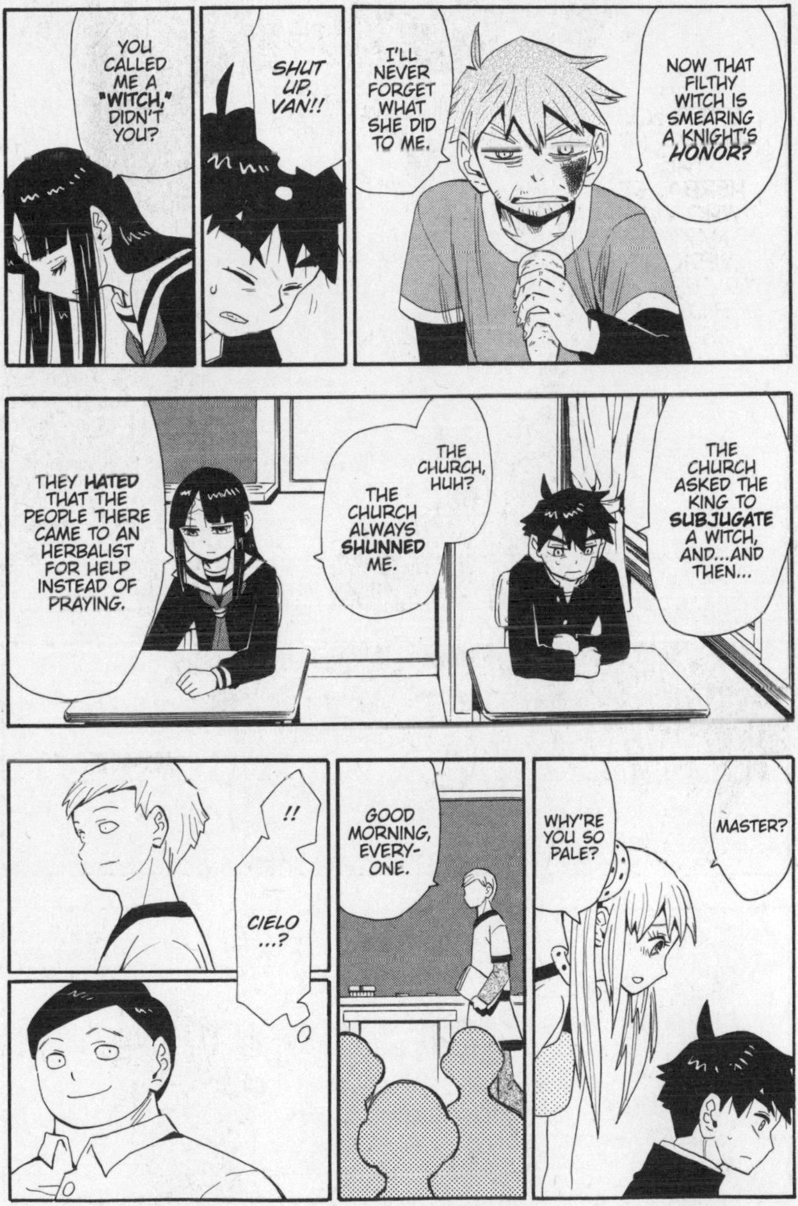
NOW THAT FILTHY WITCH IS SMEARING A KNIGHT'S HONOR?
I'LL NEVER FORGET WHAT SHE DID TO ME.
SHUT UP, VAN!!
YOU CALLED ME A "WITCH," DIDN'T YOU?
THE CHURCH ASKED THE KING TO SUBJUGATE A WITCH, AND...AND THEN...
THE CHURCH, HUH?
THE CHURCH ALWAYS SHUNNED ME.
THEY HATED THAT THE PEOPLE THERE CAME TO AN HERBALIST FOR HELP INSTEAD OF PRAYING.
MASTER?
WHY'RE YOU SO PALE?
GOOD MORNING, EVERY-ONE.
!!
CIELO ...?

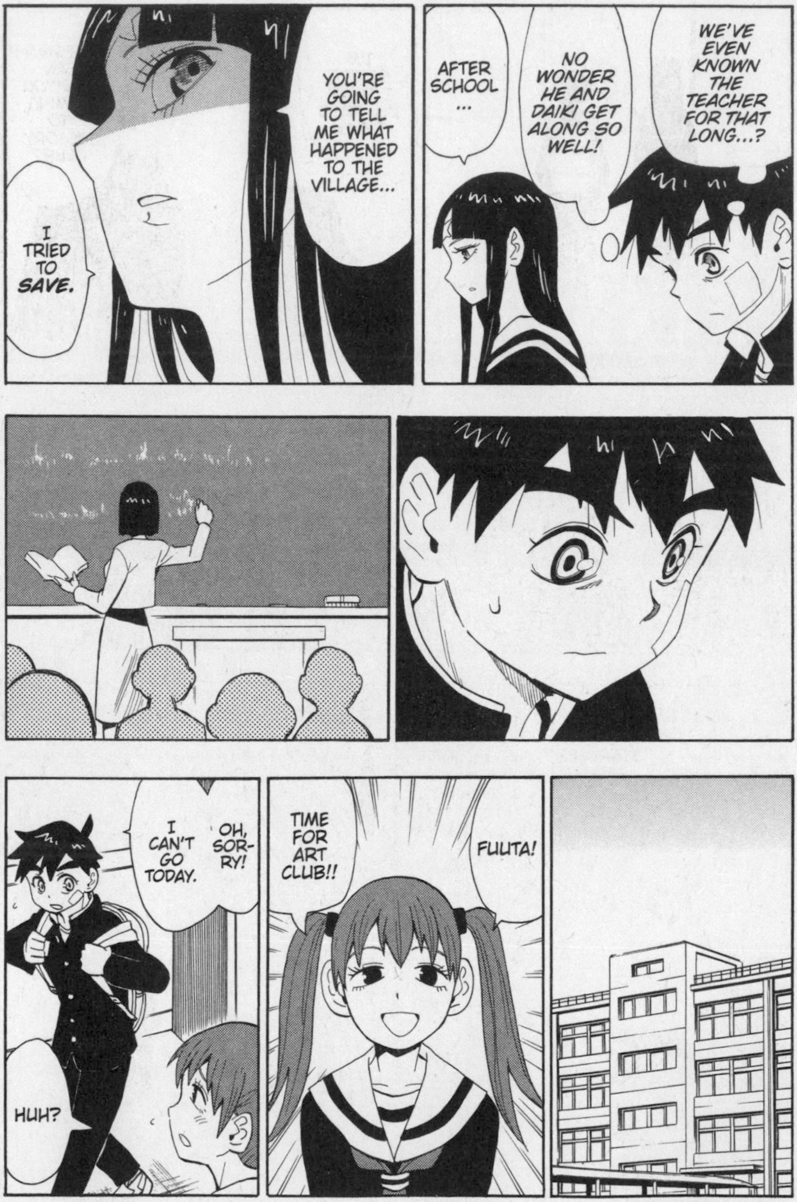
WE'VE EVEN KNOWN THE TEACHER FOR THAT LONG...?
NO WONDER HE AND DAIKI GET ALONG SO WELL!
AFTER SCHOOL ...
YOU'RE GOING TO TELL ME WHAT HAPPENED TO THE VILLAGE...
I TRIED TO SAVE.
FUUTA!
TIME FOR ART CLUB!!
OH, SOR-RY!
I CAN'T GO TODAY.
HUH?

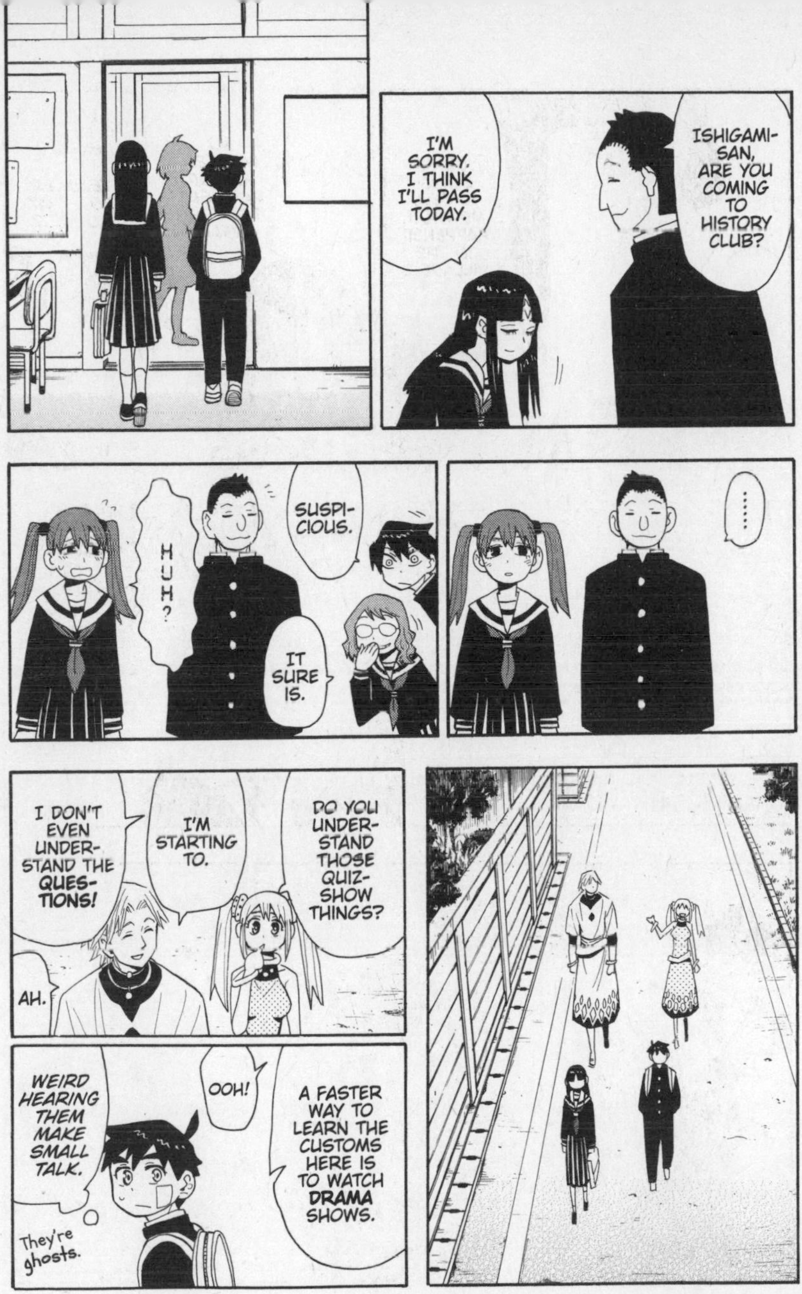
ISHIGAMI-SAN, ARE YOU COMING TO HISTORY CLUB?
I'M SORRY. I THINK I'LL PASS TODAY.
......
SUSPICIOUS.
HUH?
IT SURE IS.
DO YOU UNDERSTAND THOSE QUIZ-SHOW THINGS?
I'M STARTING TO.
I DON'T EVEN UNDERSTAND THE QUESTIONS!
AH.
A FASTER WAY TO LEARN THE CUSTOMS HERE IS TO WATCH DRAMA SHOWS.
OOH!
WEIRD HEARING THEM MAKE SMALL TALK.
They're ghosts.

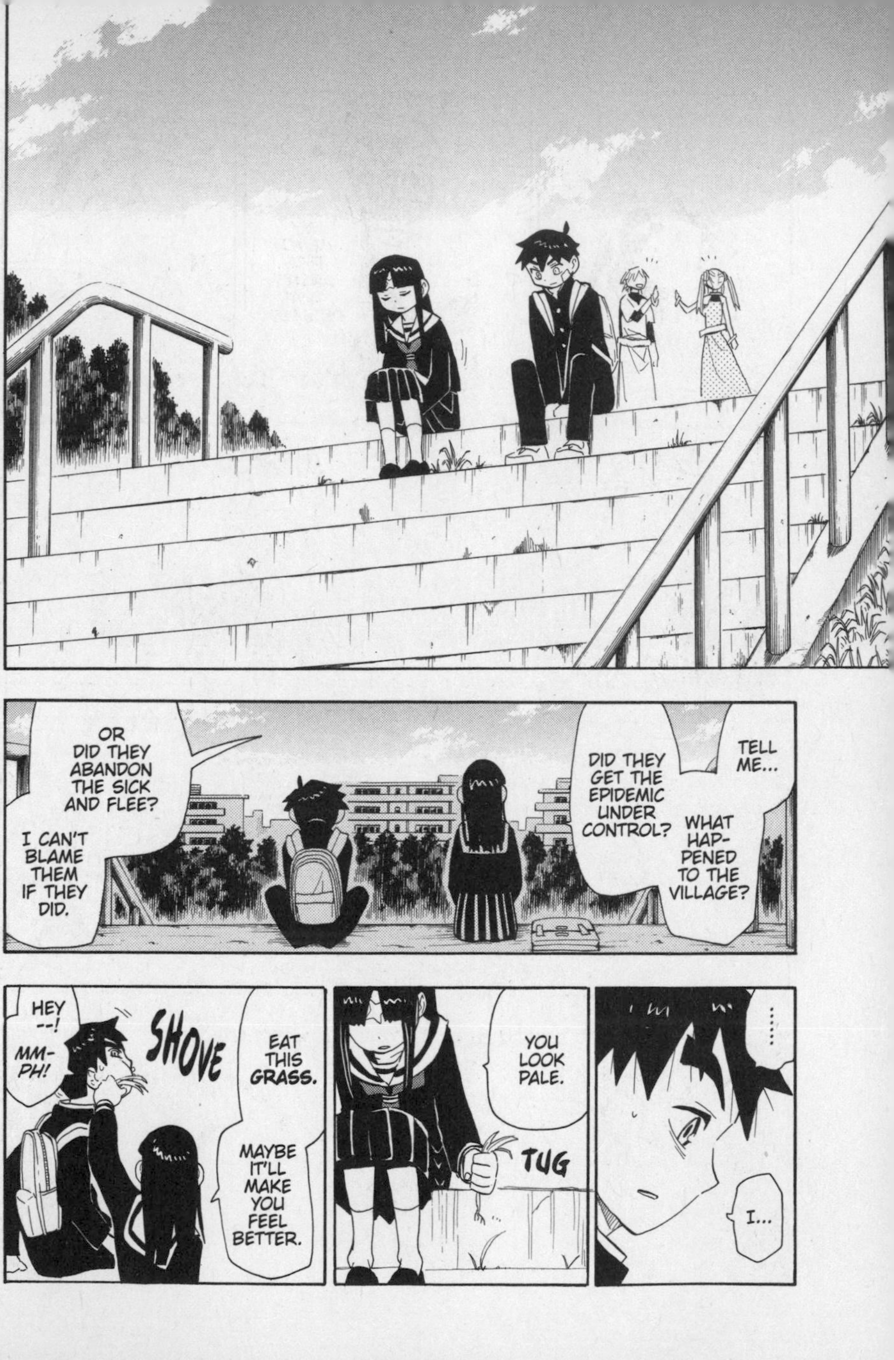

TELL ME...
DID THEY GET THE EPIDEMIC UNDER CONTROL?
WHAT HAPPENED TO THE VILLAGE?
OR DID THEY ABANDON THE SICK AND FLEE?
I CAN'T BLAME THEM IF THEY DID.
......
I...
YOU LOOK PALE.
TUG
EAT THIS GRASS.
SHOVE
HEY --!
MAYBE IT'LL MAKE YOU FEEL BETTER.
MM-PH!

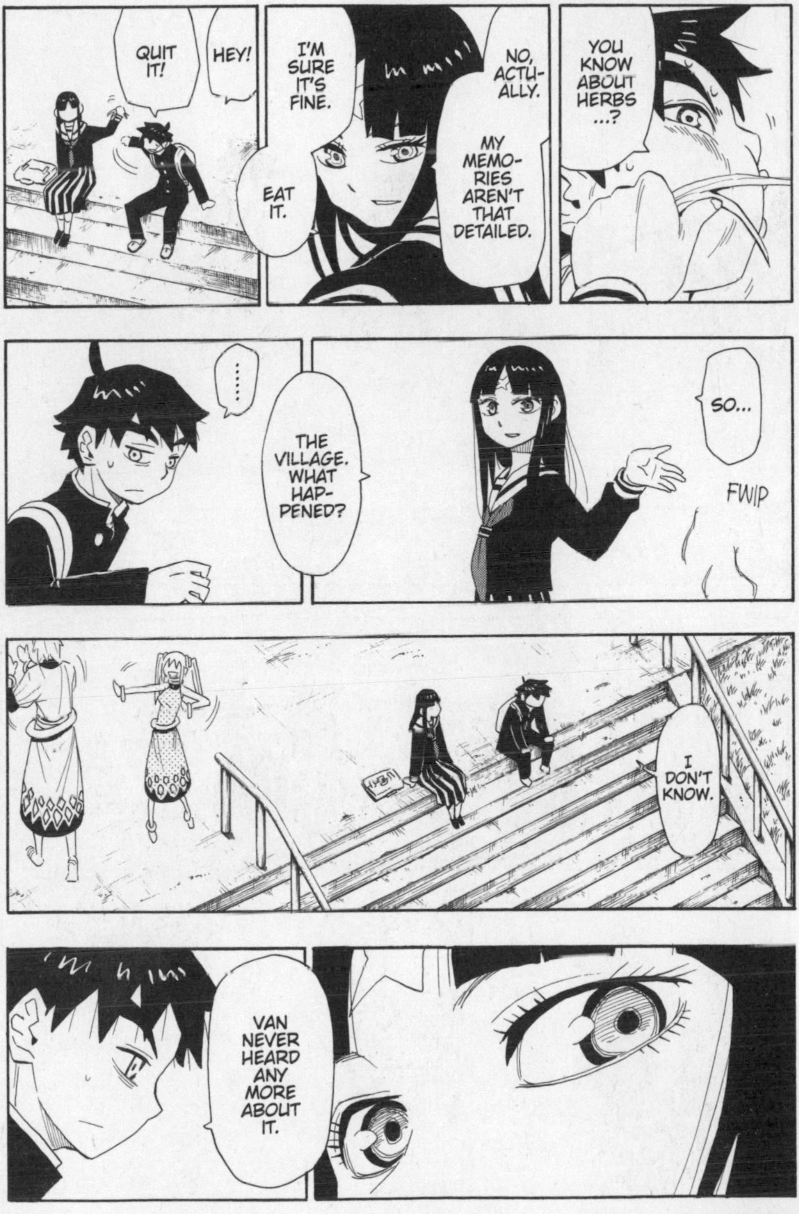
YOU KNOW ABOUT HERBS ...?
NO, ACTUALLY.
MY MEMORIES AREN'T THAT DETAILED.
I'M SURE IT'S FINE.
EAT IT.
HEY!
QUIT IT!
SO...
FWIP
THE VILLAGE. WHAT HAPPENED?
......
I DON'T KNOW.
VAN NEVER HEARD ANY MORE ABOUT IT.

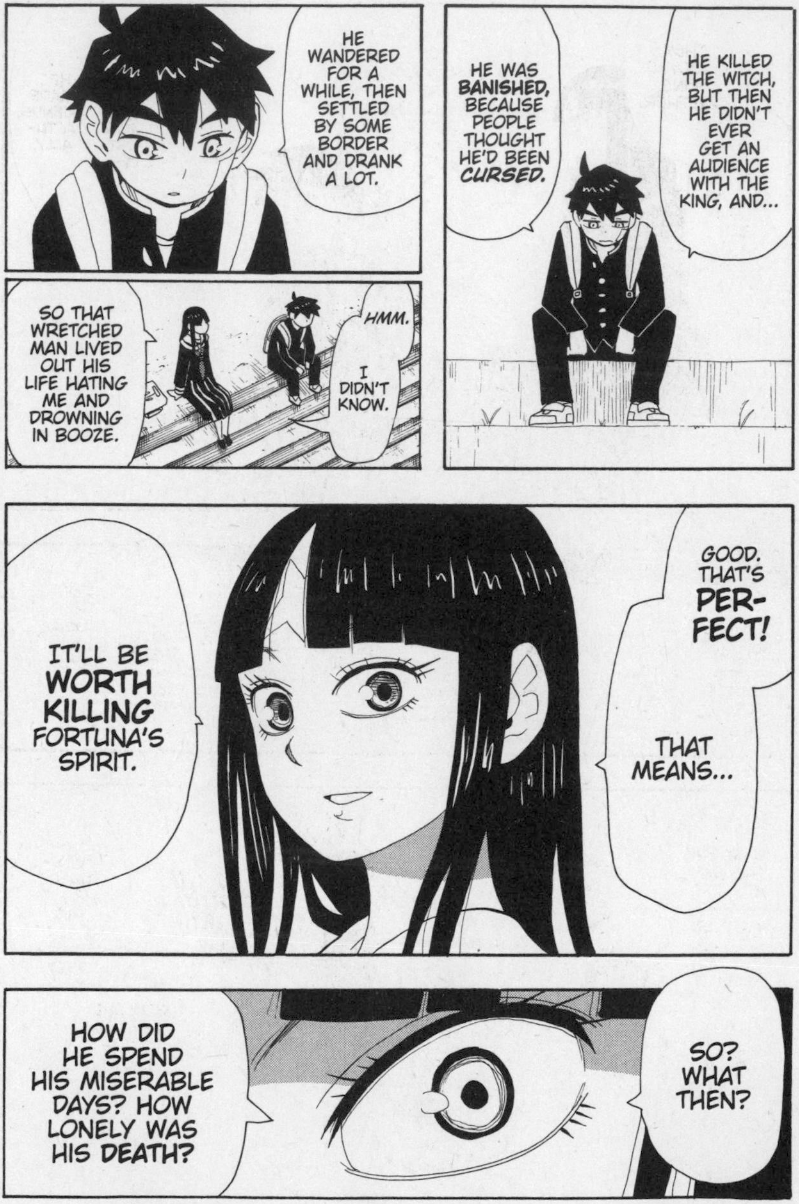
HE KILLED THE WITCH, BUT THEN HE DIDN'T EVER GET AN AUDIENCE WITH THE KING, AND...
HE WAS BANISHED, BECAUSE PEOPLE THOUGHT HE'D BEEN CURSED.
HE WANDERED FOR A WHILE, THEN SETTLED BY SOME BORDER AND DRANK A LOT.
HMM.
I DIDN'T KNOW.
SO THAT WRETCHED MAN LIVED OUT HIS LIFE HATING ME AND DROWNING IN BOOZE.
GOOD. THAT'S PER-FECT!
THAT MEANS...
IT'LL BE WORTH KILLING FORTUNA'S SPIRIT.
SO? WHAT THEN?
HOW DID HE SPEND HIS MISERABLE DAYS? HOW LONELY WAS HIS DEATH?

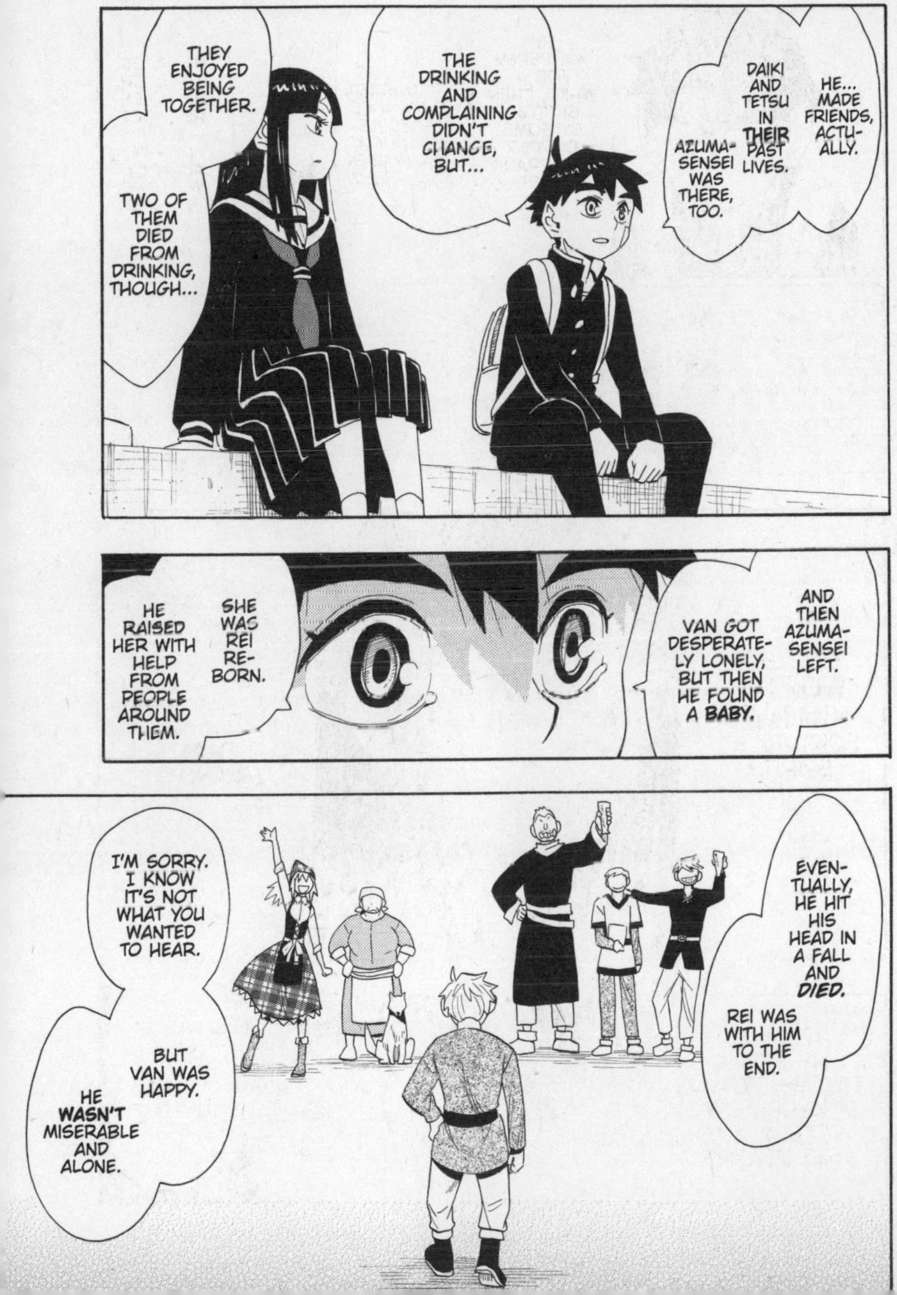
HE... MADE FRIENDS, ACTU-ALLY.
DAIKI AND TETSU IN **THEIR** PAST LIVES.
AZUMA-SENSEI WAS THERE, TOO.
THE DRINKING AND COMPLAINING DIDN'T CHANCE, BUT...
THEY ENJOYED BEING TOGETHER.
TWO OF THEM DIED FROM DRINKING, THOUGH...
AND THEN AZUMA-SENSEI LEFT.
VAN GOT DESPERATE-LY LONELY, BUT THEN HE FOUND A **BABY.**
SHE WAS REI RE-BORN.
HE RAISED HER WITH HELP FROM PEOPLE AROUND THEM.
EVEN-TUALLY, HE HIT HIS HEAD IN A FALL AND ***DIED.***
REI WAS WITH HIM TO THE END.
I'M SORRY. I KNOW IT'S NOT WHAT YOU WANTED TO HEAR.
BUT VAN WAS HAPPY.
HE **WASN'T** MISERABLE AND ALONE.

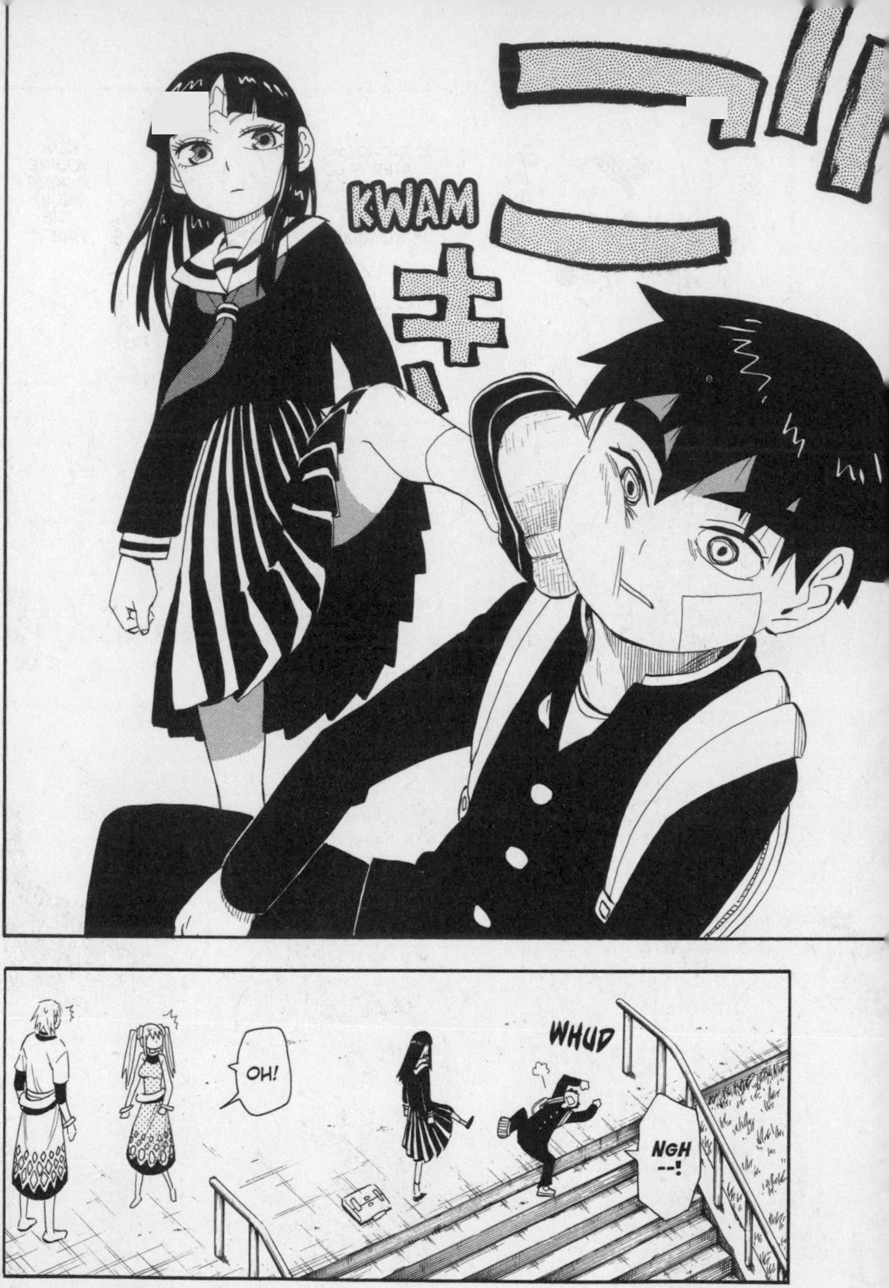
KWAM
WHUD
NGH
--!
OH!

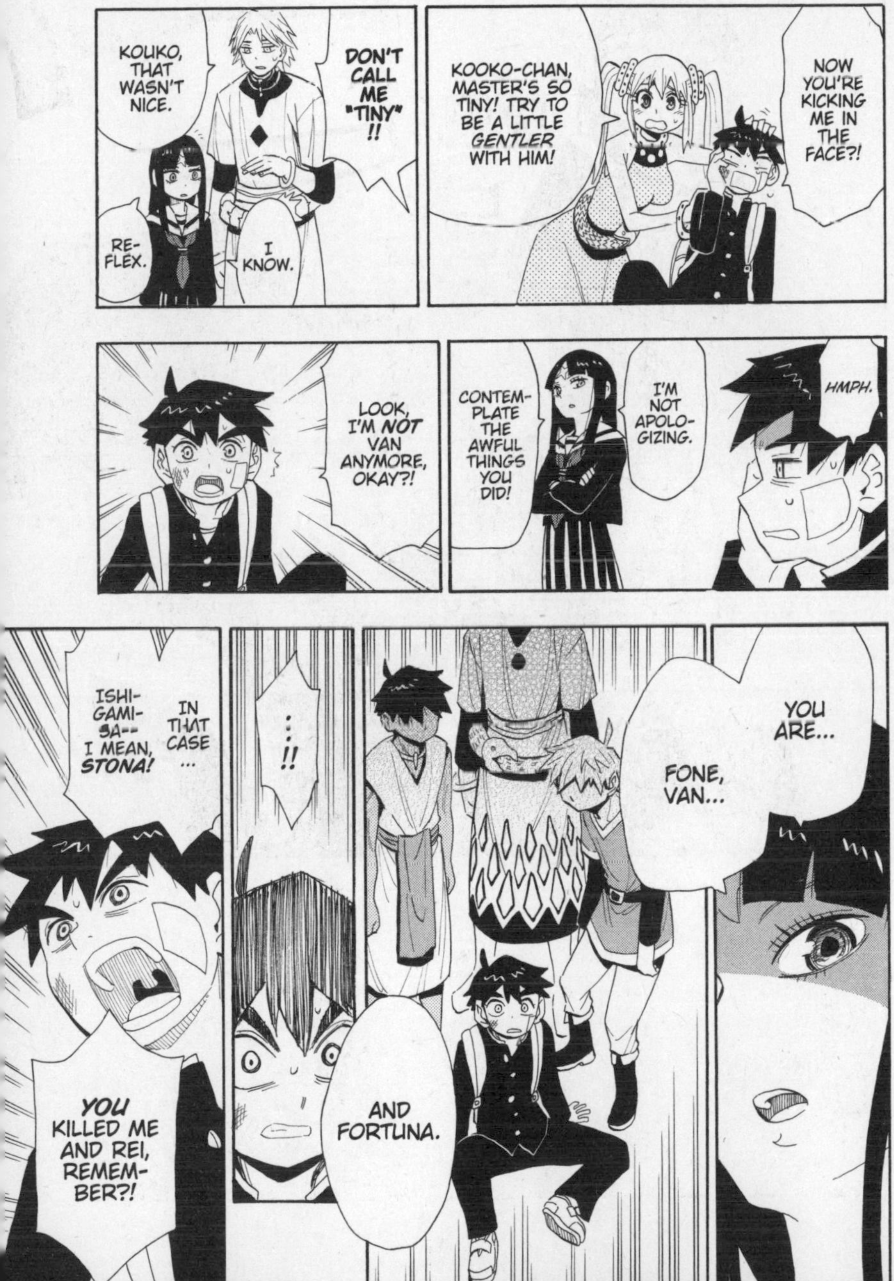
NOW YOU'RE KICKING ME IN THE FACE?!
KOOKO-CHAN, MASTER'S SO TINY! TRY TO BE A LITTLE *GENTLER* WITH HIM!
DON'T CALL ME "TINY"!!
KOUKO, THAT WASN'T NICE.
I KNOW.
RE-FLEX.
HMPH.
I'M NOT APOLO-GIZING.
CONTEM-PLATE THE AWFUL THINGS YOU DID!
LOOK, I'M ***NOT*** VAN ANYMORE, OKAY?!
YOU ARE...
FONE, VAN...
AND FORTUNA.
...!!
IN THAT CASE...
ISHI-GAMI-SA-- I MEAN, ***STONA!***
YOU KILLED ME AND REI, REMEM-BER?!

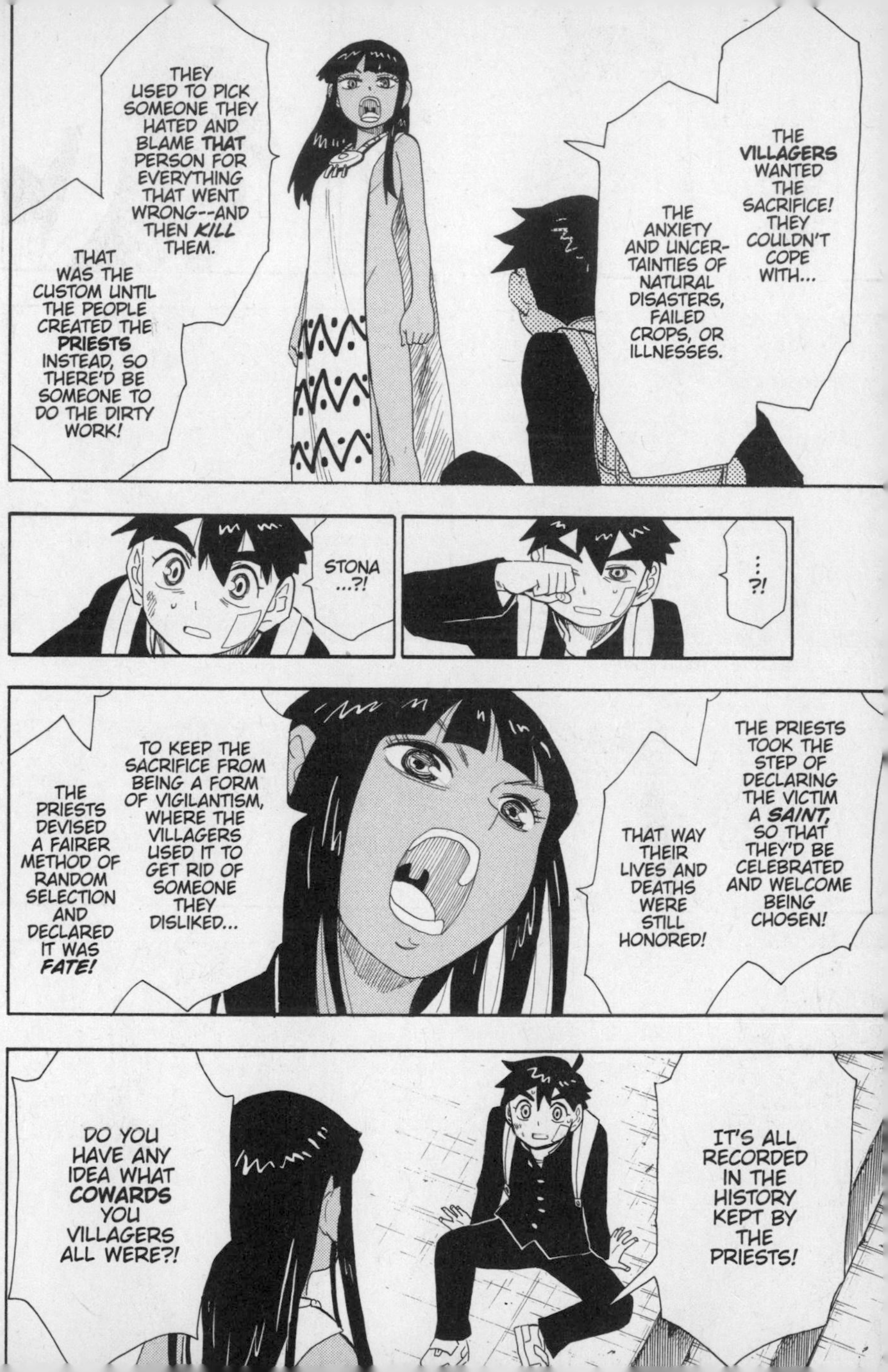
THE VILLAGERS WANTED THE SACRIFICE! THEY COULDN'T COPE WITH...
THE ANXIETY AND UNCERTAINTIES OF NATURAL DISASTERS, FAILED CROPS, OR ILLNESSES.
THEY USED TO PICK SOMEONE THEY HATED AND BLAME THAT PERSON FOR EVERYTHING THAT WENT WRONG--AND THEN KILL THEM.
THAT WAS THE CUSTOM UNTIL THE PEOPLE CREATED THE PRIESTS INSTEAD, SO THERE'D BE SOMEONE TO DO THE DIRTY WORK!
...?!
STONA ...?!
THE PRIESTS TOOK THE STEP OF DECLARING THE VICTIM A SAINT, SO THAT THEY'D BE CELEBRATED AND WELCOME BEING CHOSEN!
THAT WAY THEIR LIVES AND DEATHS WERE STILL HONORED!
TO KEEP THE SACRIFICE FROM BEING A FORM OF VIGILANTISM, WHERE THE VILLAGERS USED IT TO GET RID OF SOMEONE THEY DISLIKED...
THE PRIESTS DEVISED A FAIRER METHOD OF RANDOM SELECTION AND DECLARED IT WAS FATE!
IT'S ALL RECORDED IN THE HISTORY KEPT BY THE PRIESTS!
DO YOU HAVE ANY IDEA WHAT COWARDS YOU VILLAGERS ALL WERE?!

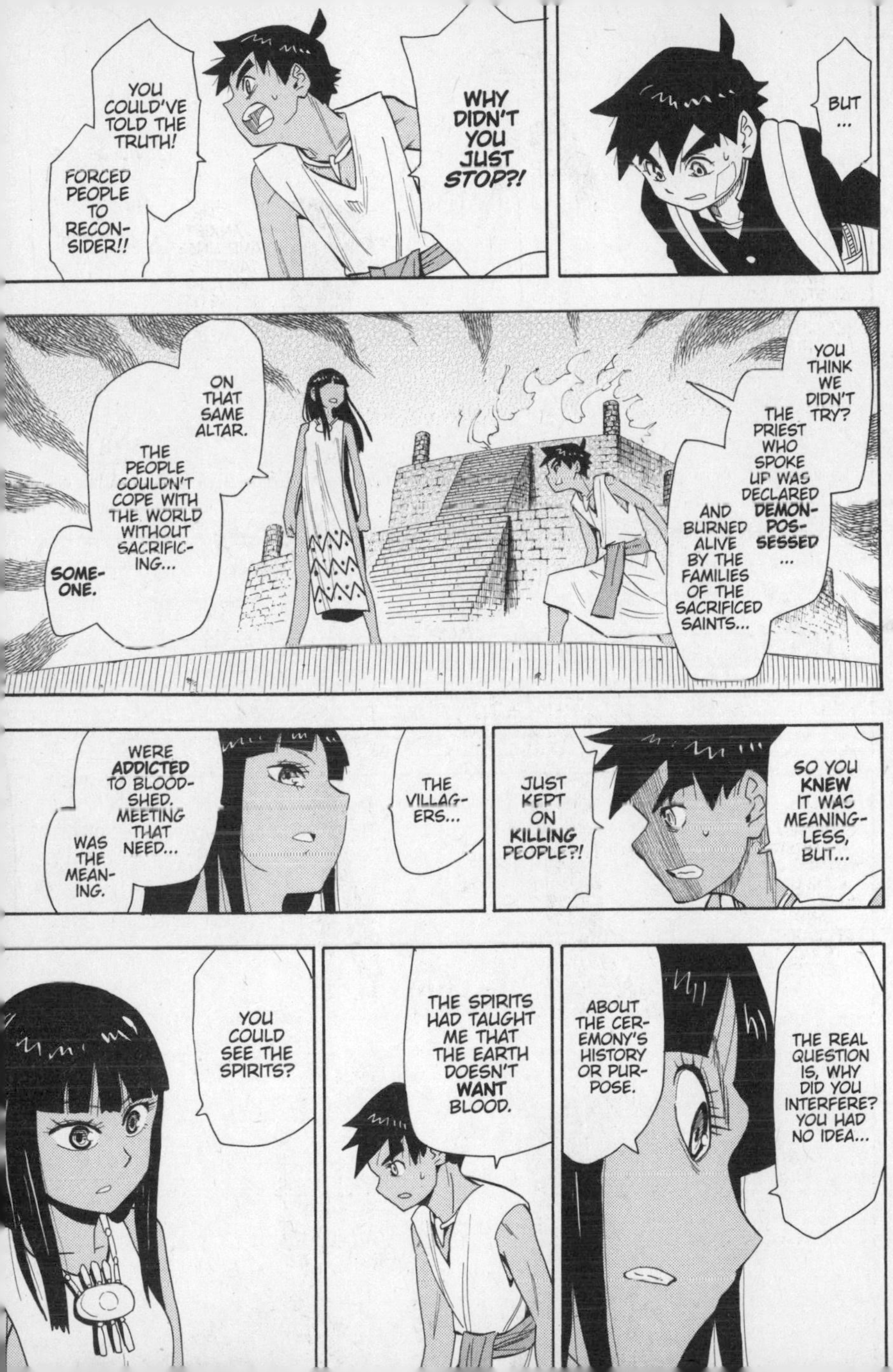
BUT...
WHY DIDN'T YOU JUST STOP?!
YOU COULD'VE TOLD THE TRUTH!
FORCED PEOPLE TO RECONSIDER!!
YOU THINK WE DIDN'T TRY?
THE PRIEST WHO SPOKE UP WAS DECLARED DEMON-POSSESSED...
AND BURNED ALIVE BY THE FAMILIES OF THE SACRIFICED SAINTS...
ON THAT SAME ALTAR.
THE PEOPLE COULDN'T COPE WITH THE WORLD WITHOUT SACRIFICING...
SOMEONE.
SO YOU KNEW IT WAS MEANINGLESS, BUT...
JUST KEPT ON KILLING PEOPLE?!
THE VILLAGERS...
WERE ADDICTED TO BLOODSHED. MEETING THAT NEED...
WAS THE MEANING.
THE REAL QUESTION IS, WHY DID YOU INTERFERE? YOU HAD NO IDEA...
ABOUT THE CEREMONY'S HISTORY OR PURPOSE.
THE SPIRITS HAD TAUGHT ME THAT THE EARTH DOESN'T WANT BLOOD.
YOU COULD SEE THE SPIRITS?

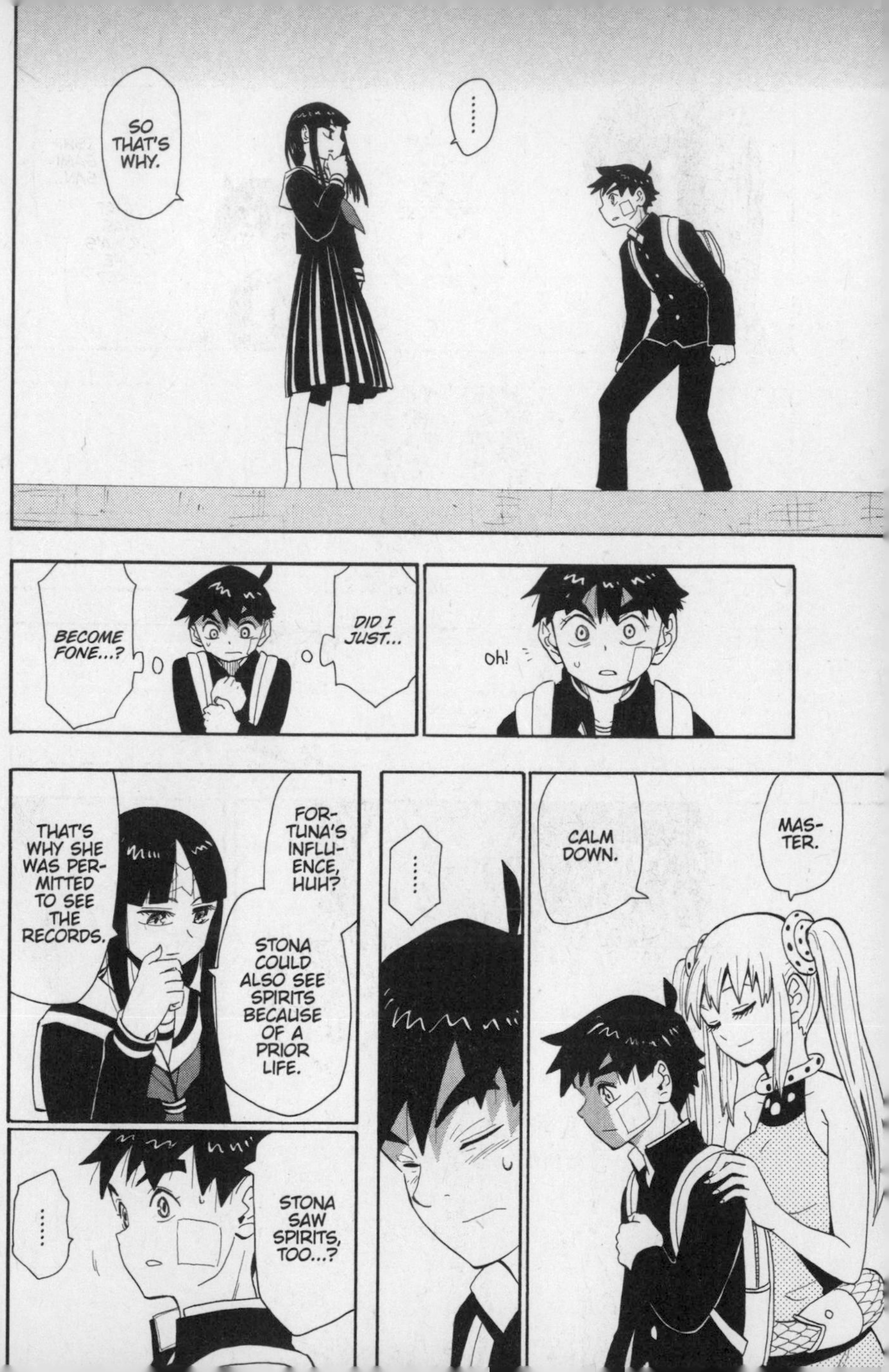
......
SO THAT'S WHY.
Oh!
DID I JUST...
BECOME FONE...?
MAS-TER.
CALM DOWN.
......
FOR-TUNA'S INFLU-ENCE, HUH?
THAT'S WHY SHE WAS PER-MITTED TO SEE THE RECORDS.
STONA COULD ALSO SEE SPIRITS BECAUSE OF A PRIOR LIFE.
STONA SAW SPIRITS, TOO...?
......

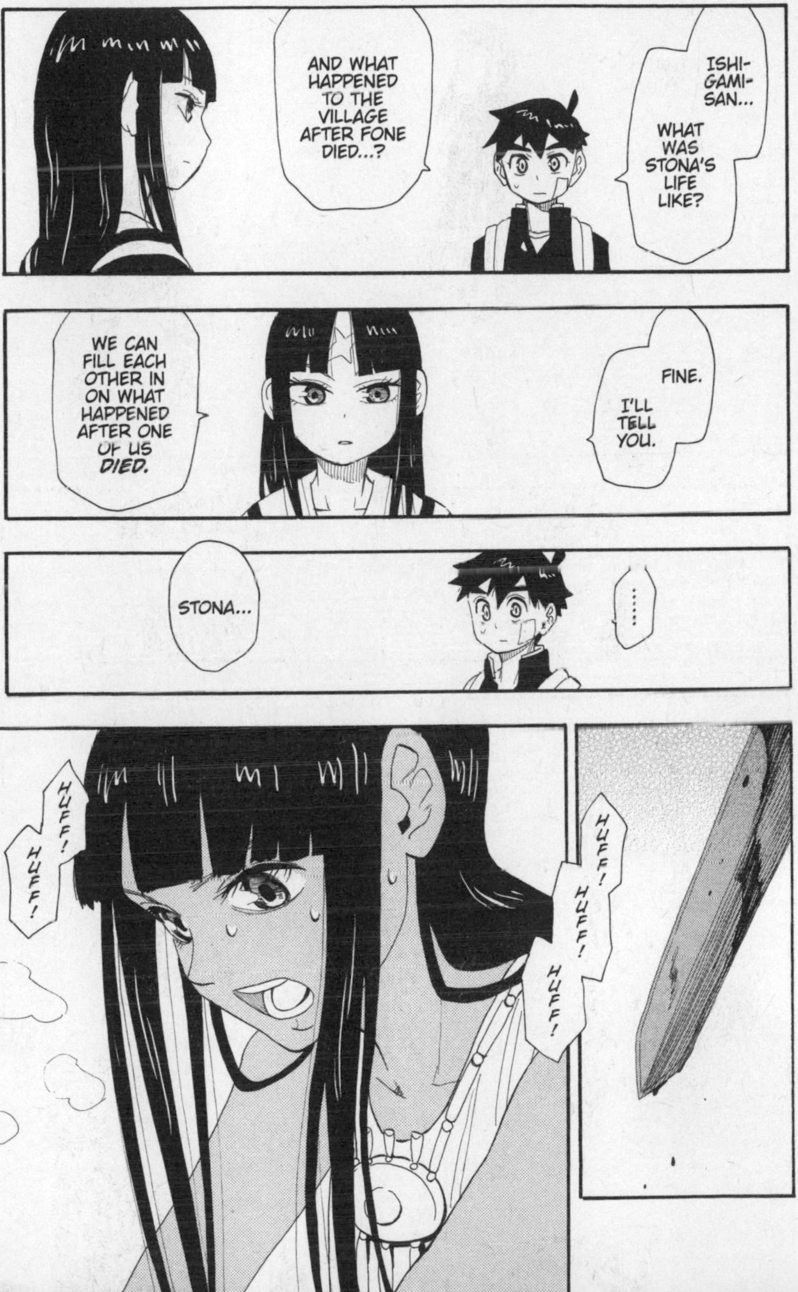
ISHI-GAMI-SAN... WHAT WAS STONA'S LIFE LIKE?
AND WHAT HAPPENED TO THE VILLAGE AFTER FONE DIED...?
FINE. I'LL TELL YOU.
WE CAN FILL EACH OTHER IN ON WHAT HAPPENED AFTER ONE OF US *DIED.*
......
STONA...
HUFF! HUFF! HUFF!
HUFF! HUFF!

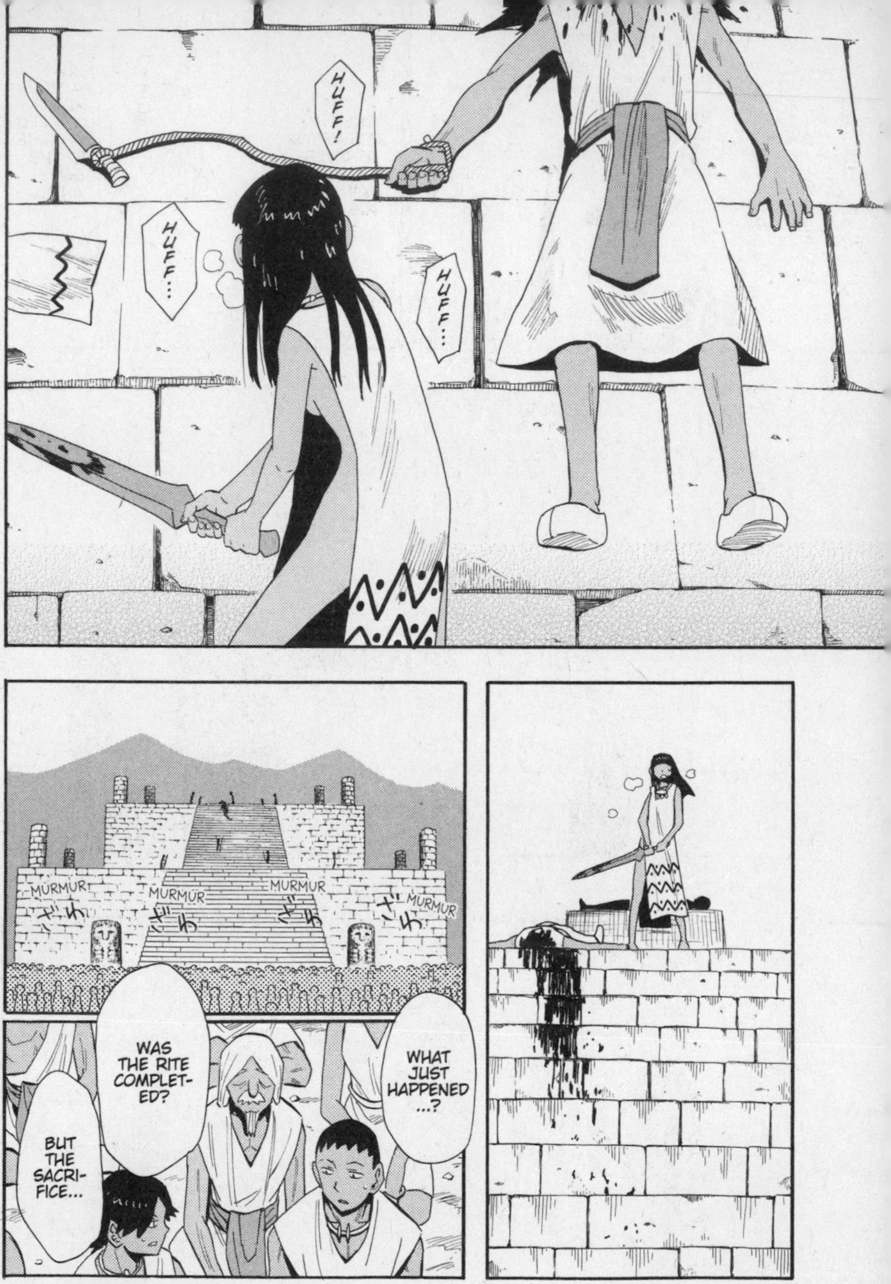
HUFF!
HUFF...
HUFF...
MURMUR
MURMUR
MURMUR
MURMUR
WHAT JUST HAPPENED...?
WAS THE RITE COMPLETED?
BUT THE SACRIFICE...

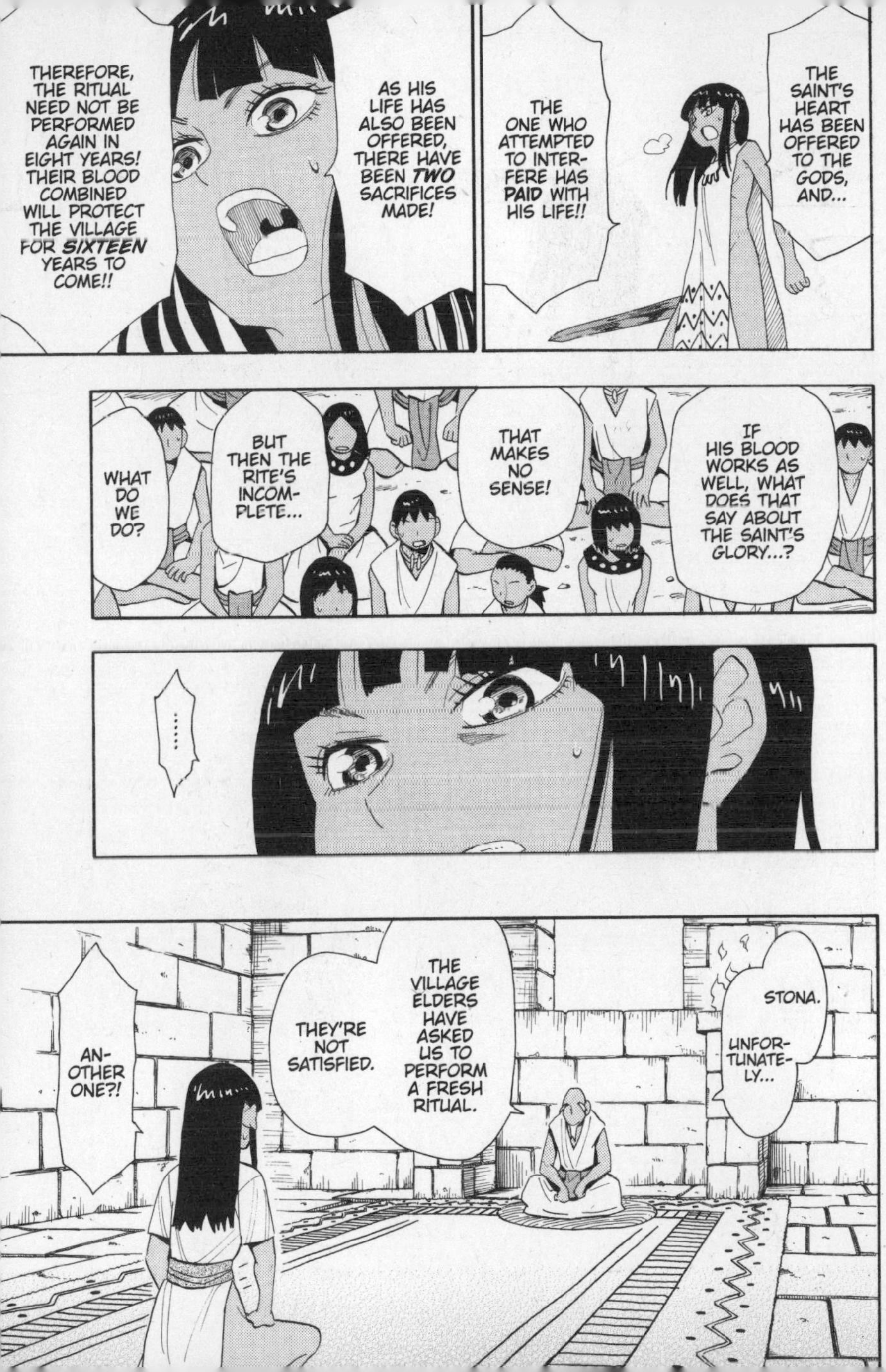
THE SAINT'S HEART HAS BEEN OFFERED TO THE GODS, AND...
THE ONE WHO ATTEMPTED TO INTERFERE HAS **PAID** WITH HIS LIFE!!
AS HIS LIFE HAS ALSO BEEN OFFERED, THERE HAVE BEEN ***TWO*** SACRIFICES MADE!
THEREFORE, THE RITUAL NEED NOT BE PERFORMED AGAIN IN EIGHT YEARS! THEIR BLOOD COMBINED WILL PROTECT THE VILLAGE FOR ***SIXTEEN*** YEARS TO COME!!
IF HIS BLOOD WORKS AS WELL, WHAT DOES THAT SAY ABOUT THE SAINT'S GLORY...?
THAT MAKES NO SENSE!
BUT THEN THE RITE'S INCOMPLETE...
WHAT DO WE DO?
......
STONA.
UNFORTUNATELY...
THE VILLAGE ELDERS HAVE ASKED US TO PERFORM A FRESH RITUAL.
THEY'RE NOT SATISFIED.
ANOTHER ONE?!

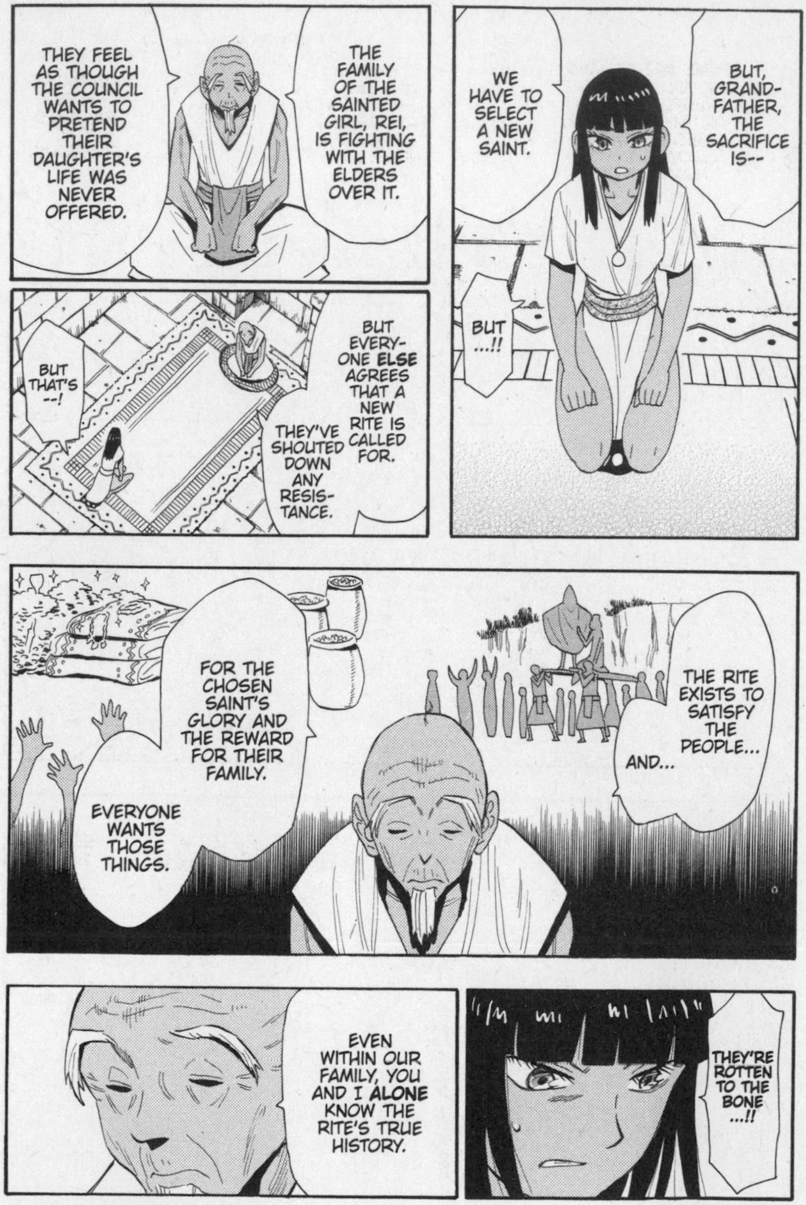
BUT, GRAND-FATHER, THE SACRIFICE IS--
WE HAVE TO SELECT A NEW SAINT.
BUT ...!!
THE FAMILY OF THE SAINTED GIRL, REI, IS FIGHTING WITH THE ELDERS OVER IT.
THEY FEEL AS THOUGH THE COUNCIL WANTS TO PRETEND THEIR DAUGHTER'S LIFE WAS NEVER OFFERED.
BUT EVERY-ONE **ELSE** AGREES THAT A NEW RITE IS CALLED FOR.
THEY'VE SHOUTED DOWN ANY RESIS-TANCE.
BUT THAT'S --!
THE RITE EXISTS TO SATISFY THE PEOPLE...
AND...
FOR THE CHOSEN SAINT'S GLORY AND THE REWARD FOR THEIR FAMILY.
EVERYONE WANTS THOSE THINGS.
THEY'RE ROTTEN TO THE BONE ...!!
EVEN WITHIN OUR FAMILY, YOU AND I **ALONE** KNOW THE RITE'S TRUE HISTORY.

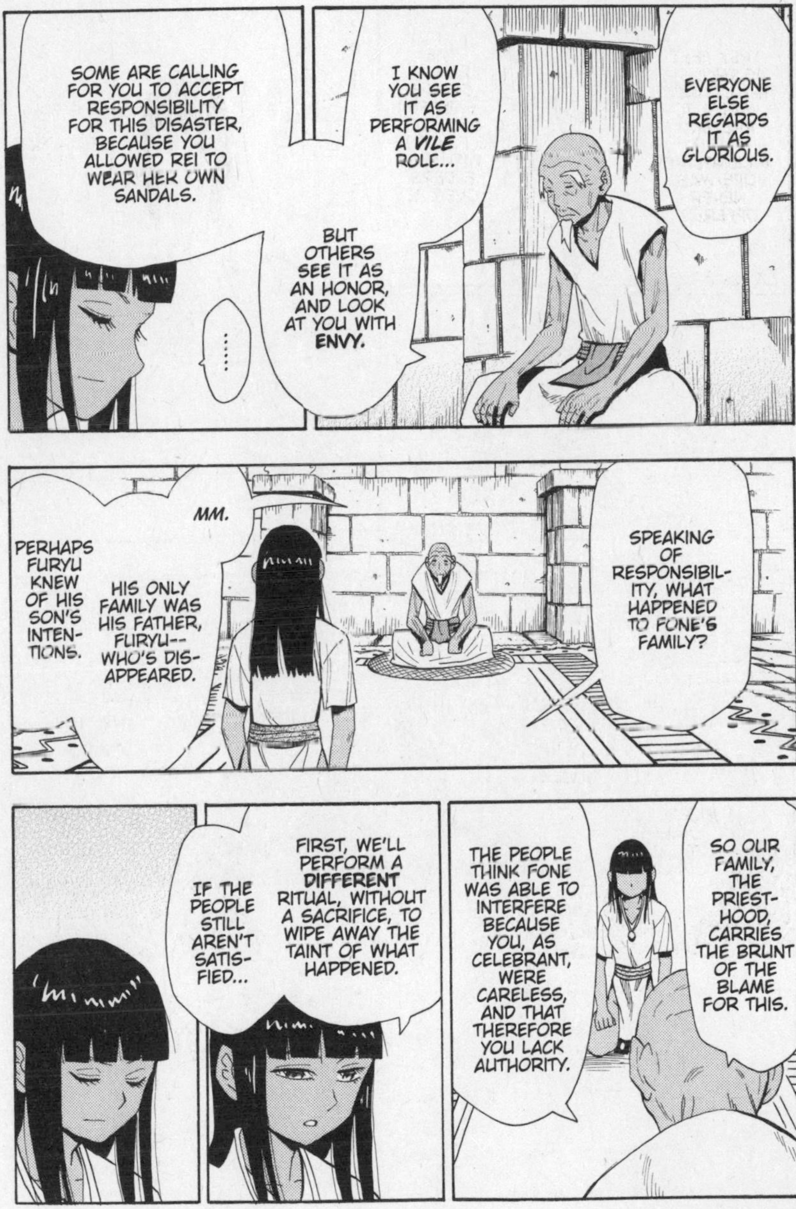
EVERYONE ELSE REGARDS IT AS GLORIOUS.
I KNOW YOU SEE IT AS PERFORMING A **VILE** ROLE...
BUT OTHERS SEE IT AS AN HONOR, AND LOOK AT YOU WITH **ENVY.**
SOME ARE CALLING FOR YOU TO ACCEPT RESPONSIBILITY FOR THIS DISASTER, BECAUSE YOU ALLOWED REI TO WEAR HER OWN SANDALS.
......
SPEAKING OF RESPONSIBIL-ITY, WHAT HAPPENED TO FONE'S FAMILY?
MM.
HIS ONLY FAMILY WAS HIS FATHER, FURYU-- WHO'S DIS-APPEARED.
PERHAPS FURYU KNEW OF HIS SON'S INTEN-TIONS.
SO OUR FAMILY, THE PRIEST-HOOD, CARRIES THE BRUNT OF THE BLAME FOR THIS.
THE PEOPLE THINK FONE WAS ABLE TO INTERFERE BECAUSE YOU, AS CELEBRANT, WERE CARELESS, AND THAT THEREFORE YOU LACK AUTHORITY.
FIRST, WE'LL PERFORM A **DIFFERENT** RITUAL, WITHOUT A SACRIFICE, TO WIPE AWAY THE TAINT OF WHAT HAPPENED.
IF THE PEOPLE STILL AREN'T SATIS-FIED...

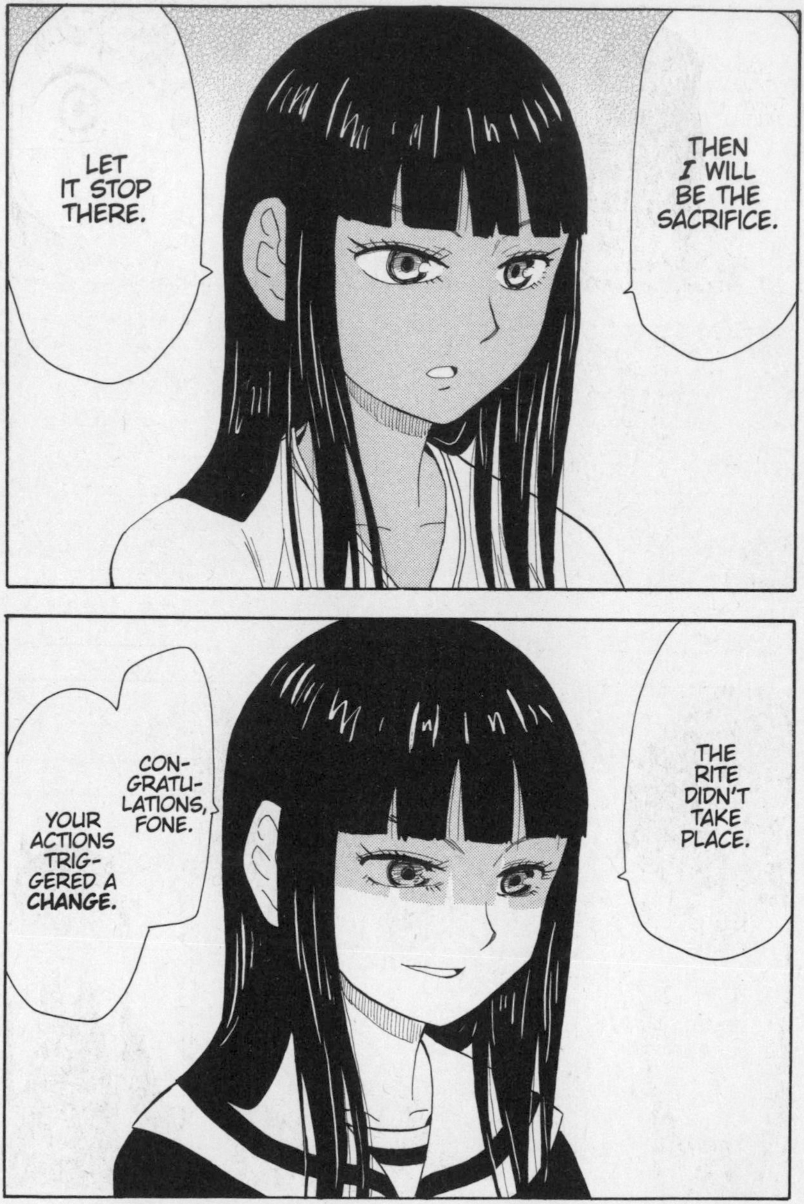
THEN *I* WILL BE THE SACRIFICE.
LET IT STOP THERE.
THE RITE DIDN'T TAKE PLACE.
CON-GRATU-LATIONS, FONE.
YOUR ACTIONS TRIG-GERED A CHANGE.

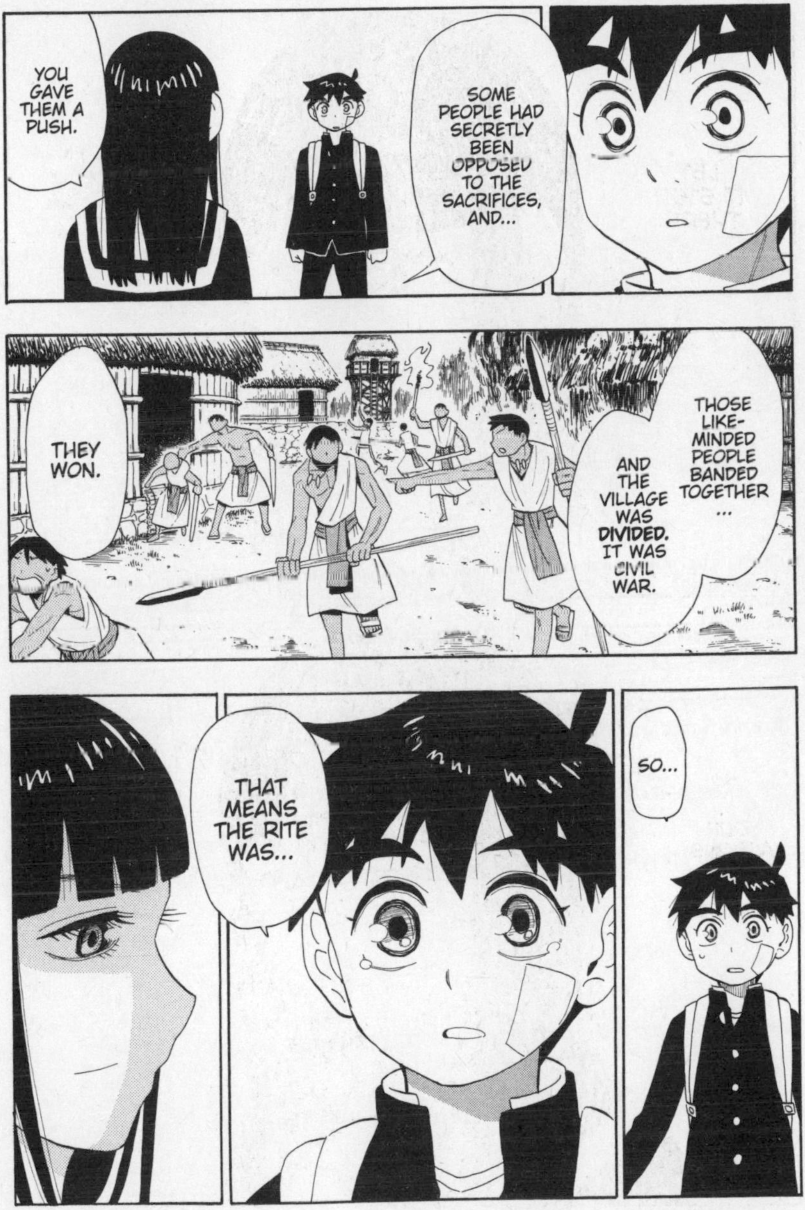
SOME PEOPLE HAD SECRETLY BEEN OPPOSED TO THE SACRIFICES, AND...
YOU GAVE THEM A PUSH.
THOSE LIKE-MINDED PEOPLE BANDED TOGETHER ...
AND THE VILLAGE WAS DIVIDED. IT WAS CIVIL WAR.
THEY WON.
SO...
THAT MEANS THE RITE WAS...

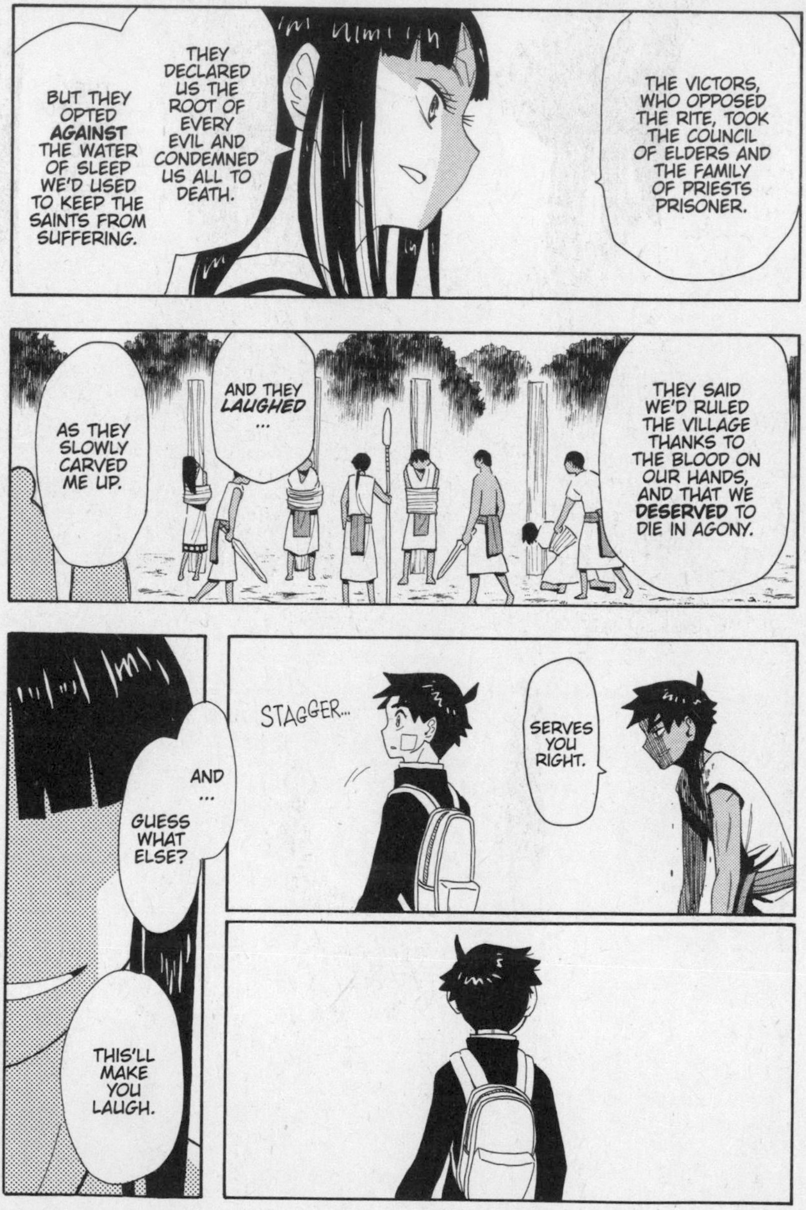
THE VICTORS, WHO OPPOSED THE RITE, TOOK THE COUNCIL OF ELDERS AND THE FAMILY OF PRIESTS PRISONER.
THEY DECLARED US THE ROOT OF EVERY EVIL AND CONDEMNED US ALL TO DEATH.
BUT THEY OPTED **AGAINST** THE WATER OF SLEEP WE'D USED TO KEEP THE SAINTS FROM SUFFERING.
THEY SAID WE'D RULED THE VILLAGE THANKS TO THE BLOOD ON OUR HANDS, AND THAT WE **DESERVED** TO DIE IN AGONY.
AND THEY ***LAUGHED*** ...
AS THEY SLOWLY CARVED ME UP.
SERVES YOU RIGHT.
STAGGER...
AND ... GUESS WHAT ELSE?
THIS'LL MAKE YOU LAUGH.

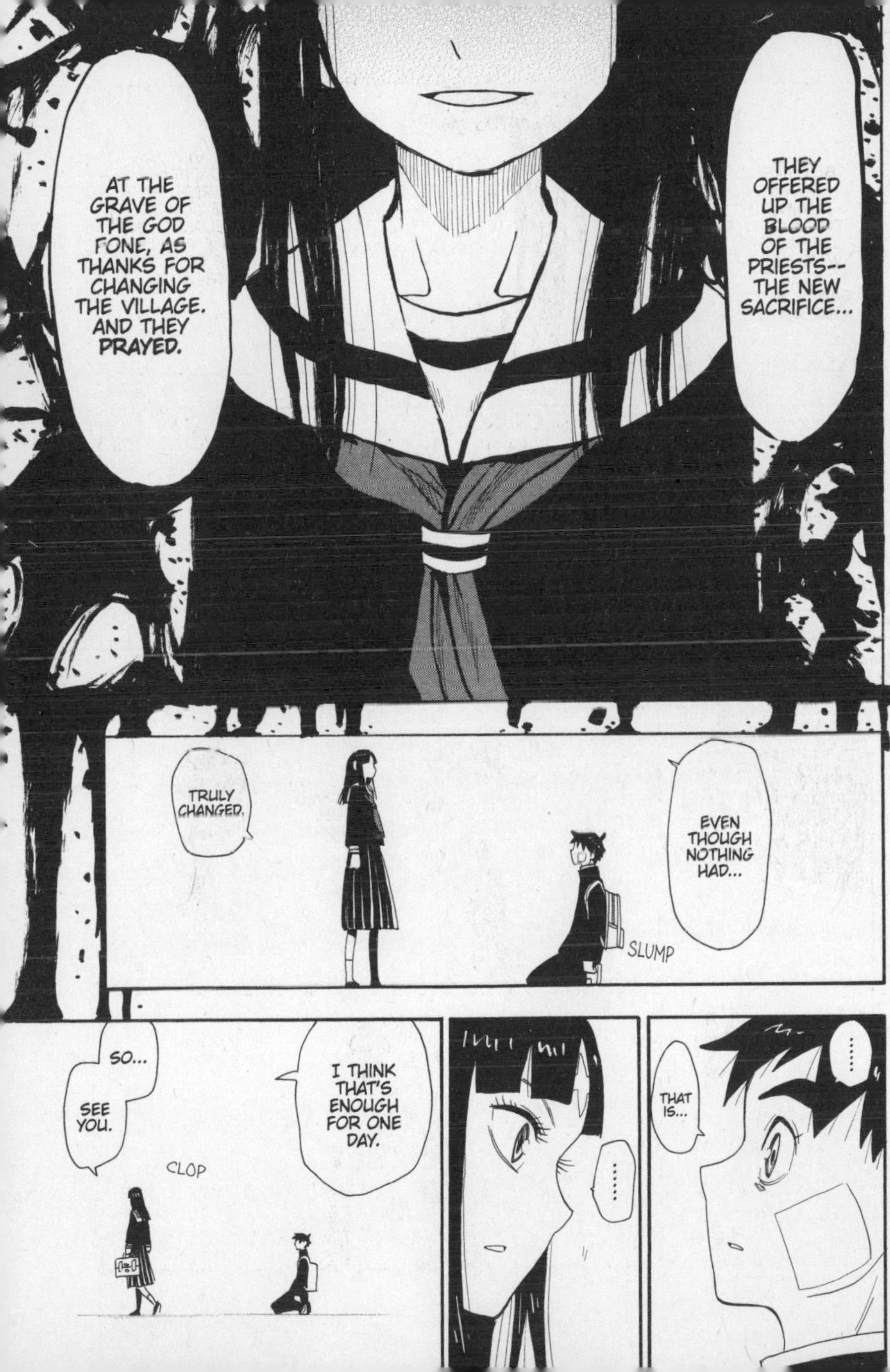
THEY OFFERED UP THE BLOOD OF THE PRIESTS-- THE NEW SACRIFICE...
AT THE GRAVE OF THE GOD FONE, AS THANKS FOR CHANGING THE VILLAGE. AND THEY PRAYED.
EVEN THOUGH NOTHING HAD...
SLUMP
TRULY CHANGED.
......
THAT IS...
......
I THINK THAT'S ENOUGH FOR ONE DAY.
SO...
SEE YOU.
CLOP

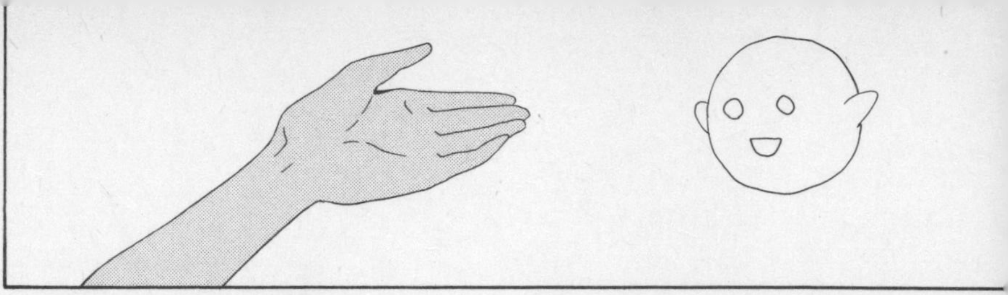

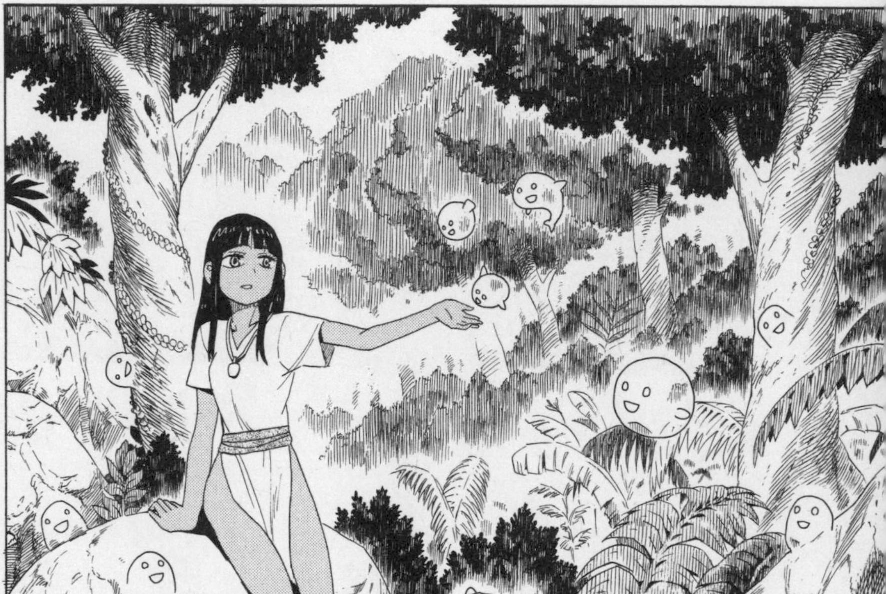

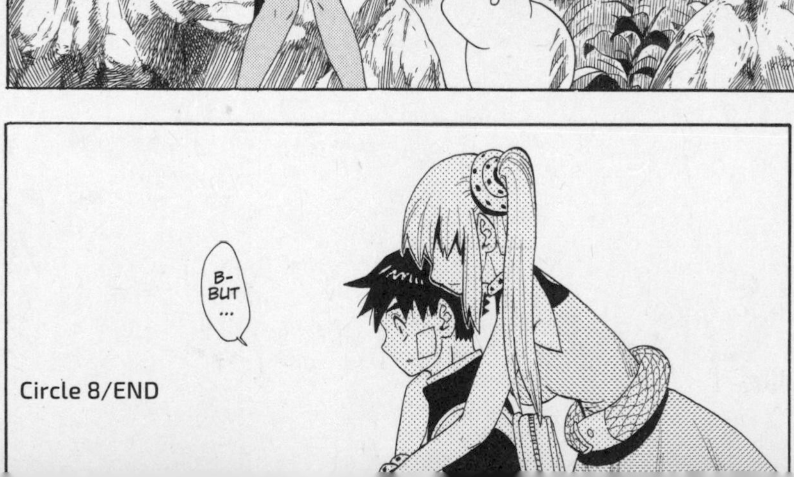
B-BUT ...

Circle 8/END

Spirit Circle

Rei

Circle 9
Dream

100 STRIKES

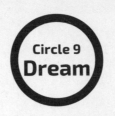

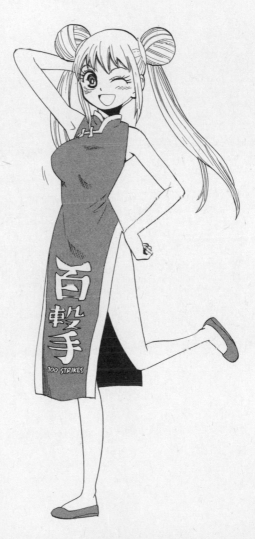

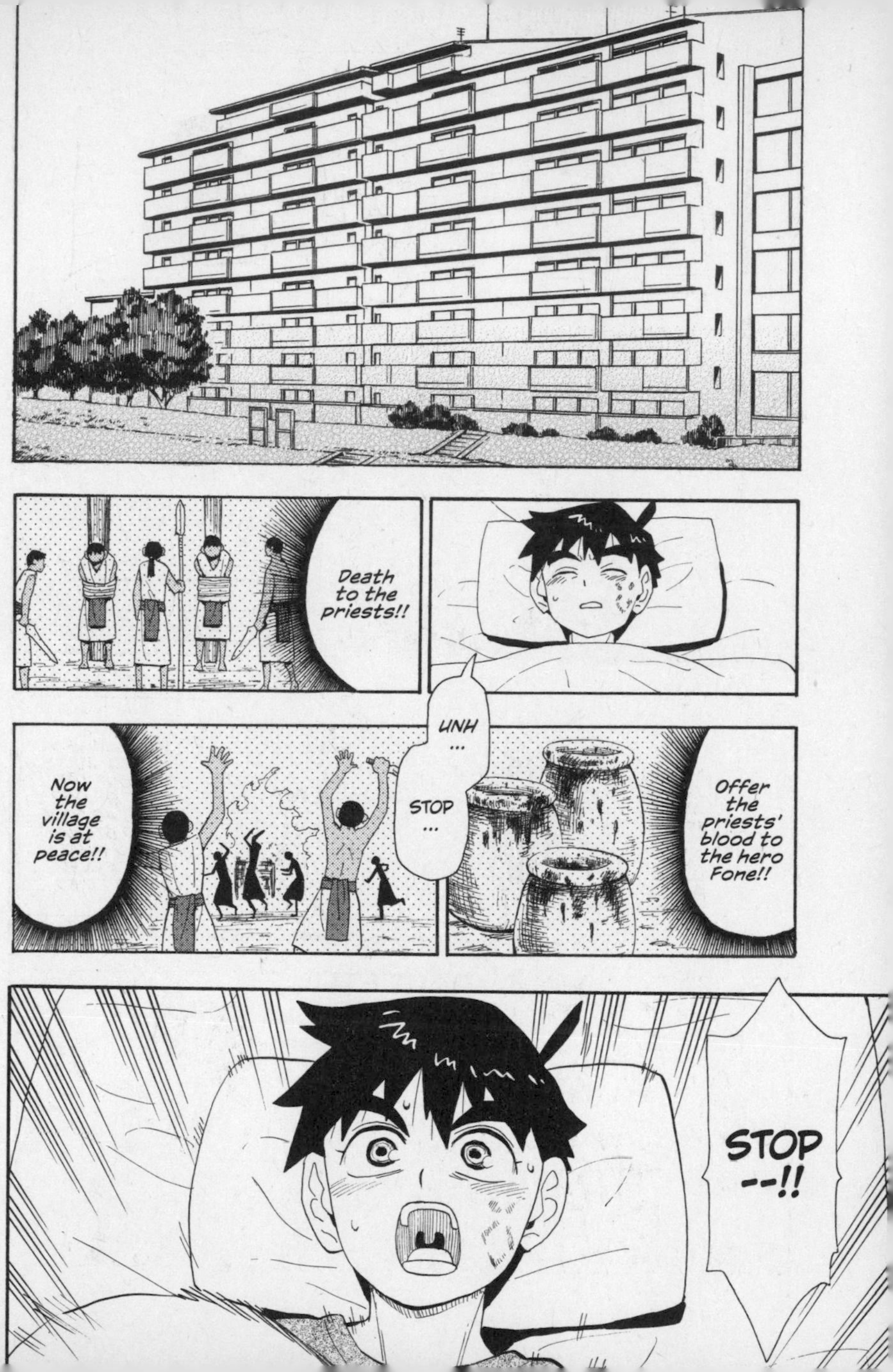
Death to the priests!!
UNH ... STOP ...
Offer the priests' blood to the hero Fone!!
Now the village is at peace!!
STOP --!!

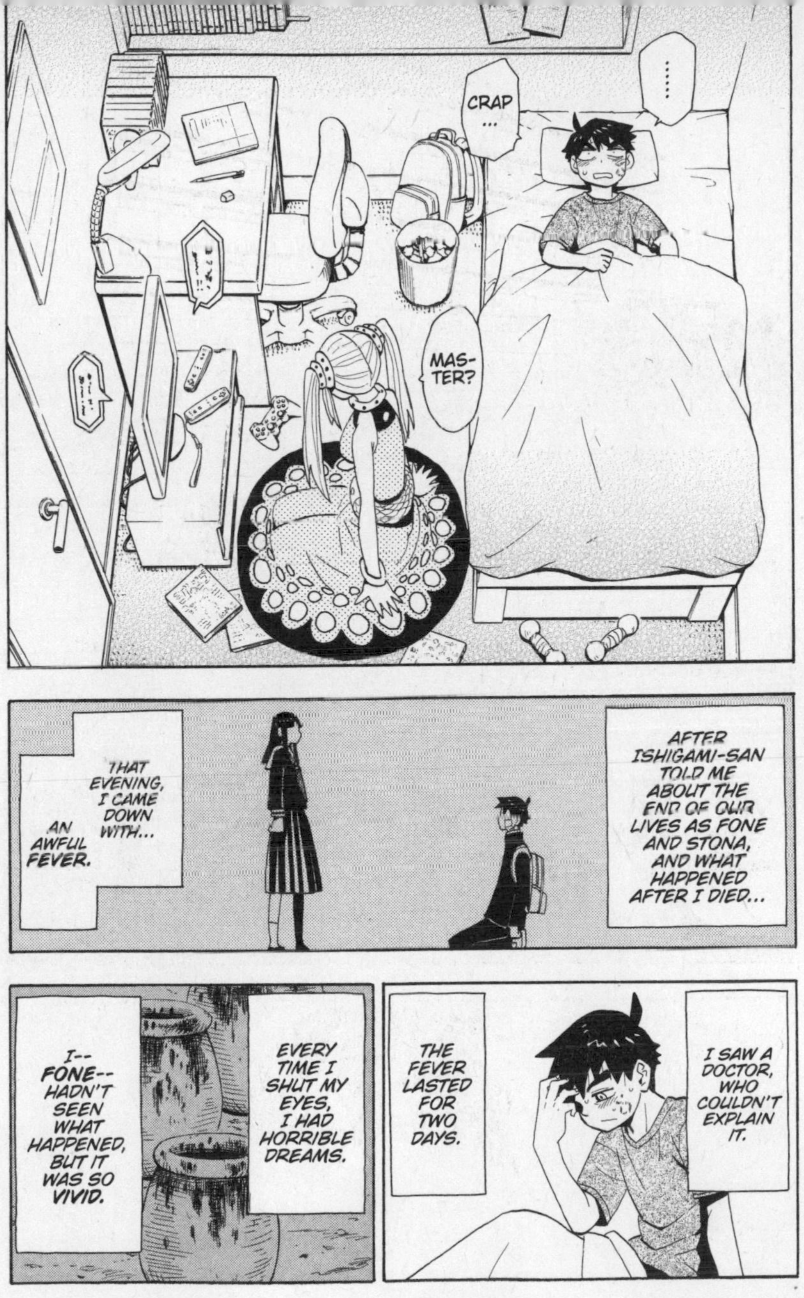
......
CRAP ...
MAS-TER?
AFTER ISHIGAMI-SAN TOLD ME ABOUT THE END OF OUR LIVES AS FONE AND STONA, AND WHAT HAPPENED AFTER I DIED...
THAT EVENING, I CAME DOWN WITH...
AN AWFUL FEVER.
I SAW A DOCTOR, WHO COULDN'T EXPLAIN IT.
THE FEVER LASTED FOR TWO DAYS.
EVERY TIME I SHUT MY EYES, I HAD HORRIBLE DREAMS.
I-- FONE-- HADN'T SEEN WHAT HAPPENED, BUT IT WAS SO VIVID.

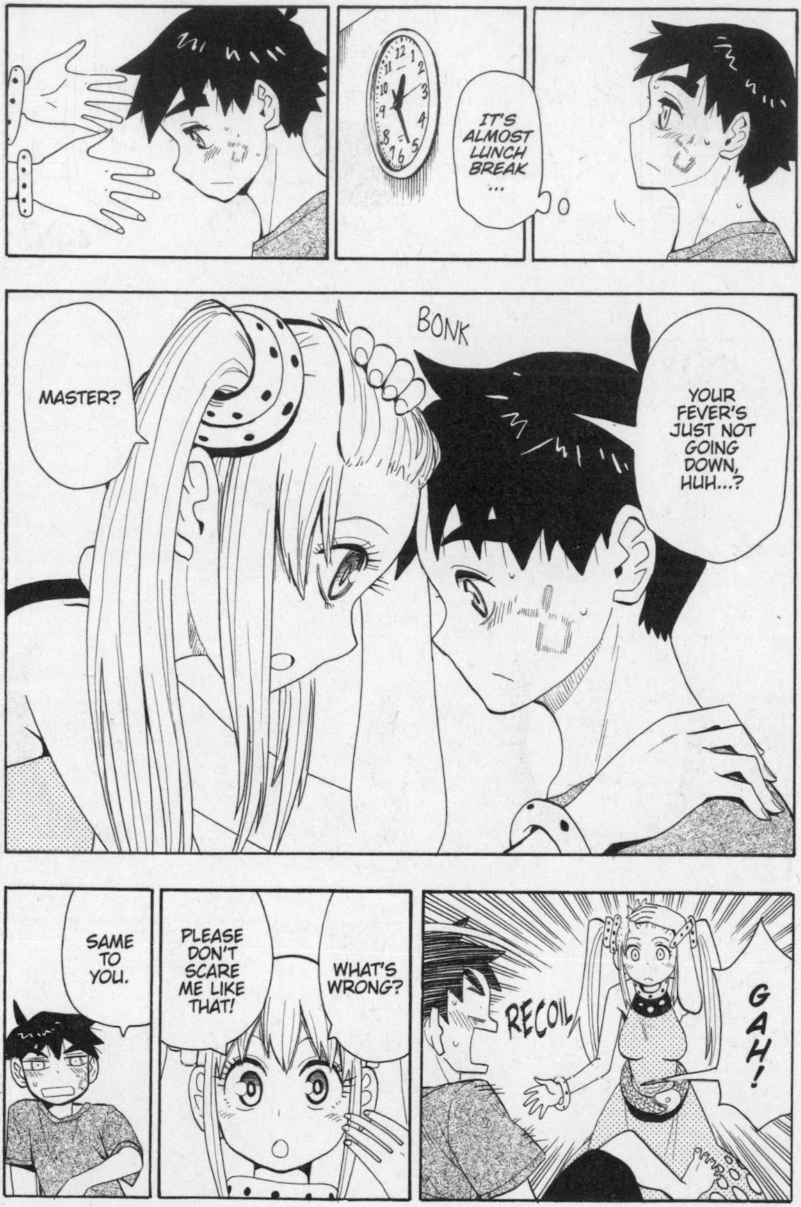
IT'S ALMOST LUNCH BREAK ...
YOUR FEVER'S JUST NOT GOING DOWN, HUH...?
BONK
MASTER?
GAH!
RECOIL
WHAT'S WRONG?
PLEASE DON'T SCARE ME LIKE THAT!
SAME TO YOU.

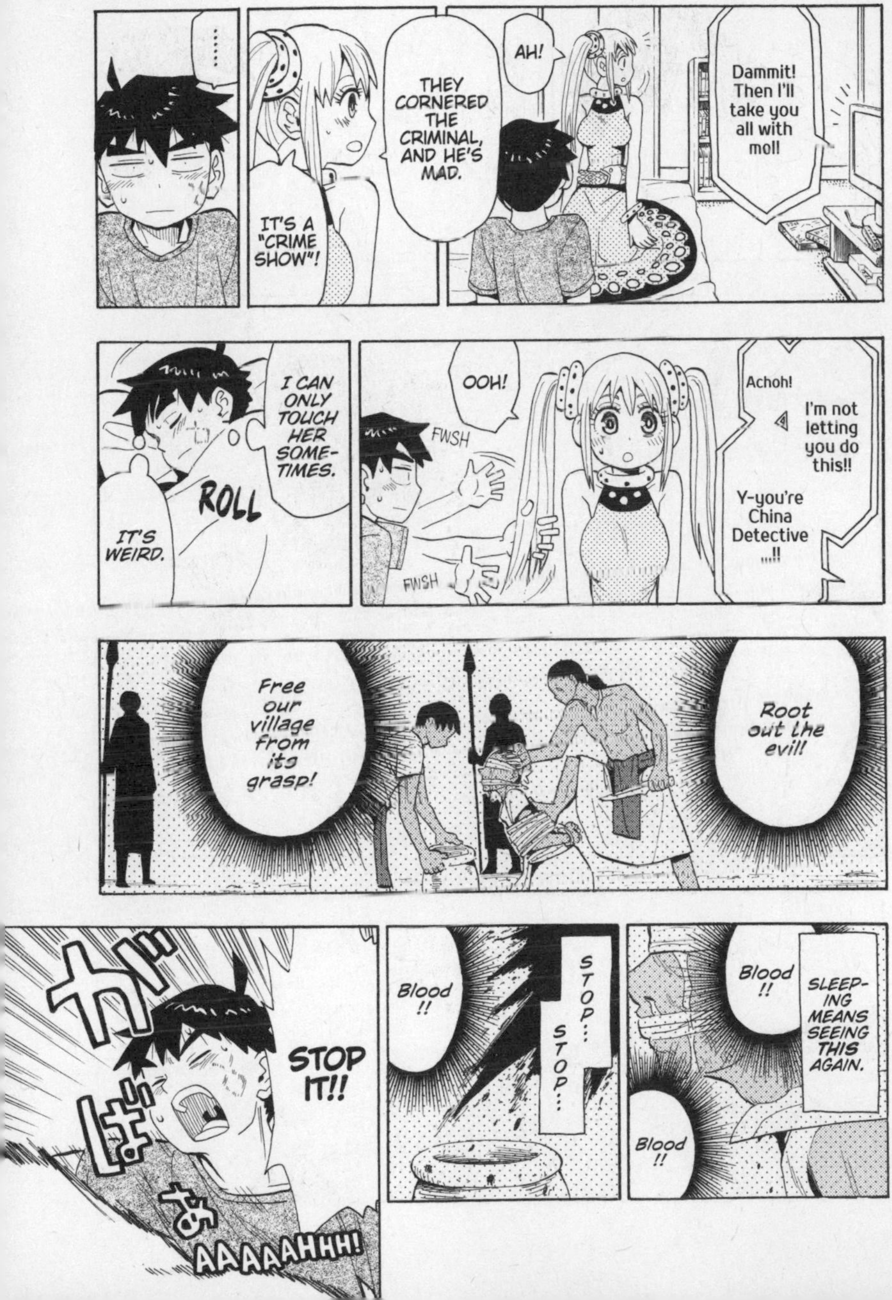
Dammit! Then I'll take you all with me!!
AH!
THEY CORNERED THE CRIMINAL, AND HE'S MAD.
IT'S A "CRIME SHOW"!
......
Achoh!
I'm not letting you do this!!
Y-you're China Detective ...!!
OOH!
FWSH
FWSH
I CAN ONLY TOUCH HER SOME-TIMES.
ROLL
IT'S WEIRD.
Root out the evil!
Free our village from its grasp!
SLEEP-ING MEANS SEEING THIS AGAIN.
Blood!!
Blood!!
STOP...
STOP...
Blood!!
STOP IT!!
AAAAAHHH!

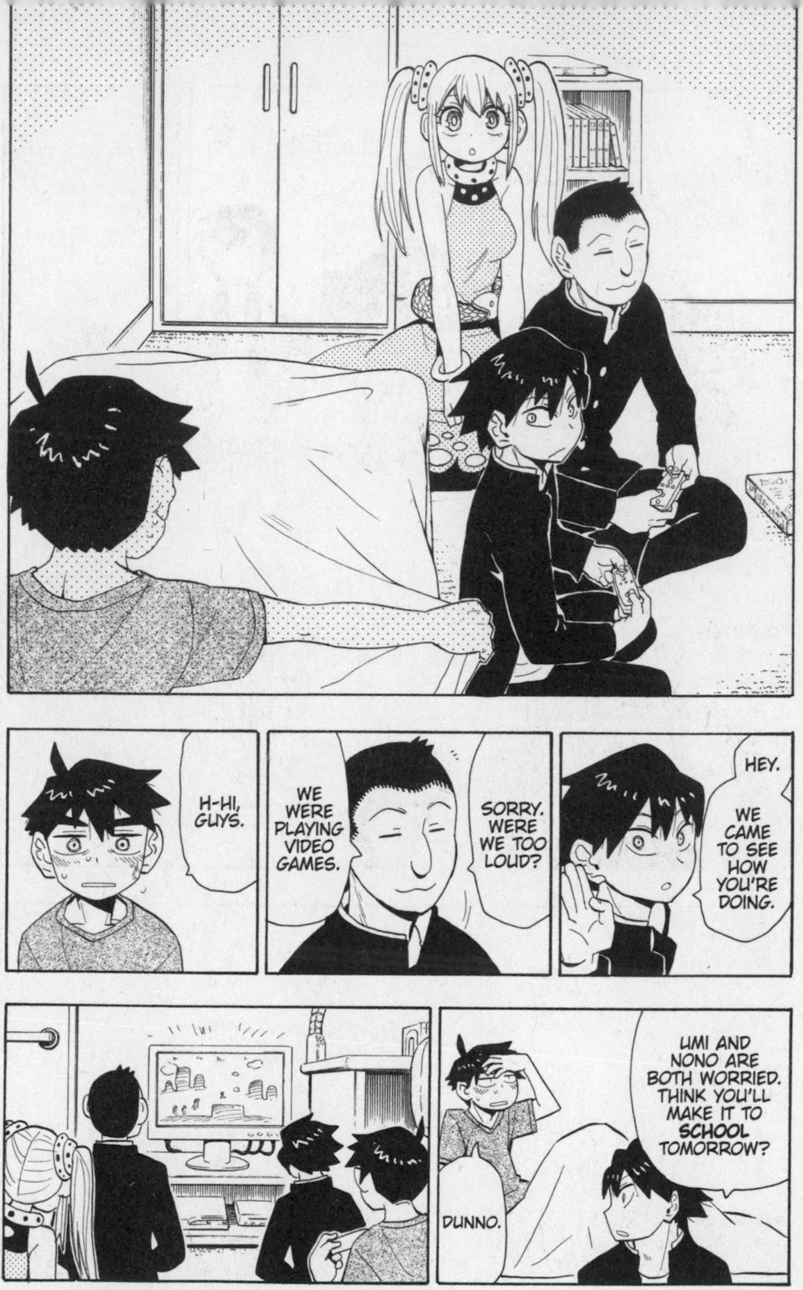
HEY.
WE CAME TO SEE HOW YOU'RE DOING.
SORRY. WERE WE TOO LOUD?
WE WERE PLAYING VIDEO GAMES.
H-HI, GUYS.
UMI AND NONO ARE BOTH WORRIED. THINK YOU'LL MAKE IT TO **SCHOOL** TOMORROW?
DUNNO.

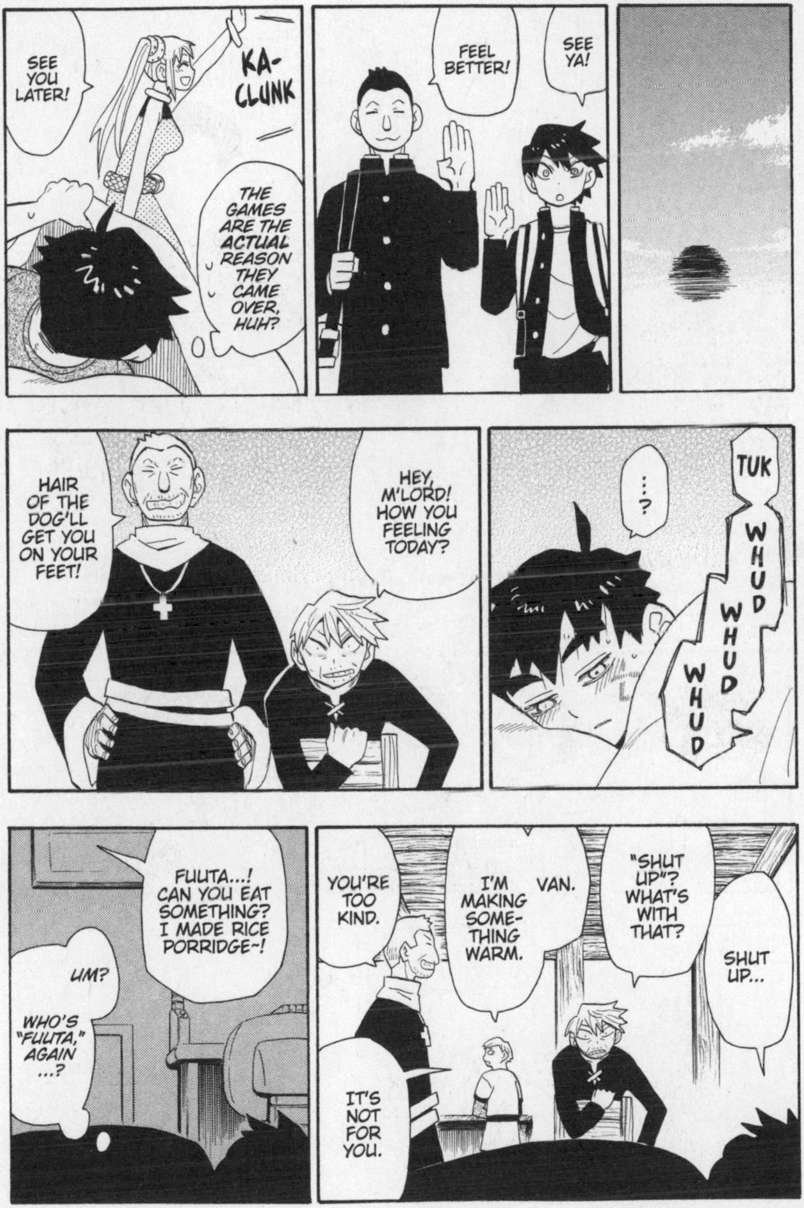
SEE YA!
FEEL BETTER!
KA-CLUNK
SEE YOU LATER!
THE GAMES ARE THE ACTUAL REASON THEY CAME OVER, HUH?
TUK
WHUD WHUD WHUD WHUD
...?
HEY, M'LORD! HOW YOU FEELING TODAY?
HAIR OF THE DOG'LL GET YOU ON YOUR FEET!
SHUT UP...
"SHUT UP"? WHAT'S WITH THAT?
VAN.
I'M MAKING SOME-THING WARM.
YOU'RE TOO KIND.
IT'S NOT FOR YOU.
FUUTA...! CAN YOU EAT SOMETHING? I MADE RICE PORRIDGE~!
UM?
WHO'S "FUUTA," AGAIN ...?

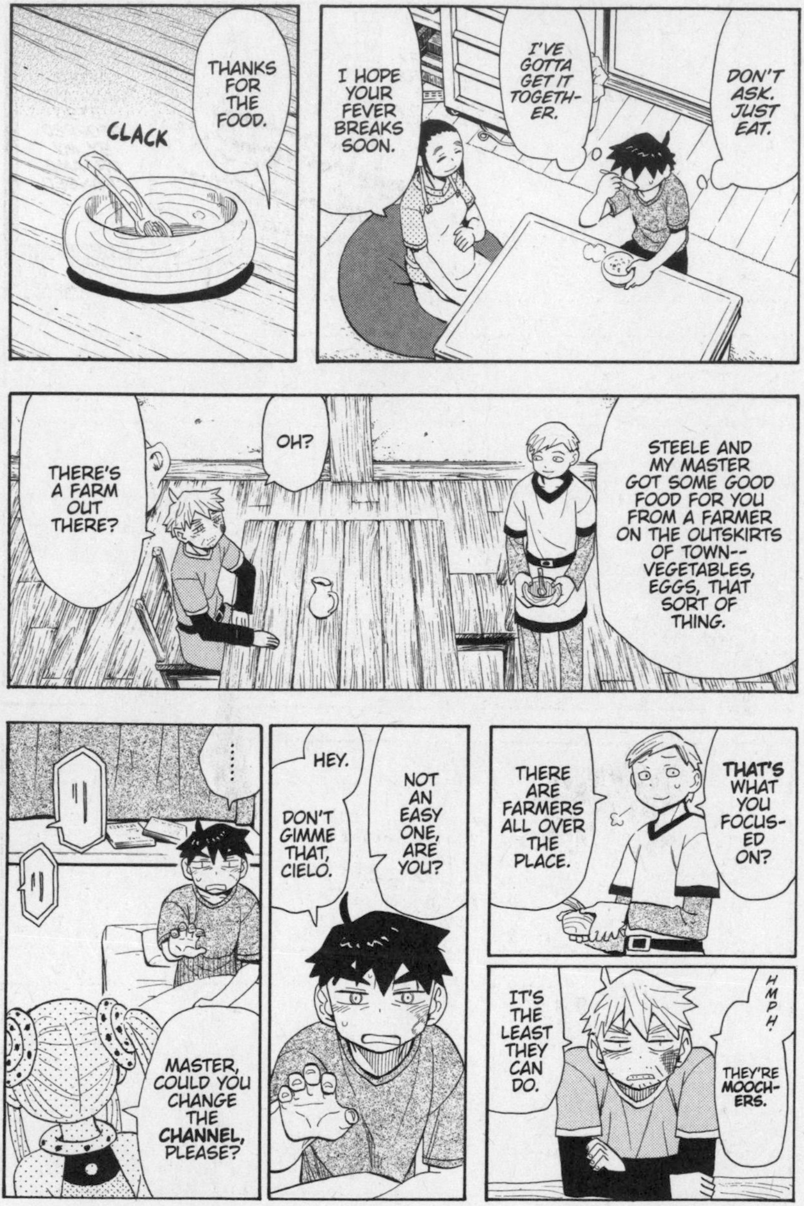
DON'T ASK. JUST EAT.
I'VE GOTTA GET IT TOGETHER.
I HOPE YOUR FEVER BREAKS SOON.
THANKS FOR THE FOOD.
CLACK
STEELE AND MY MASTER GOT SOME GOOD FOOD FOR YOU FROM A FARMER ON THE OUTSKIRTS OF TOWN--VEGETABLES, EGGS, THAT SORT OF THING.
OH?
THERE'S A FARM OUT THERE?
THAT'S WHAT YOU FOCUSED ON?
THERE ARE FARMERS ALL OVER THE PLACE.
HMPH.
THEY'RE MOOCHERS.
IT'S THE LEAST THEY CAN DO.
NOT AN EASY ONE, ARE YOU?
HEY.
DON'T GIMME THAT, CIELO.
......
MASTER, COULD YOU CHANGE THE CHANNEL, PLEASE?

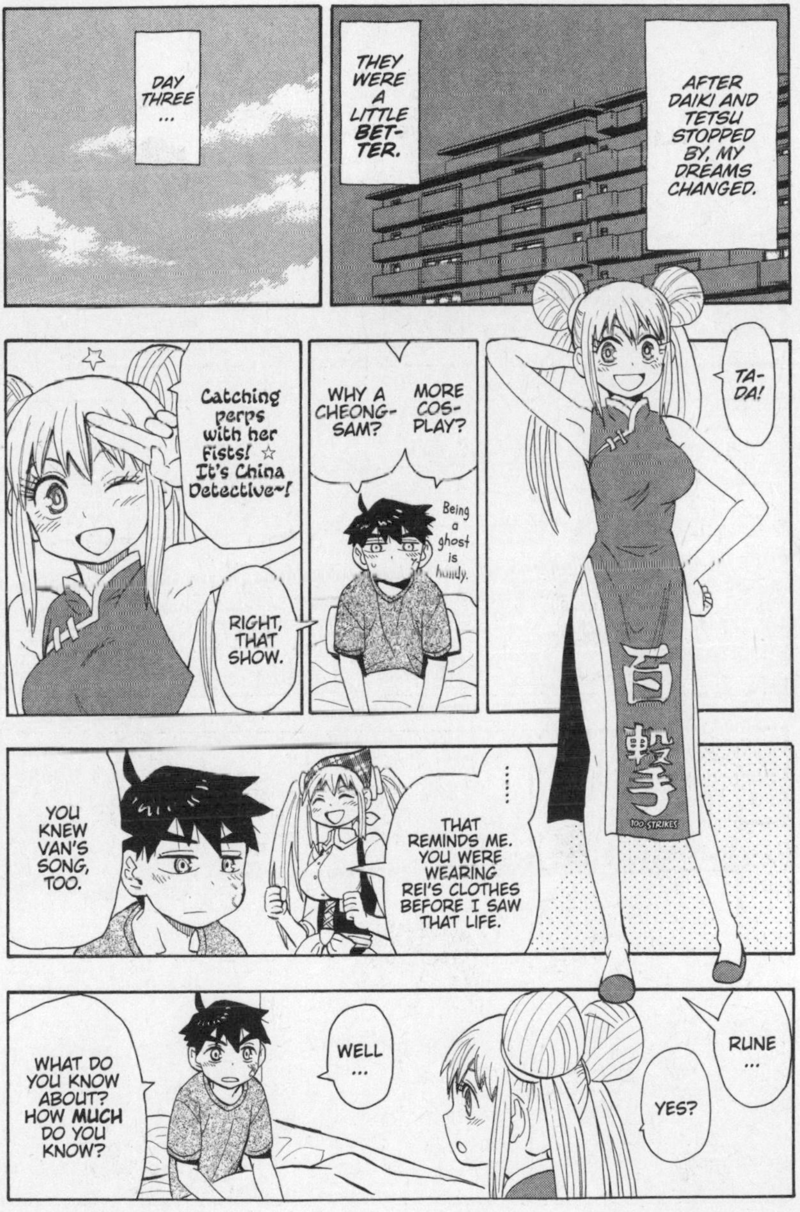
AFTER DAIKI AND TETSU STOPPED BY, MY DREAMS CHANGED.
THEY WERE A LITTLE BET-TER.
DAY THREE ...
TA-DA!
100 STRIKES
MORE COS-PLAY?
WHY A CHEONG-SAM?
Being a ghost is handy.
Catching perps with her Fists! ☆ It's China Detective~!
RIGHT, THAT SHOW.
......
THAT REMINDS ME. YOU WERE WEARING REI'S CLOTHES BEFORE I SAW THAT LIFE.
YOU KNEW VAN'S SONG, TOO.
RUNE ...
YES?
WELL ...
WHAT DO YOU KNOW ABOUT? HOW MUCH DO YOU KNOW?

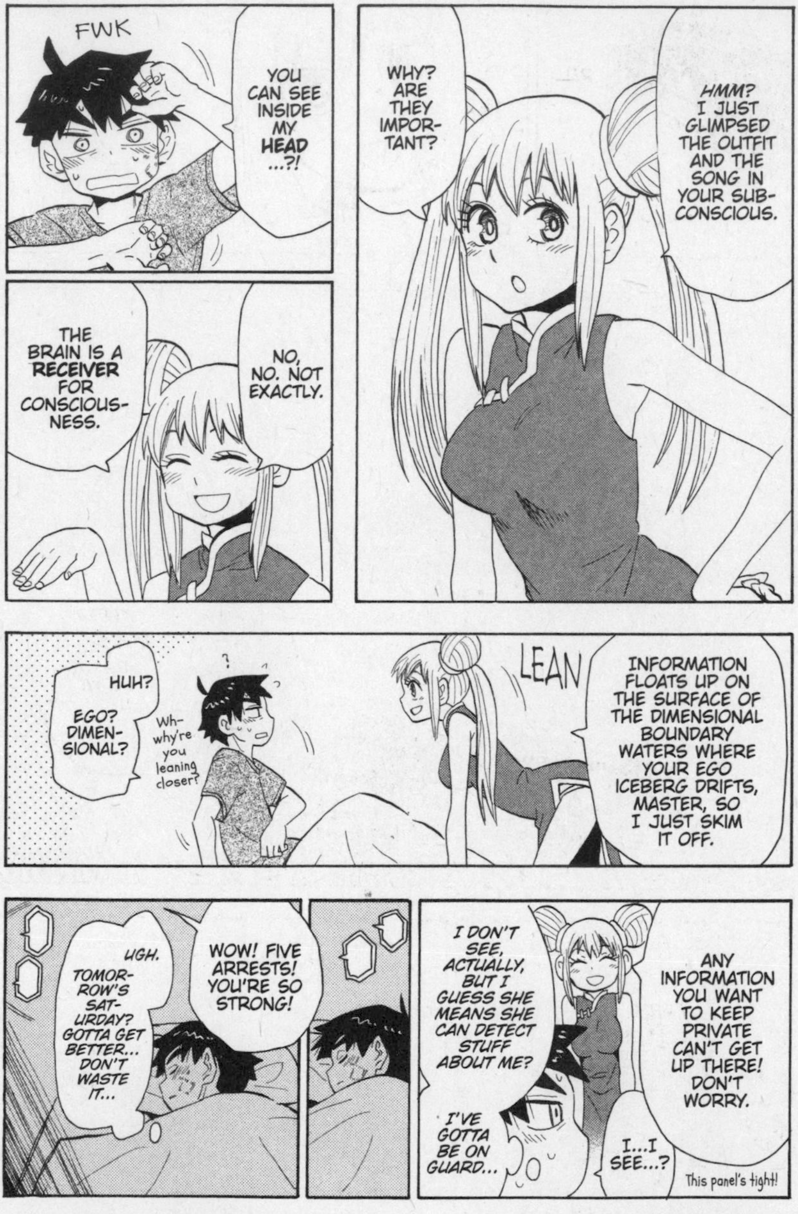
HMM? I JUST GLIMPSED THE OUTFIT AND THE SONG IN YOUR SUB-CONSCIOUS.
WHY? ARE THEY IMPOR-TANT?
FWK
YOU CAN SEE INSIDE MY HEAD ...?!
NO, NO. NOT EXACTLY.
THE BRAIN IS A RECEIVER FOR CONSCIOUS-NESS.
INFORMATION FLOATS UP ON THE SURFACE OF THE DIMENSIONAL BOUNDARY WATERS WHERE YOUR EGO ICEBERG DRIFTS, MASTER, SO I JUST SKIM IT OFF.
LEAN
Wh-why're you leaning closer?
HUH?
EGO? DIMEN-SIONAL?
ANY INFORMATION YOU WANT TO KEEP PRIVATE CAN'T GET UP THERE! DON'T WORRY.
I DON'T SEE, ACTUALLY, BUT I GUESS SHE MEANS SHE CAN DETECT STUFF ABOUT ME?
I...I SEE...?
I'VE GOTTA BE ON GUARD...
This panel's tight!
WOW! FIVE ARRESTS! YOU'RE SO STRONG!
UGH. TOMOR-ROW'S SAT-URDAY? GOTTA GET BETTER... DON'T WASTE IT...

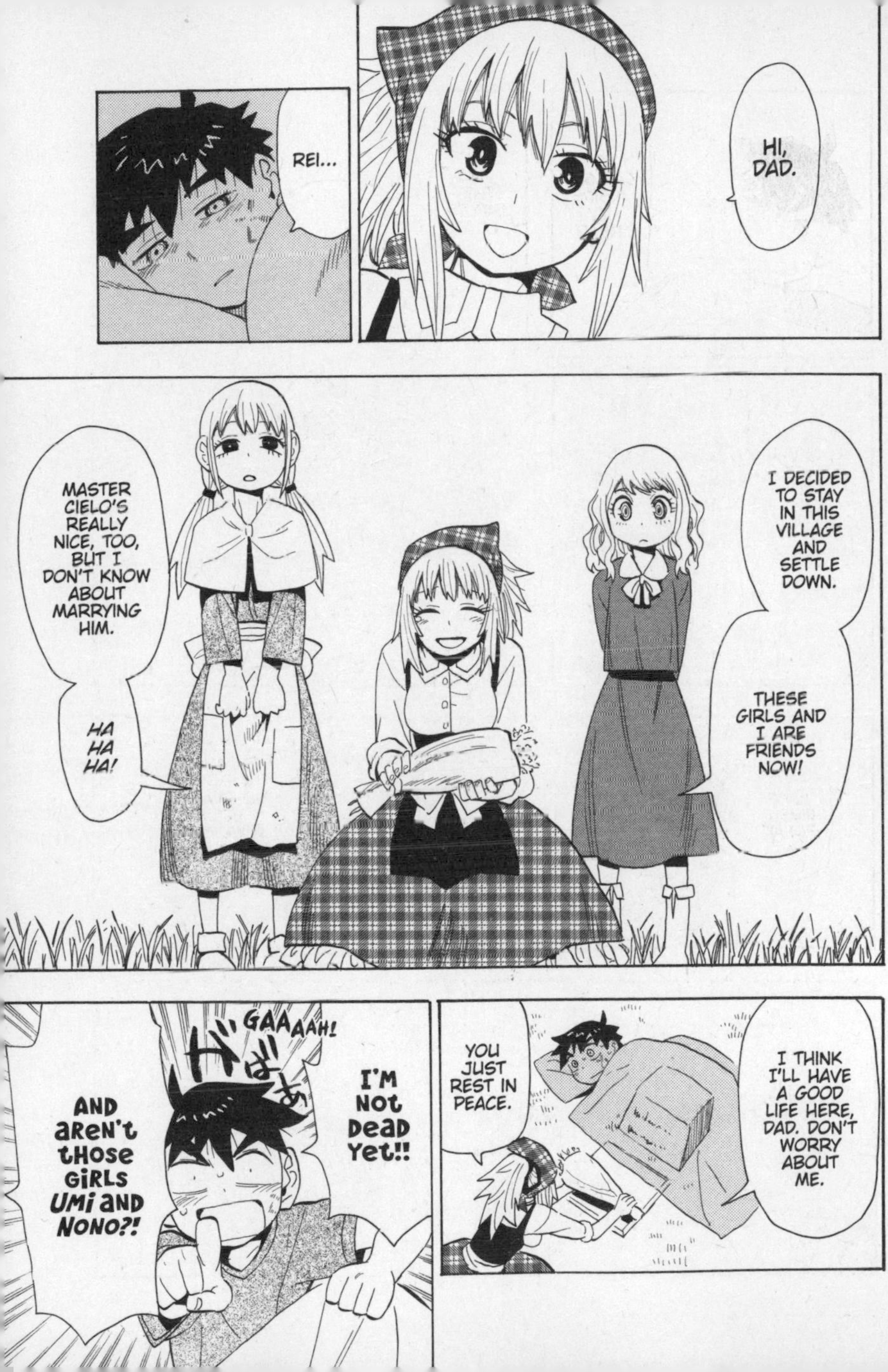
HI, DAD.
REI...
I DECIDED TO STAY IN THIS VILLAGE AND SETTLE DOWN.
THESE GIRLS AND I ARE FRIENDS NOW!
MASTER CIELO'S REALLY NICE, TOO, BUT I DON'T KNOW ABOUT MARRYING HIM.
HA HA HA!
I THINK I'LL HAVE A GOOD LIFE HERE, DAD. DON'T WORRY ABOUT ME.
YOU JUST REST IN PEACE.
I'M NOT DEAD YET!!
GAAAAH!
AND AREN'T THOSE GIRLS UMI AND NONO?!

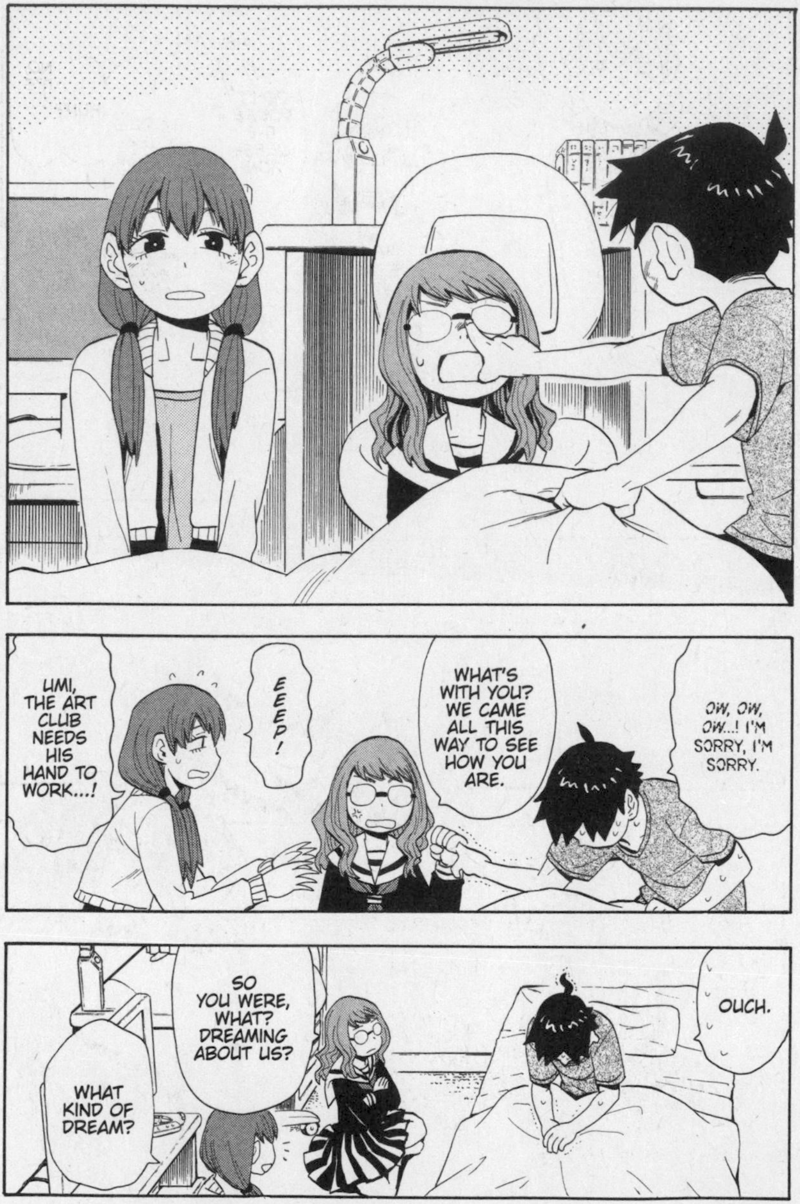
OW, OW, OW...! I'M SORRY, I'M SORRY.
WHAT'S WITH YOU? WE CAME ALL THIS WAY TO SEE HOW YOU ARE.
EEEP!
UMI, THE ART CLUB NEEDS HIS HAND TO WORK...!
OUCH.
SO YOU WERE, WHAT? DREAMING ABOUT US?
WHAT KIND OF DREAM?

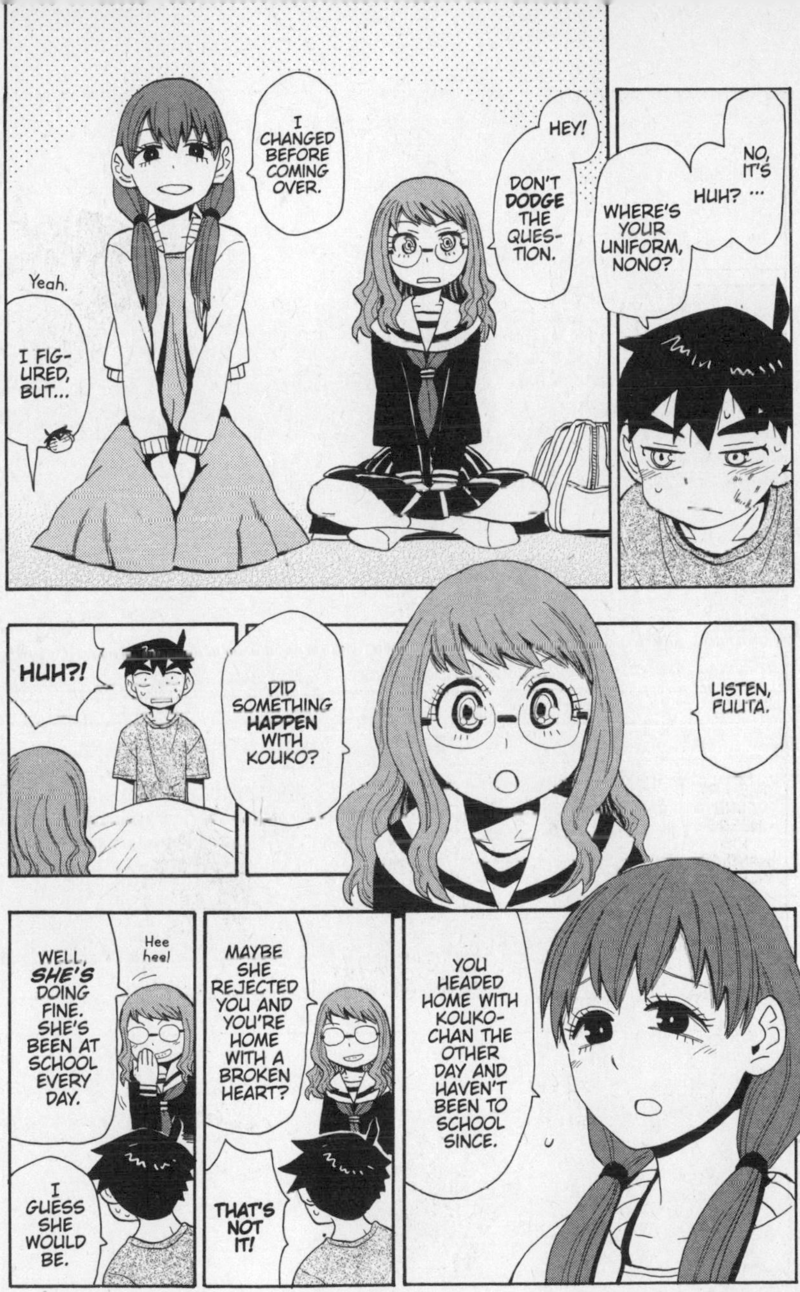

NO, IT'S HUH? …
WHERE'S YOUR UNIFORM, NONO?
HEY!
DON'T DODGE THE QUES-TION.
I CHANGED BEFORE COMING OVER.
Yeah.
I FIG-URED, BUT…
LISTEN, FUUTA.
DID SOMETHING HAPPEN WITH KOUKO?
HUH?!
YOU HEADED HOME WITH KOUKO-CHAN THE OTHER DAY AND HAVEN'T BEEN TO SCHOOL SINCE.
MAYBE SHE REJECTED YOU AND YOU'RE HOME WITH A BROKEN HEART?
THAT'S NOT IT!
Hee hee!
WELL, SHE'S DOING FINE. SHE'S BEEN AT SCHOOL EVERY DAY.
I GUESS SHE WOULD BE.

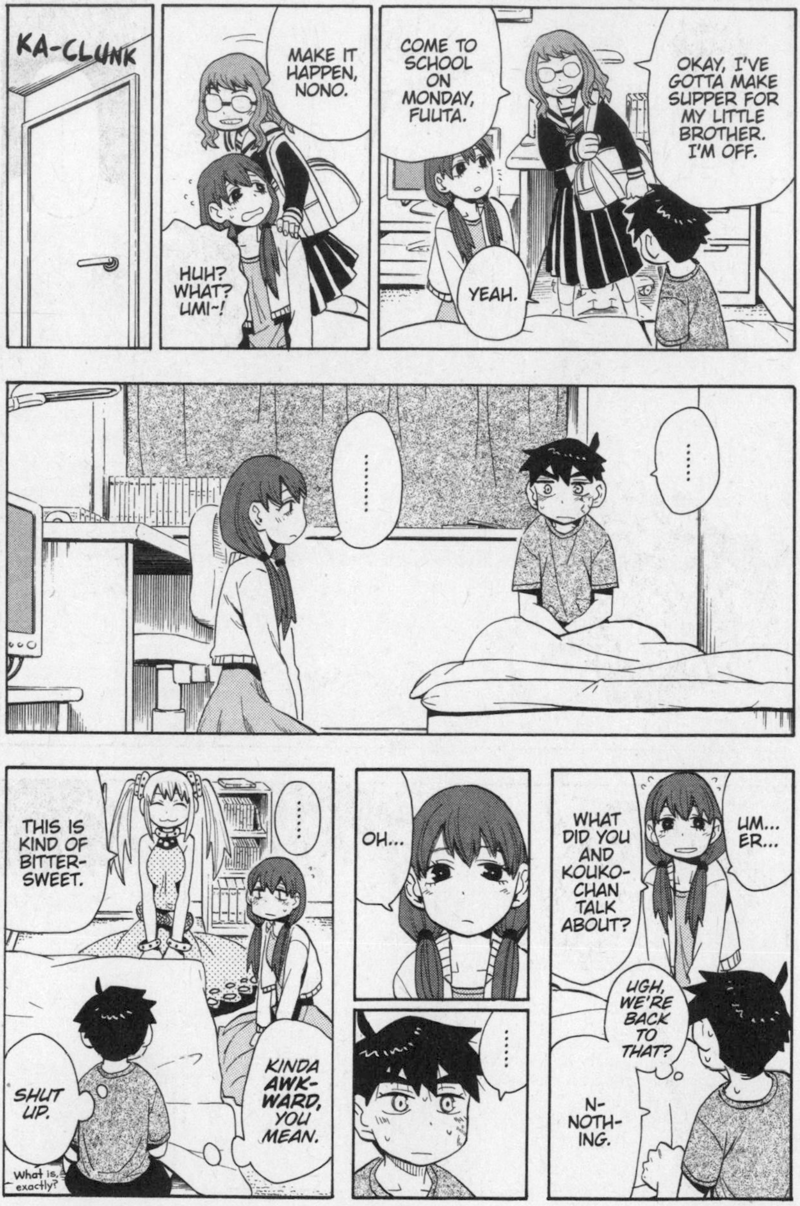
OKAY, I'VE GOTTA MAKE SUPPER FOR MY LITTLE BROTHER. I'M OFF.
COME TO SCHOOL ON MONDAY, FUUTA.
YEAH.
MAKE IT HAPPEN, NONO.
HUH? WHAT? UMI~!
KA-CLUNK
......
......
UM... ER...
WHAT DID YOU AND KOUKO-CHAN TALK ABOUT?
UGH, WE'RE BACK TO THAT?
N-NOTH-ING.
OH...
......
......
THIS IS KIND OF BITTER-SWEET.
KINDA AWK-WARD, YOU MEAN.
SHUT UP.
What is, exactly?

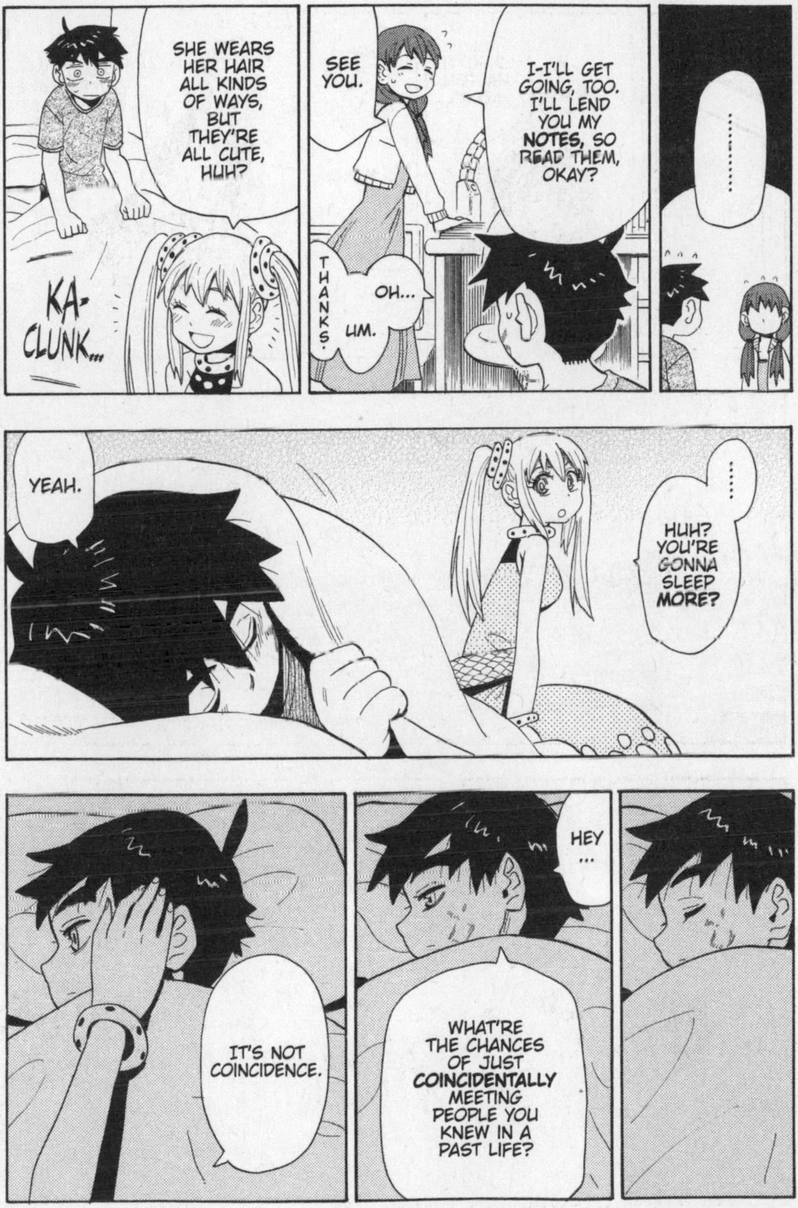
......
I-I'LL GET GOING, TOO. I'LL LEND YOU MY NOTES, SO READ THEM, OKAY?
SEE YOU.
OH... UM.
THANKS.
SHE WEARS HER HAIR ALL KINDS OF WAYS, BUT THEY'RE ALL CUTE, HUH?
KA-CLUNK...
......
HUH? YOU'RE GONNA SLEEP MORE?
YEAH.
HEY...
WHAT'RE THE CHANCES OF JUST COINCIDENTALLY MEETING PEOPLE YOU KNEW IN A PAST LIFE?
IT'S NOT COINCIDENCE.

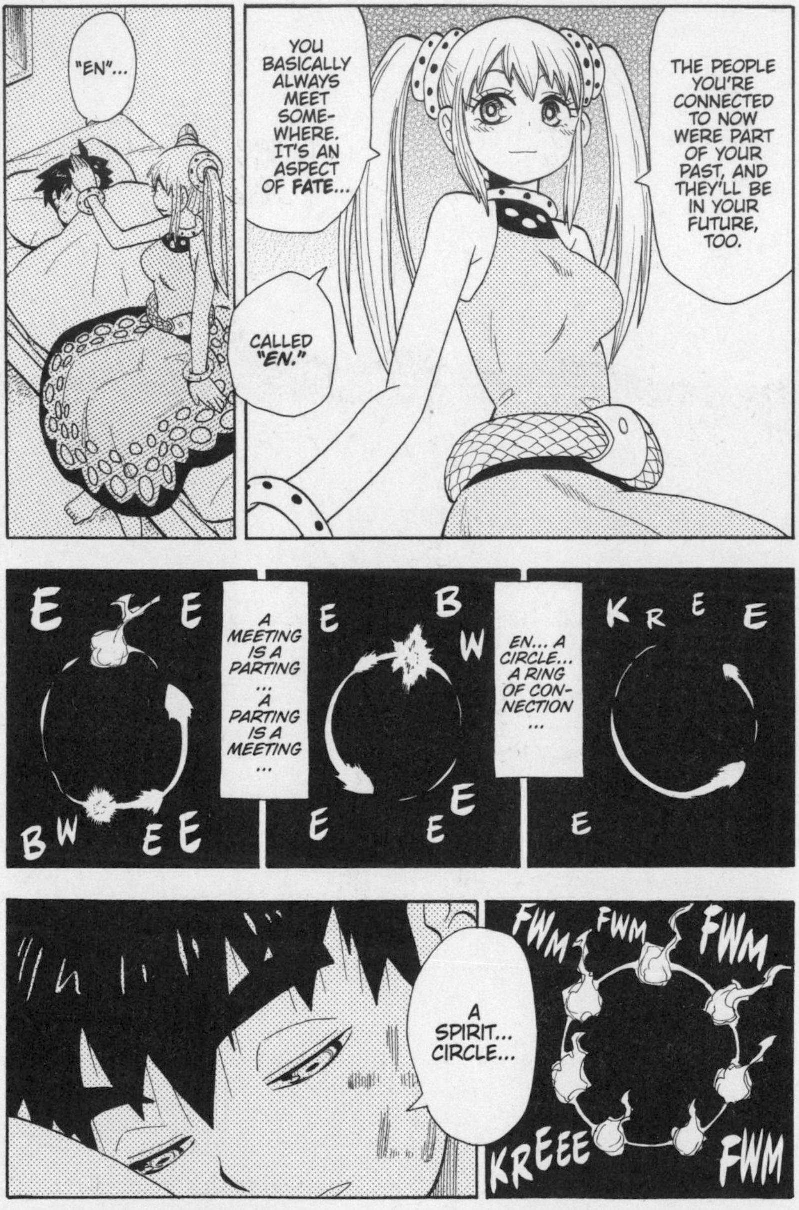
THE PEOPLE YOU'RE CONNECTED TO NOW WERE PART OF YOUR PAST, AND THEY'LL BE IN YOUR FUTURE, TOO.
YOU BASICALLY ALWAYS MEET SOME-WHERE. IT'S AN ASPECT OF **FATE**...
CALLED ***"EN."***
"EN"...
KREEE
E
EN... A CIRCLE... A RING OF CON-NECTION ...
BW
E
EEE
A MEETING IS A PARTING ... A PARTING IS A MEETING ...
EE
BW
EE
FWM
FWM
FWM
FWM
KREEE
A SPIRIT... CIRCLE...

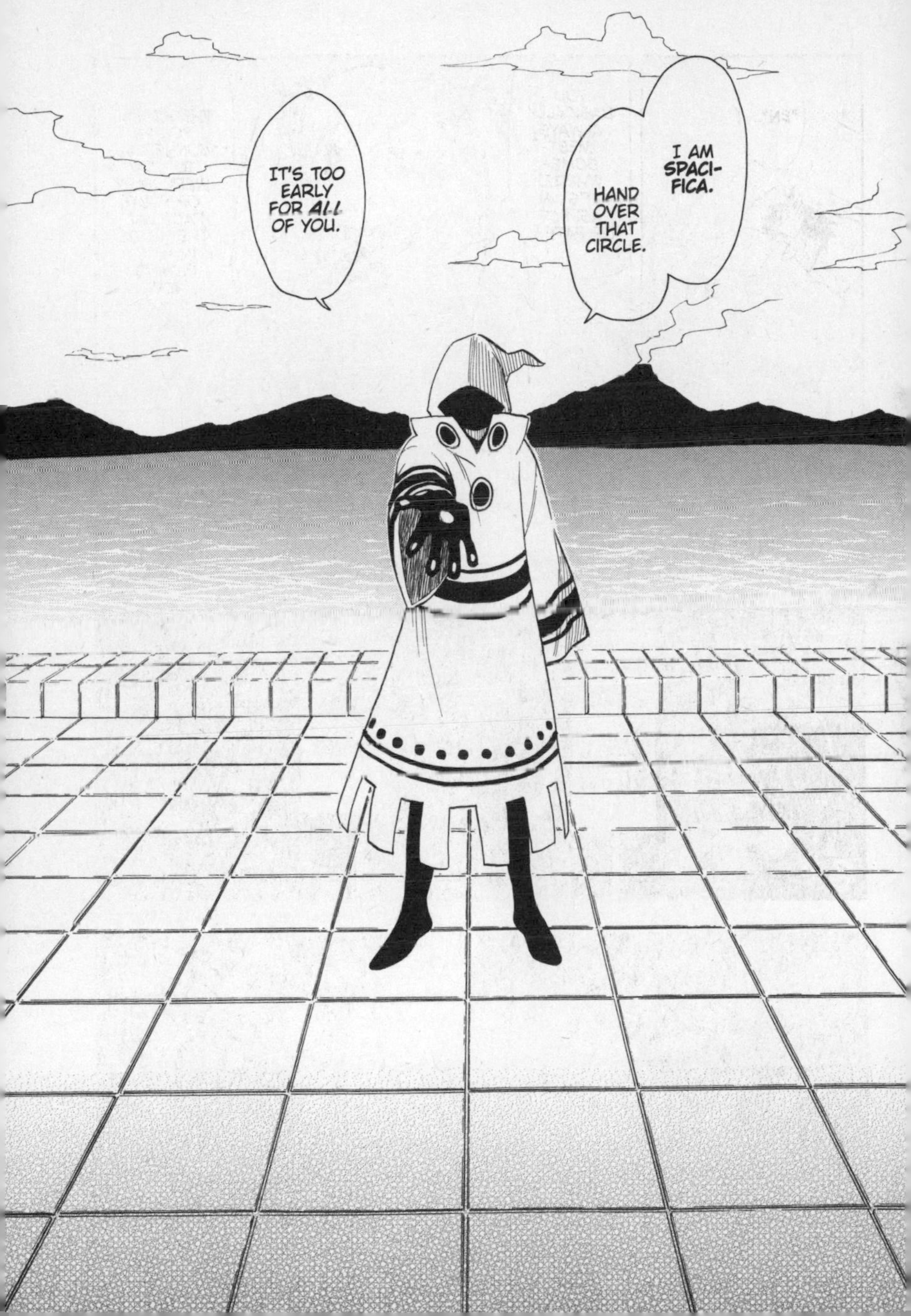
I AM SPACI-FICA.
HAND OVER THAT CIRCLE.
IT'S TOO EARLY FOR ALL OF YOU.

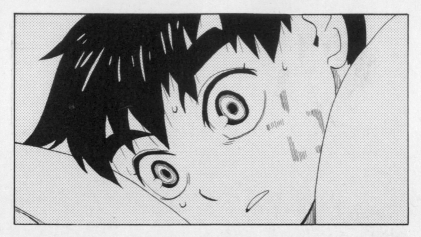

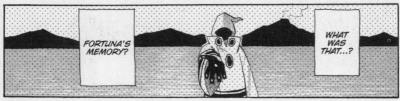

WHAT WAS THAT...?
FORTUNA'S MEMORY?
"It's too early...
"For all of you."
WHY AM I STARTING TO SMILE ...?
AM I FEELING FORTUNA'S EMOTIONS ...?
WHAT'S SO FUNNY, FORTUNA ...?

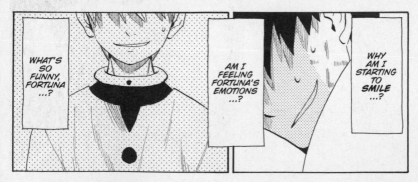

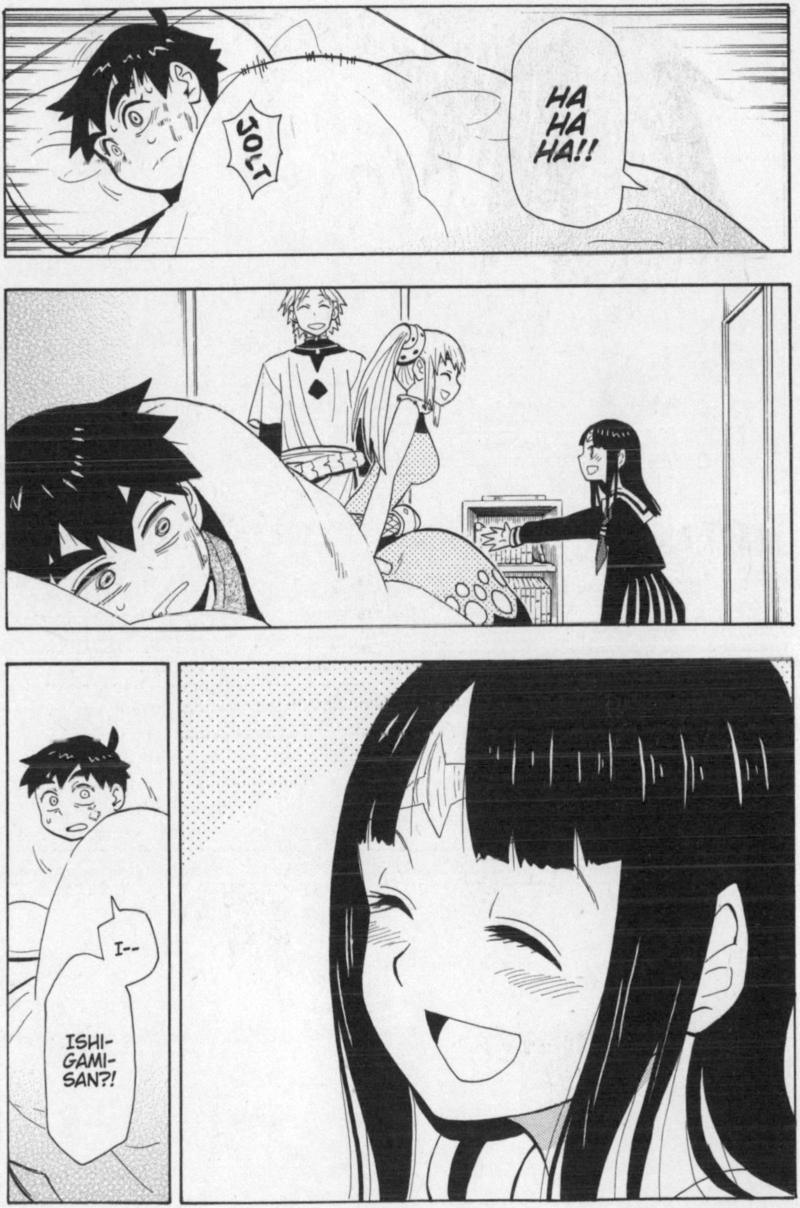
HA HA HA!!
JOLT
I--
ISHI-GAMI-SAN?!

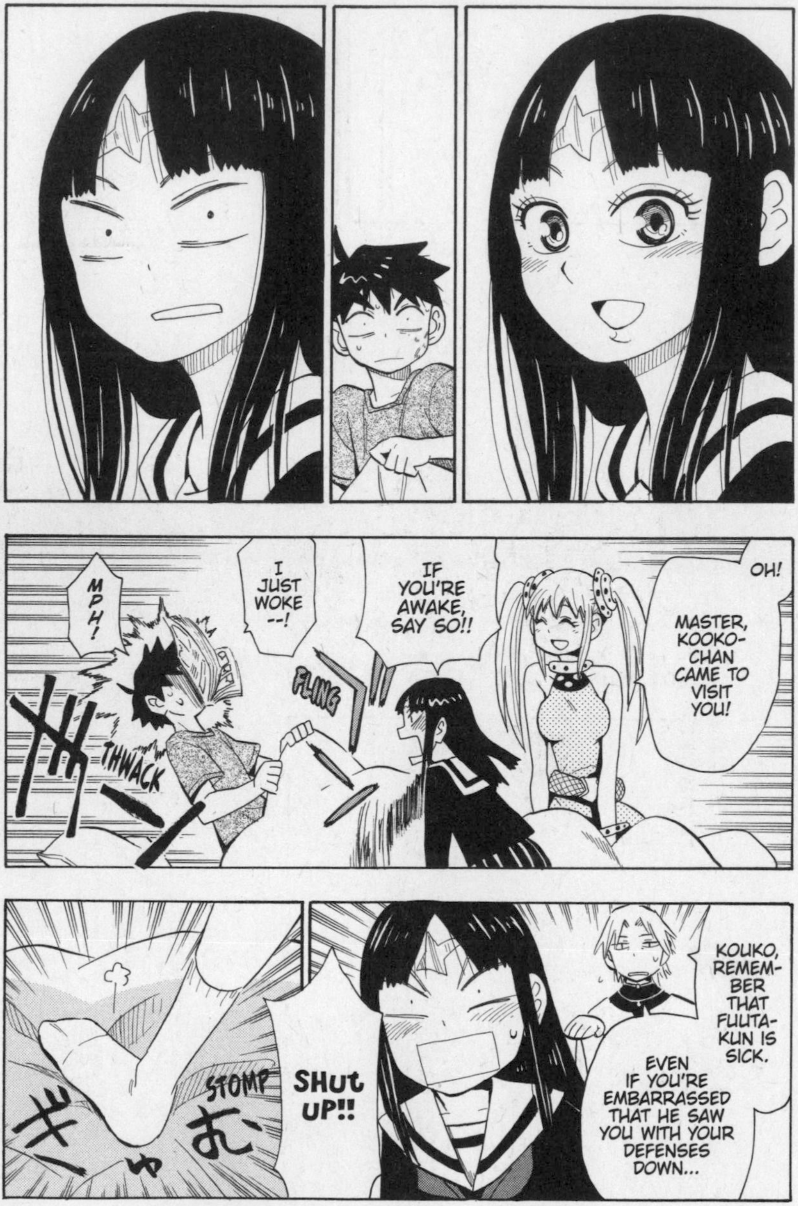
OH!
MASTER, KOOKO-CHAN CAME TO VISIT YOU!
IF YOU'RE AWAKE, SAY SO!!
FLING
I JUST WOKE --!
MPH!
THWACK
KOUKO, REMEMBER THAT FUUTA-KUN IS SICK.
EVEN IF YOU'RE EMBARRASSED THAT HE SAW YOU WITH YOUR DEFENSES DOWN...
SHUt UP!!
STOMP
ぎゅむ

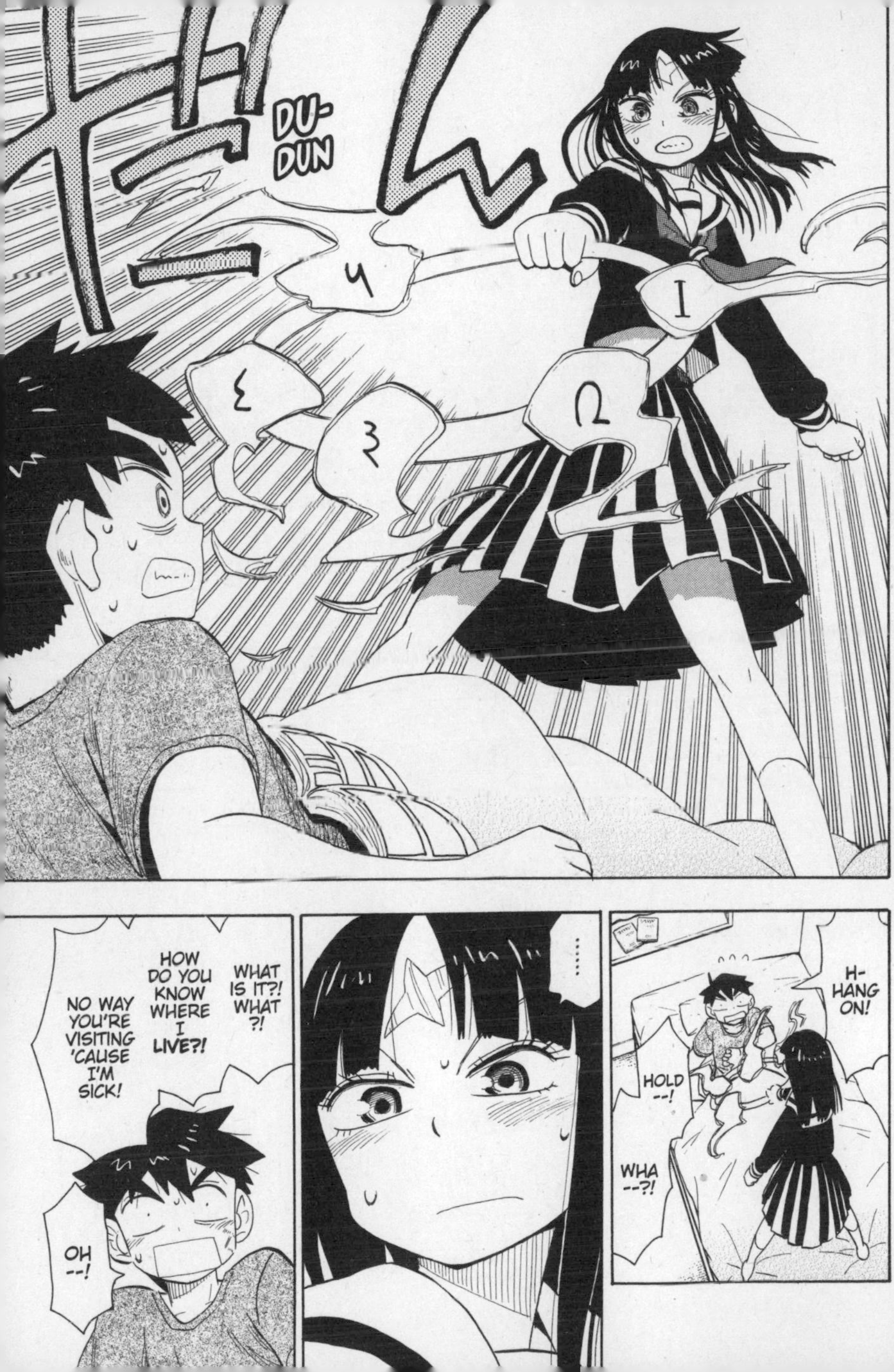
DU-DUN
H-HANG ON!
HOLD --!
WHA --?!
......
WHAT IS IT?! WHAT ?!
HOW DO YOU KNOW WHERE I LIVE?!
NO WAY YOU'RE VISITING 'CAUSE I'M SICK!
OH --!

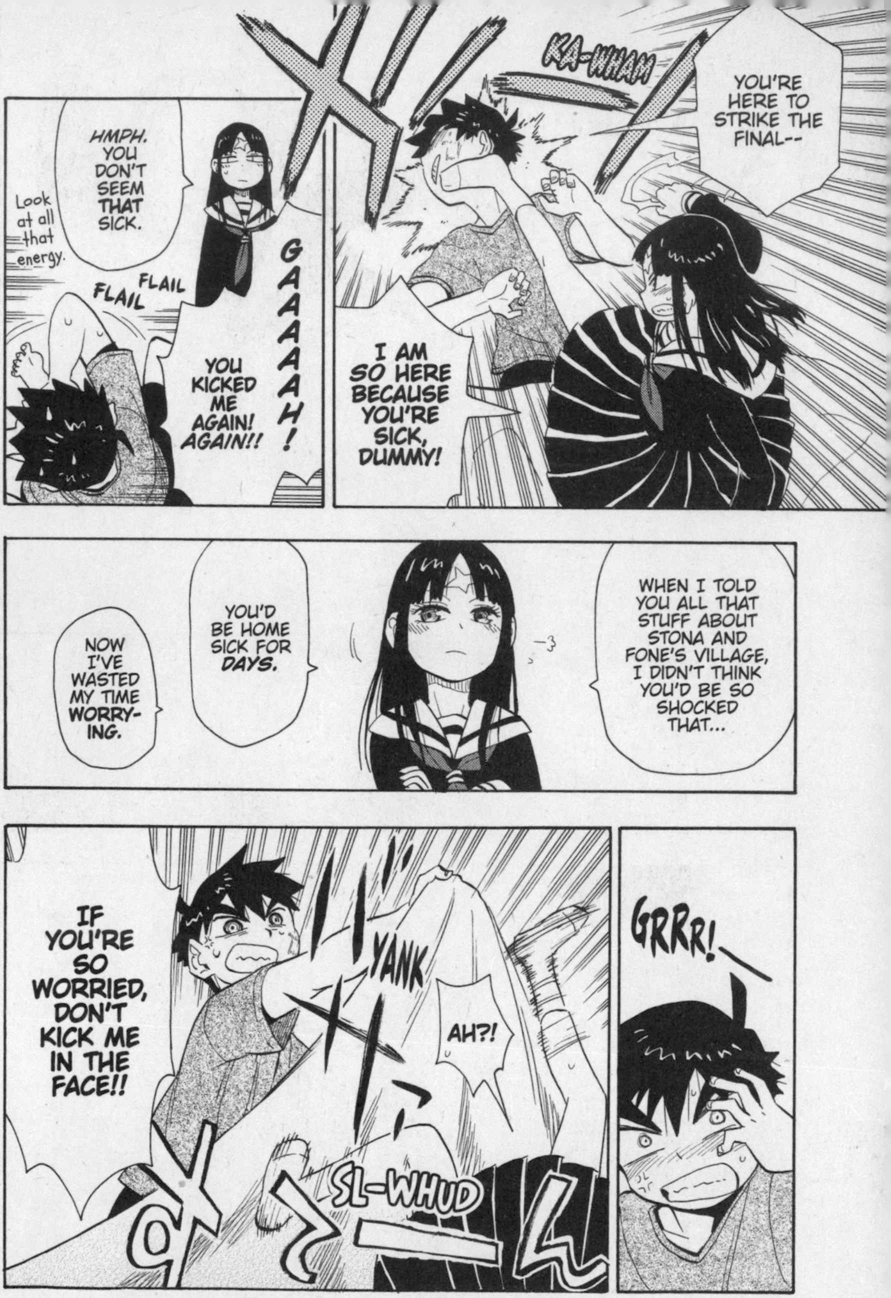
KA-WHAM
YOU'RE HERE TO STRIKE THE FINAL--
I AM SO HERE BECAUSE YOU'RE SICK, DUMMY!
GAAAAAAH!
YOU KICKED ME AGAIN! AGAIN!!
HMPH. YOU DON'T SEEM THAT SICK.
Look at all that energy.
FLAIL
FLAIL
WHEN I TOLD YOU ALL THAT STUFF ABOUT STONA AND FONE'S VILLAGE, I DIDN'T THINK YOU'D BE SO SHOCKED THAT...
YOU'D BE HOME SICK FOR DAYS.
NOW I'VE WASTED MY TIME WORRYING.
GRRR!
YANK
IF YOU'RE SO WORRIED, DON'T KICK ME IN THE FACE!!
AH?!
SL-WHUD

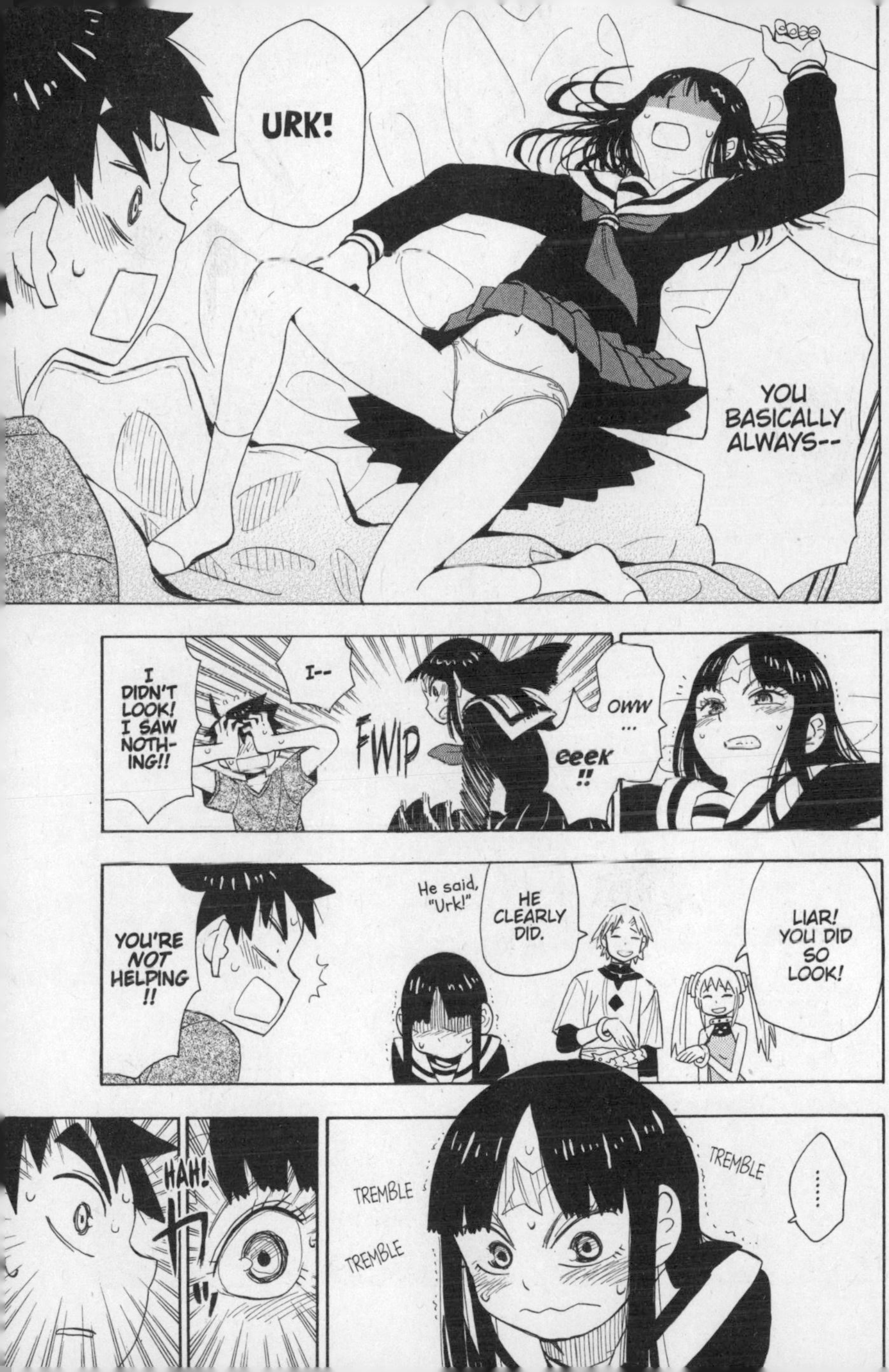
YOU BASICALLY ALWAYS--
URK!
OWW ...
eeek!!
FWIP
I--
I DIDN'T LOOK! I SAW NOTHING!!
LIAR! YOU DID SO LOOK!
HE CLEARLY DID.
He said, "Urk!"
YOU'RE NOT HELPING!!
......
TREMBLE
TREMBLE
TREMBLE
HAH!

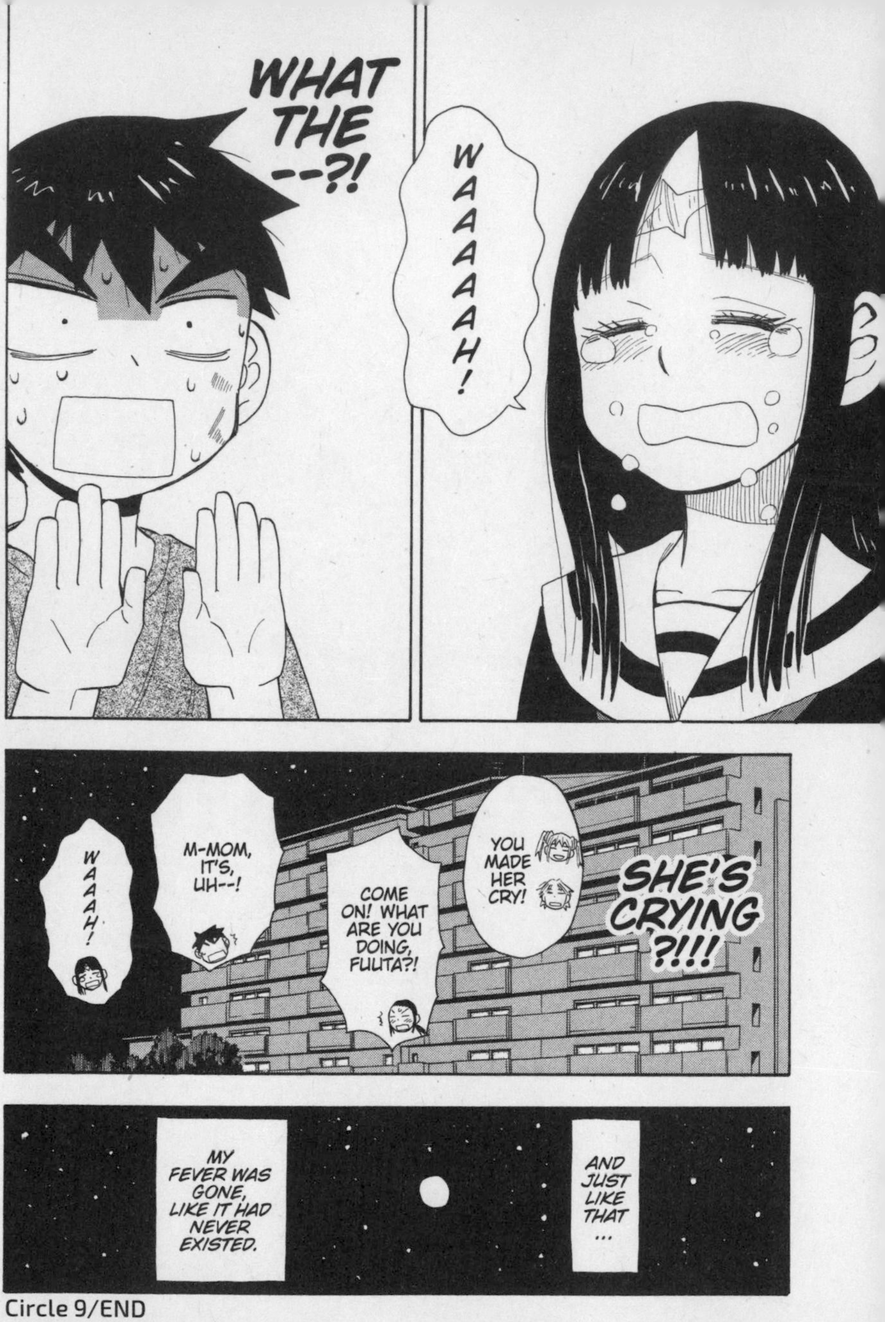
WAAAAAAH!
WHAT THE --?!
SHE'S CRYING ?!!!
YOU MADE HER CRY!
COME ON! WHAT ARE YOU DOING, FUUTA?!
M-MOM, IT'S, UH--!
WAAAAH!
AND JUST LIKE THAT ...
MY FEVER WAS GONE, LIKE IT HAD NEVER EXISTED.

Circle 9/END

Spirit Circle

Tetsu

Circle 10
Flor 1

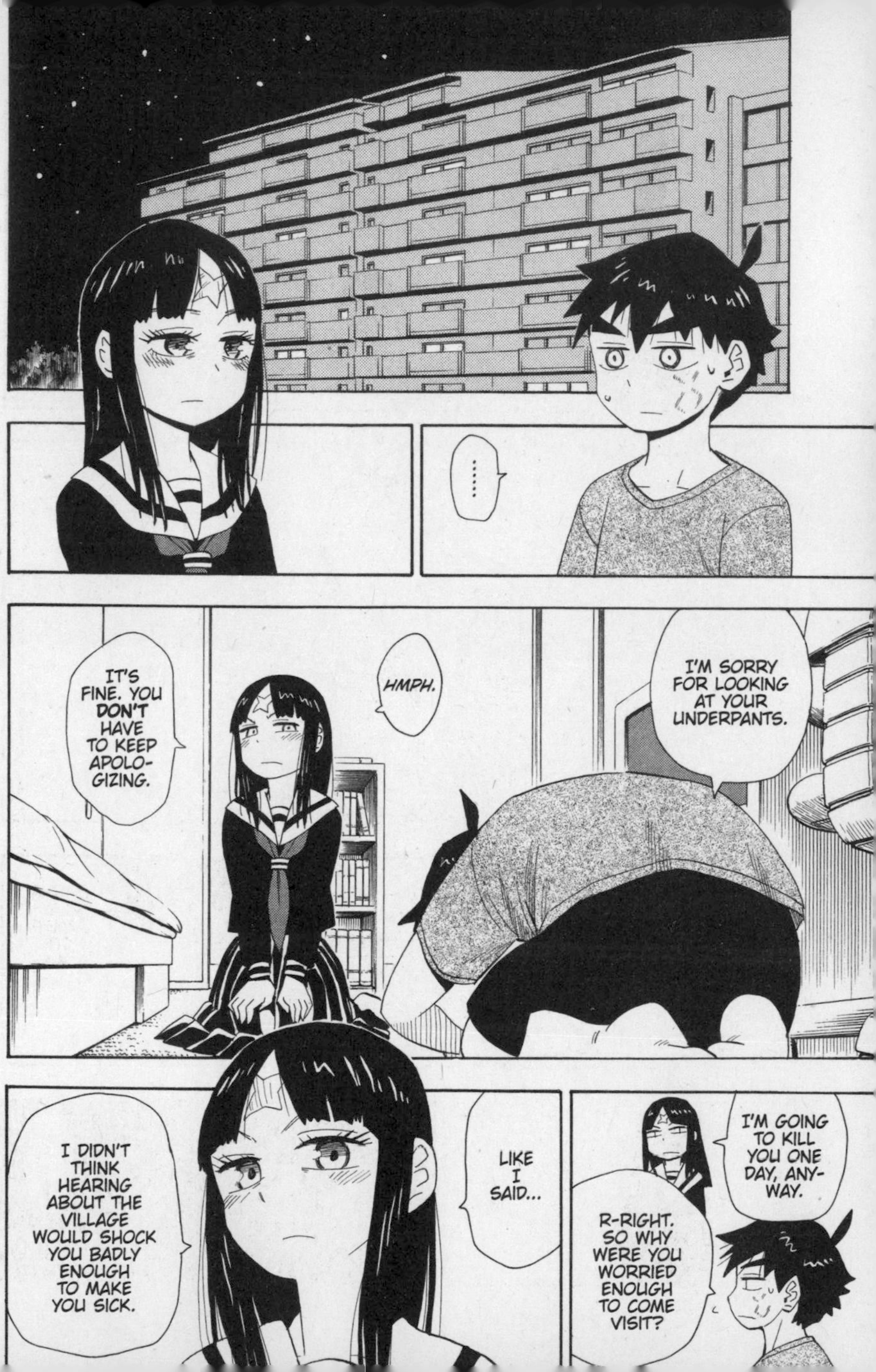
......
I'M SORRY FOR LOOKING AT YOUR UNDERPANTS.
HMPH.
IT'S FINE. YOU DON'T HAVE TO KEEP APOLOGIZING.
I'M GOING TO KILL YOU ONE DAY, ANYWAY.
R-RIGHT. SO WHY WERE YOU WORRIED ENOUGH TO COME VISIT?
LIKE I SAID...
I DIDN'T THINK HEARING ABOUT THE VILLAGE WOULD SHOCK YOU BADLY ENOUGH TO MAKE YOU SICK.

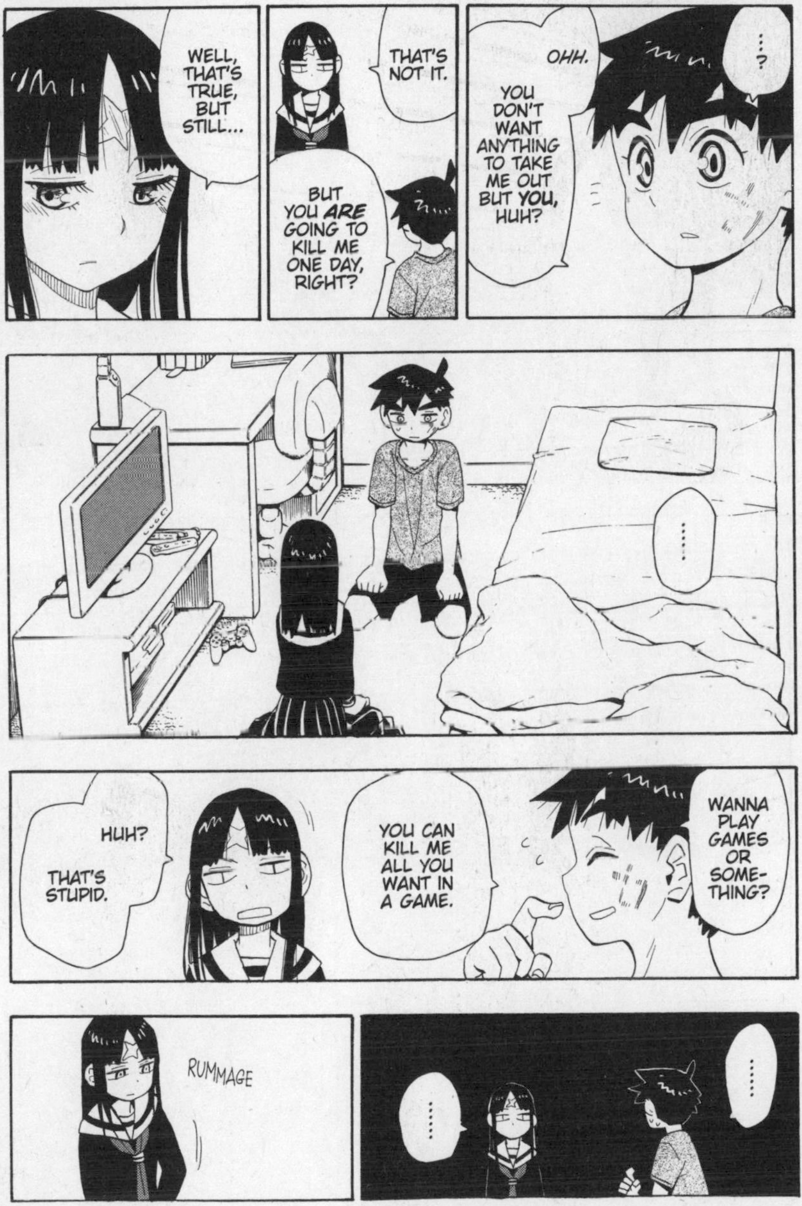
...?
OHH.
YOU DON'T WANT ANYTHING TO TAKE ME OUT BUT YOU, HUH?
THAT'S NOT IT.
BUT YOU ARE GOING TO KILL ME ONE DAY, RIGHT?
WELL, THAT'S TRUE, BUT STILL...
......
WANNA PLAY GAMES OR SOME-THING?
YOU CAN KILL ME ALL YOU WANT IN A GAME.
HUH?
THAT'S STUPID.
......
......
RUMMAGE

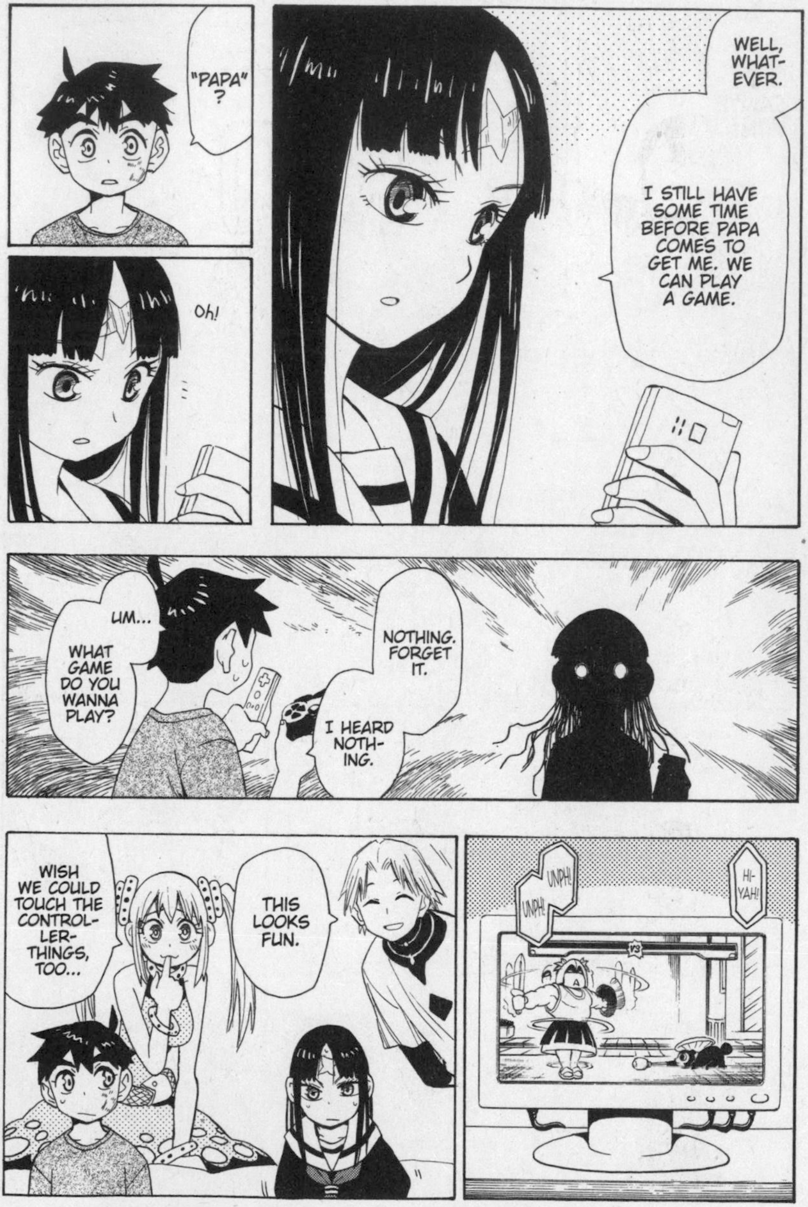
WELL, WHATEVER.
I STILL HAVE SOME TIME BEFORE PAPA COMES TO GET ME. WE CAN PLAY A GAME.
"PAPA"?
Oh!
NOTHING. FORGET IT.
I HEARD NOTHING.
UM...
WHAT GAME DO YOU WANNA PLAY?
HI-YAH!
UNPH!
UNPH!
THIS LOOKS FUN.
WISH WE COULD TOUCH THE CONTROLLER-THINGS, TOO...

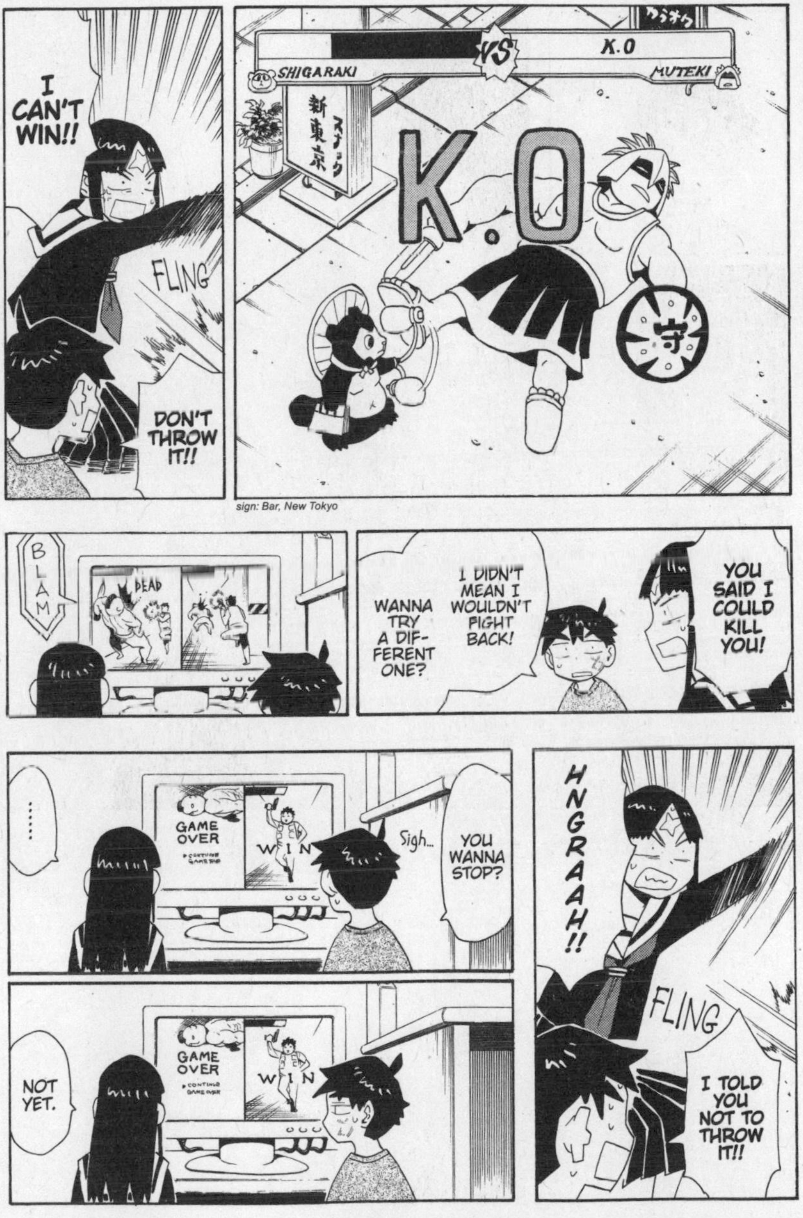
カラオケ
VS
K.O
SHIGARAKI
MUTEKI
新東京 スナック
K.O
守
I CAN'T WIN!!
FLING
DON'T THROW IT!!
YOU SAID I COULD KILL YOU!
I DIDN'T MEAN I WOULDN'T FIGHT BACK!
WANNA TRY A DIF-FERENT ONE?
BLAM
DEAD
HNGRAAH!!
FLING
I TOLD YOU NOT TO THROW IT!!
YOU WANNA STOP?
Sigh...
GAME OVER
WIN
......
GAME OVER
WIN
NOT YET.
sign: Bar, New Tokyo

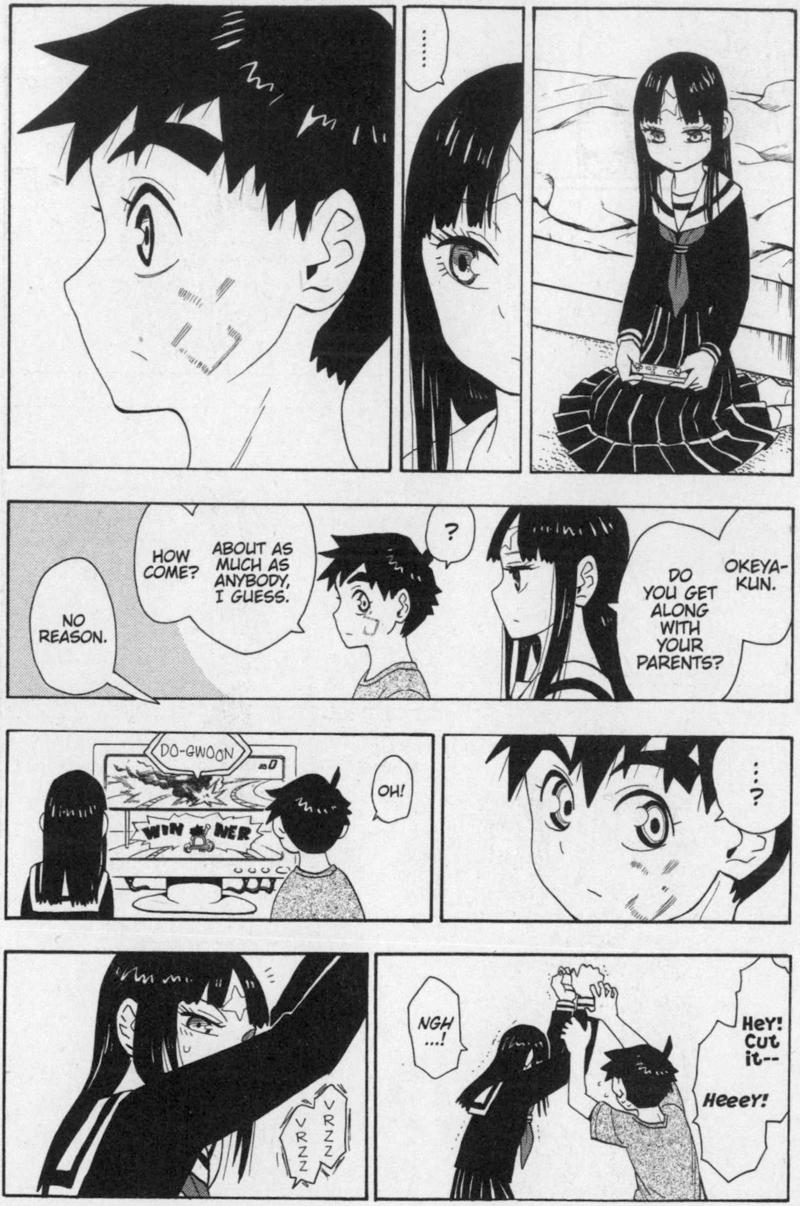
......
OKEYA-KUN.
DO YOU GET ALONG WITH YOUR PARENTS?
?
ABOUT AS MUCH AS ANYBODY, I GUESS.
HOW COME?
NO REASON.
...?
OH!
DO-GWOON
WIN NER
Hey! Cut it--
Heeey!
NGH ...!
VRZZ VRZZ

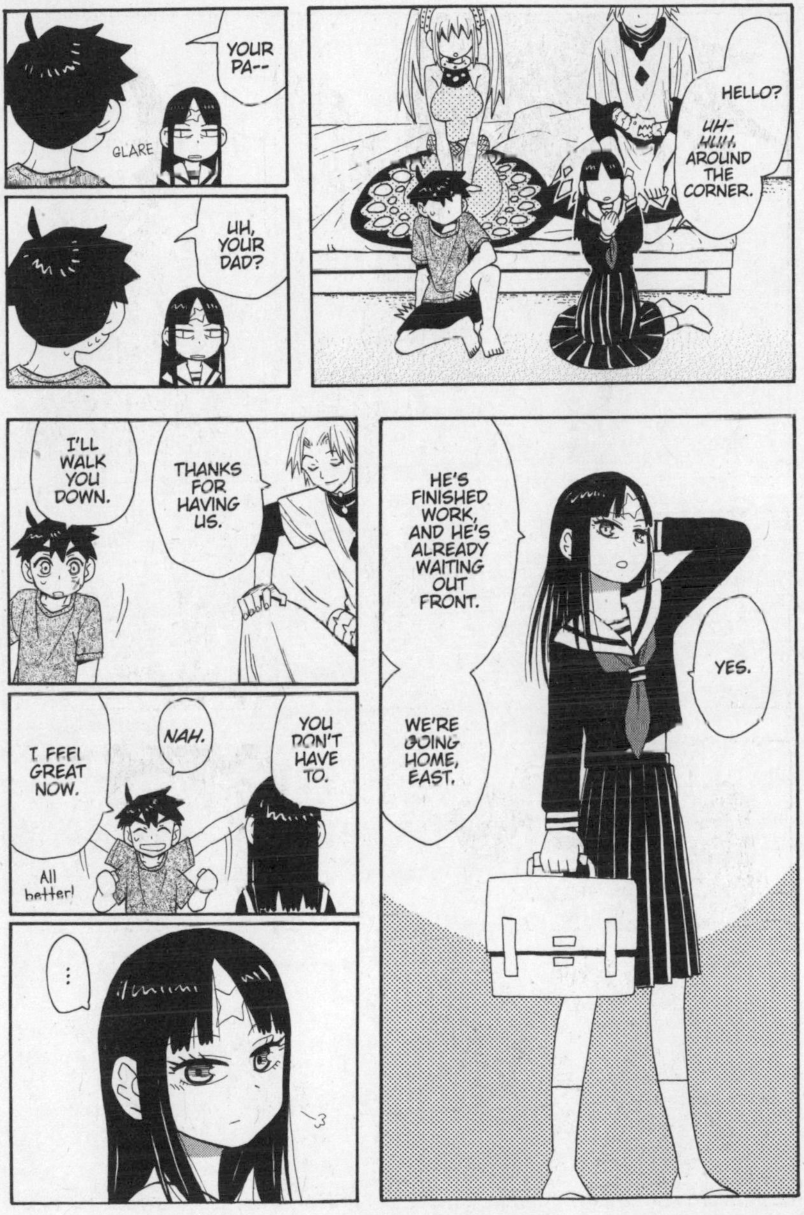
HELLO?
UH-HUH, AROUND THE CORNER.
YOUR PA--
GLARE
UH, YOUR DAD?
HE'S FINISHED WORK, AND HE'S ALREADY WAITING OUT FRONT.
YES.
WE'RE GOING HOME, EAST.
THANKS FOR HAVING US.
I'LL WALK YOU DOWN.
YOU DON'T HAVE TO.
NAH.
I FEEL GREAT NOW.
All better!
...

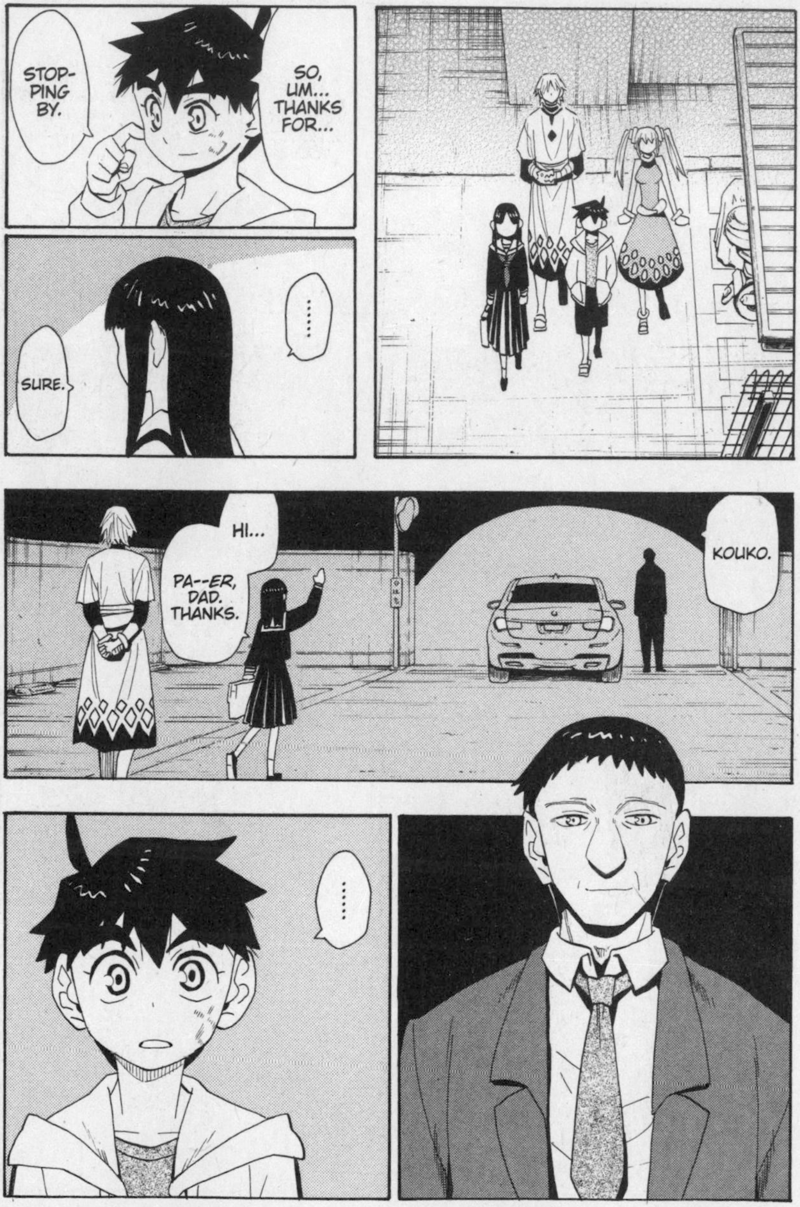
SO, UM... THANKS FOR...
STOP-PING BY.
......
SURE.
KOUKO.
HI... PA--ER, DAD. THANKS.
......

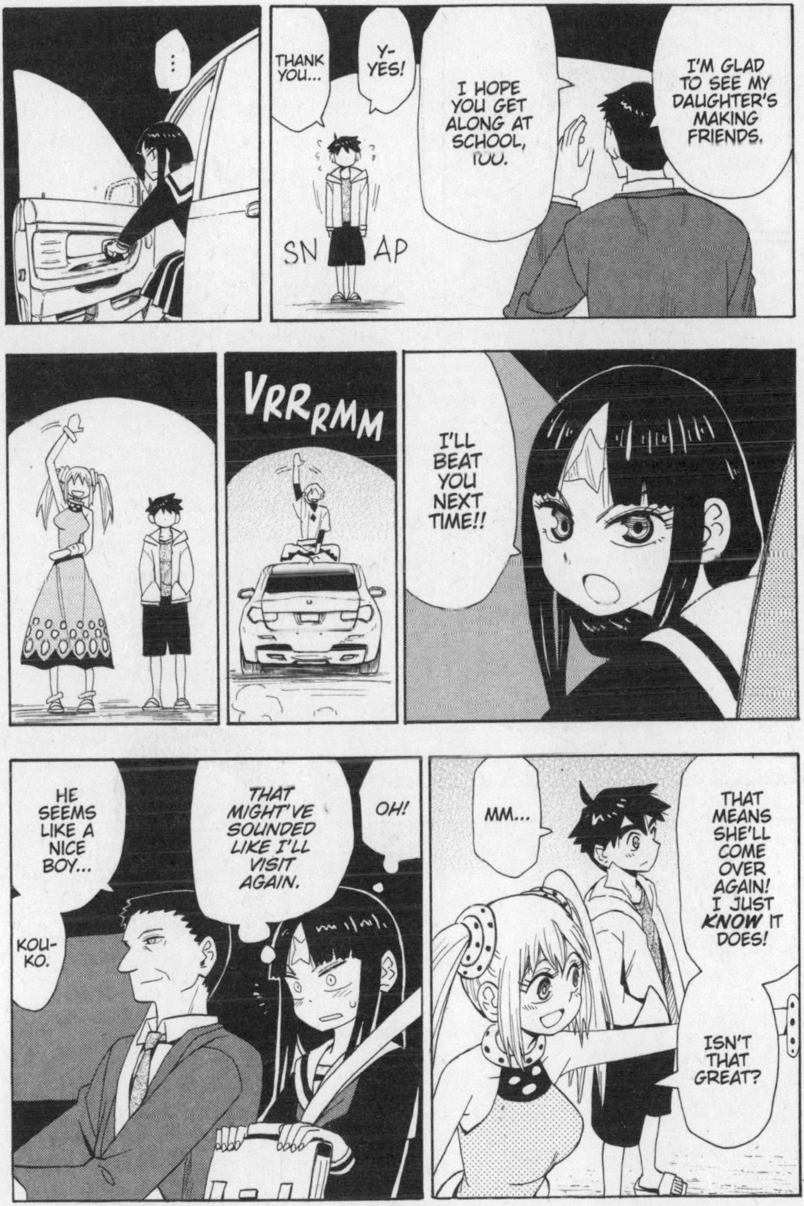
I'M GLAD TO SEE MY DAUGHTER'S MAKING FRIENDS.
I HOPE YOU GET ALONG AT SCHOOL, TOO.
Y- YES!
THANK YOU...
SN AP
...
I'LL BEAT YOU NEXT TIME!!
VRRRMM
THAT MEANS SHE'LL COME OVER AGAIN! I JUST KNOW IT DOES!
MM...
ISN'T THAT GREAT?
OH!
THAT MIGHT'VE SOUNDED LIKE I'LL VISIT AGAIN.
HE SEEMS LIKE A NICE BOY...
KOU- KO.

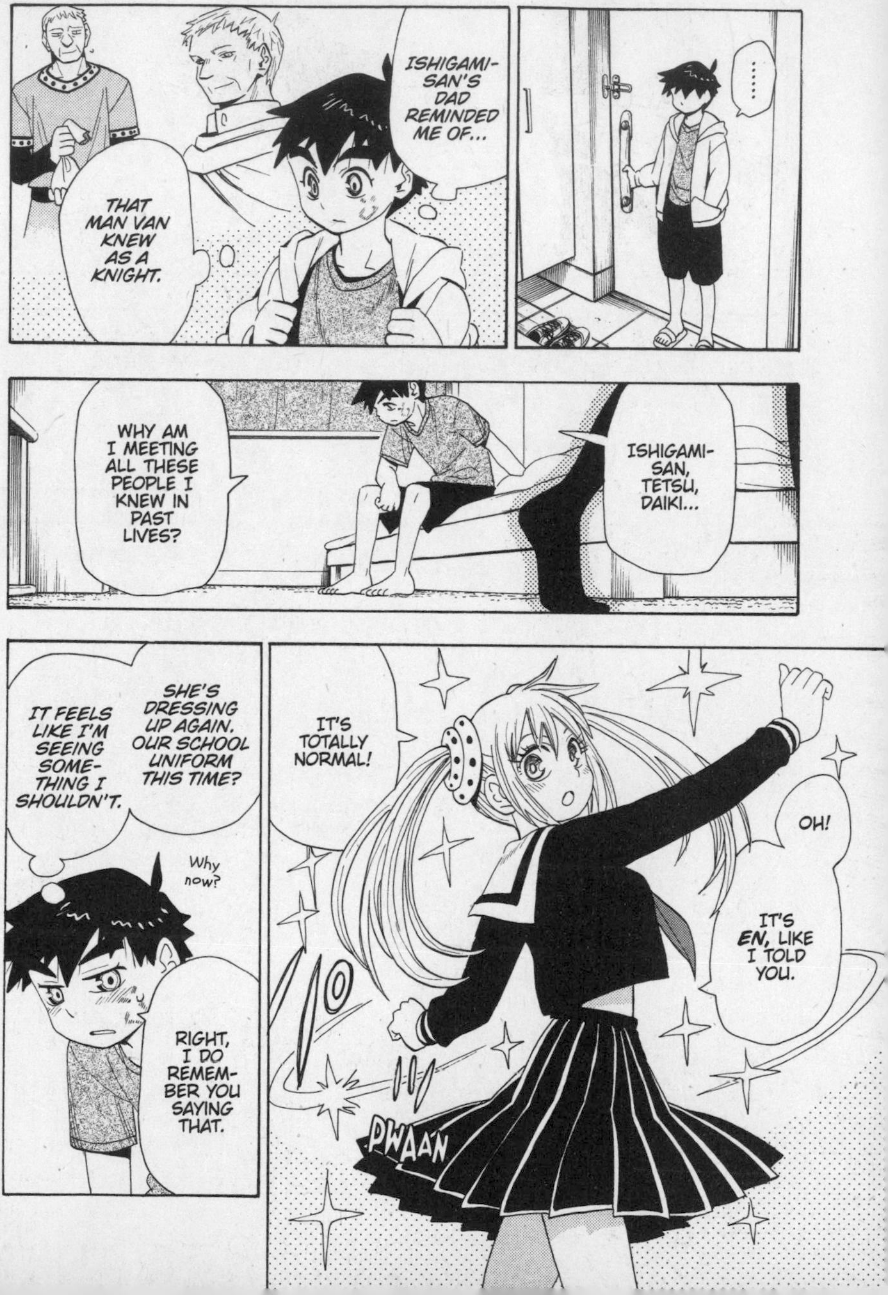
......
ISHIGAMI-SAN'S DAD REMINDED ME OF...
THAT MAN VAN KNEW AS A KNIGHT.
ISHIGAMI-SAN, TETSU, DAIKI...
WHY AM I MEETING ALL THESE PEOPLE I KNEW IN PAST LIVES?
IT'S TOTALLY NORMAL!
OH!
IT'S EN, LIKE I TOLD YOU.
PWAAN
SHE'S DRESSING UP AGAIN. OUR SCHOOL UNIFORM THIS TIME?
IT FEELS LIKE I'M SEEING SOME-THING I SHOULDN'T.
Why now?
RIGHT, I DO REMEMBER YOU SAYING THAT.

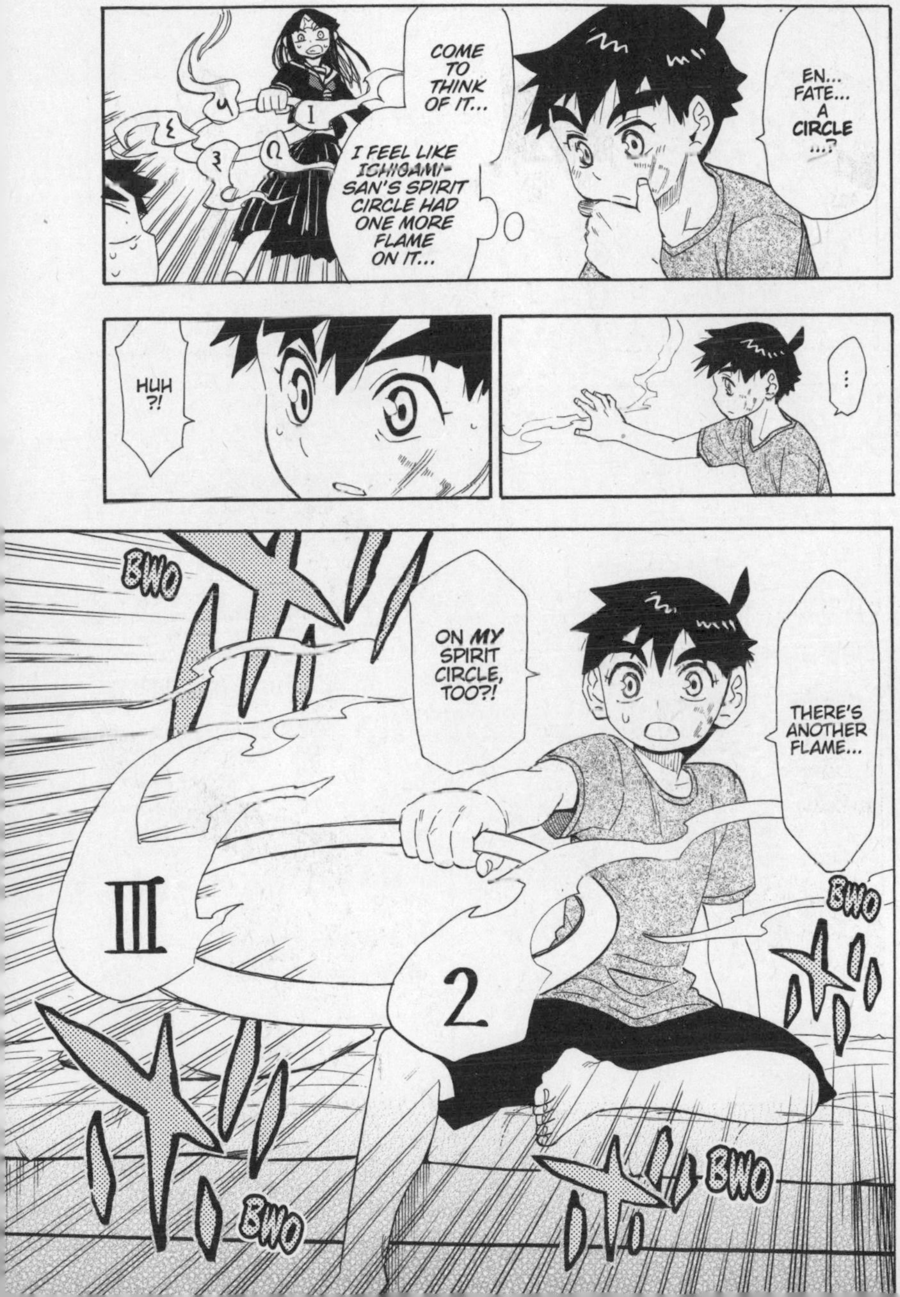
EN... FATE... A CIRCLE ...?
COME TO THINK OF IT...
I FEEL LIKE ICHIGAMI-SAN'S SPIRIT CIRCLE HAD ONE MORE FLAME ON IT...
...
HUH ?!
THERE'S ANOTHER FLAME...
ON MY SPIRIT CIRCLE, TOO?!
BWO
BWO
BWO
BWO

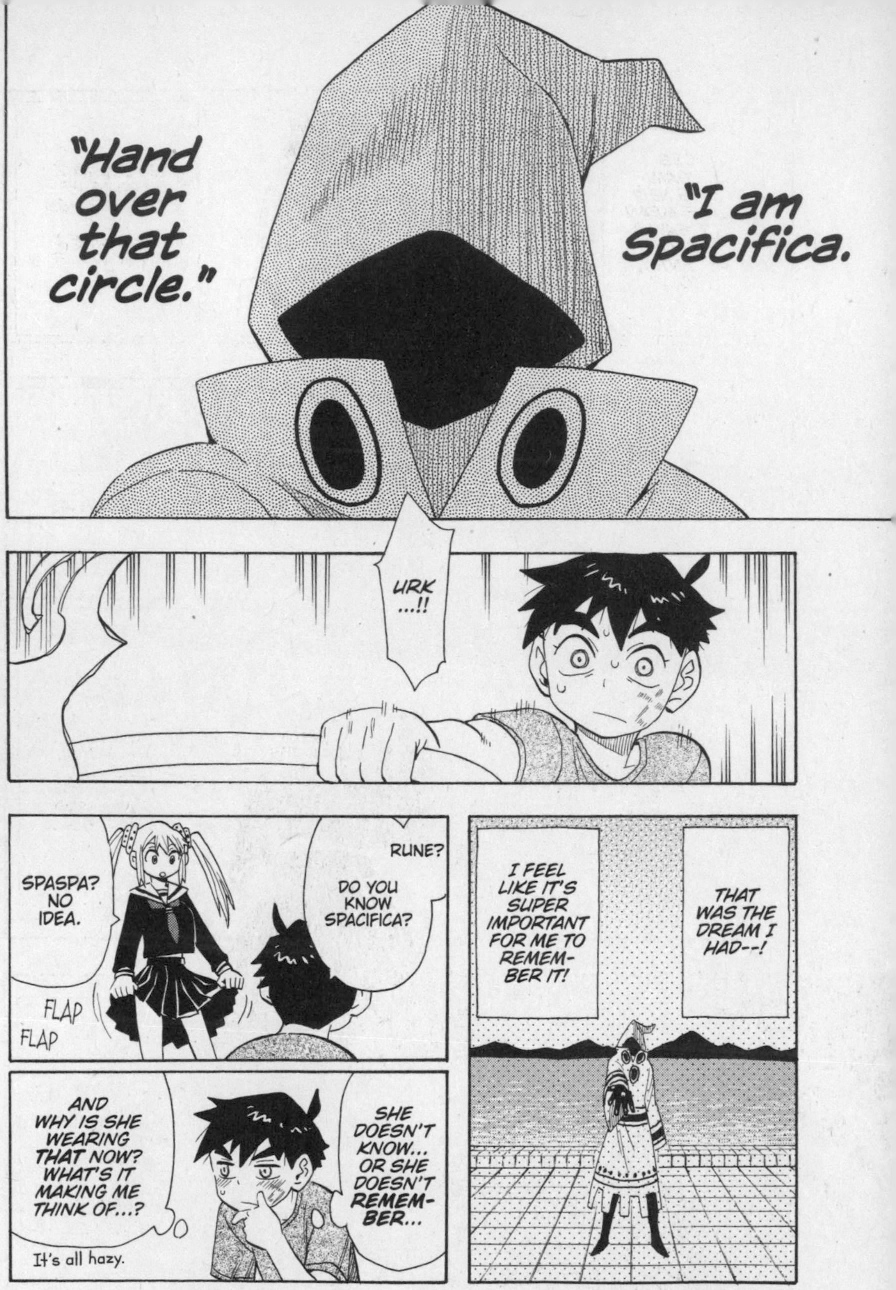
"I am Spacifica.
"Hand over that circle."
URK ...!!
THAT WAS THE DREAM I HAD--!
I FEEL LIKE IT'S SUPER IMPORTANT FOR ME TO REMEMBER IT!
RUNE?
DO YOU KNOW SPACIFICA?
SPASPA? NO IDEA.
FLAP FLAP
SHE DOESN'T KNOW... OR SHE DOESN'T REMEMBER...
AND WHY IS SHE WEARING THAT NOW? WHAT'S IT MAKING ME THINK OF...?
It's all hazy.

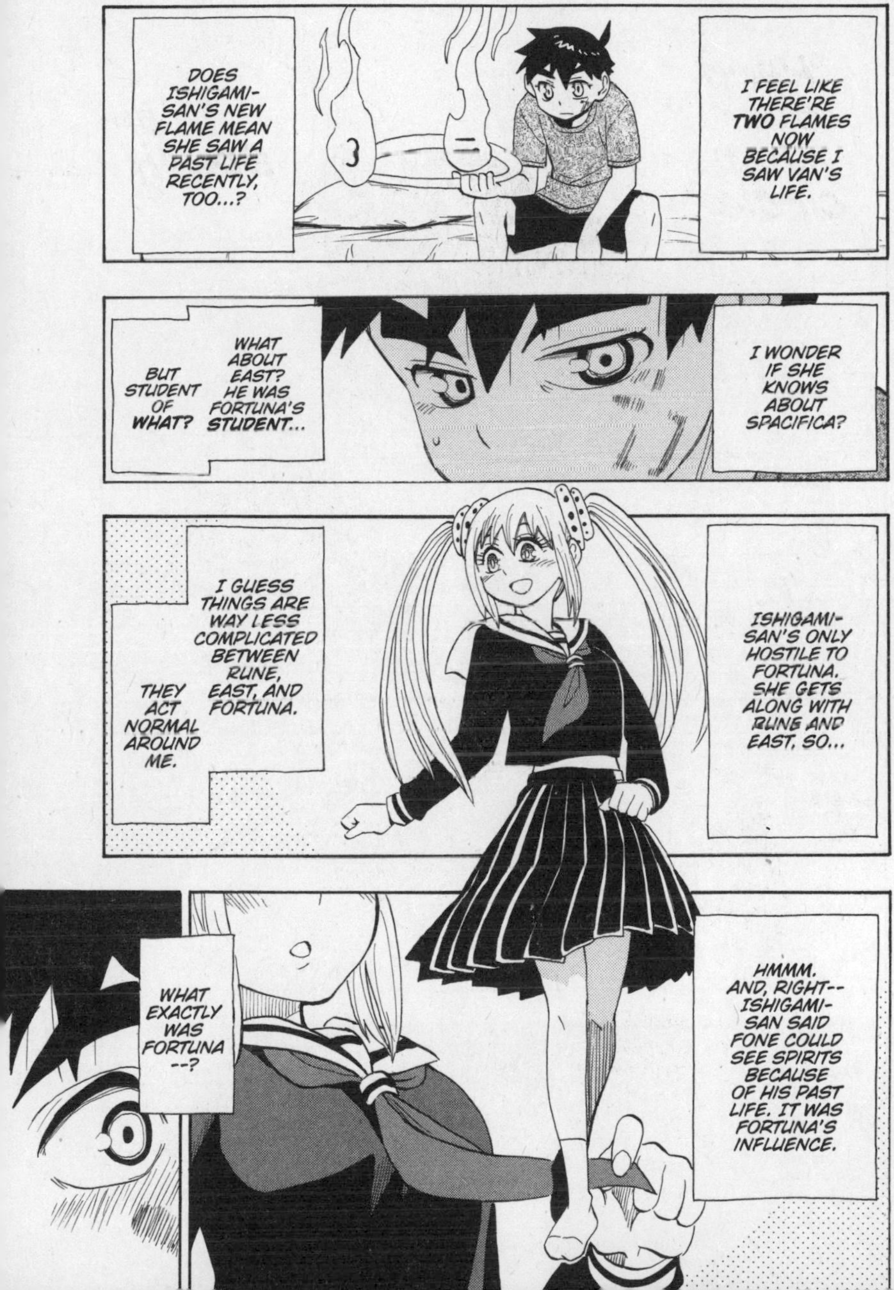
I FEEL LIKE THERE'RE TWO FLAMES NOW BECAUSE I SAW VAN'S LIFE.
DOES ISHIGAMI-SAN'S NEW FLAME MEAN SHE SAW A PAST LIFE RECENTLY, TOO...?
I WONDER IF SHE KNOWS ABOUT SPACIFICA?
WHAT ABOUT EAST? HE WAS FORTUNA'S STUDENT...
BUT STUDENT OF WHAT?
ISHIGAMI-SAN'S ONLY HOSTILE TO FORTUNA. SHE GETS ALONG WITH RUNE AND EAST, SO...
I GUESS THINGS ARE WAY LESS COMPLICATED BETWEEN RUNE, EAST, AND FORTUNA.
THEY ACT NORMAL AROUND ME.
HMMM. AND, RIGHT-- ISHIGAMI-SAN SAID FONE COULD SEE SPIRITS BECAUSE OF HIS PAST LIFE. IT WAS FORTUNA'S INFLUENCE.
WHAT EXACTLY WAS FORTUNA --?

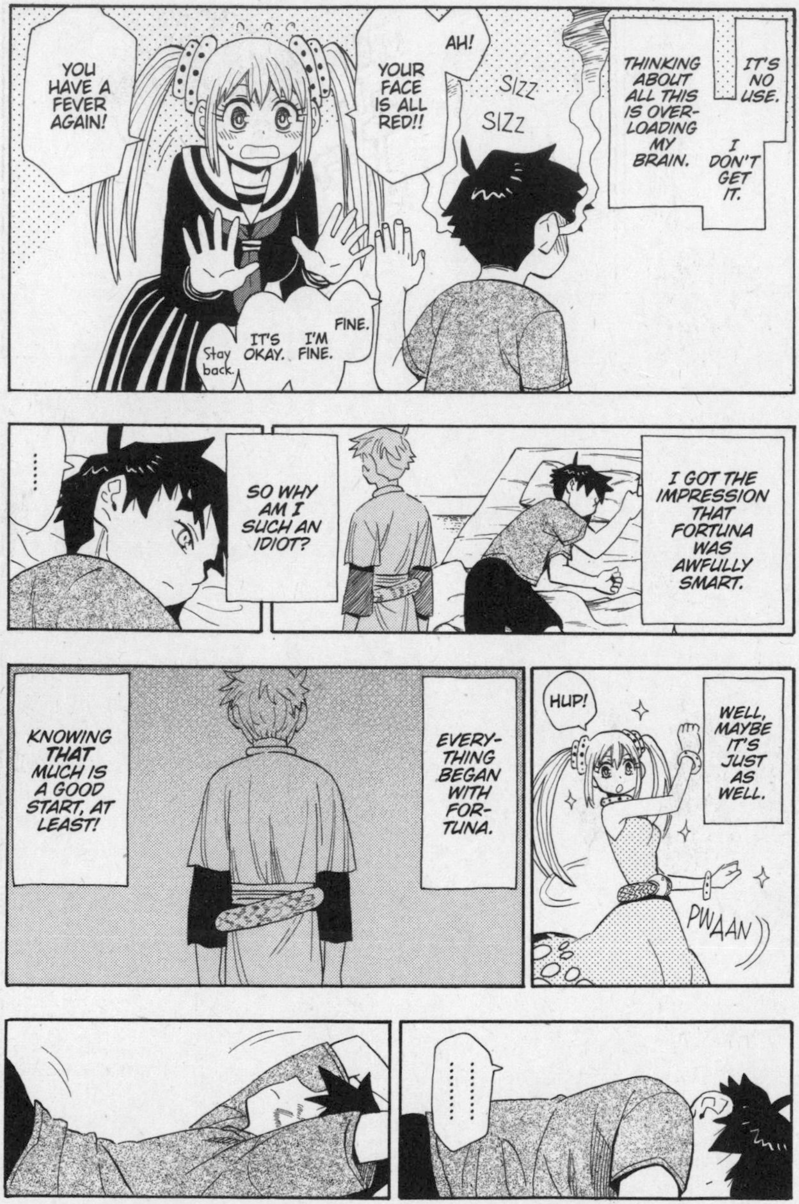
IT'S NO USE.
I DON'T GET IT.
THINKING ABOUT ALL THIS IS OVER-LOADING MY BRAIN.
SIZZ
SIZZ
AH!
YOUR FACE IS ALL RED!!
YOU HAVE A FEVER AGAIN!
FINE.
I'M FINE.
IT'S OKAY.
Stay back.
I GOT THE IMPRESSION THAT FORTUNA WAS AWFULLY SMART.
SO WHY AM I SUCH AN IDIOT?
......
WELL, MAYBE IT'S JUST AS WELL.
HUP!
PWAAN
EVERY-THING BEGAN WITH FOR-TUNA.
KNOWING THAT MUCH IS A GOOD START, AT LEAST!
......

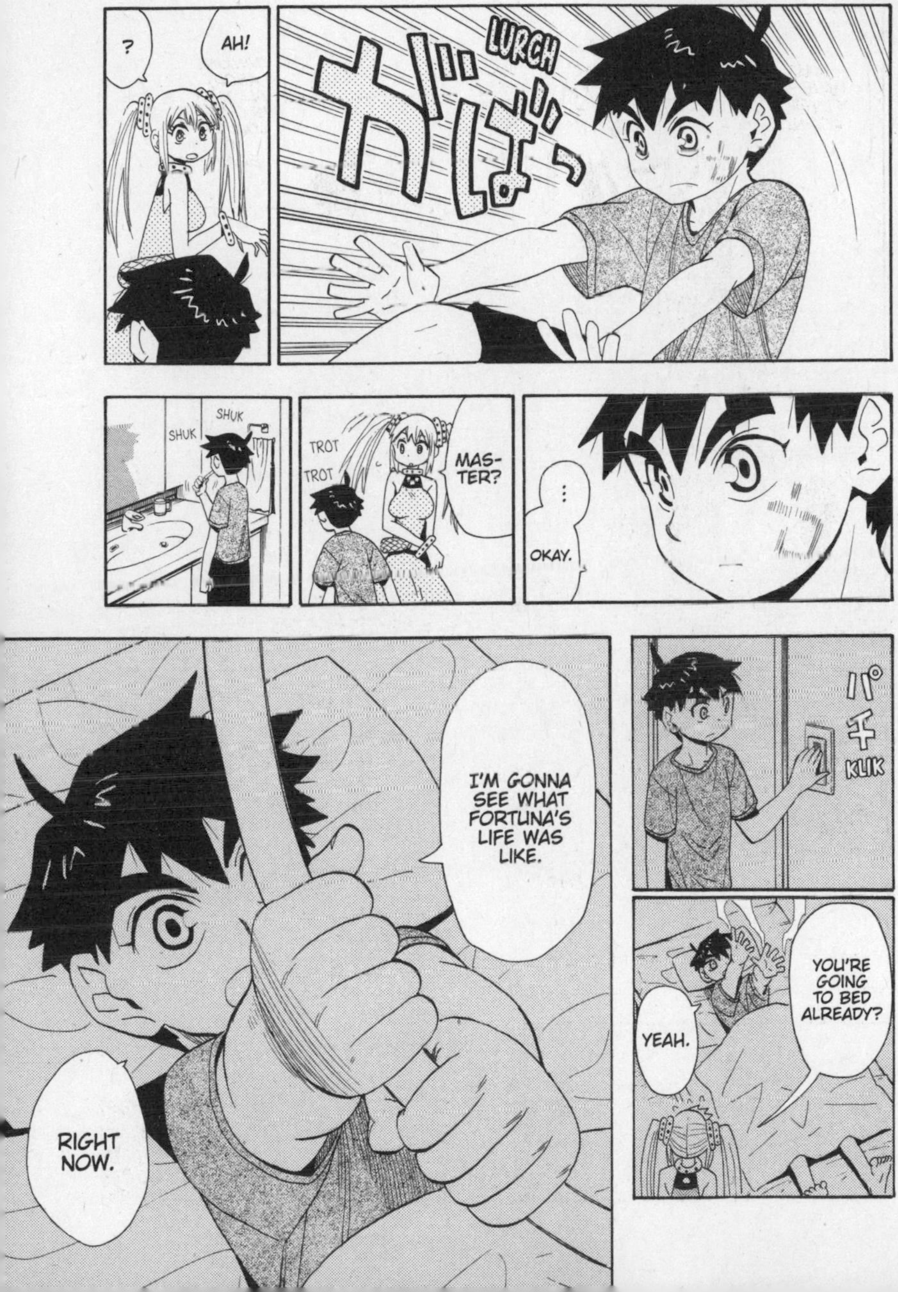
LURCH
がばっ
AH!
?
TROT
TROT
MAS-TER?
...
OKAY.
SHUK
SHUK
パチ
KLIK
YOU'RE GOING TO BED ALREADY?
YEAH.
I'M GONNA SEE WHAT FORTUNA'S LIFE WAS LIKE.
RIGHT NOW.

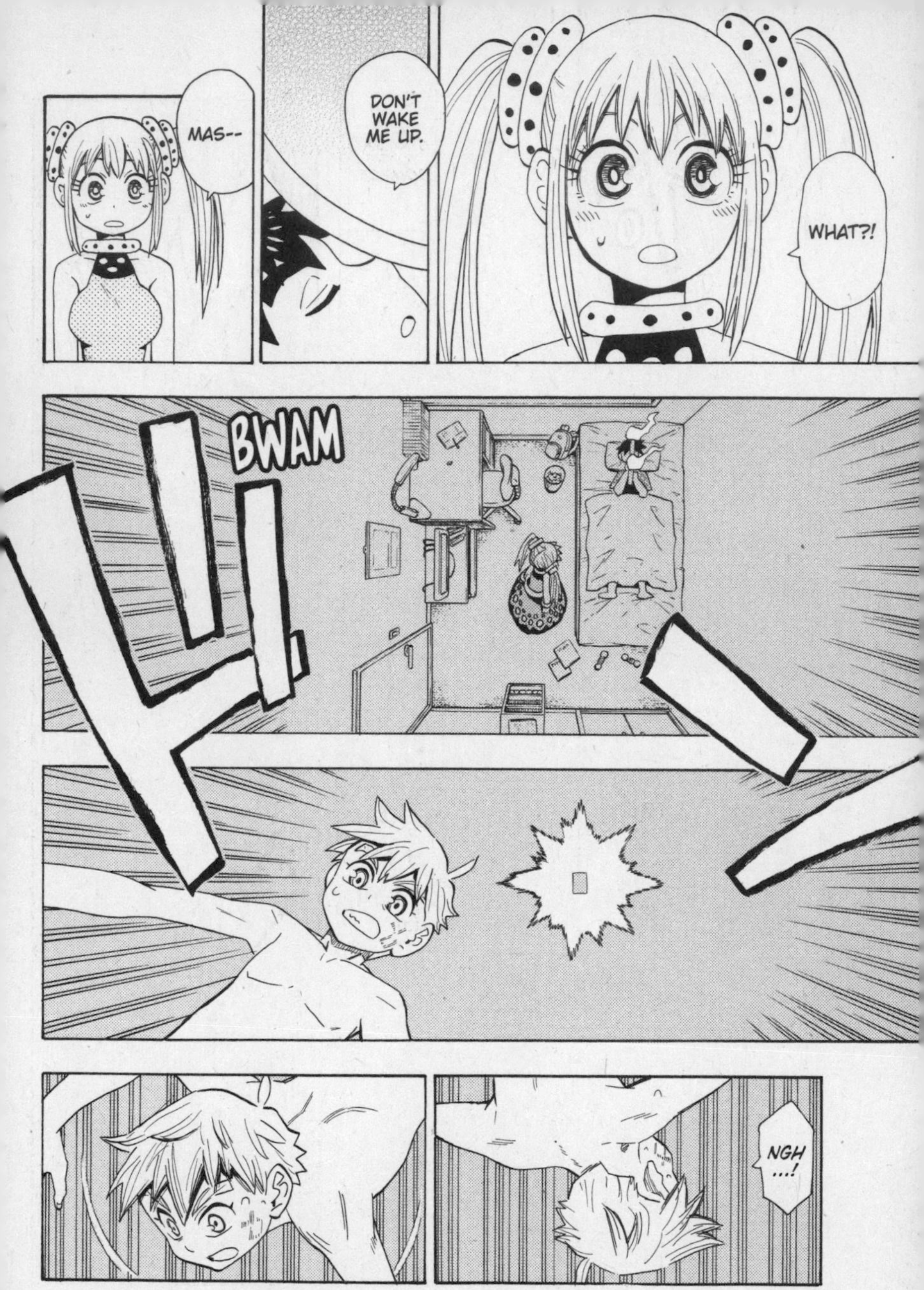
WHAT?!
DON'T WAKE ME UP.
MAS--
BWAM
NGH...!

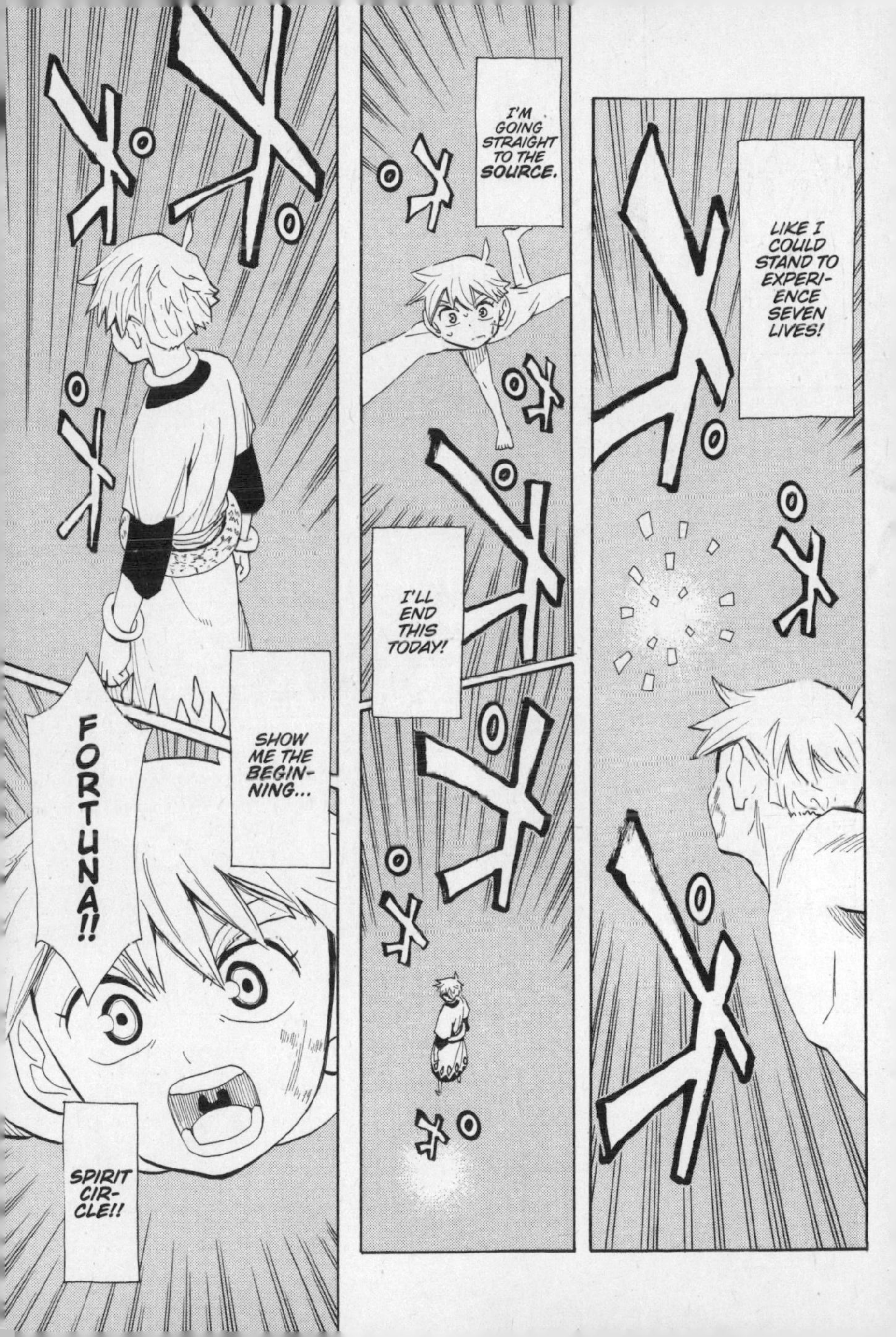
LIKE I COULD STAND TO EXPERIENCE SEVEN LIVES!
I'M GOING STRAIGHT TO THE SOURCE.
I'LL END THIS TODAY!
SHOW ME THE BEGINNING...
FORTUNA!!
SPIRIT CIRCLE!!

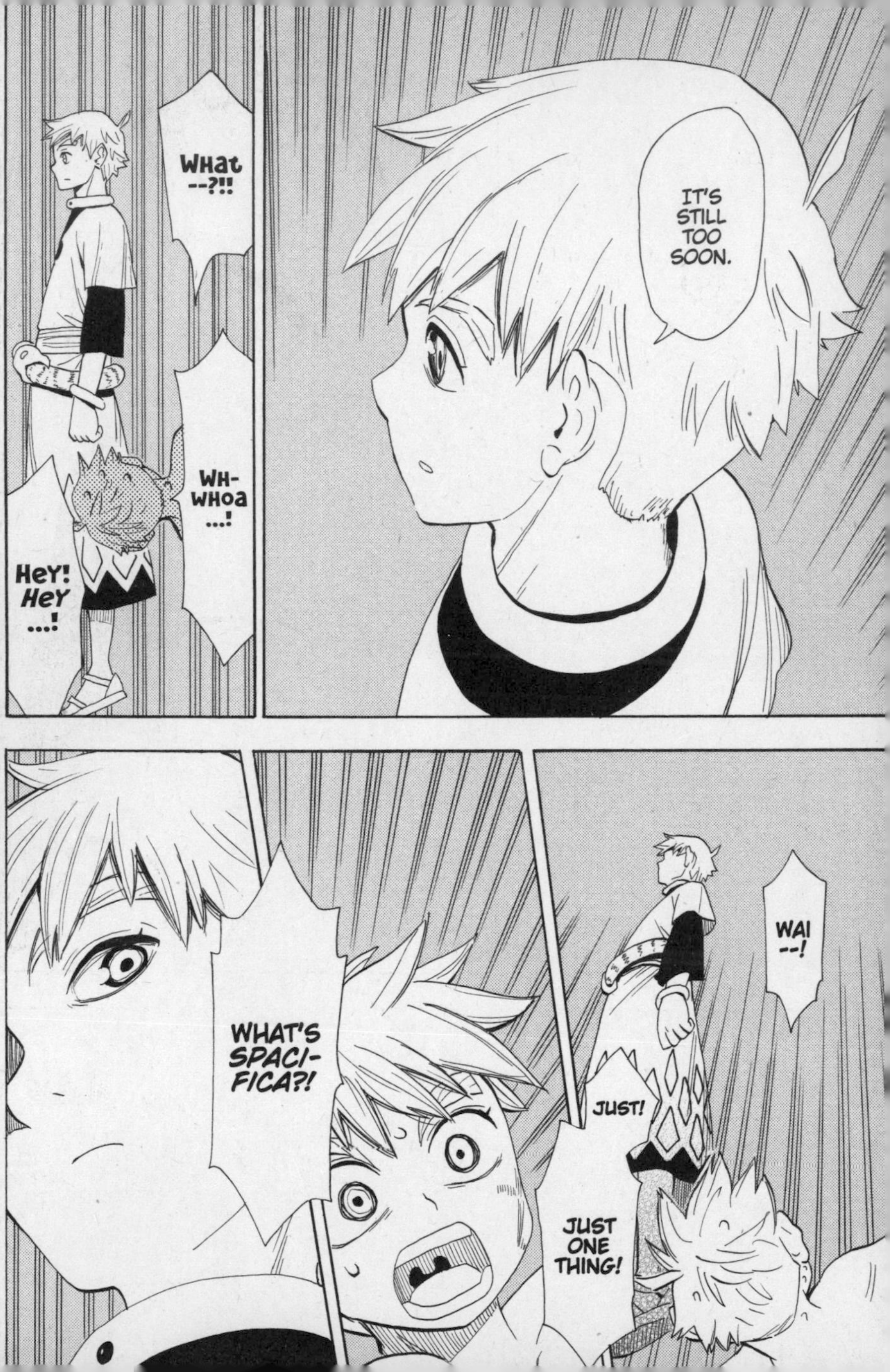
IT'S STILL TOO SOON.
What--?!!
WH-WHOA...!
Hey! Hey...!
WAI--!
JUST!
JUST ONE THING!
WHAT'S SPACI-FICA?!

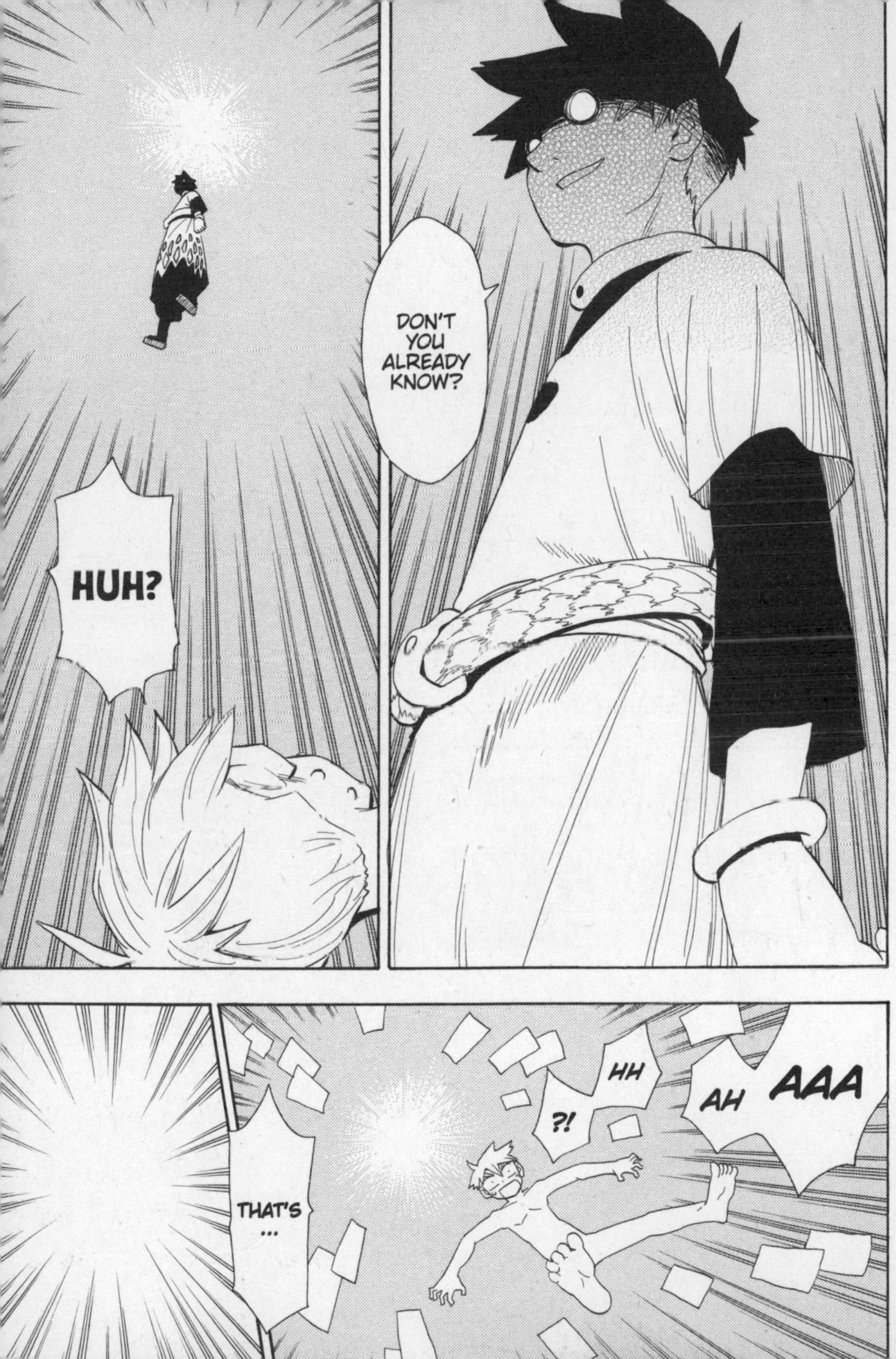
DON'T YOU ALREADY KNOW?
HUH?
AH AAA
HH ?!
THAT'S ...

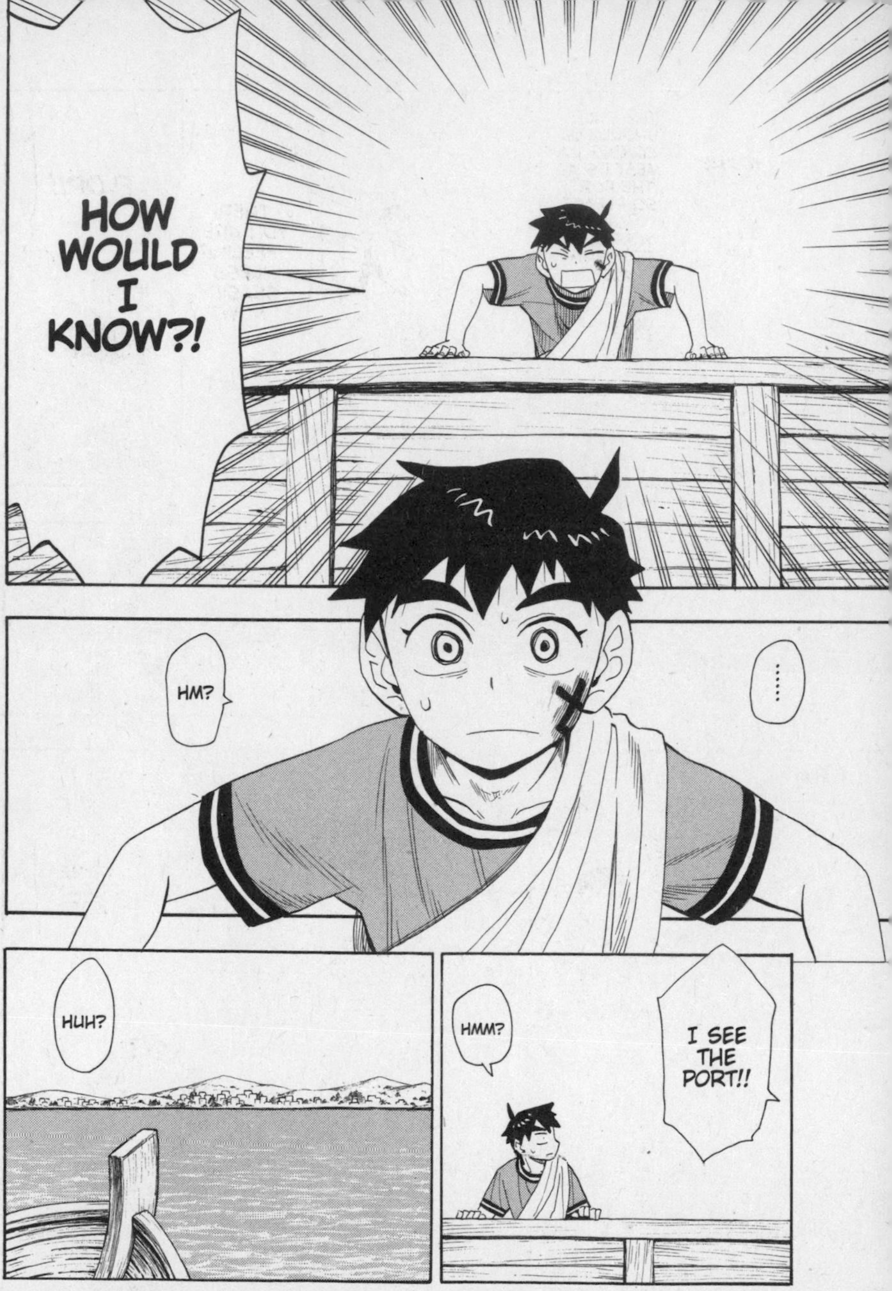
HOW WOULD I KNOW?!
......
HM?
I SEE THE PORT!!
HMM?
HUH?

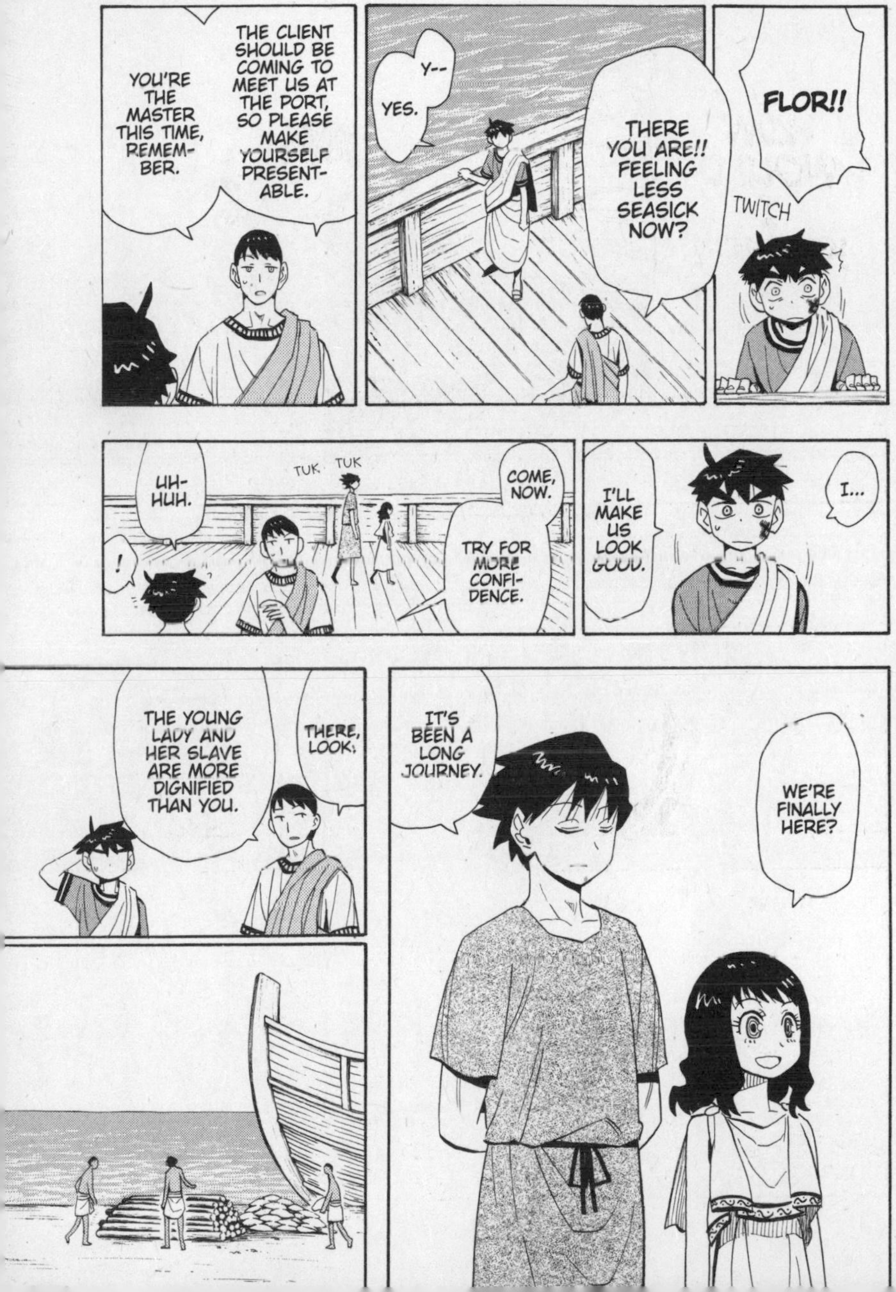
FLOR!!
TWITCH
THERE YOU ARE!! FEELING LESS SEASICK NOW?
Y--
YES.
THE CLIENT SHOULD BE COMING TO MEET US AT THE PORT, SO PLEASE MAKE YOURSELF PRESENTABLE.
YOU'RE THE MASTER THIS TIME, REMEMBER.
I...
I'LL MAKE US LOOK GOOD.
COME, NOW.
TRY FOR MORE CONFIDENCE.
TUK TUK
UH-HUH.
!
WE'RE FINALLY HERE?
IT'S BEEN A LONG JOURNEY.
THERE, LOOK.
THE YOUNG LADY AND HER SLAVE ARE MORE DIGNIFIED THAN YOU.

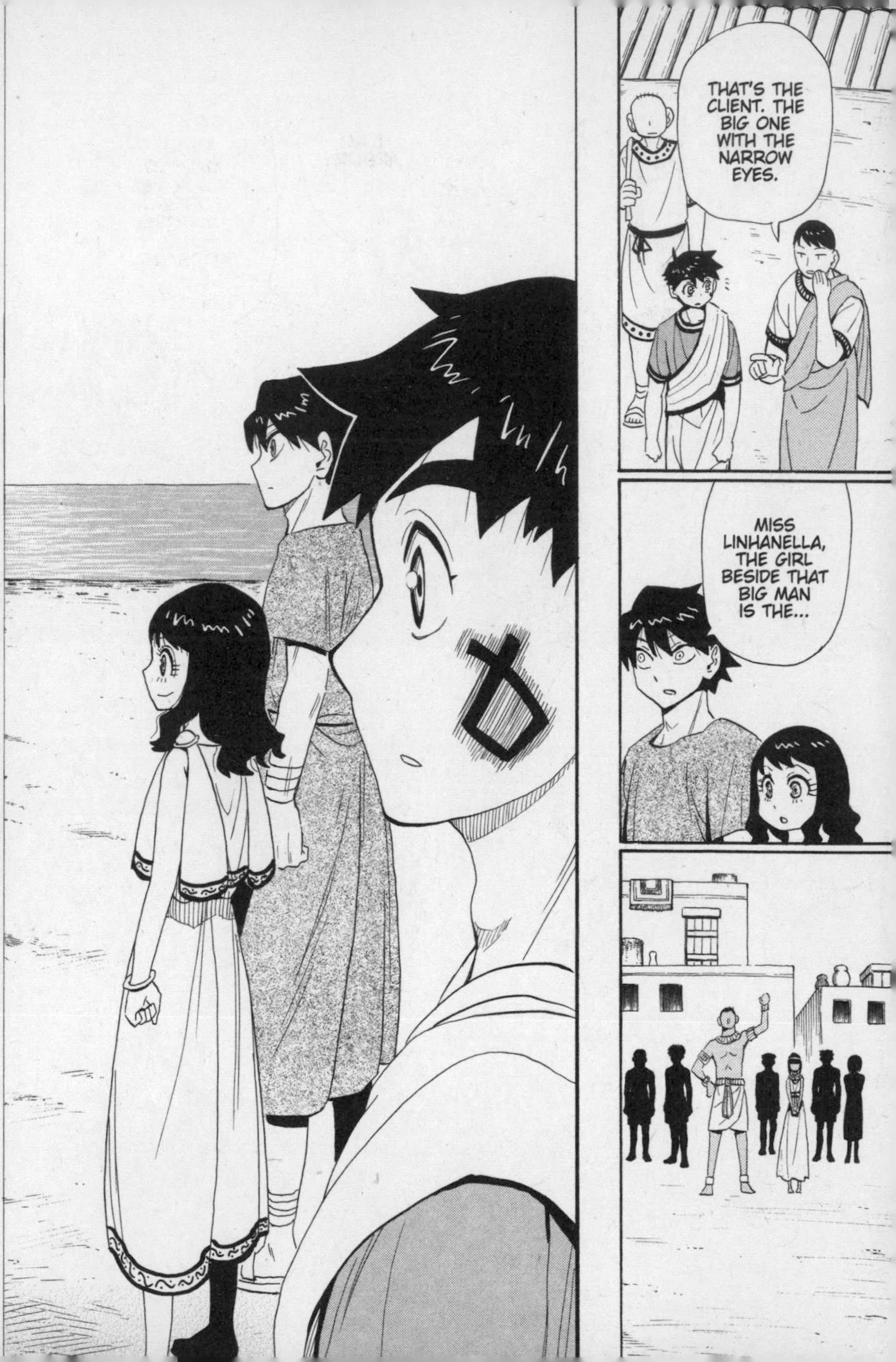
THAT'S THE CLIENT. THE BIG ONE WITH THE NARROW EYES.
MISS LINHANELLA, THE GIRL BESIDE THAT BIG MAN IS THE...

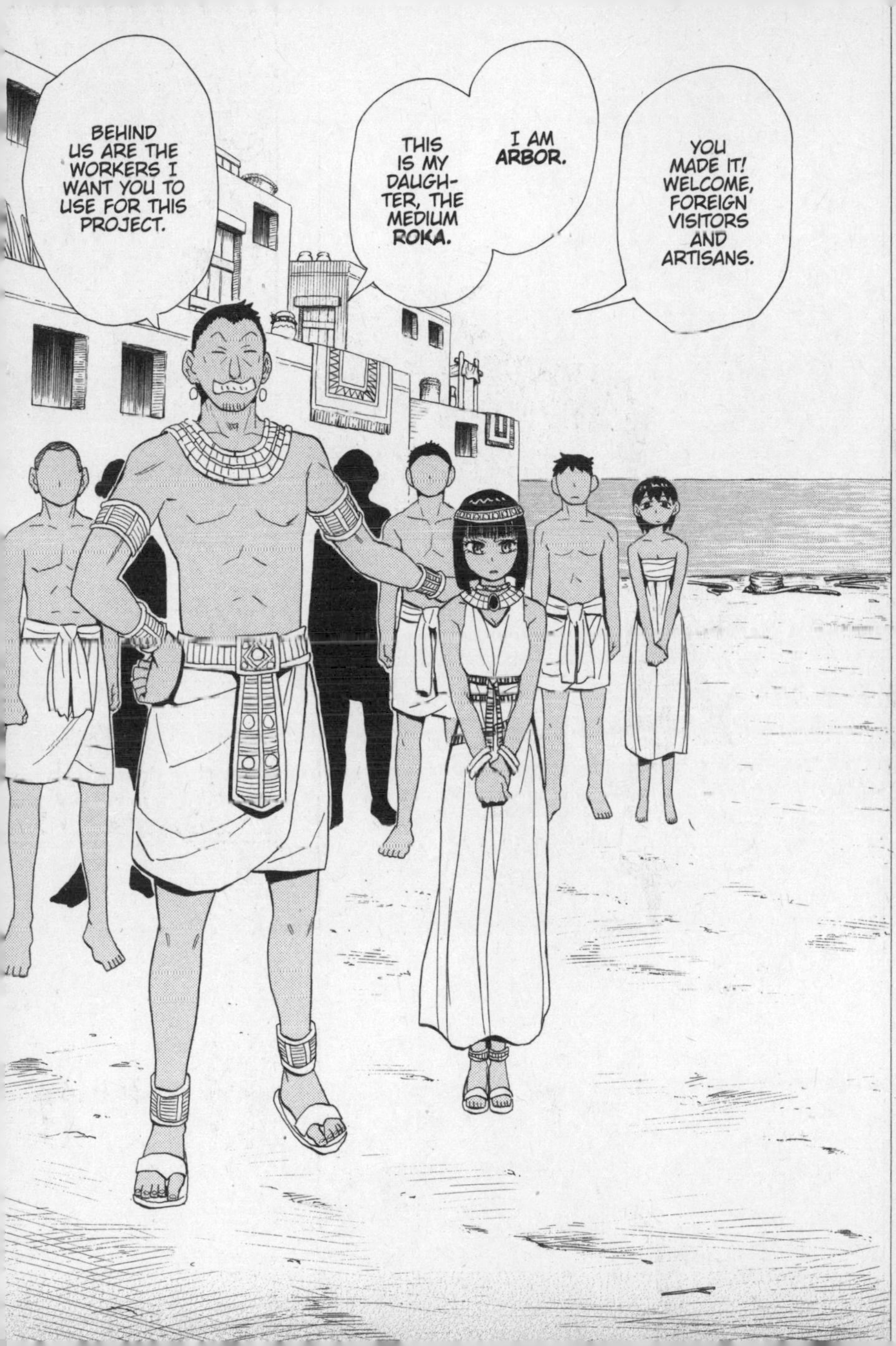
YOU MADE IT! WELCOME, FOREIGN VISITORS AND ARTISANS.
I AM ARBOR.
THIS IS MY DAUGH-TER, THE MEDIUM ROKA.
BEHIND US ARE THE WORKERS I WANT YOU TO USE FOR THIS PROJECT.

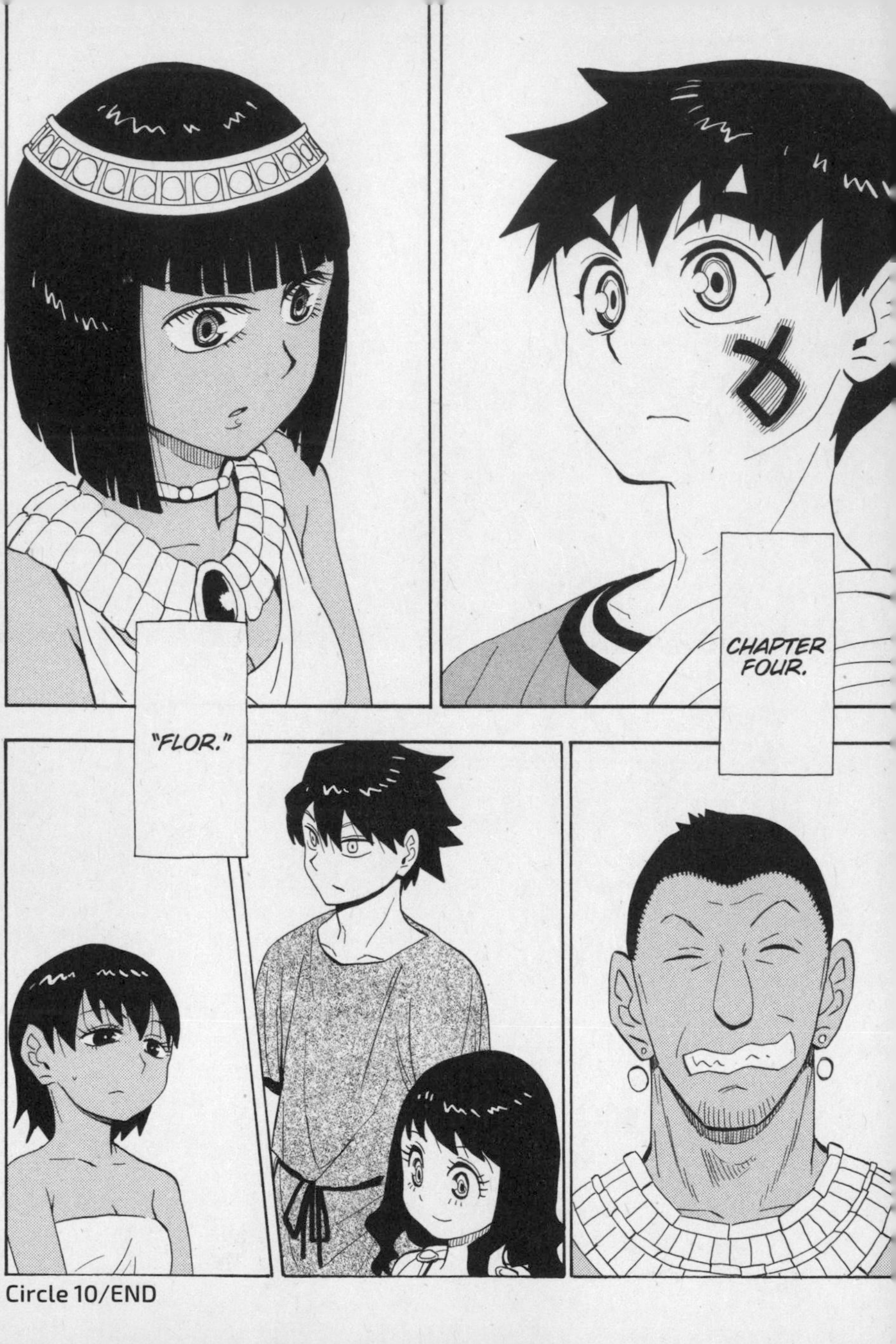
CHAPTER FOUR.
"FLOR."

Circle 10/END

Spirit Circle

Umi

Circle 11
Flor 2

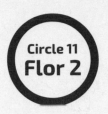

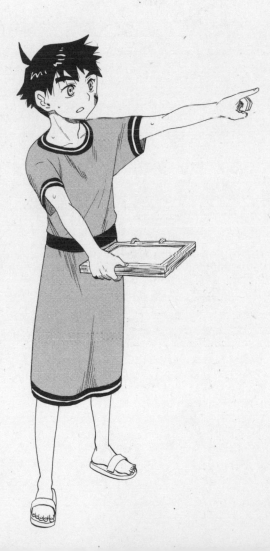

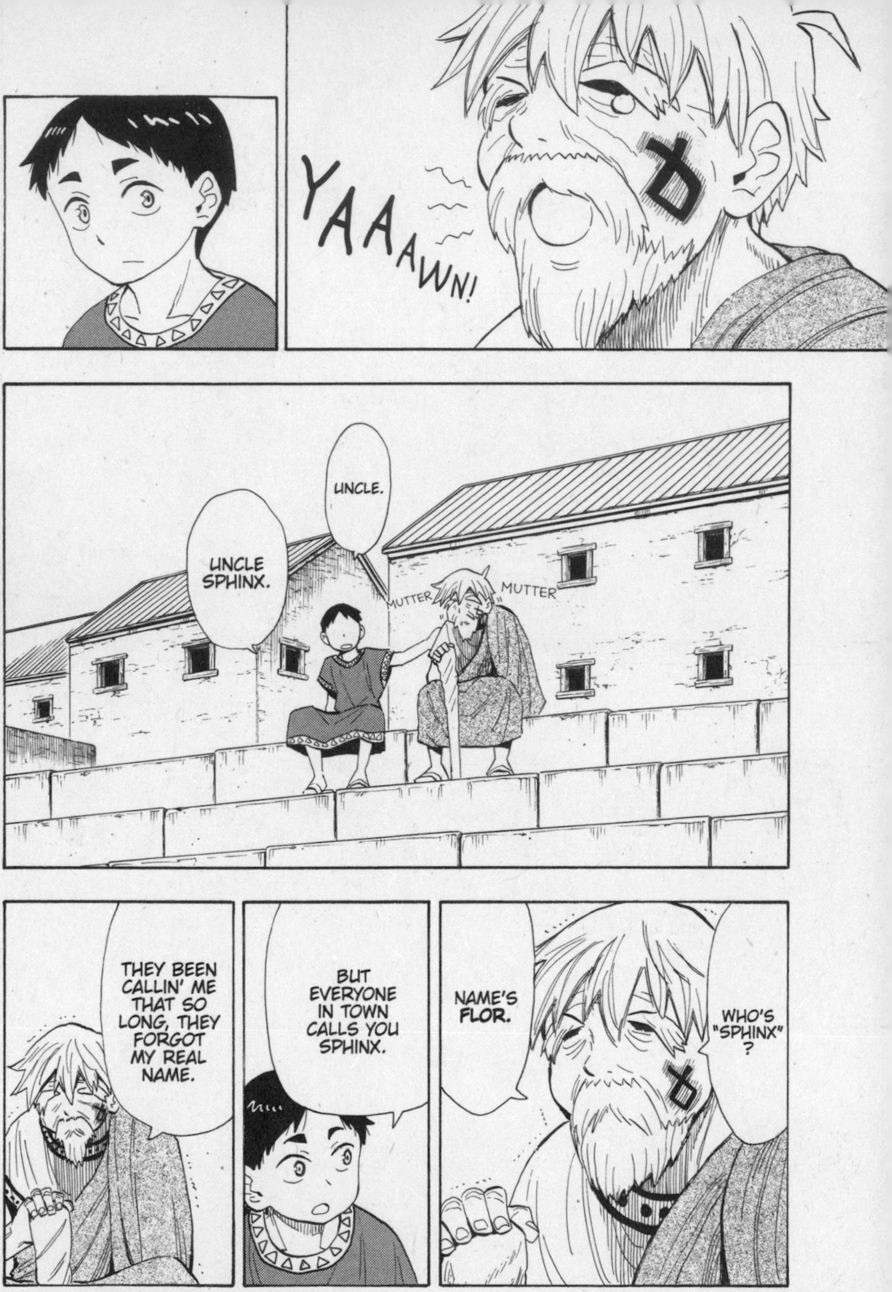
YAAAAWN!
UNCLE.
MUTTER MUTTER
UNCLE SPHINX.
WHO'S "SPHINX"?
NAME'S FLOR.
BUT EVERYONE IN TOWN CALLS YOU SPHINX.
THEY BEEN CALLIN' ME THAT SO LONG, THEY FORGOT MY REAL NAME.

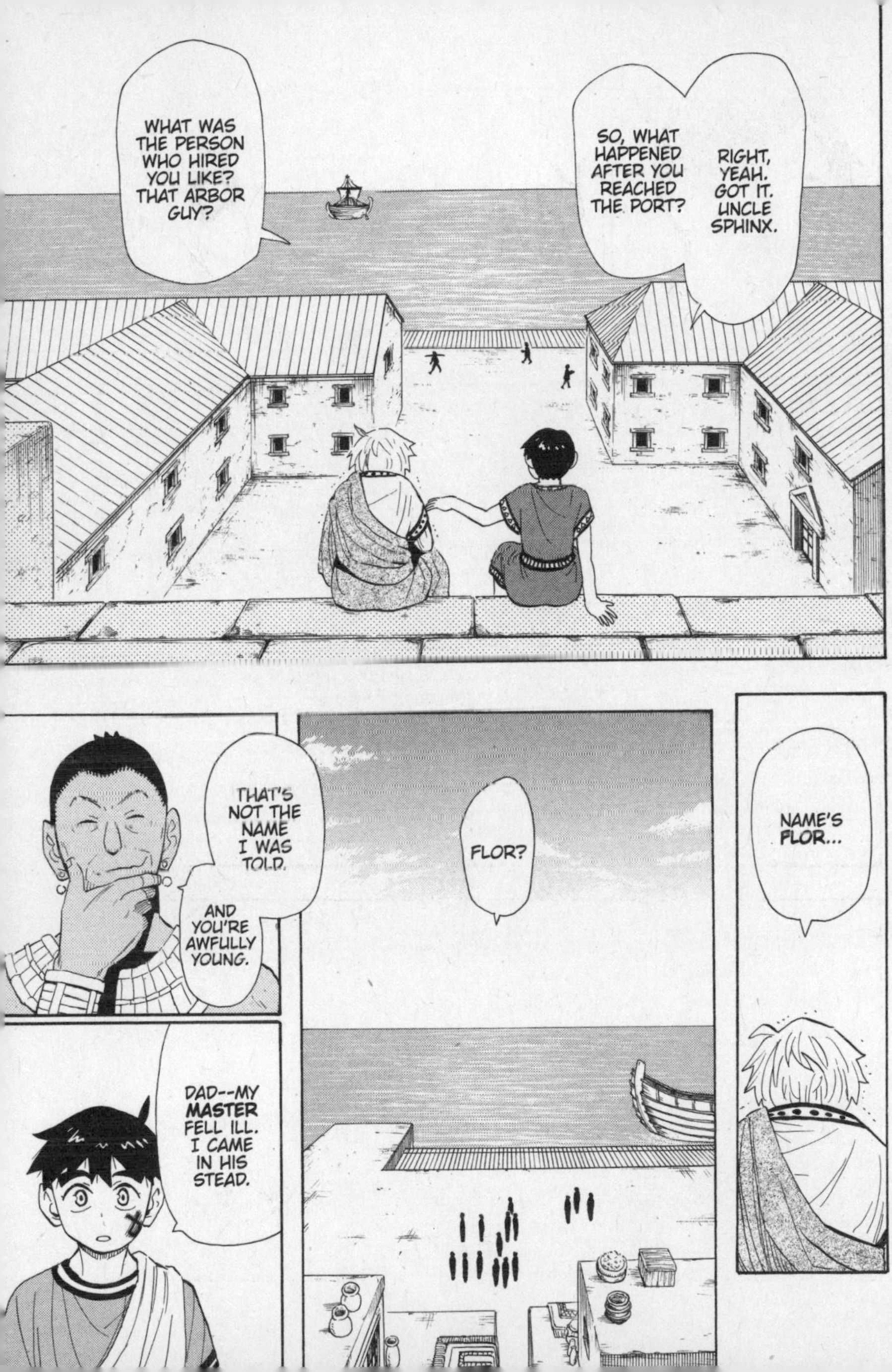
RIGHT, YEAH. GOT IT. UNCLE SPHINX.
SO, WHAT HAPPENED AFTER YOU REACHED THE PORT?
WHAT WAS THE PERSON WHO HIRED YOU LIKE? THAT ARBOR GUY?
NAME'S FLOR...
FLOR?
THAT'S NOT THE NAME I WAS TOLD.
AND YOU'RE AWFULLY YOUNG.
DAD--MY MASTER FELL ILL. I CAME IN HIS STEAD.

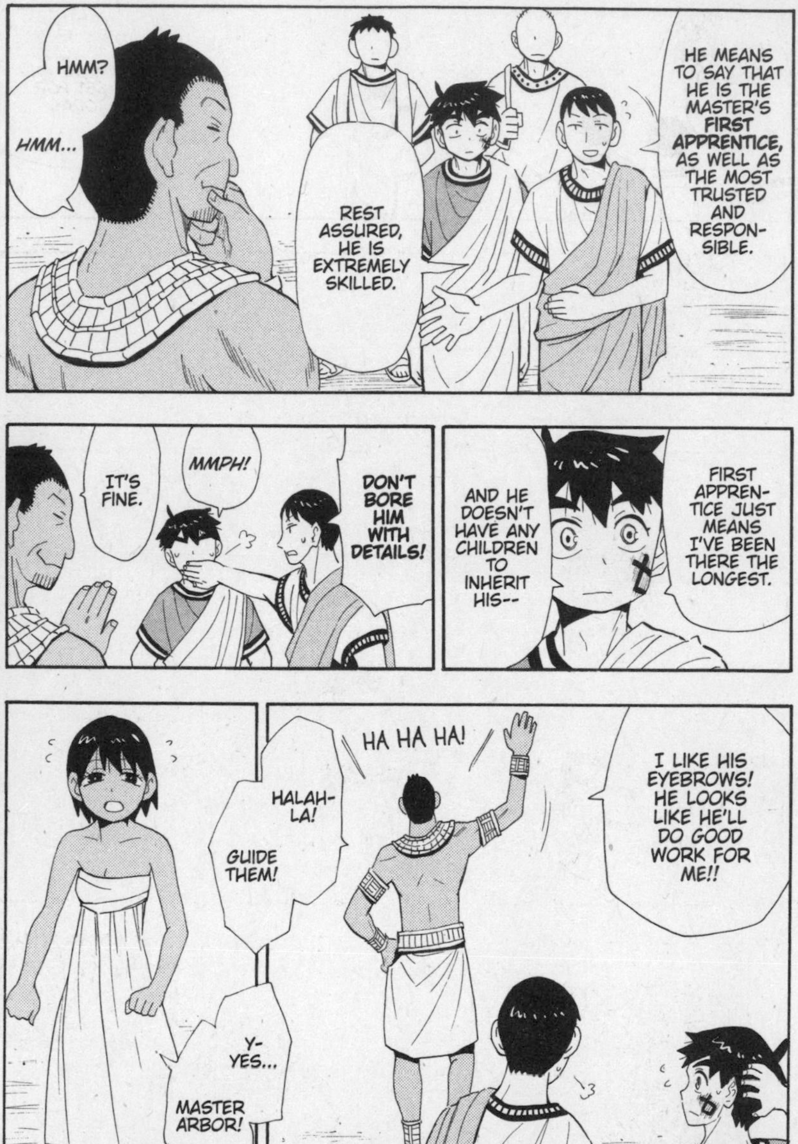
HE MEANS TO SAY THAT HE IS THE MASTER'S FIRST APPRENTICE, AS WELL AS THE MOST TRUSTED AND RESPONSIBLE.
REST ASSURED, HE IS EXTREMELY SKILLED.
HMM?
HMM...
FIRST APPRENTICE JUST MEANS I'VE BEEN THERE THE LONGEST.
AND HE DOESN'T HAVE ANY CHILDREN TO INHERIT HIS--
DON'T BORE HIM WITH DETAILS!
MMPH!
IT'S FINE.
I LIKE HIS EYEBROWS! HE LOOKS LIKE HE'LL DO GOOD WORK FOR ME!!
HA HA HA!
HALAH-LA!
GUIDE THEM!
Y-YES...
MASTER ARBOR!

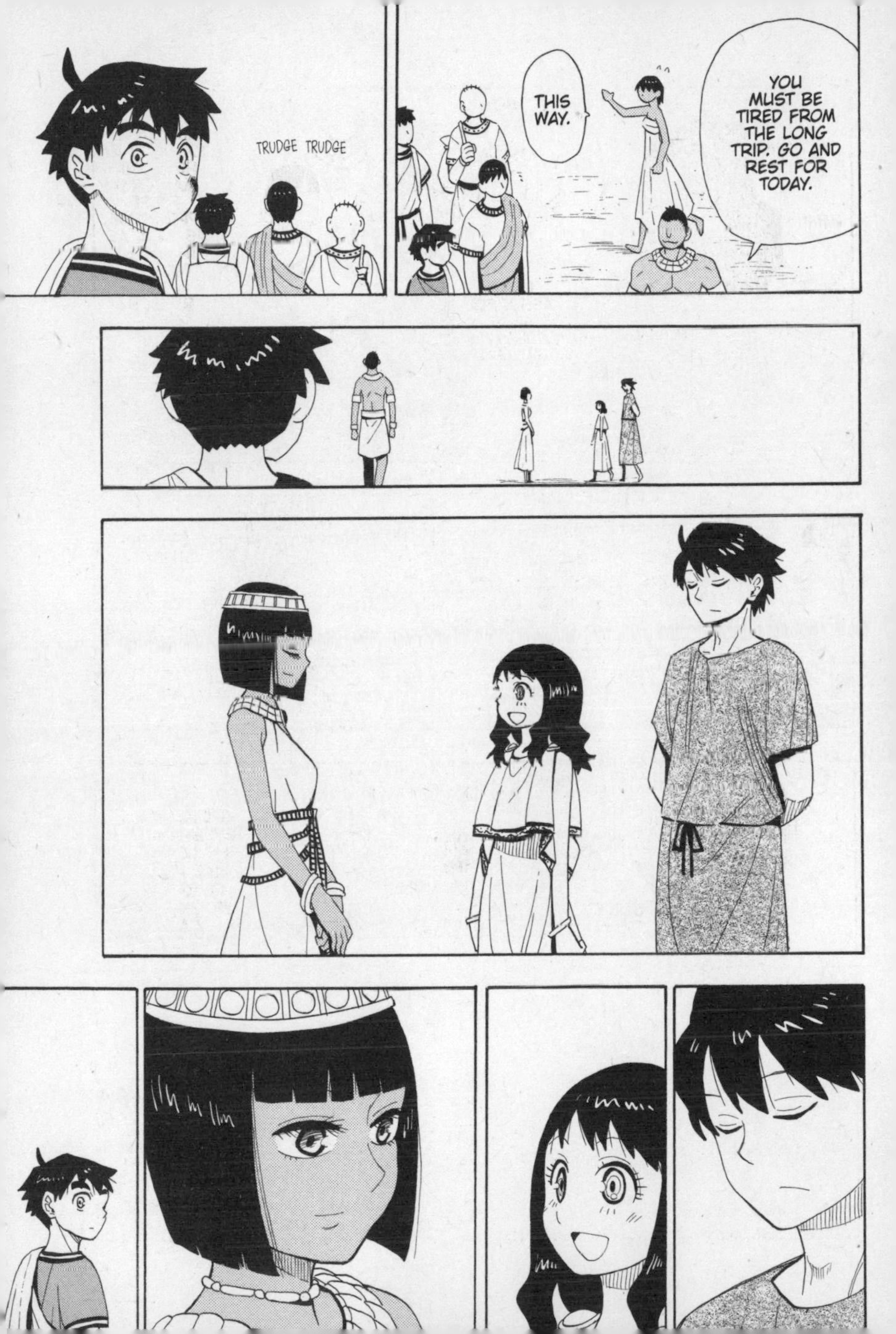
YOU MUST BE TIRED FROM THE LONG TRIP. GO AND REST FOR TODAY.
THIS WAY.
TRUDGE TRUDGE

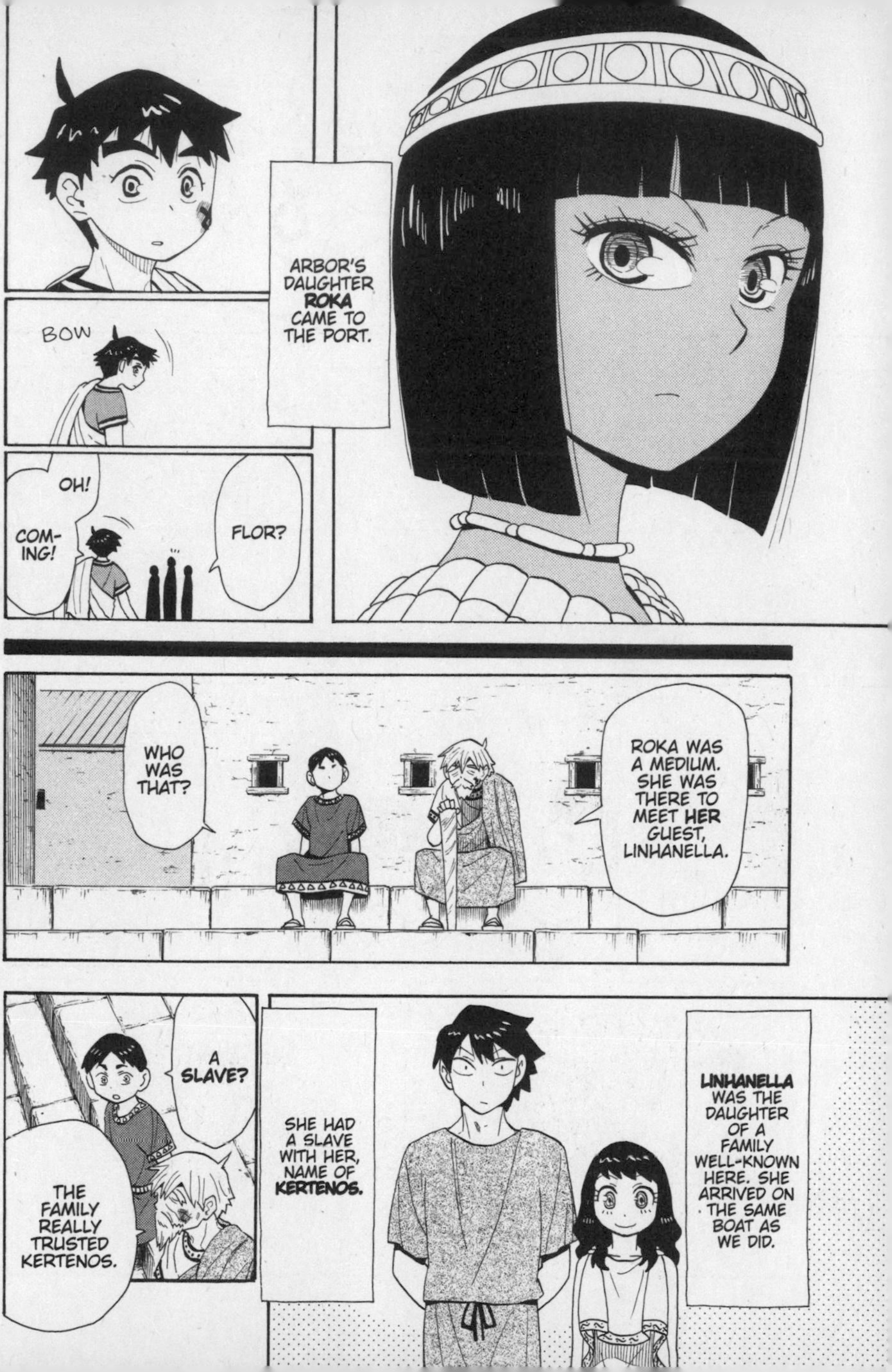
ARBOR'S DAUGHTER ROKA CAME TO THE PORT.
BOW
FLOR?
OH!
COM-ING!
ROKA WAS A MEDIUM. SHE WAS THERE TO MEET HER GUEST, LINHANELLA.
WHO WAS THAT?
LINHANELLA WAS THE DAUGHTER OF A FAMILY WELL-KNOWN HERE. SHE ARRIVED ON THE SAME BOAT AS WE DID.
SHE HAD A SLAVE WITH HER, NAME OF KERTENOS.
A SLAVE?
THE FAMILY REALLY TRUSTED KERTENOS.

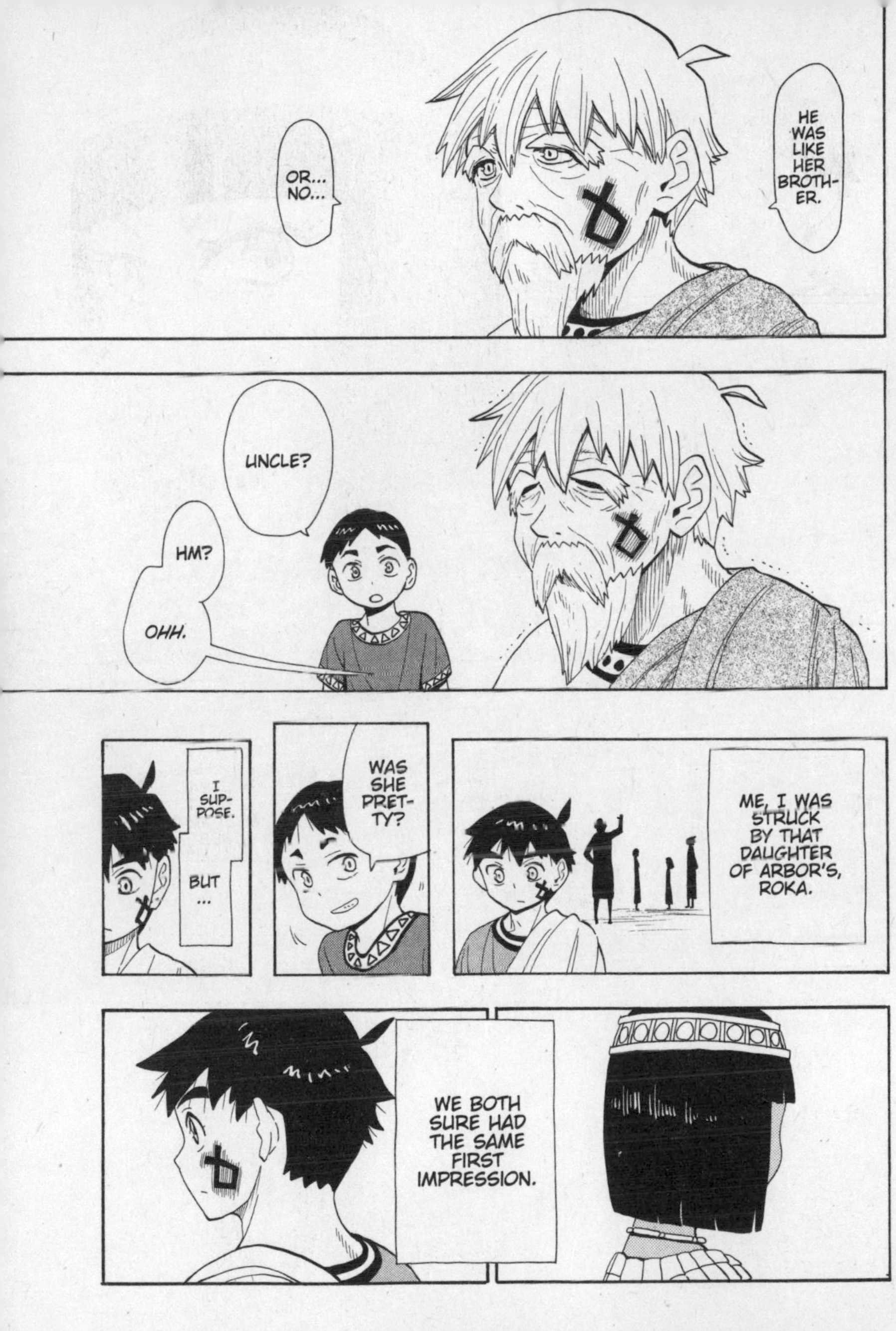
HE WAS LIKE HER BROTHER.
OR... NO...
UNCLE?
HM?
OHH.
ME, I WAS STRUCK BY THAT DAUGHTER OF ARBOR'S, ROKA.
WAS SHE PRETTY?
I SUPPOSE.
BUT...
WE BOTH SURE HAD THE SAME FIRST IMPRESSION.

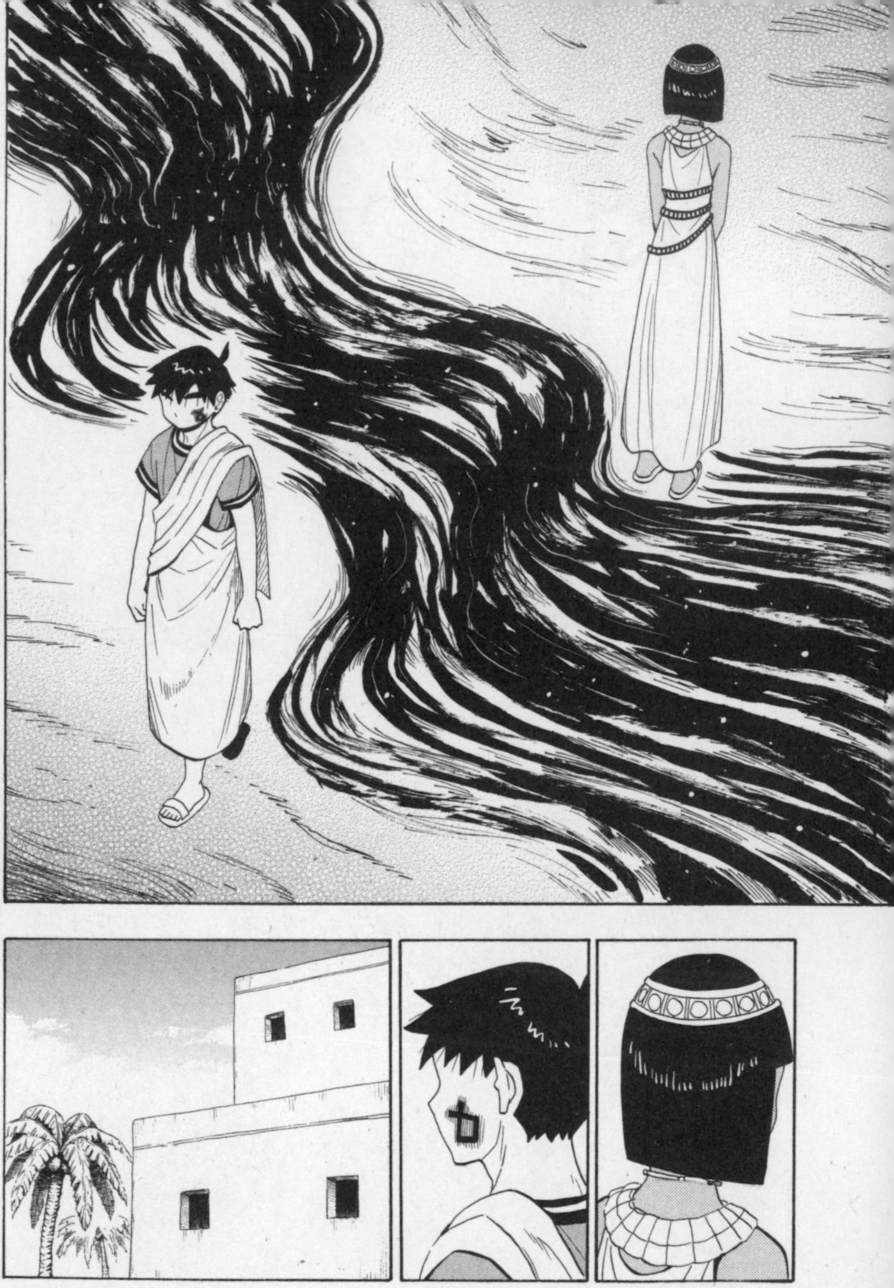

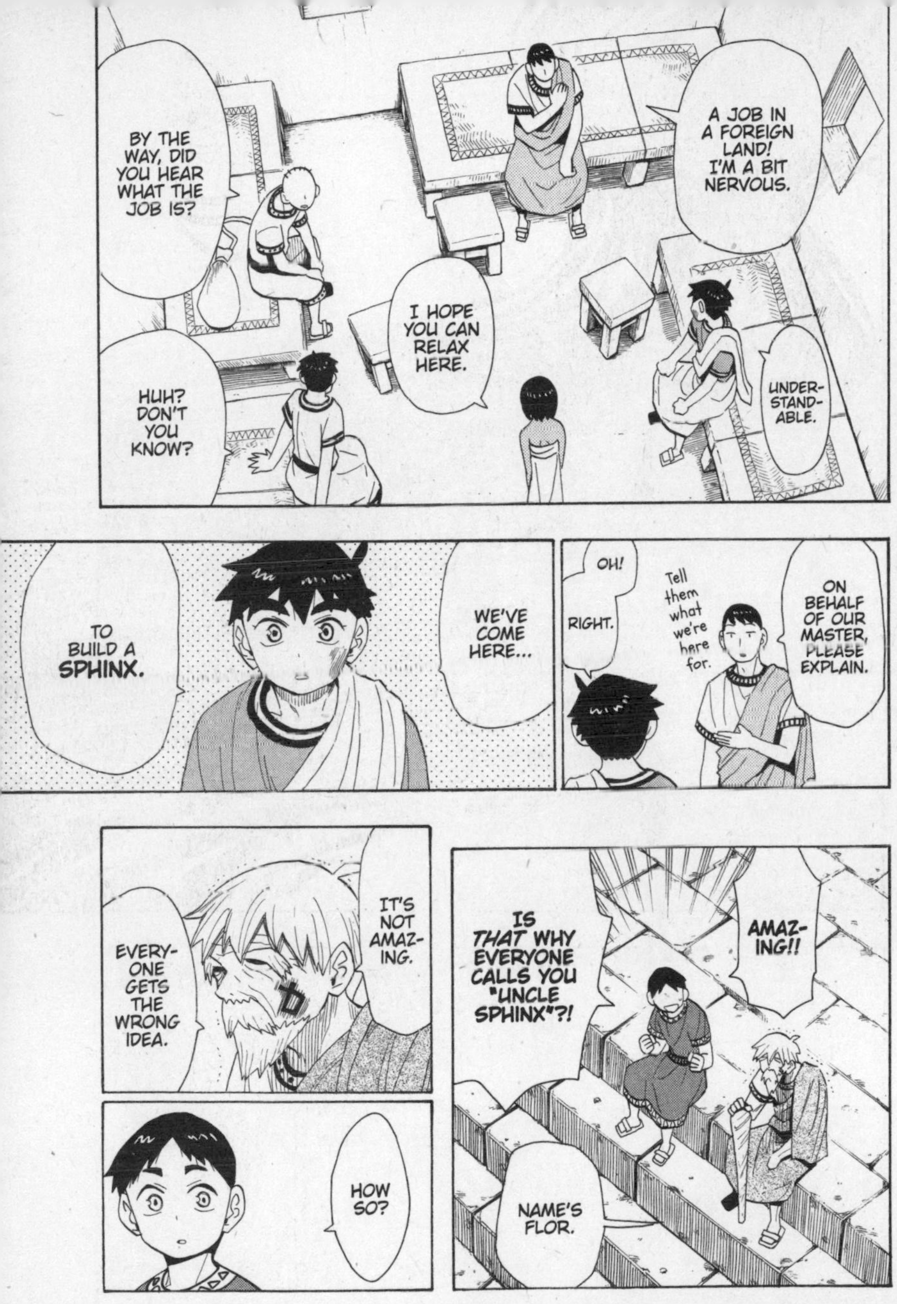
A JOB IN A FOREIGN LAND! I'M A BIT NERVOUS.
UNDER-STAND-ABLE.
I HOPE YOU CAN RELAX HERE.
BY THE WAY, DID YOU HEAR WHAT THE JOB IS?
HUH? DON'T YOU KNOW?
ON BEHALF OF OUR MASTER, PLEASE EXPLAIN.
Tell them what we're here for.
OH!
RIGHT.
WE'VE COME HERE...
TO BUILD A **SPHINX.**
AMAZ-ING!!
IS *THAT* WHY EVERYONE CALLS YOU "UNCLE SPHINX"?!
NAME'S FLOR.
IT'S NOT AMAZ-ING.
EVERY-ONE GETS THE WRONG IDEA.
HOW SO?

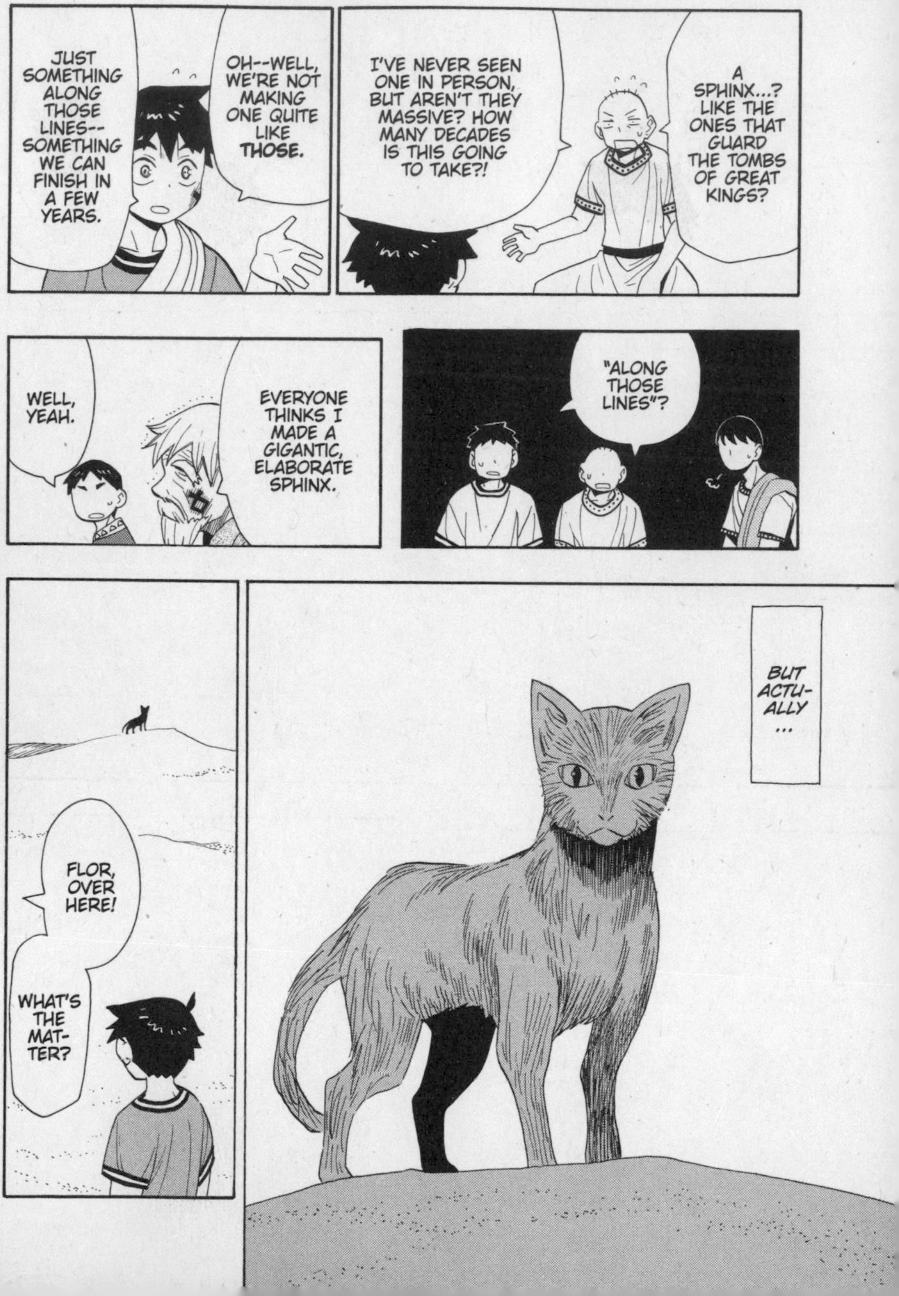
A SPHINX...? LIKE THE ONES THAT GUARD THE TOMBS OF GREAT KINGS?
I'VE NEVER SEEN ONE IN PERSON, BUT AREN'T THEY MASSIVE? HOW MANY DECADES IS THIS GOING TO TAKE?!
OH--WELL, WE'RE NOT MAKING ONE QUITE LIKE **THOSE.**
JUST SOMETHING ALONG THOSE LINES-- SOMETHING WE CAN FINISH IN A FEW YEARS.
"ALONG THOSE LINES"?
EVERYONE THINKS I MADE A GIGANTIC, ELABORATE SPHINX.
WELL, YEAH.
BUT ACTU-ALLY...
FLOR, OVER HERE!
WHAT'S THE MAT-TER?

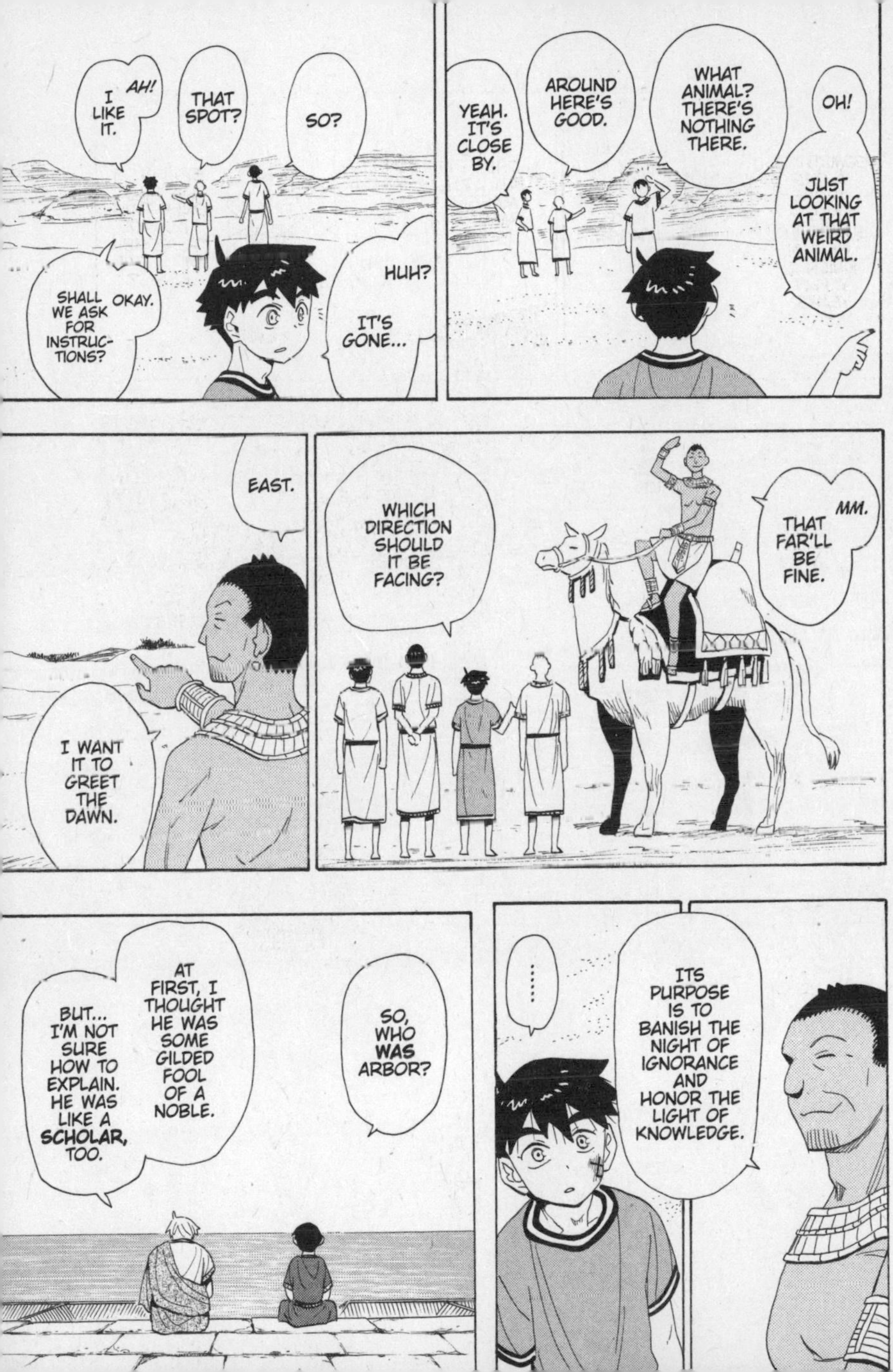
OH!
JUST LOOKING AT THAT WEIRD ANIMAL.
WHAT ANIMAL? THERE'S NOTHING THERE.
AROUND HERE'S GOOD.
YEAH. IT'S CLOSE BY.
SO?
THAT SPOT?
AH! I LIKE IT.
HUH?
IT'S GONE...
OKAY.
SHALL WE ASK FOR INSTRUC- TIONS?
MM. THAT FAR'LL BE FINE.
WHICH DIRECTION SHOULD IT BE FACING?
EAST.
I WANT IT TO GREET THE DAWN.
ITS PURPOSE IS TO BANISH THE NIGHT OF IGNORANCE AND HONOR THE LIGHT OF KNOWLEDGE.
......
SO, WHO **WAS** ARBOR?
AT FIRST, I THOUGHT HE WAS SOME GILDED FOOL OF A NOBLE.
BUT... I'M NOT SURE HOW TO EXPLAIN. HE WAS LIKE A **SCHOLAR**, TOO.

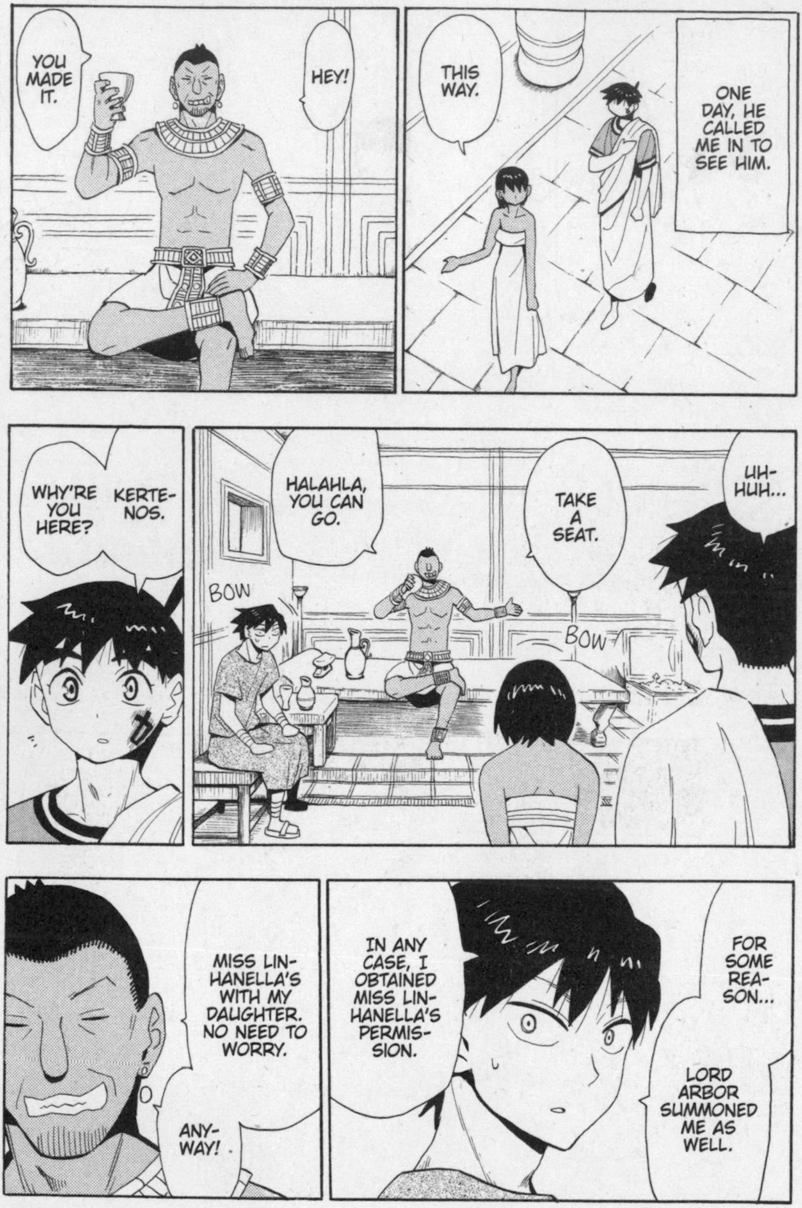
ONE DAY, HE CALLED ME IN TO SEE HIM.
THIS WAY.
HEY!
YOU MADE IT.
UH-HUH...
TAKE A SEAT.
BOW
HALAHLA, YOU CAN GO.
BOW
KERTE-NOS.
WHY'RE YOU HERE?
FOR SOME REA-SON...
LORD ARBOR SUMMONED ME AS WELL.
IN ANY CASE, I OBTAINED MISS LIN-HANELLA'S PERMIS-SION.
MISS LIN-HANELLA'S WITH MY DAUGHTER. NO NEED TO WORRY.
ANY-WAY!

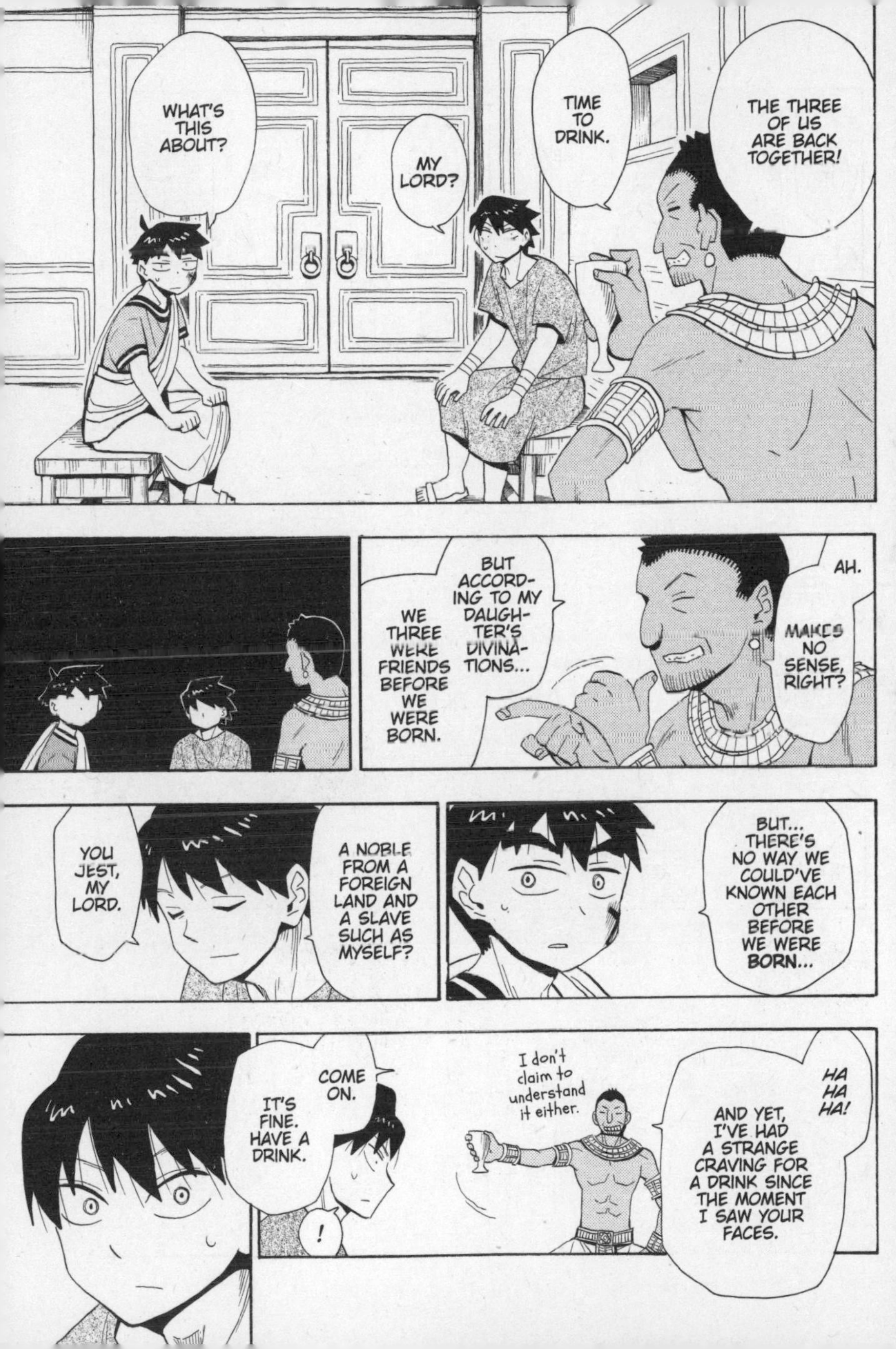
THE THREE OF US ARE BACK TOGETHER!
TIME TO DRINK.
MY LORD?
WHAT'S THIS ABOUT?
AH.
MAKES NO SENSE, RIGHT?
BUT ACCORDING TO MY DAUGHTER'S DIVINATIONS...
WE THREE WERE FRIENDS BEFORE WE WERE BORN.
BUT... THERE'S NO WAY WE COULD'VE KNOWN EACH OTHER BEFORE WE WERE BORN...
A NOBLE FROM A FOREIGN LAND AND A SLAVE SUCH AS MYSELF?
YOU JEST, MY LORD.
HA HA HA!
AND YET, I'VE HAD A STRANGE CRAVING FOR A DRINK SINCE THE MOMENT I SAW YOUR FACES.
I don't claim to understand it either.
COME ON.
IT'S FINE. HAVE A DRINK.
!

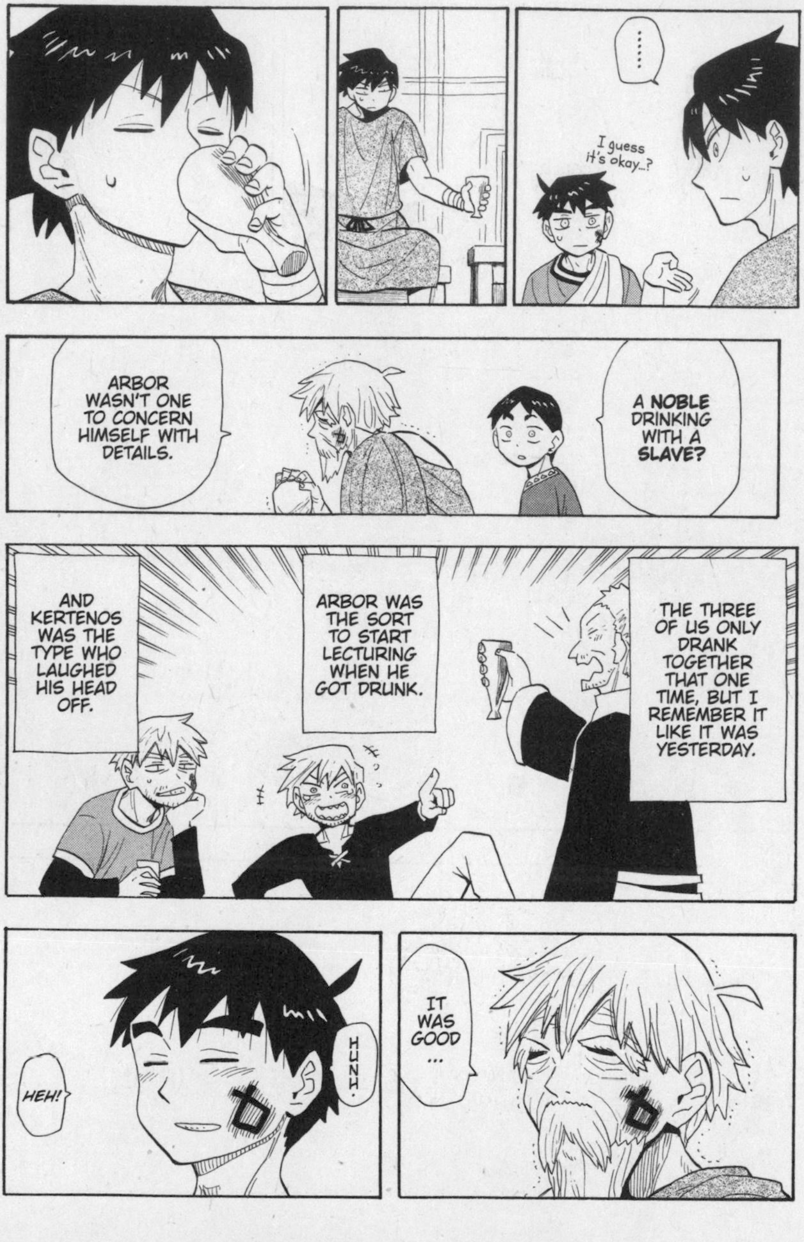

......
I guess it's okay...?
A NOBLE DRINKING WITH A SLAVE?
ARBOR WASN'T ONE TO CONCERN HIMSELF WITH DETAILS.
THE THREE OF US ONLY DRANK TOGETHER THAT ONE TIME, BUT I REMEMBER IT LIKE IT WAS YESTERDAY.
ARBOR WAS THE SORT TO START LECTURING WHEN HE GOT DRUNK.
AND KERTENOS WAS THE TYPE WHO LAUGHED HIS HEAD OFF.
IT WAS GOOD ...
HUNH.
HEH!

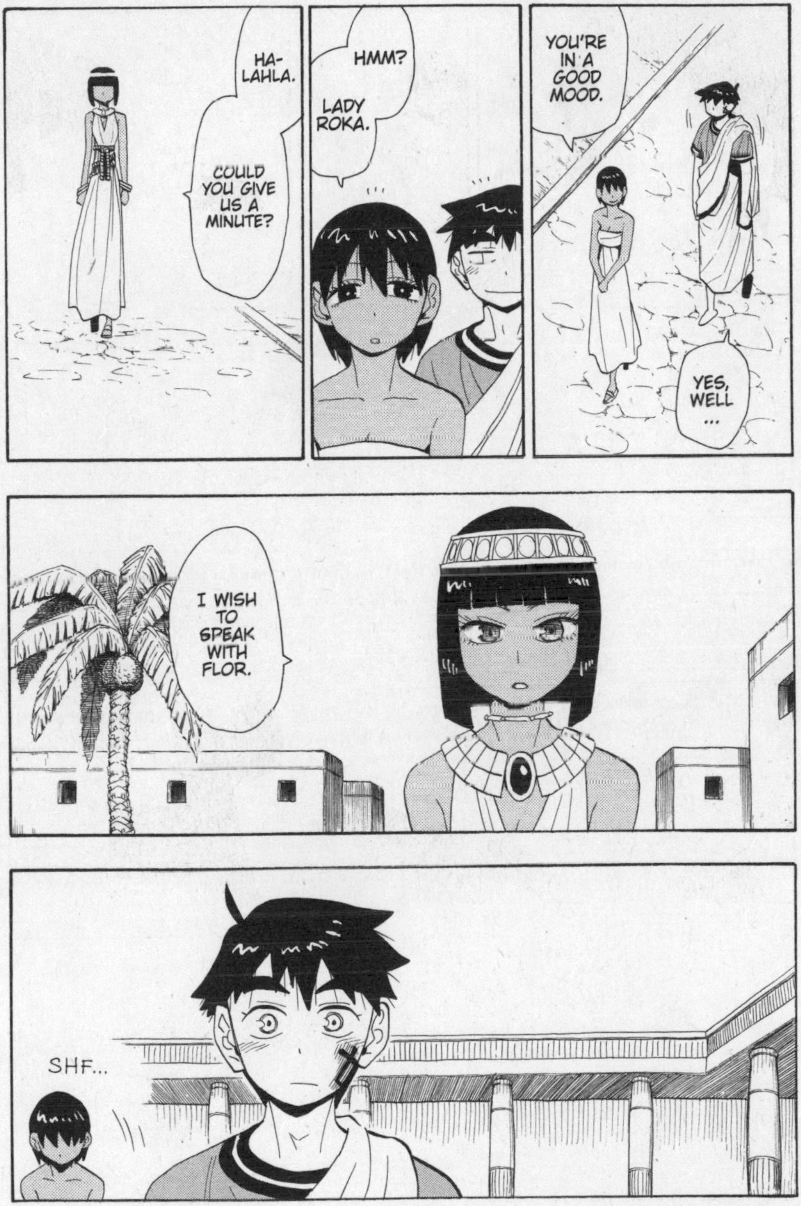
YOU'RE IN A GOOD MOOD.
YES, WELL ...
HMM?
LADY ROKA.
HA-LAHLA.
COULD YOU GIVE US A MINUTE?
I WISH TO SPEAK WITH FLOR.
SHF...

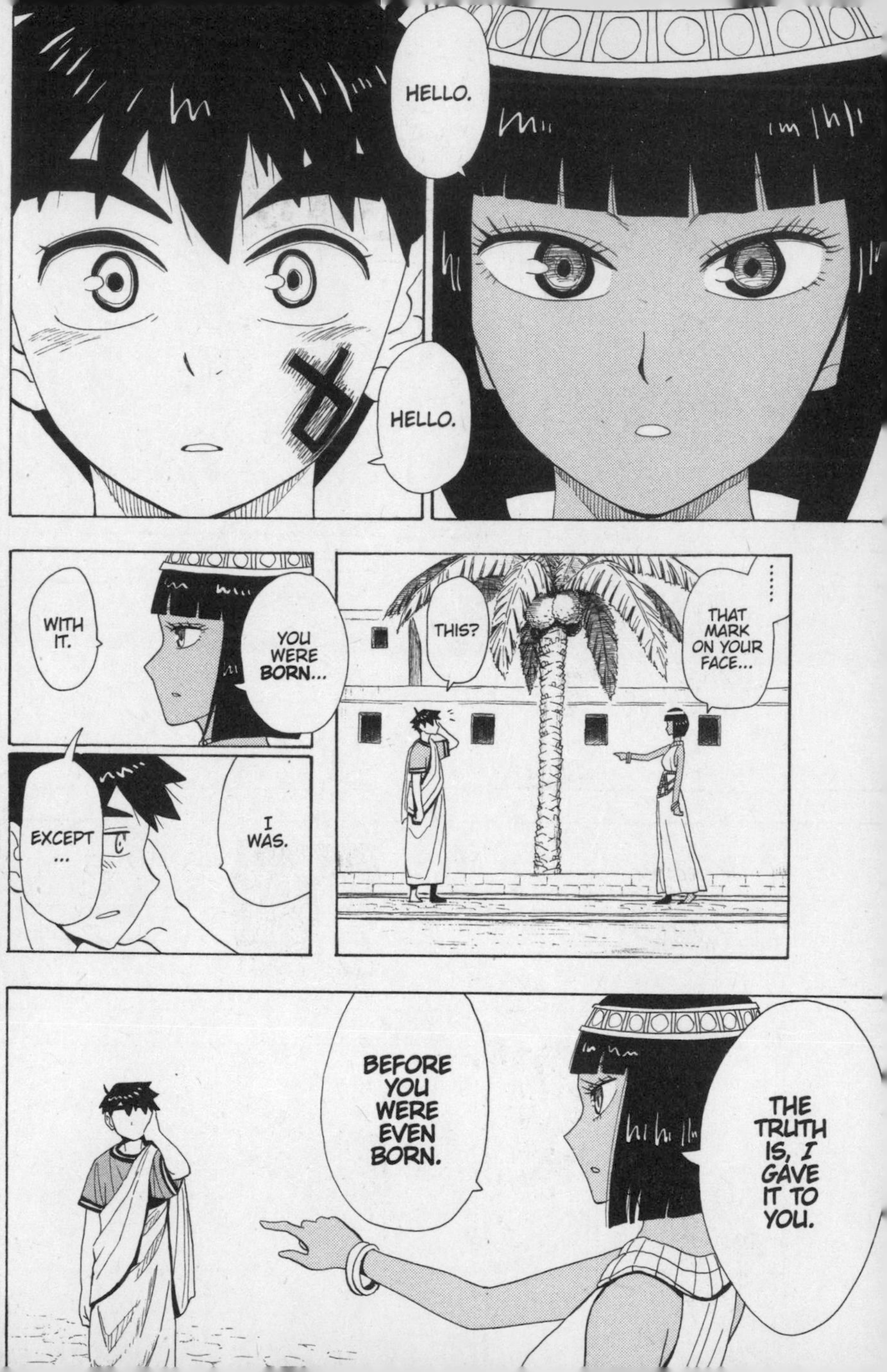
HELLO.
HELLO.
......
THAT MARK ON YOUR FACE...
THIS?
YOU WERE BORN...
WITH IT.
I WAS.
EXCEPT ...
THE TRUTH IS, *I* GAVE IT TO YOU.
BEFORE YOU WERE EVEN BORN.

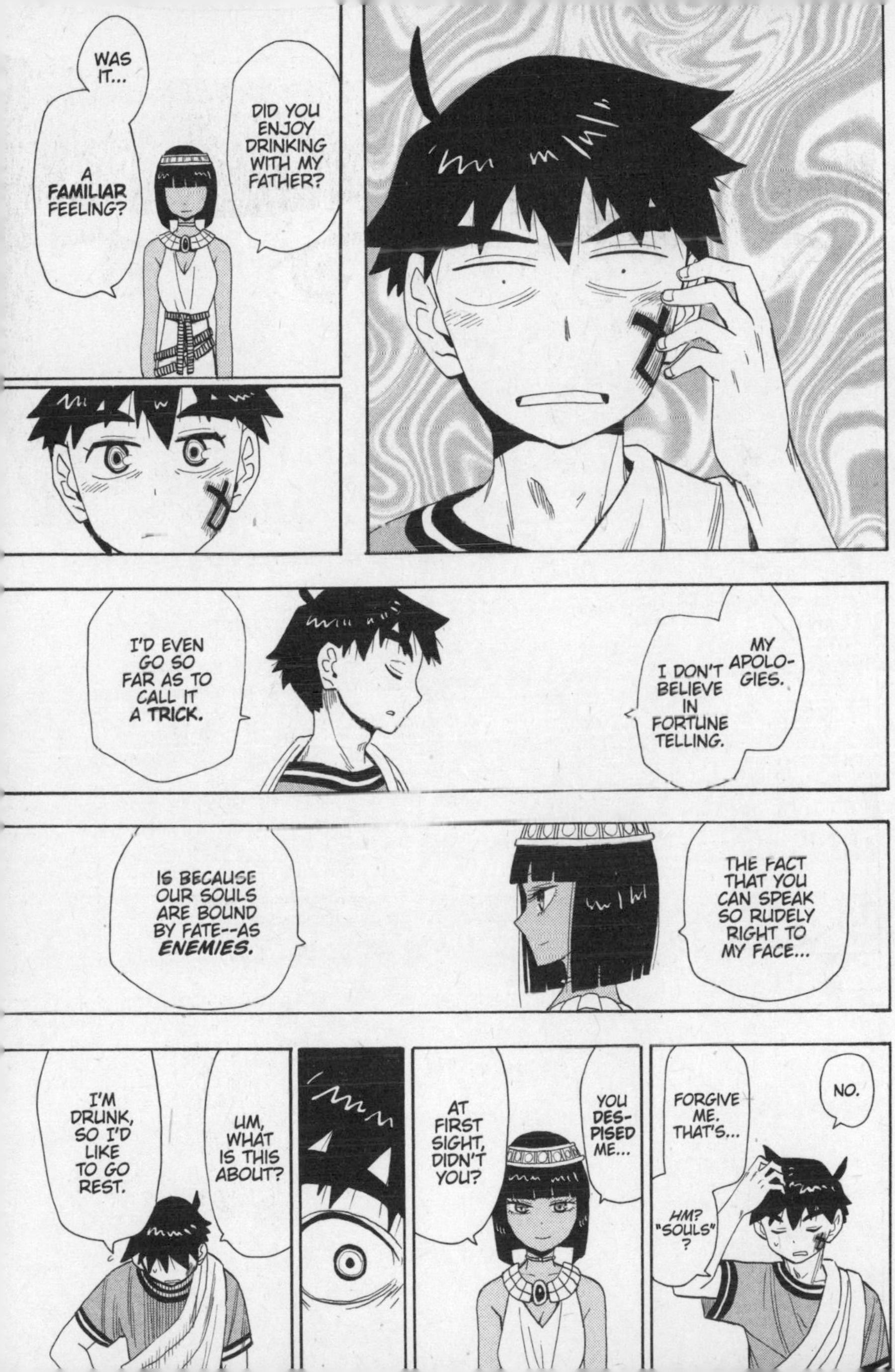
DID YOU ENJOY DRINKING WITH MY FATHER?
WAS IT... A FAMILIAR FEELING?
MY APOLOGIES.
I DON'T BELIEVE IN FORTUNE TELLING.
I'D EVEN GO SO FAR AS TO CALL IT A TRICK.
THE FACT THAT YOU CAN SPEAK SO RUDELY RIGHT TO MY FACE...
IS BECAUSE OUR SOULS ARE BOUND BY FATE--AS ENEMIES.
NO.
FORGIVE ME. THAT'S...
HM? "SOULS"?
YOU DESPISED ME...
AT FIRST SIGHT, DIDN'T YOU?
UM, WHAT IS THIS ABOUT?
I'M DRUNK, SO I'D LIKE TO GO REST.

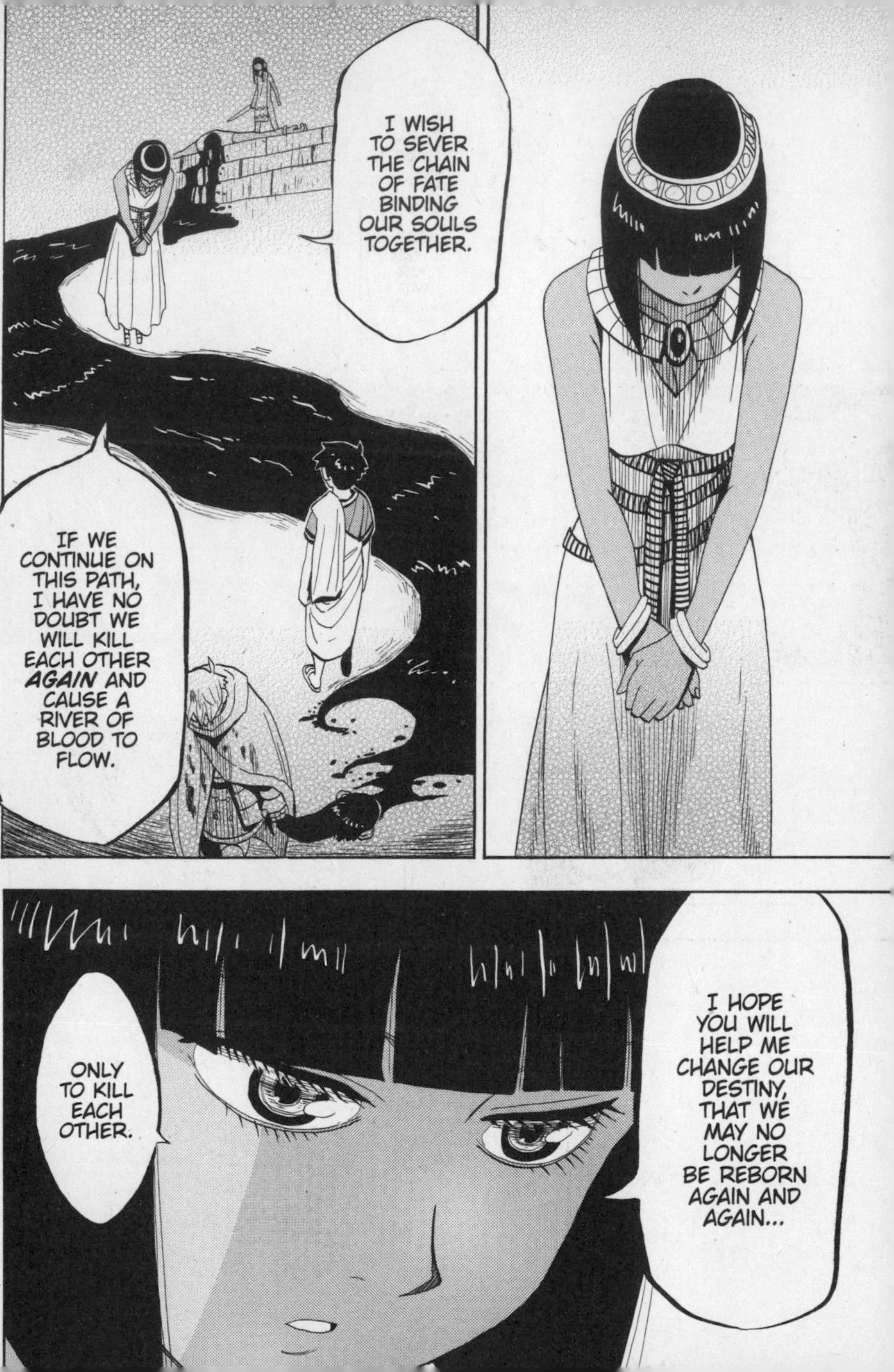
I WISH TO SEVER THE CHAIN OF FATE BINDING OUR SOULS TOGETHER.
IF WE CONTINUE ON THIS PATH, I HAVE NO DOUBT WE WILL KILL EACH OTHER *AGAIN* AND CAUSE A RIVER OF BLOOD TO FLOW.
I HOPE YOU WILL HELP ME CHANGE OUR DESTINY, THAT WE MAY NO LONGER BE REBORN AGAIN AND AGAIN...
ONLY TO KILL EACH OTHER.

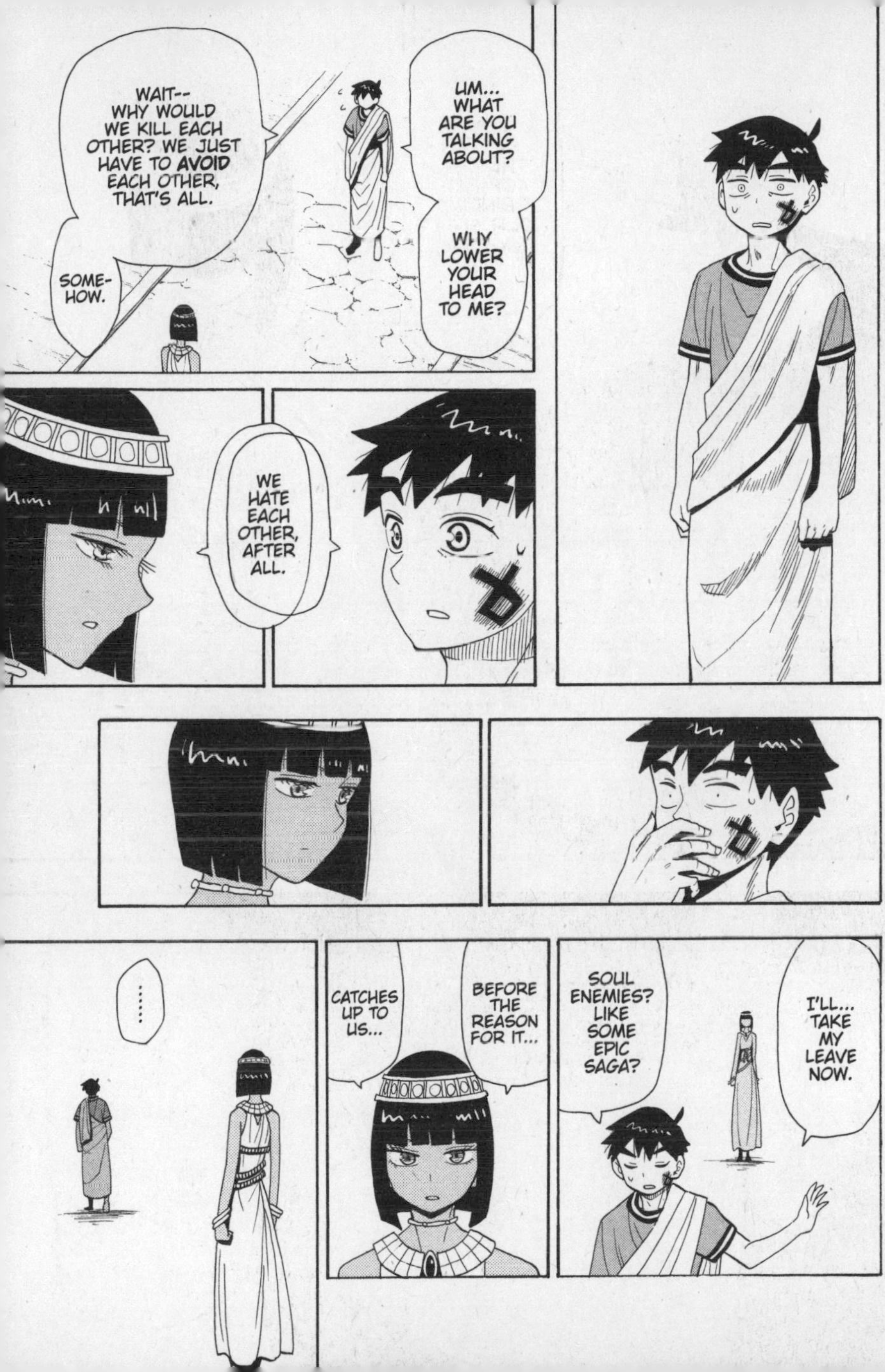
UM... WHAT ARE YOU TALKING ABOUT?
WHY LOWER YOUR HEAD TO ME?
WAIT-- WHY WOULD WE KILL EACH OTHER? WE JUST HAVE TO **AVOID** EACH OTHER, THAT'S ALL.
SOME-HOW.
WE HATE EACH OTHER, AFTER ALL.
I'LL... TAKE MY LEAVE NOW.
SOUL ENEMIES? LIKE SOME EPIC SAGA?
BEFORE THE REASON FOR IT...
CATCHES UP TO US...
......

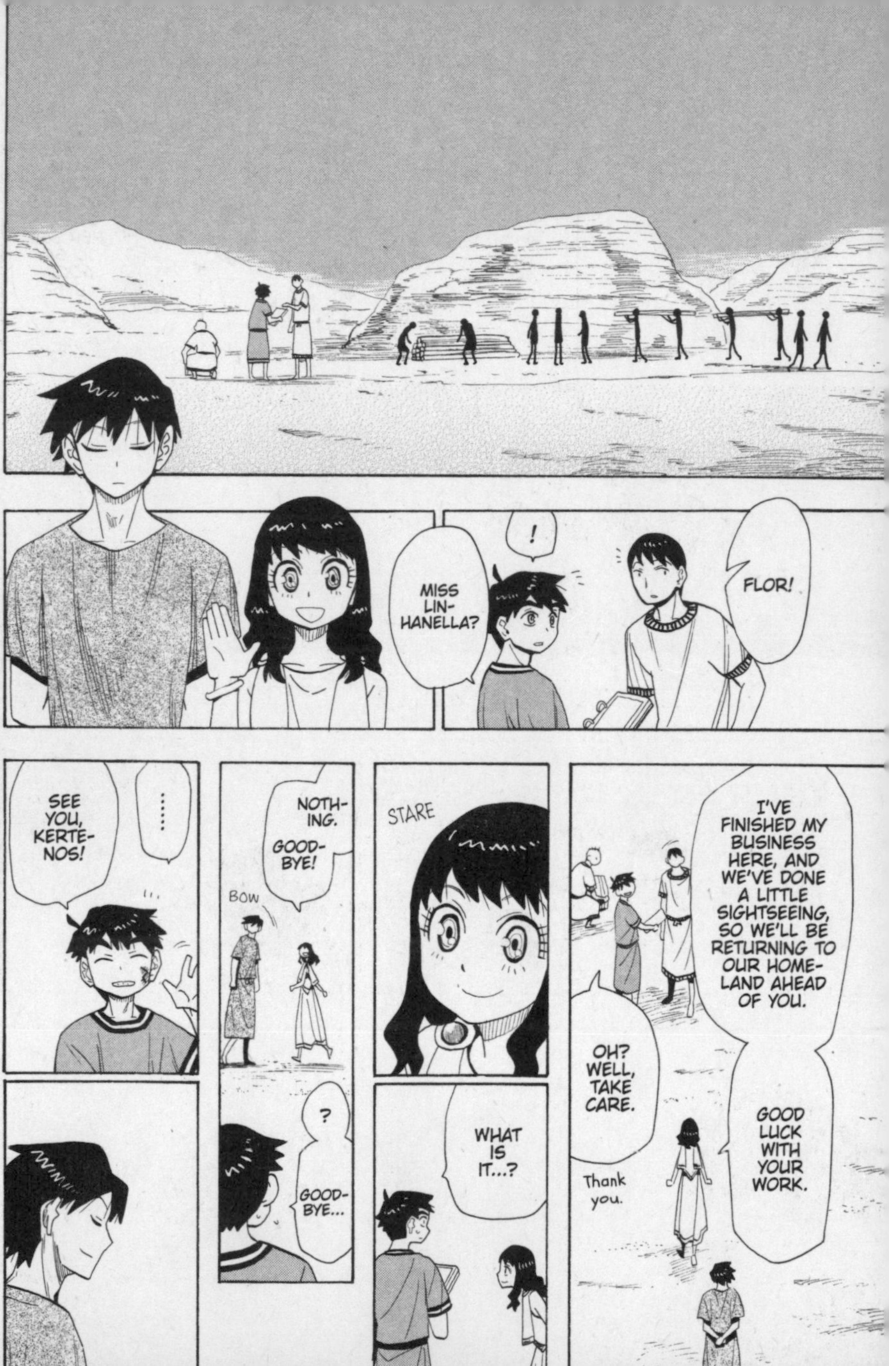
FLOR!
!
MISS LIN-HANELLA?
I'VE FINISHED MY BUSINESS HERE, AND WE'VE DONE A LITTLE SIGHTSEEING, SO WE'LL BE RETURNING TO OUR HOMELAND AHEAD OF YOU.
OH? WELL, TAKE CARE.
GOOD LUCK WITH YOUR WORK.
Thank you.
STARE
NOTHING.
GOOD-BYE!
BOW
......
SEE YOU, KERTENOS!
WHAT IS IT...?
?
GOOD-BYE...

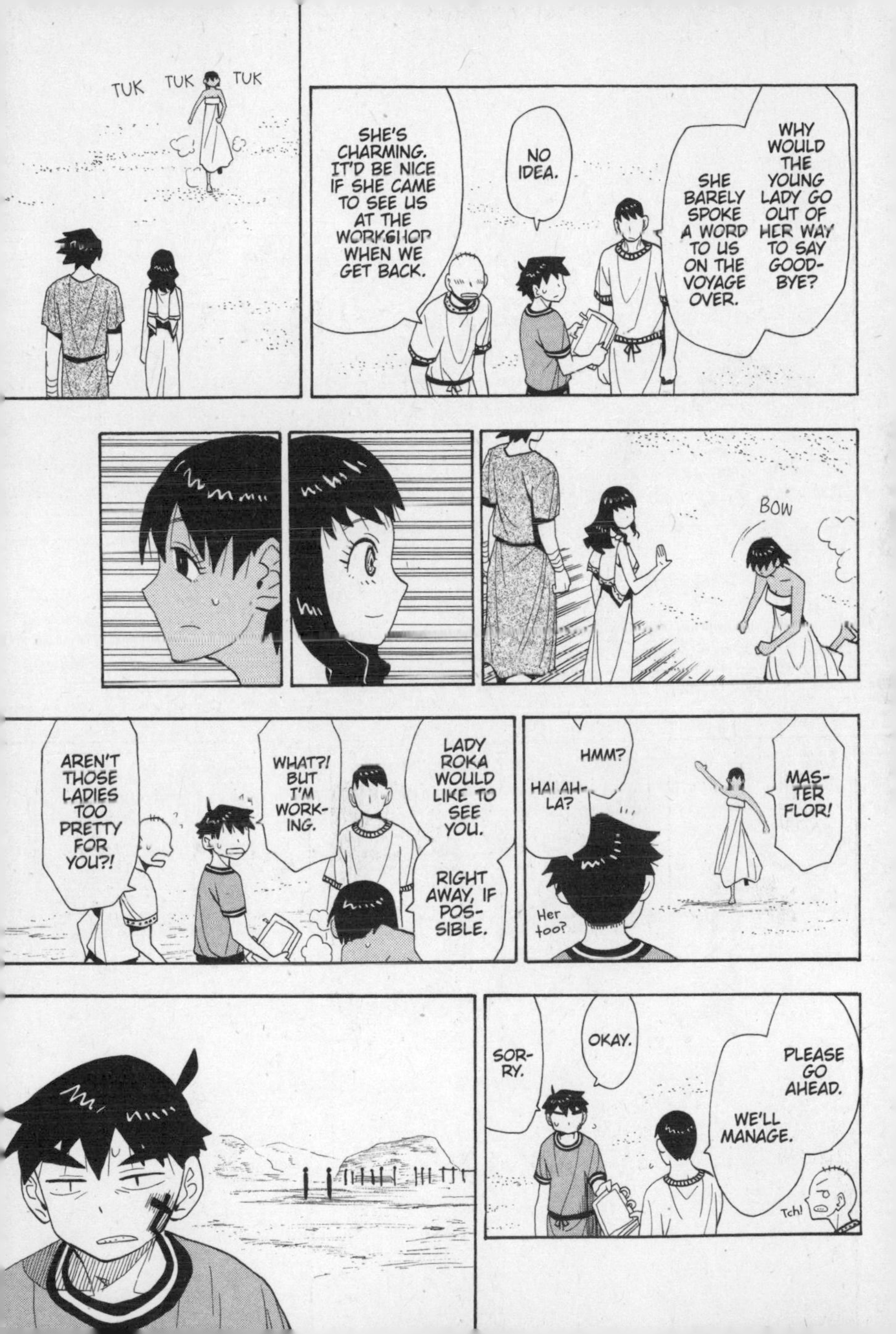
WHY WOULD THE YOUNG LADY GO OUT OF HER WAY TO SAY GOOD-BYE?
SHE BARELY SPOKE A WORD TO US ON THE VOYAGE OVER.
NO IDEA.
SHE'S CHARMING. IT'D BE NICE IF SHE CAME TO SEE US AT THE WORKSHOP WHEN WE GET BACK.
TUK TUK TUK
BOW
MAS-TER FLOR!
HMM?
HAI AH-LA?
Her too?
LADY ROKA WOULD LIKE TO SEE YOU.
RIGHT AWAY, IF POS-SIBLE.
WHAT?! BUT I'M WORK-ING.
AREN'T THOSE LADIES TOO PRETTY FOR YOU?!
PLEASE GO AHEAD.
WE'LL MANAGE.
OKAY.
SOR-RY.
Tch!

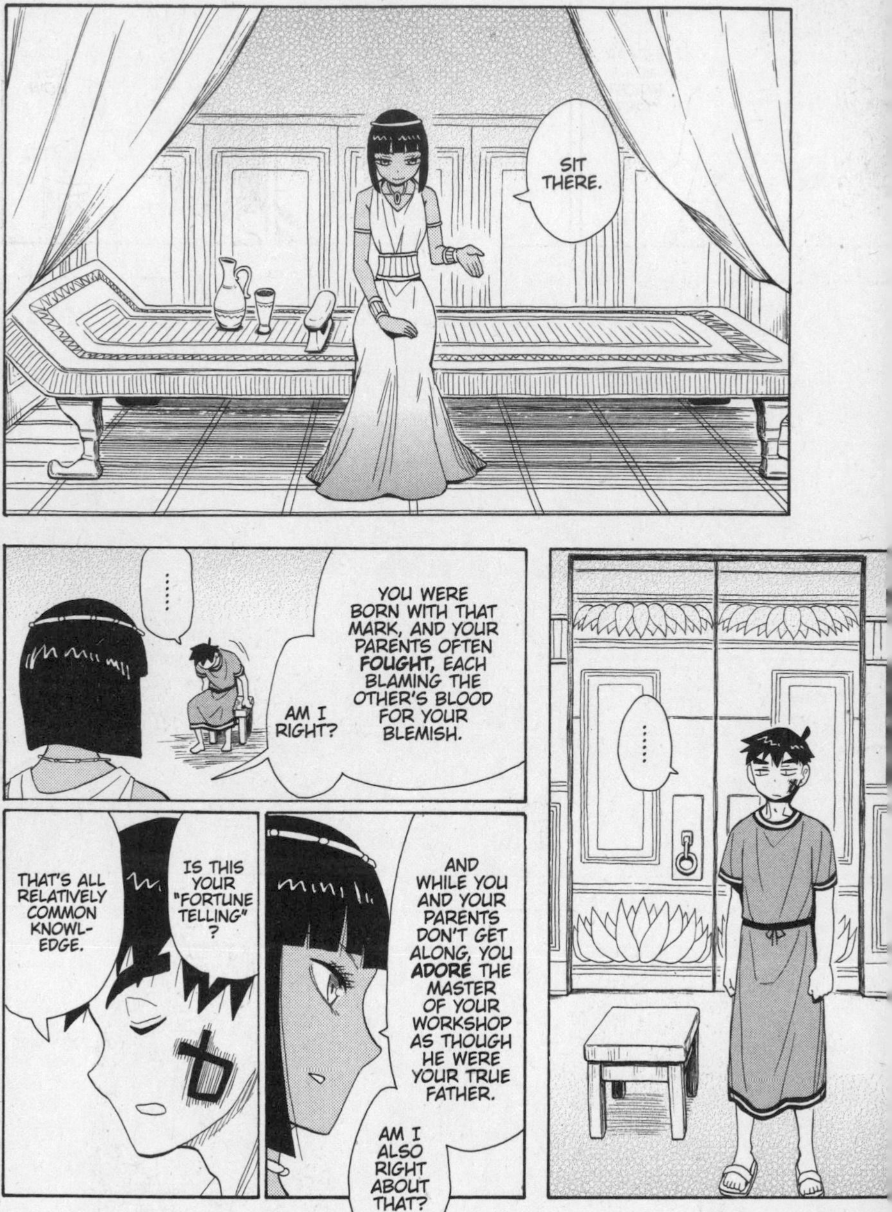
SIT THERE.
......
YOU WERE BORN WITH THAT MARK, AND YOUR PARENTS OFTEN FOUGHT, EACH BLAMING THE OTHER'S BLOOD FOR YOUR BLEMISH.
AM I RIGHT?
......
AND WHILE YOU AND YOUR PARENTS DON'T GET ALONG, YOU ADORE THE MASTER OF YOUR WORKSHOP AS THOUGH HE WERE YOUR TRUE FATHER.
AM I ALSO RIGHT ABOUT THAT?
IS THIS YOUR "FORTUNE TELLING"?
THAT'S ALL RELATIVELY COMMON KNOWLEDGE.

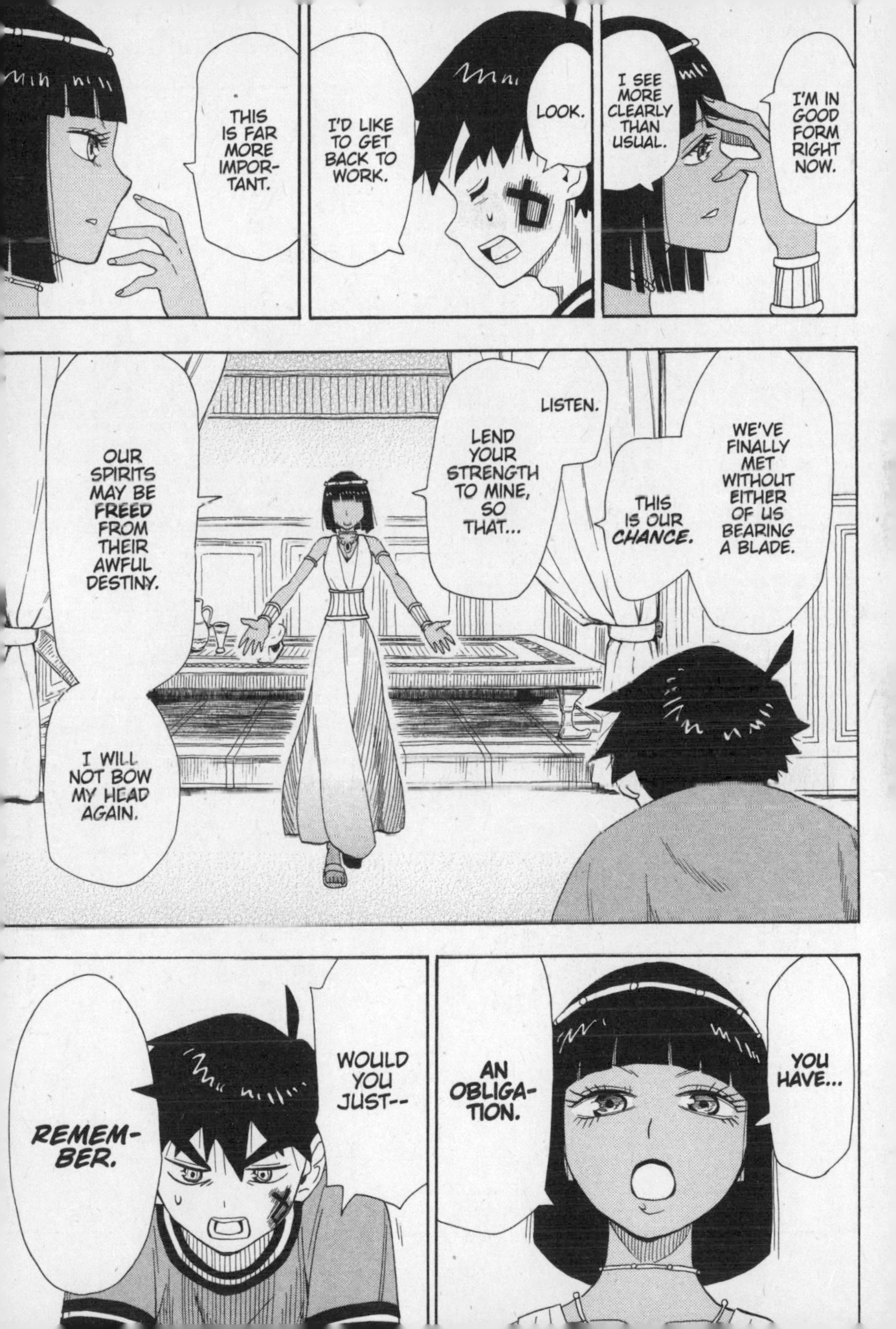
I'M IN GOOD FORM RIGHT NOW.
I SEE MORE CLEARLY THAN USUAL.
LOOK.
I'D LIKE TO GET BACK TO WORK.
THIS IS FAR MORE IMPORTANT.
WE'VE FINALLY MET WITHOUT EITHER OF US BEARING A BLADE.
THIS IS OUR *CHANCE.*
LISTEN.
LEND YOUR STRENGTH TO MINE, SO THAT...
OUR SPIRITS MAY BE FREED FROM THEIR AWFUL DESTINY.
I WILL NOT BOW MY HEAD AGAIN.
YOU HAVE...
AN OBLIGATION.
WOULD YOU JUST--
REMEMBER.

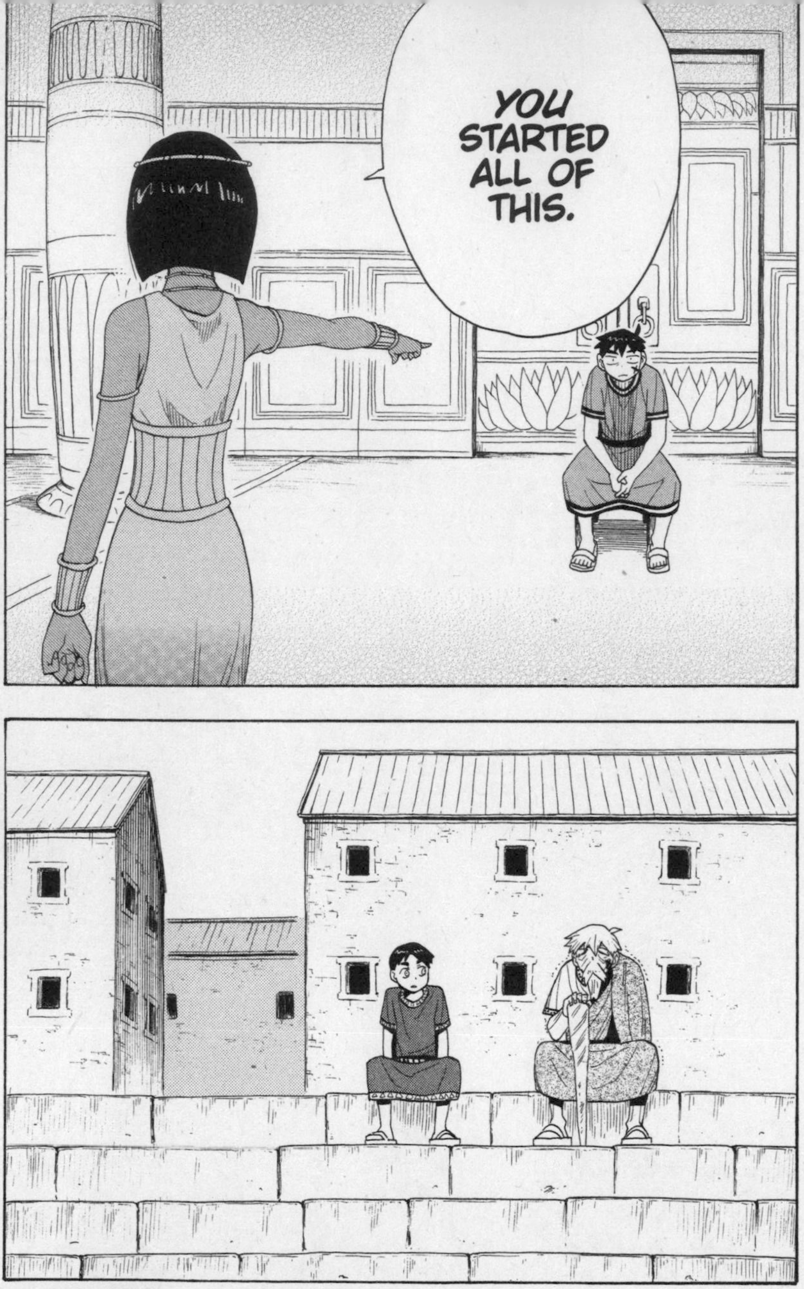
YOU STARTED ALL OF THIS.

Circle 11/END

Spirit Circle

Daiki

Circle 12
Flor 3

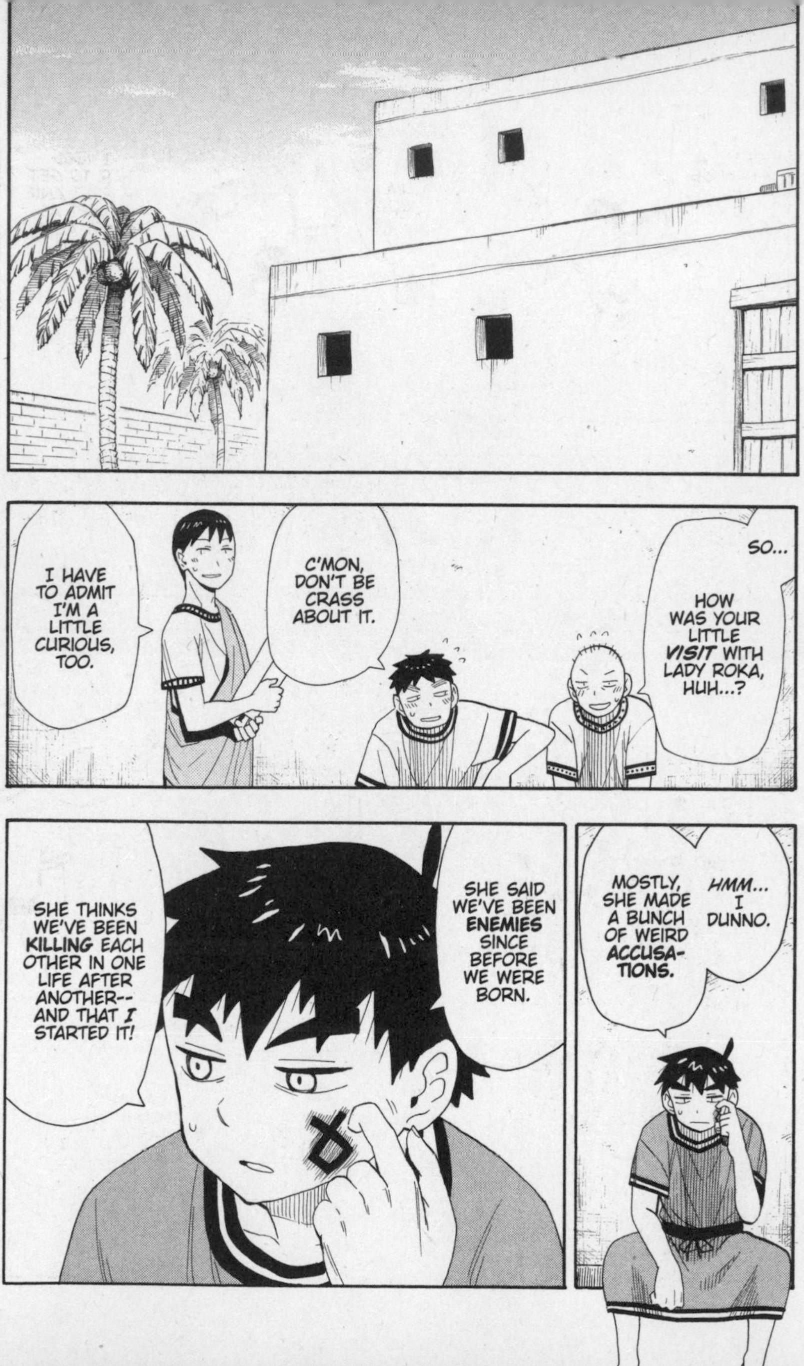
SO...
HOW WAS YOUR LITTLE *VISIT* WITH LADY ROKA, HUH...?
C'MON, DON'T BE CRASS ABOUT IT.
I HAVE TO ADMIT I'M A LITTLE CURIOUS, TOO.
HMM... I DUNNO.
MOSTLY, SHE MADE A BUNCH OF WEIRD **ACCUSA-TIONS.**
SHE SAID WE'VE BEEN **ENEMIES** SINCE BEFORE WE WERE BORN.
SHE THINKS WE'VE BEEN **KILLING** EACH OTHER IN ONE LIFE AFTER ANOTHER-- AND THAT *I* STARTED IT!

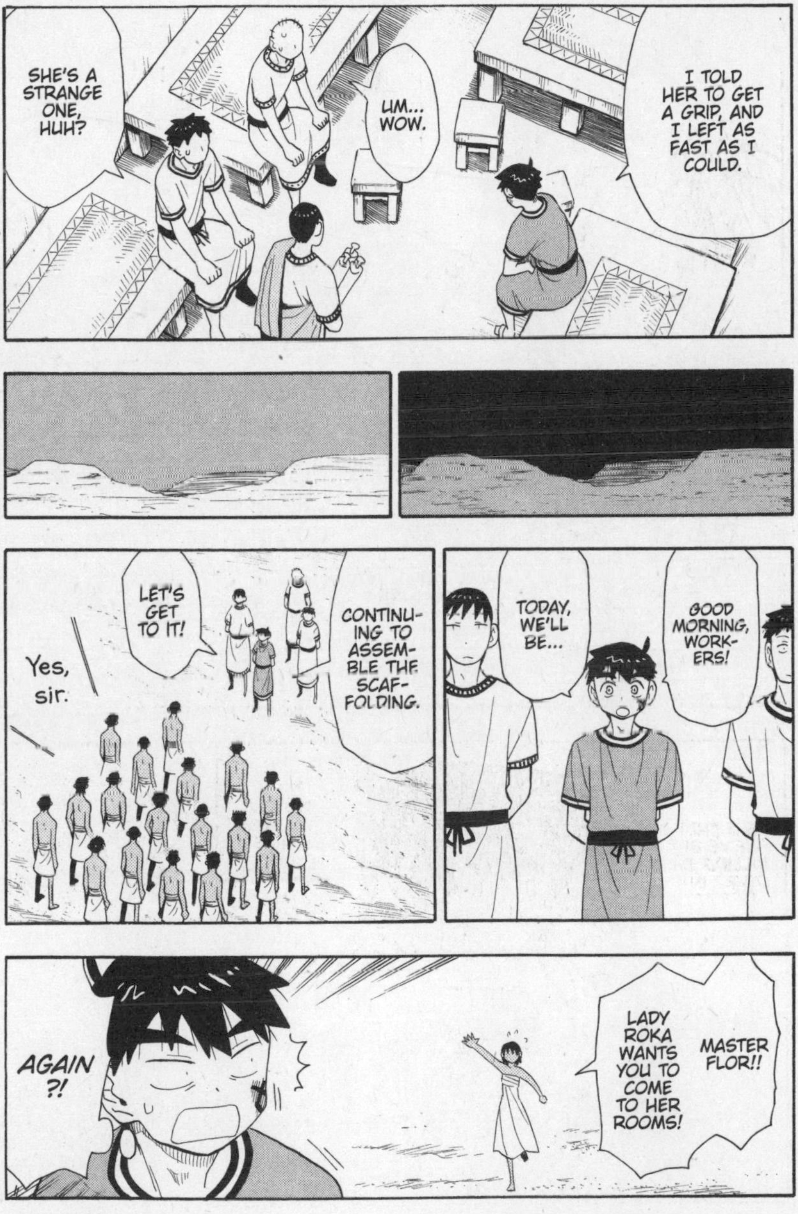
I TOLD HER TO GET A GRIP, AND I LEFT AS FAST AS I COULD.
UM... WOW.
SHE'S A STRANGE ONE, HUH?
GOOD MORNING, WORKERS!
TODAY, WE'LL BE...
CONTINUING TO ASSEMBLE THE SCAFFOLDING.
LET'S GET TO IT!
Yes, sir.
MASTER FLOR!!
LADY ROKA WANTS YOU TO COME TO HER ROOMS!
AGAIN?!

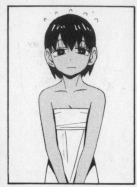

SHE'S OUR CLIENT'S DAUGHTER. YOU SHOULD PROBABLY GO.
WHAT IF SHE KNIFES HIM?
FOOL! WHY WOULD SHE?
I'LL COME.
THANKS FOR BRINGING THE MESSAGE.
I'M SORRY TO DISRUPT YOUR WORK.
WELCOME. YOU LOOK WELL AGAIN TODAY.
I HAD AN INTER-ESTING VISION.
LISTEN, I CAME HERE TO **WORK.**
I DIDN'T CROSS THE OCEAN JUST TO SIT HERE AND LISTEN TO YOUR FANTAS--

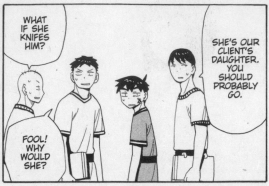

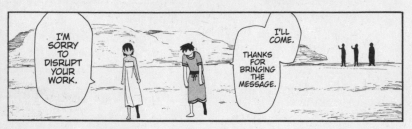

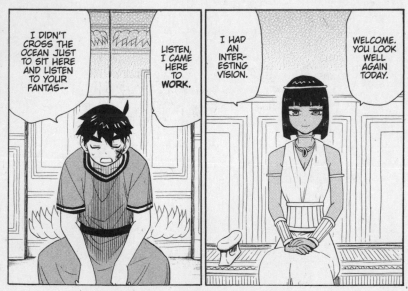

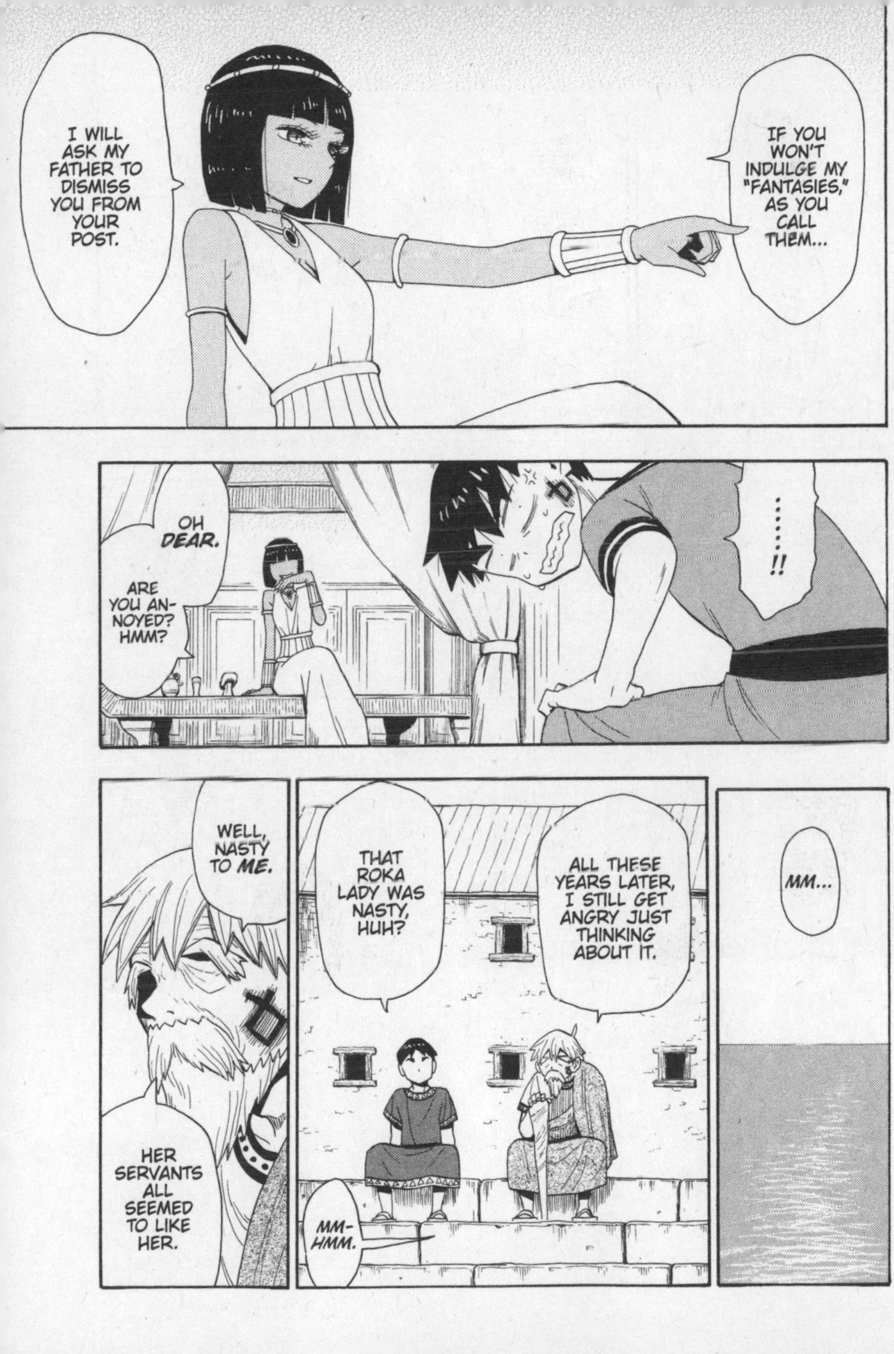
IF YOU WON'T INDULGE MY "FANTASIES," AS YOU CALL THEM...
I WILL ASK MY FATHER TO DISMISS YOU FROM YOUR POST.
......!!
OH *DEAR*.
ARE YOU AN-NOYED? HMM?
MM...
ALL THESE YEARS LATER, I STILL GET ANGRY JUST THINKING ABOUT IT.
THAT ROKA LADY WAS NASTY, HUH?
MM-HMM.
WELL, NASTY TO *ME*.
HER SERVANTS ALL SEEMED TO LIKE HER.

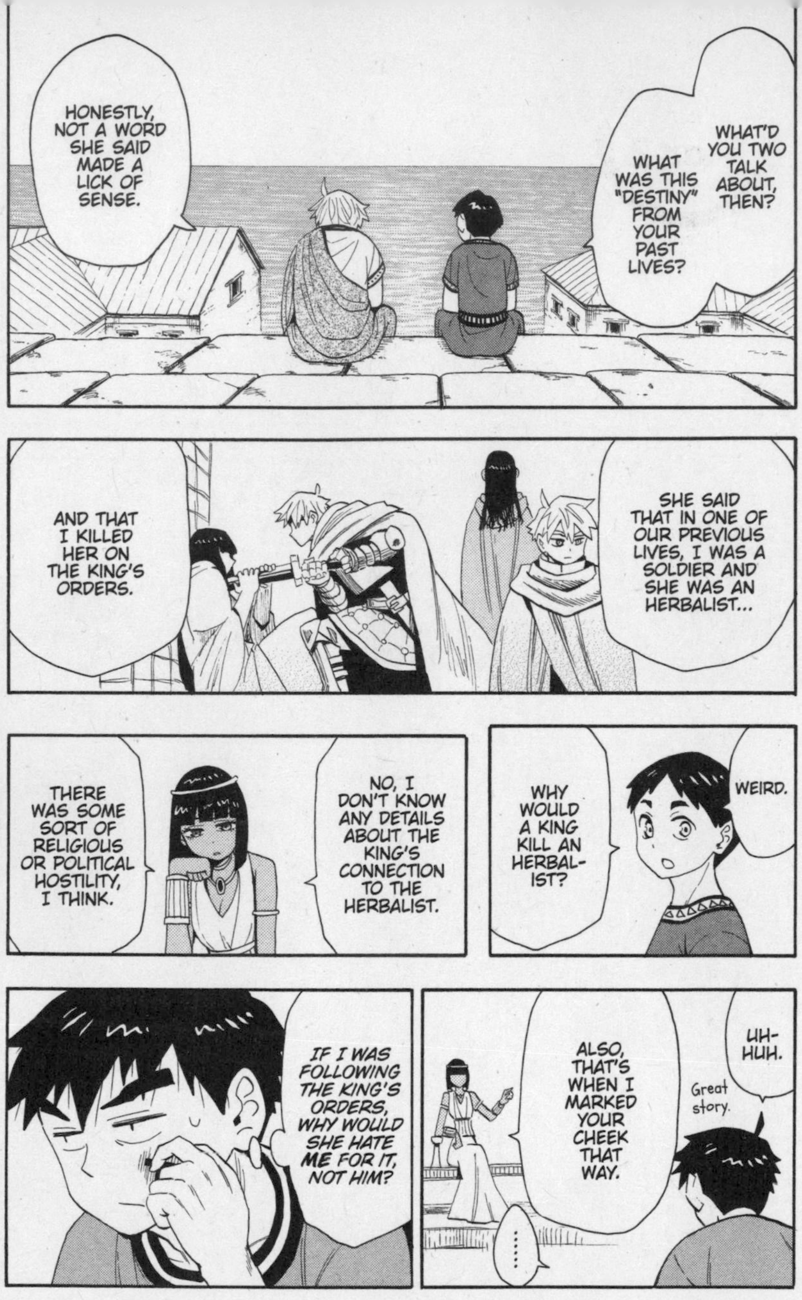
WHAT'D YOU TWO TALK ABOUT, THEN?
WHAT WAS THIS "DESTINY" FROM YOUR PAST LIVES?
HONESTLY, NOT A WORD SHE SAID MADE A LICK OF SENSE.
SHE SAID THAT IN ONE OF OUR PREVIOUS LIVES, I WAS A SOLDIER AND SHE WAS AN HERBALIST...
AND THAT I KILLED HER ON THE KING'S ORDERS.
WEIRD.
WHY WOULD A KING KILL AN HERBAL-IST?
NO, I DON'T KNOW ANY DETAILS ABOUT THE KING'S CONNECTION TO THE HERBALIST.
THERE WAS SOME SORT OF RELIGIOUS OR POLITICAL HOSTILITY, I THINK.
UH-HUH.
Great story.
ALSO, THAT'S WHEN I MARKED YOUR CHEEK THAT WAY.
......
IF I WAS FOLLOWING THE KING'S ORDERS, WHY WOULD SHE HATE *ME* FOR IT, NOT HIM?

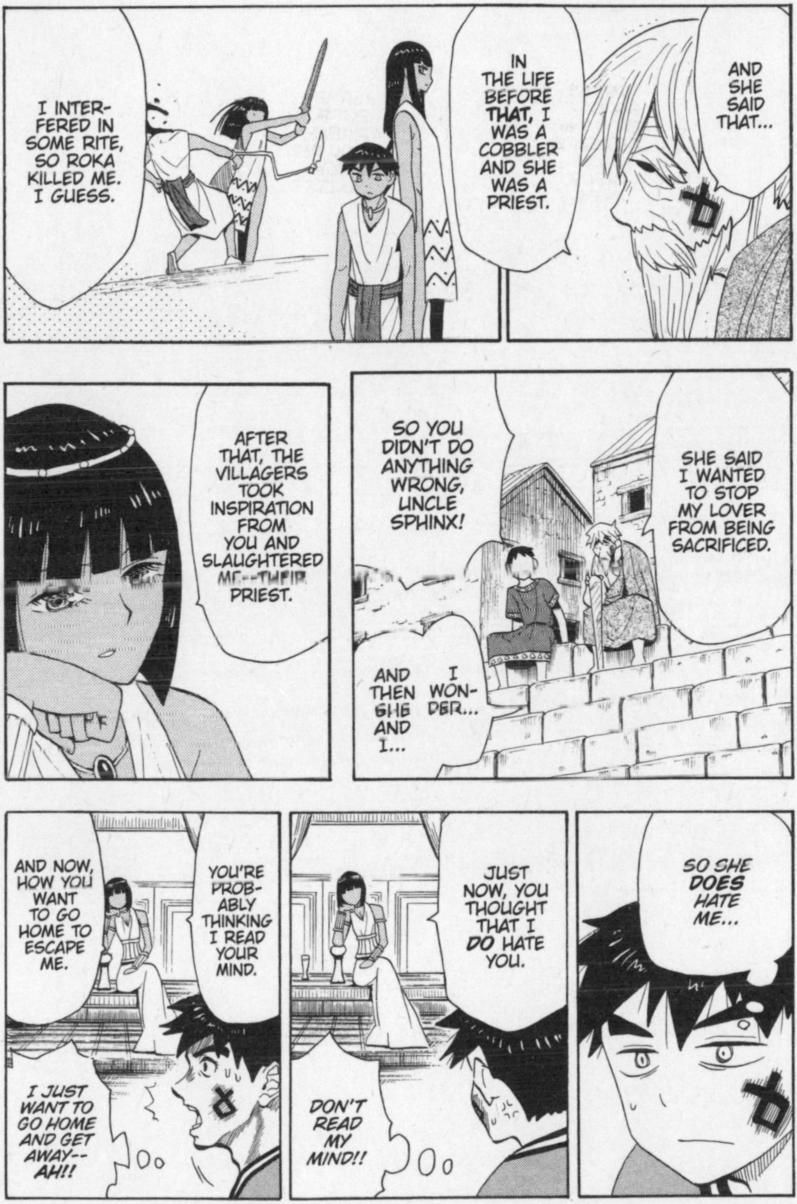
AND SHE SAID THAT...
IN THE LIFE BEFORE THAT, I WAS A COBBLER AND SHE WAS A PRIEST.
I INTERFERED IN SOME RITE, SO ROKA KILLED ME. I GUESS.
SHE SAID I WANTED TO STOP MY LOVER FROM BEING SACRIFICED.
SO YOU DIDN'T DO ANYTHING WRONG, UNCLE SPHINX!
I WONDER...
AND THEN SHE AND I...
AFTER THAT, THE VILLAGERS TOOK INSPIRATION FROM YOU AND SLAUGHTERED ME--THEIR PRIEST.
SO SHE DOES HATE ME...
JUST NOW, YOU THOUGHT THAT I DO HATE YOU.
DON'T READ MY MIND!!
YOU'RE PROBABLY THINKING I READ YOUR MIND.
AND NOW, HOW YOU WANT TO GO HOME TO ESCAPE ME.
I JUST WANT TO GO HOME AND GET AWAY--AH!!

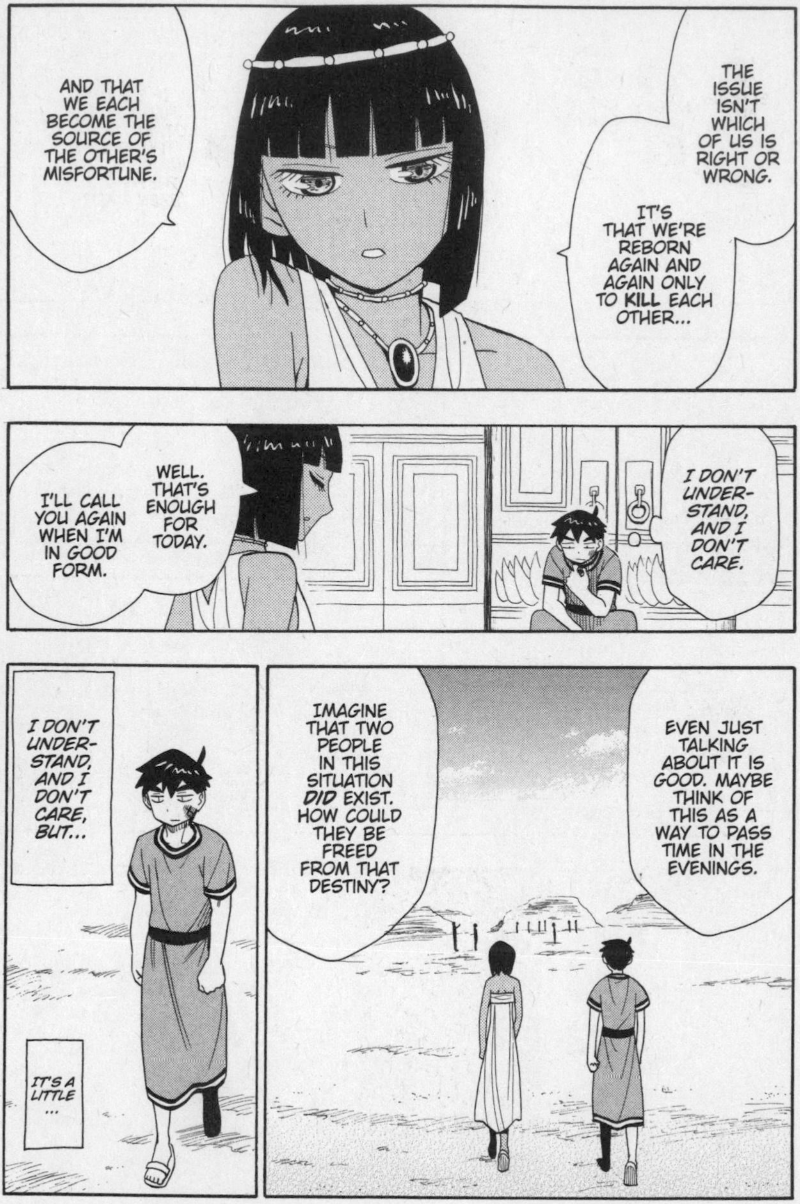
THE ISSUE ISN'T WHICH OF US IS RIGHT OR WRONG.
IT'S THAT WE'RE REBORN AGAIN AND AGAIN ONLY TO **KILL** EACH OTHER...
AND THAT WE EACH BECOME THE SOURCE OF THE OTHER'S MISFORTUNE.
I DON'T UNDERSTAND, AND I DON'T CARE.
WELL. THAT'S ENOUGH FOR TODAY.
I'LL CALL YOU AGAIN WHEN I'M IN GOOD FORM.
EVEN JUST TALKING ABOUT IT IS GOOD. MAYBE THINK OF THIS AS A WAY TO PASS TIME IN THE EVENINGS.
IMAGINE THAT TWO PEOPLE IN THIS SITUATION *DID* EXIST. HOW COULD THEY BE FREED FROM THAT DESTINY?
I DON'T UNDERSTAND, AND I DON'T CARE, BUT...
IT'S A LITTLE ...

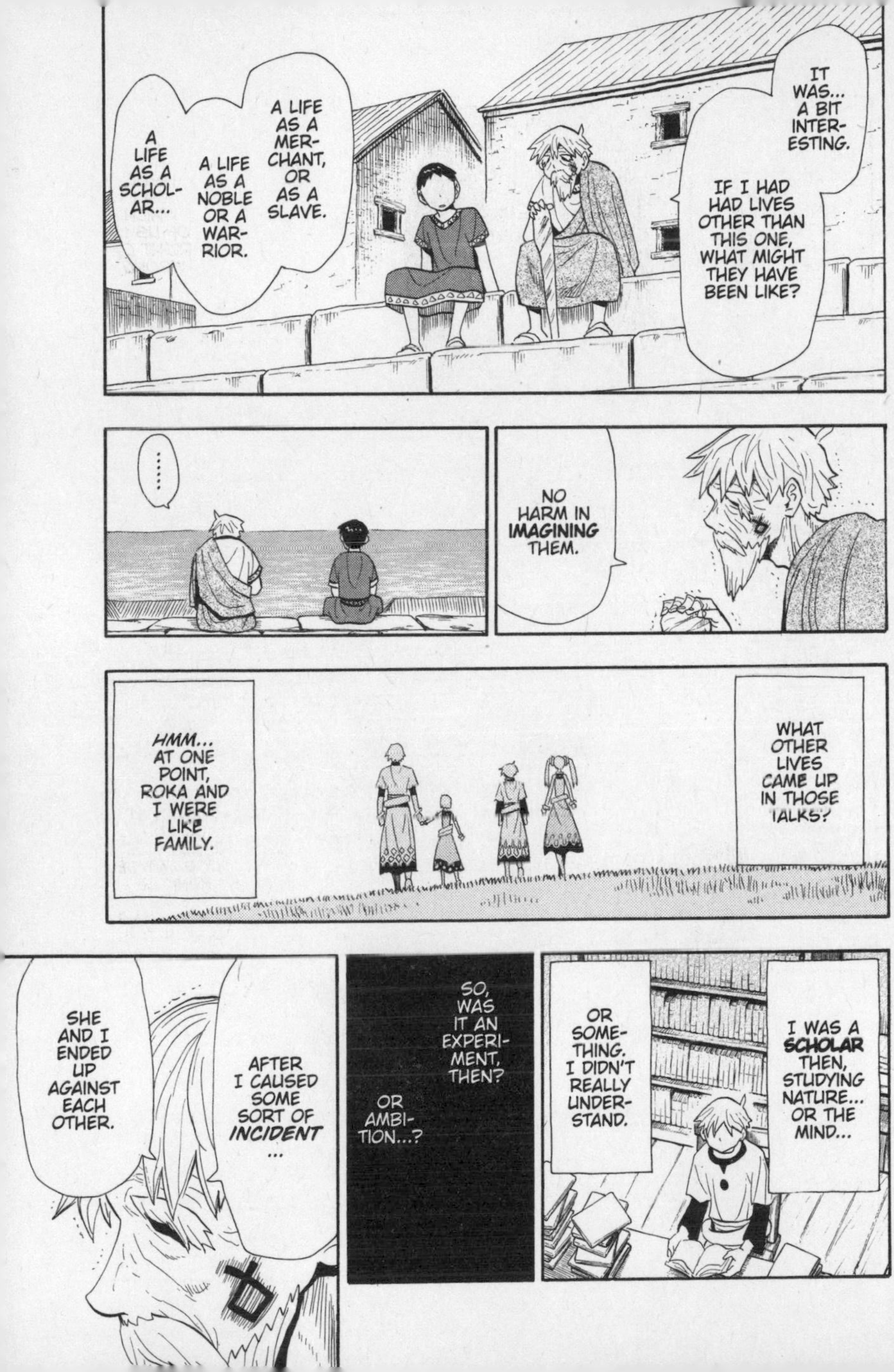
IT WAS... A BIT INTERESTING.
IF I HAD HAD LIVES OTHER THAN THIS ONE, WHAT MIGHT THEY HAVE BEEN LIKE?
A LIFE AS A SCHOLAR... A LIFE AS A NOBLE OR A WARRIOR. A LIFE AS A MERCHANT, OR AS A SLAVE.
NO HARM IN IMAGINING THEM.
......
WHAT OTHER LIVES CAME UP IN THOSE TALKS?
HMM... AT ONE POINT, ROKA AND I WERE LIKE FAMILY.
I WAS A SCHOLAR THEN, STUDYING NATURE... OR THE MIND...
OR SOMETHING. I DIDN'T REALLY UNDERSTAND.
SO, WAS IT AN EXPERIMENT, THEN?
OR AMBITION...?
AFTER I CAUSED SOME SORT OF INCIDENT...
SHE AND I ENDED UP AGAINST EACH OTHER.

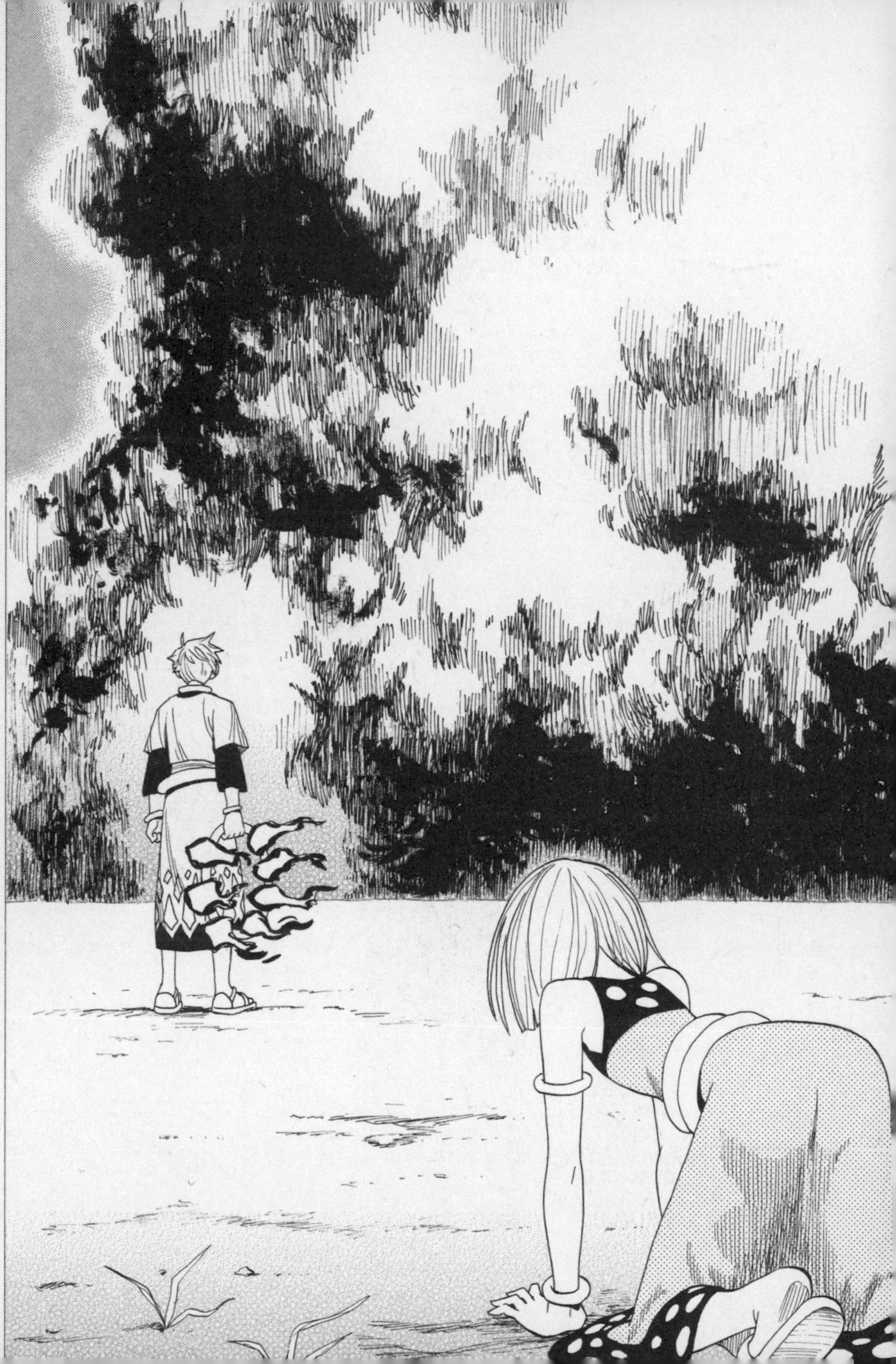

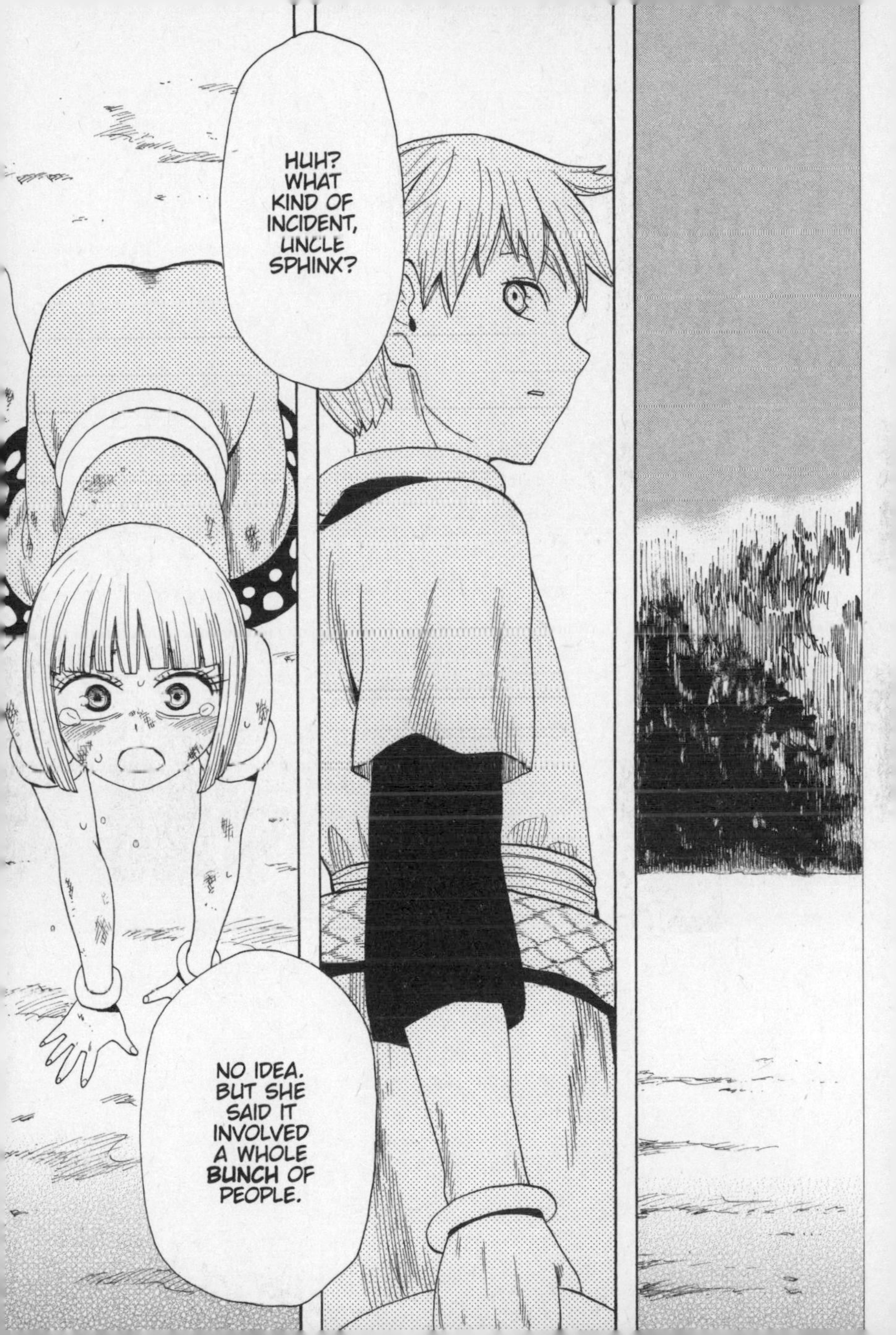
HUH? WHAT KIND OF INCIDENT, UNCLE SPHINX?
NO IDEA. BUT SHE SAID IT INVOLVED A WHOLE BUNCH OF PEOPLE.

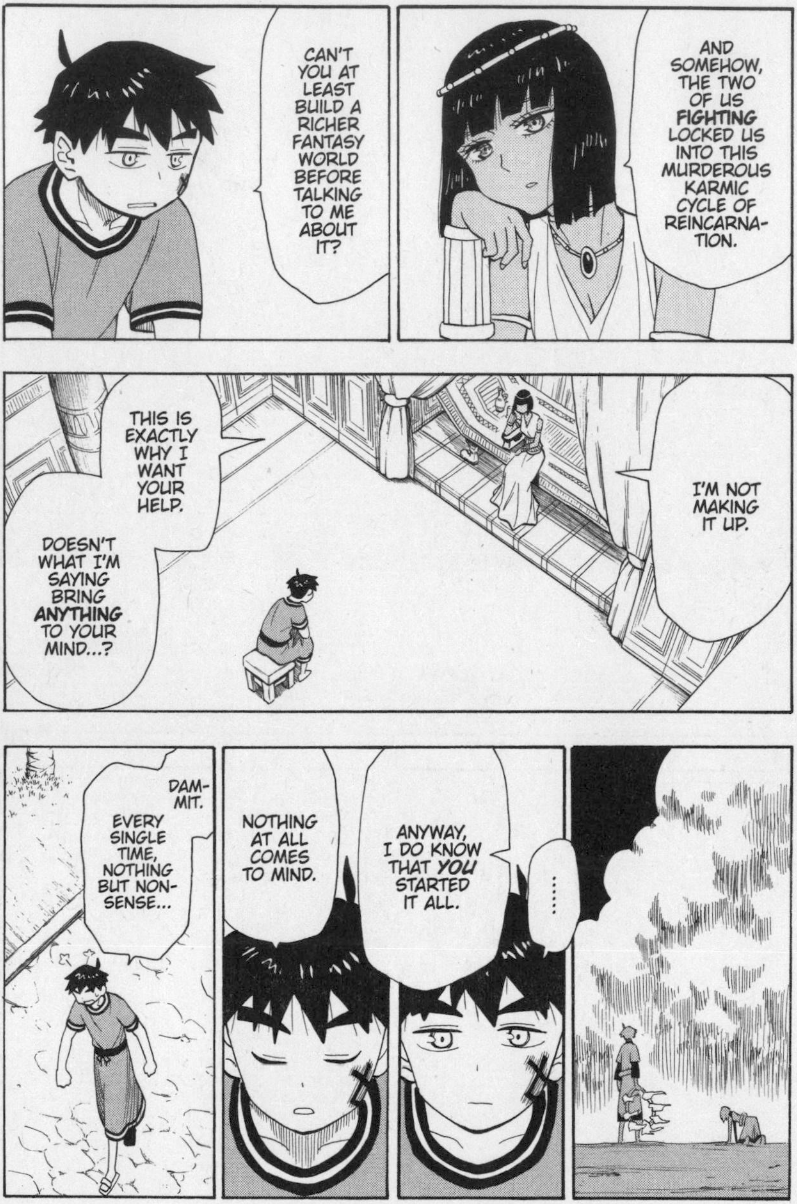
AND SOMEHOW, THE TWO OF US **FIGHTING** LOCKED US INTO THIS MURDEROUS KARMIC CYCLE OF REINCARNATION.
CAN'T YOU AT LEAST BUILD A RICHER FANTASY WORLD BEFORE TALKING TO ME ABOUT IT?
I'M NOT MAKING IT UP.
THIS IS EXACTLY WHY I WANT YOUR HELP.
DOESN'T WHAT I'M SAYING BRING **ANYTHING** TO YOUR MIND...?
......
ANYWAY, I DO KNOW THAT *YOU* STARTED IT ALL.
NOTHING AT ALL COMES TO MIND.
DAMMIT.
EVERY SINGLE TIME, NOTHING BUT NONSENSE...

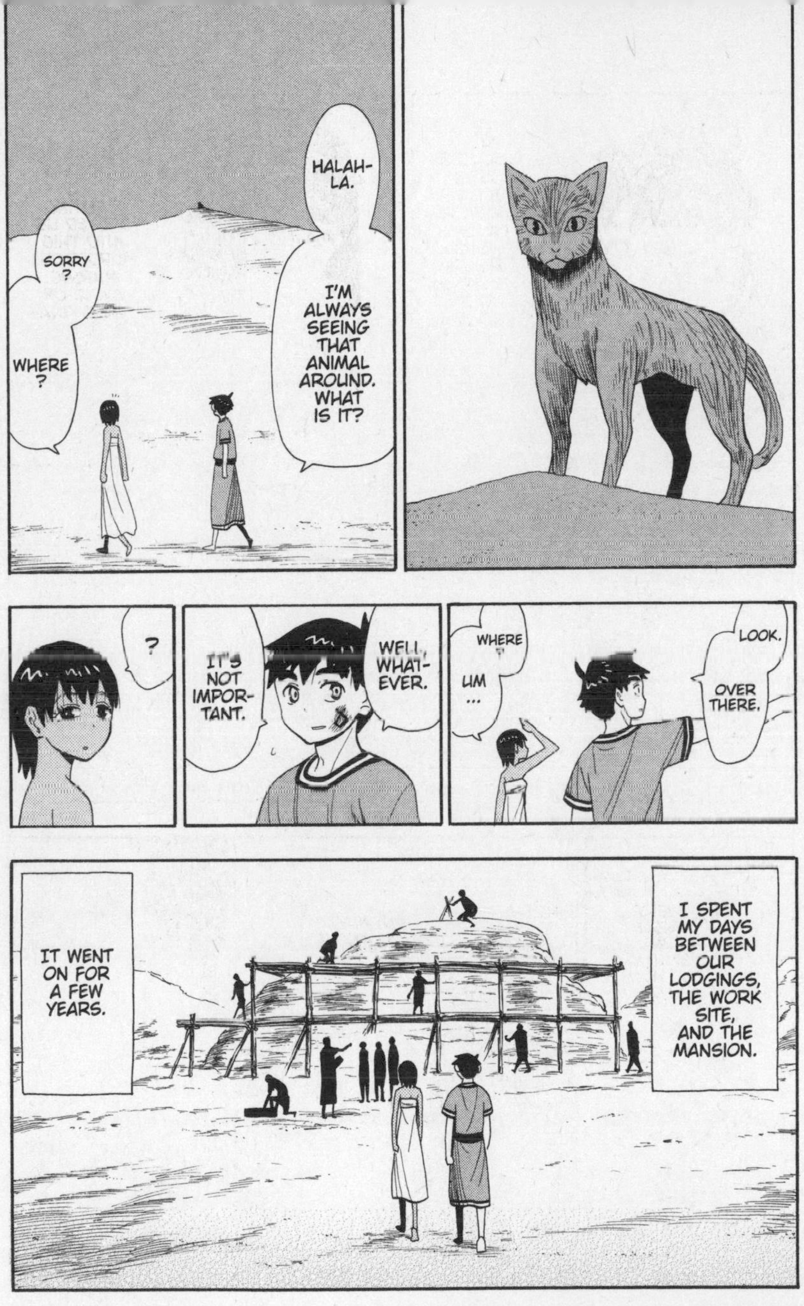
HALAH-LA.
I'M ALWAYS SEEING THAT ANIMAL AROUND. WHAT IS IT?
SORRY?
WHERE?
LOOK.
OVER THERE.
WHERE?
UM...
WELL, WHATEVER.
IT'S NOT IMPORTANT.
?
I SPENT MY DAYS BETWEEN OUR LODGINGS, THE WORK SITE, AND THE MANSION.
IT WENT ON FOR A FEW YEARS.

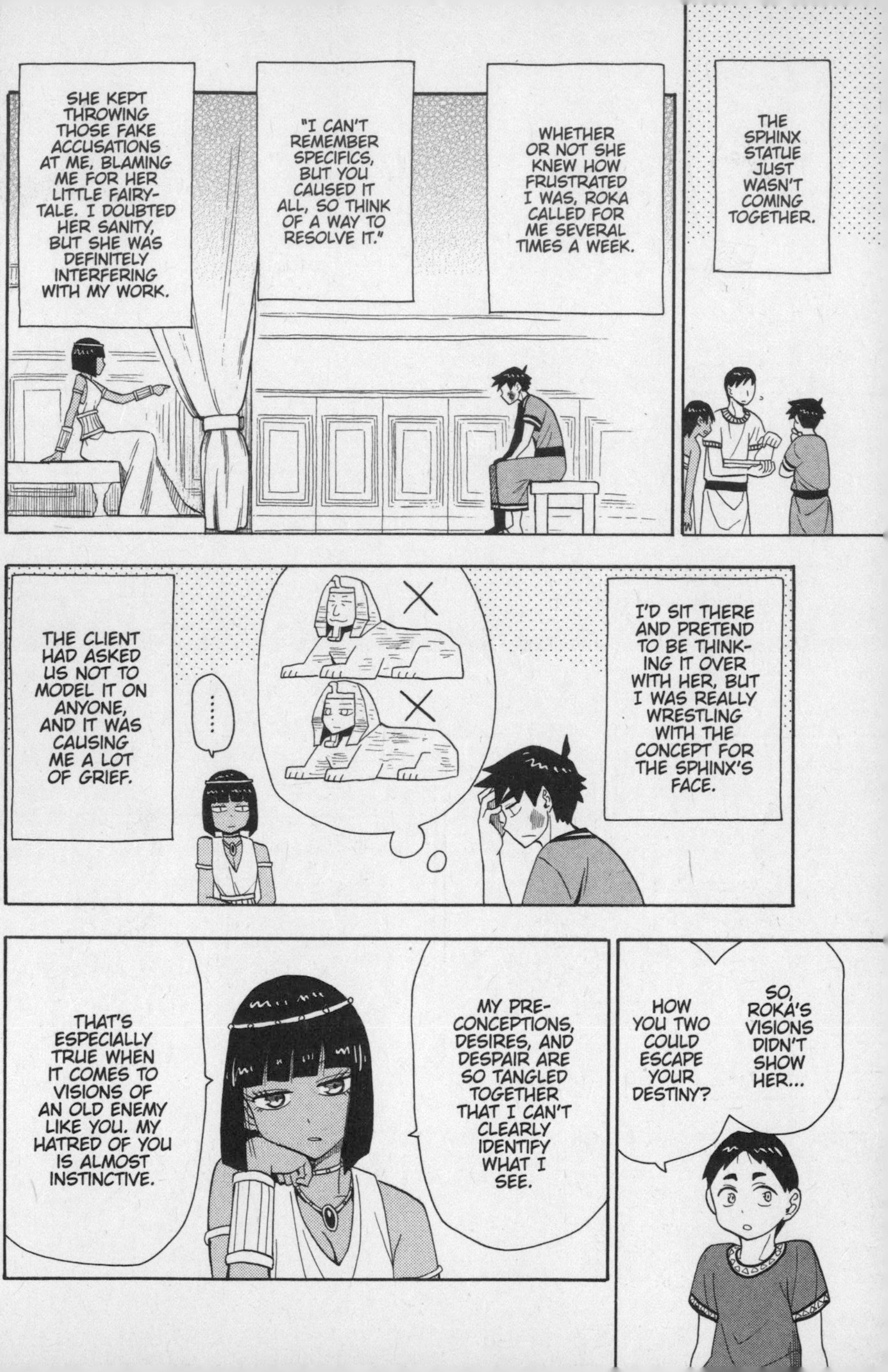
THE SPHINX STATUE JUST WASN'T COMING TOGETHER.
WHETHER OR NOT SHE KNEW HOW FRUSTRATED I WAS, ROKA CALLED FOR ME SEVERAL TIMES A WEEK.
"I CAN'T REMEMBER SPECIFICS, BUT YOU CAUSED IT ALL, SO THINK OF A WAY TO RESOLVE IT."
SHE KEPT THROWING THOSE FAKE ACCUSATIONS AT ME, BLAMING ME FOR HER LITTLE FAIRY-TALE. I DOUBTED HER SANITY, BUT SHE WAS DEFINITELY INTERFERING WITH MY WORK.
I'D SIT THERE AND PRETEND TO BE THINKING IT OVER WITH HER, BUT I WAS REALLY WRESTLING WITH THE CONCEPT FOR THE SPHINX'S FACE.
......
THE CLIENT HAD ASKED US NOT TO MODEL IT ON ANYONE, AND IT WAS CAUSING ME A LOT OF GRIEF.
SO, ROKA'S VISIONS DIDN'T SHOW HER...
HOW YOU TWO COULD ESCAPE YOUR DESTINY?
MY PRECONCEPTIONS, DESIRES, AND DESPAIR ARE SO TANGLED TOGETHER THAT I CAN'T CLEARLY IDENTIFY WHAT I SEE.
THAT'S ESPECIALLY TRUE WHEN IT COMES TO VISIONS OF AN OLD ENEMY LIKE YOU. MY HATRED OF YOU IS ALMOST INSTINCTIVE.

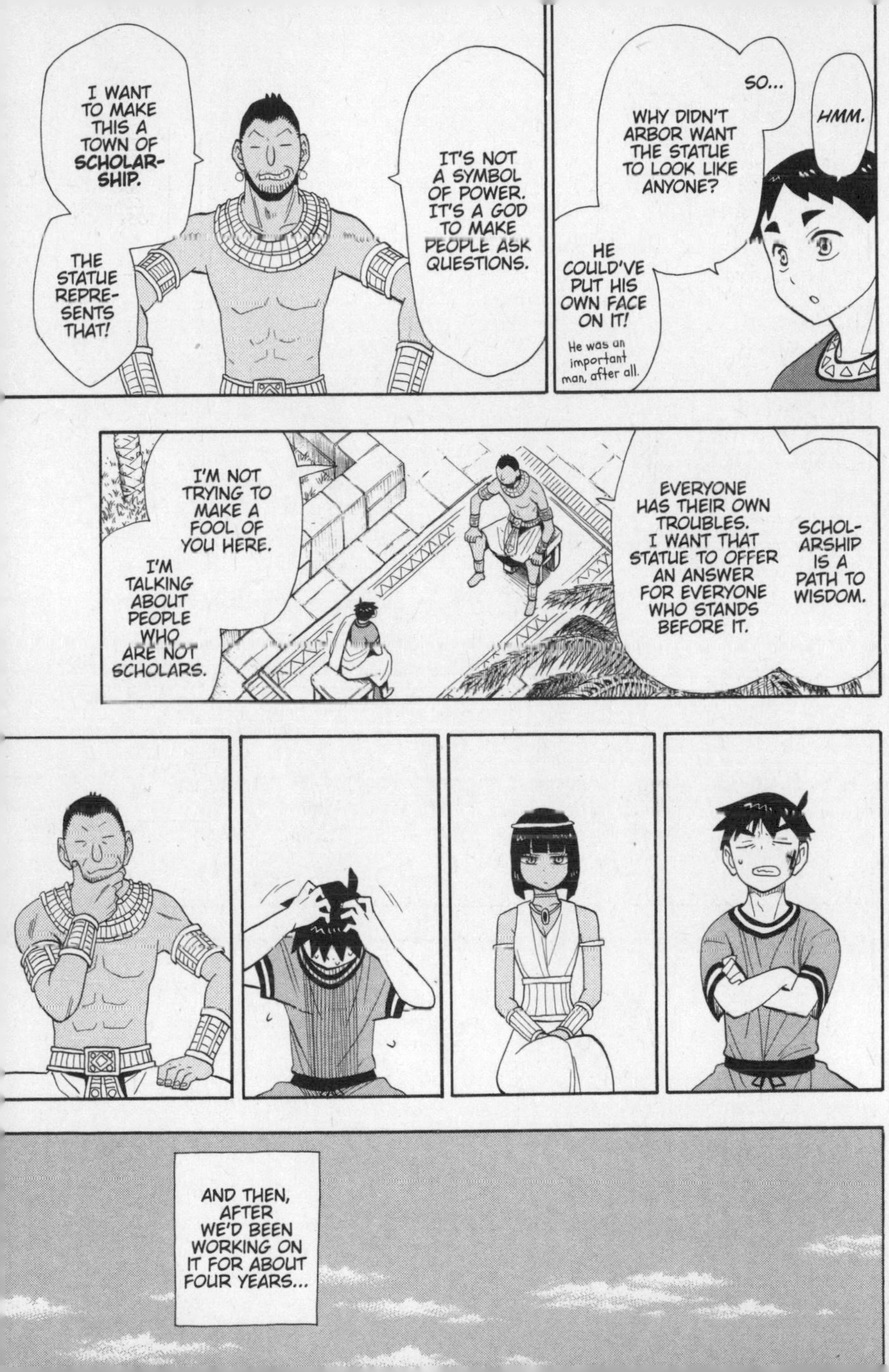
HMM.
SO... WHY DIDN'T ARBOR WANT THE STATUE TO LOOK LIKE ANYONE? HE COULD'VE PUT HIS OWN FACE ON IT!
He was an important man, after all.
IT'S NOT A SYMBOL OF POWER. IT'S A GOD TO MAKE PEOPLE ASK QUESTIONS.
I WANT TO MAKE THIS A TOWN OF SCHOLARSHIP.
THE STATUE REPRESENTS THAT!
SCHOLARSHIP IS A PATH TO WISDOM.
EVERYONE HAS THEIR OWN TROUBLES. I WANT THAT STATUE TO OFFER AN ANSWER FOR EVERYONE WHO STANDS BEFORE IT.
I'M NOT TRYING TO MAKE A FOOL OF YOU HERE.
I'M TALKING ABOUT PEOPLE WHO ARE NOT SCHOLARS.
AND THEN, AFTER WE'D BEEN WORKING ON IT FOR ABOUT FOUR YEARS...

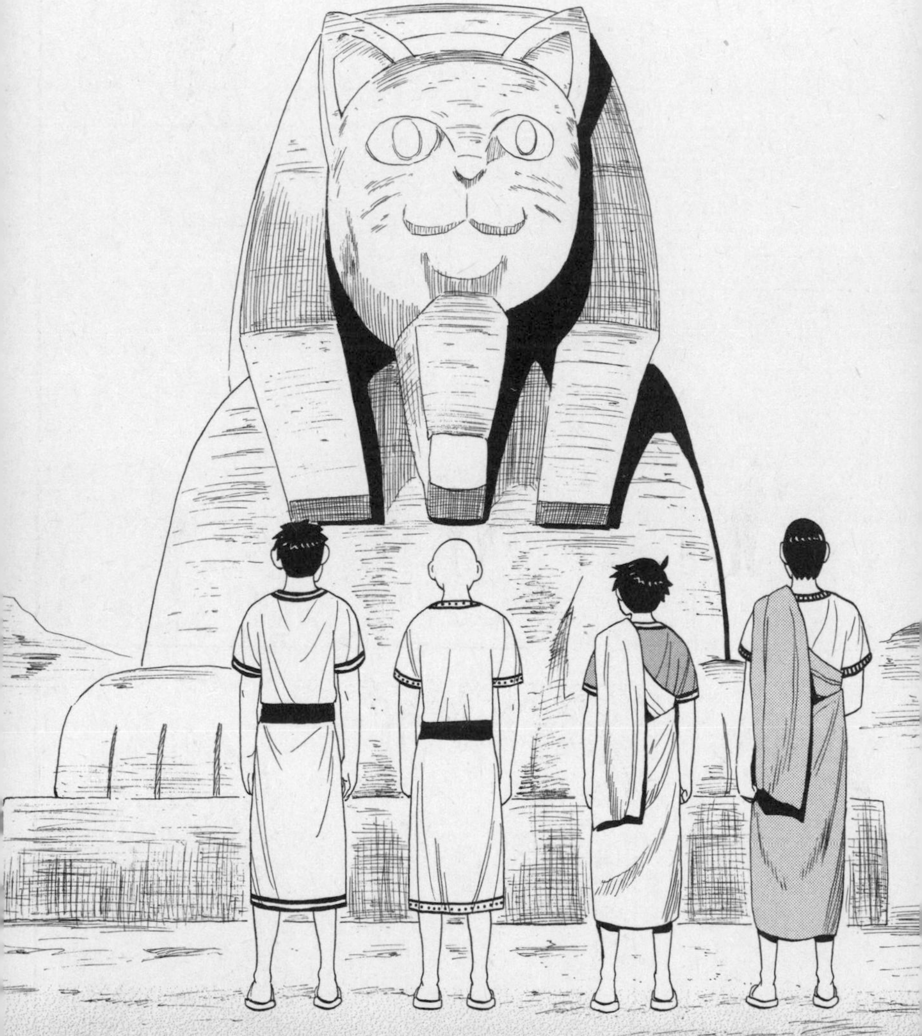

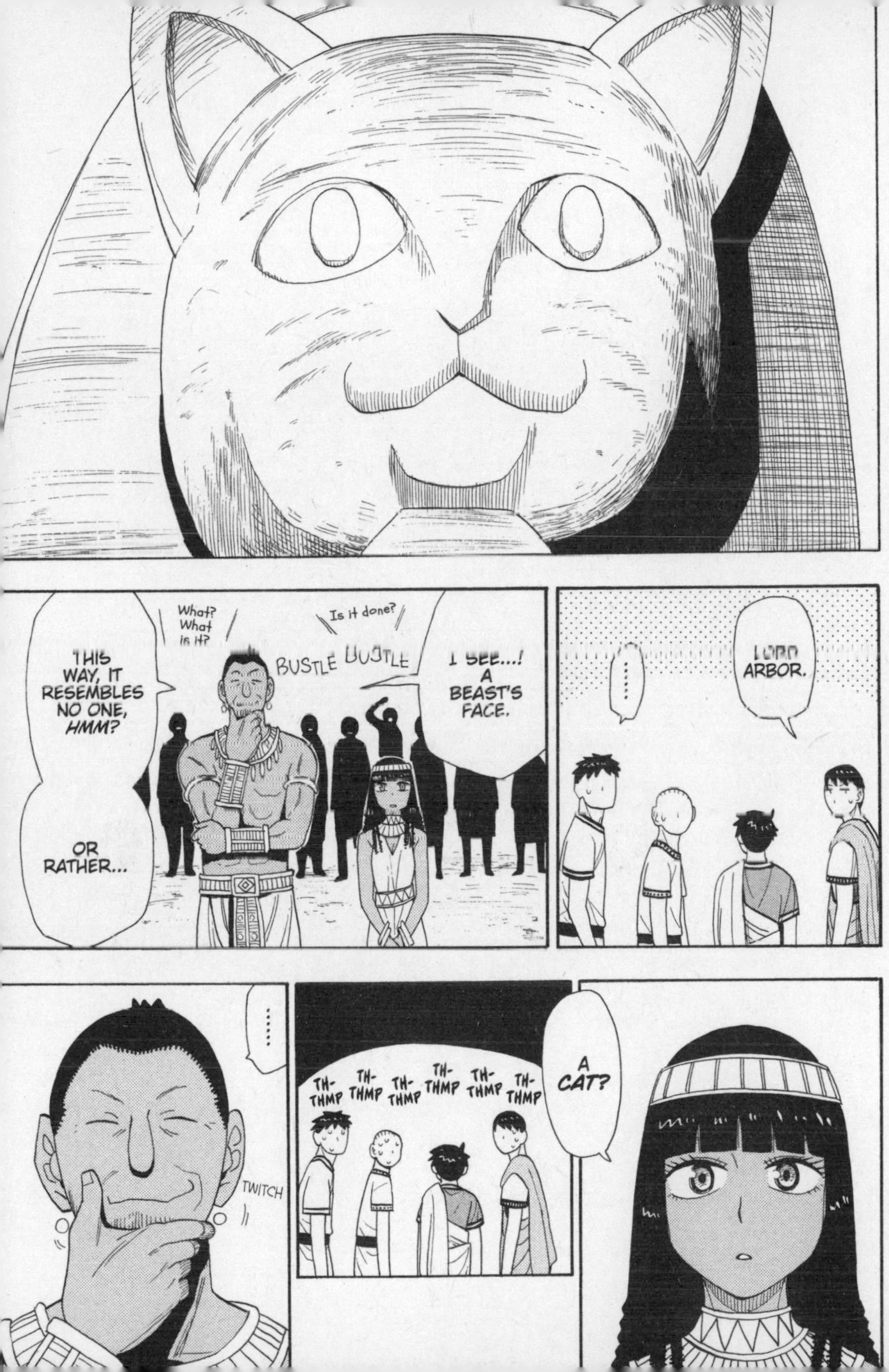
LORD ARBOR.
......
I SEE...! A BEAST'S FACE.
Is it done?
BUSTLE BUSTLE
What? What is it?
THIS WAY, IT RESEMBLES NO ONE, *HMM?*
OR RATHER...
A *CAT?*
TH-THMP TH-THMP TH-THMP TH-THMP TH-THMP TH-THMP
......
TWITCH

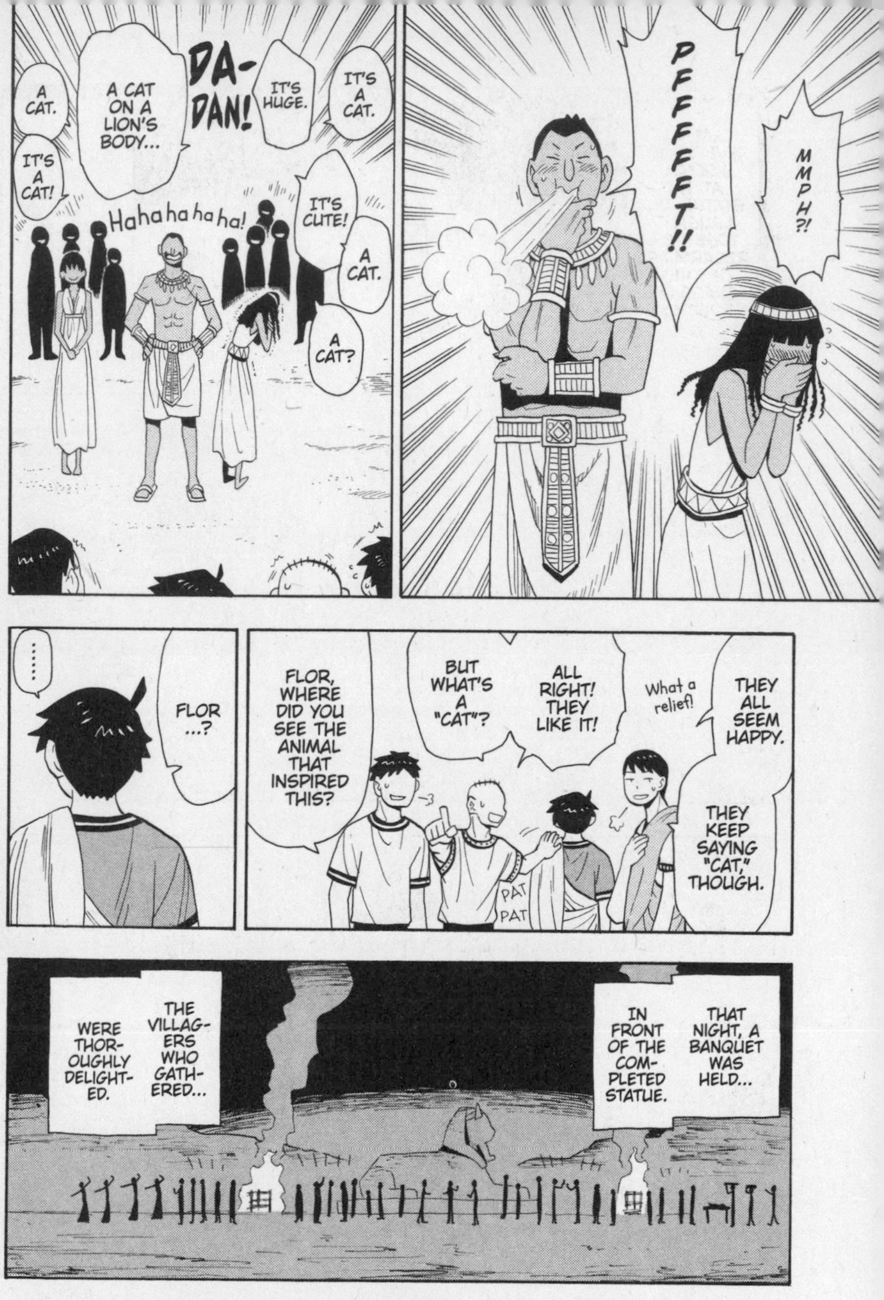
MMPH?!
PFFFFFT!!
IT'S A CAT.
IT'S HUGE.
DA-DAN!
A CAT ON A LION'S BODY...
A CAT.
IT'S A CAT!
Hahaha ha ha!
IT'S CUTE!
A CAT.
A CAT?
THEY ALL SEEM HAPPY.
What a relief!
THEY KEEP SAYING "CAT," THOUGH.
ALL RIGHT! THEY LIKE IT!
BUT WHAT'S A "CAT"?
FLOR, WHERE DID YOU SEE THE ANIMAL THAT INSPIRED THIS?
PAT PAT
FLOR ...?
......
THAT NIGHT, A BANQUET WAS HELD...
IN FRONT OF THE COMPLETED STATUE.
THE VILLAGERS WHO GATHERED...
WERE THOROUGHLY DELIGHTED.

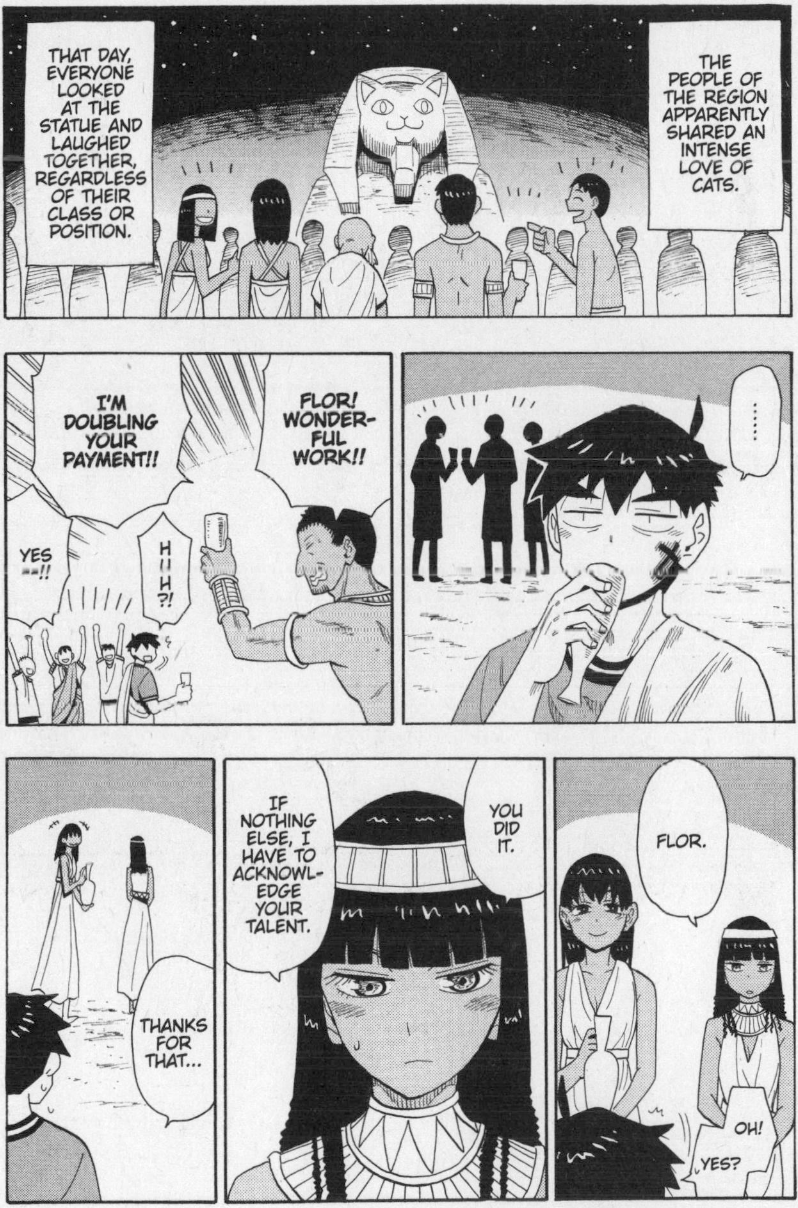
THE PEOPLE OF THE REGION APPARENTLY SHARED AN INTENSE LOVE OF CATS.
THAT DAY, EVERYONE LOOKED AT THE STATUE AND LAUGHED TOGETHER, REGARDLESS OF THEIR CLASS OR POSITION.
......
FLOR! WONDERFUL WORK!!
I'M DOUBLING YOUR PAYMENT!!
HUH?!
YES--!!
FLOR.
OH! YES?
YOU DID IT.
IF NOTHING ELSE, I HAVE TO ACKNOWLEDGE YOUR TALENT.
THANKS FOR THAT...

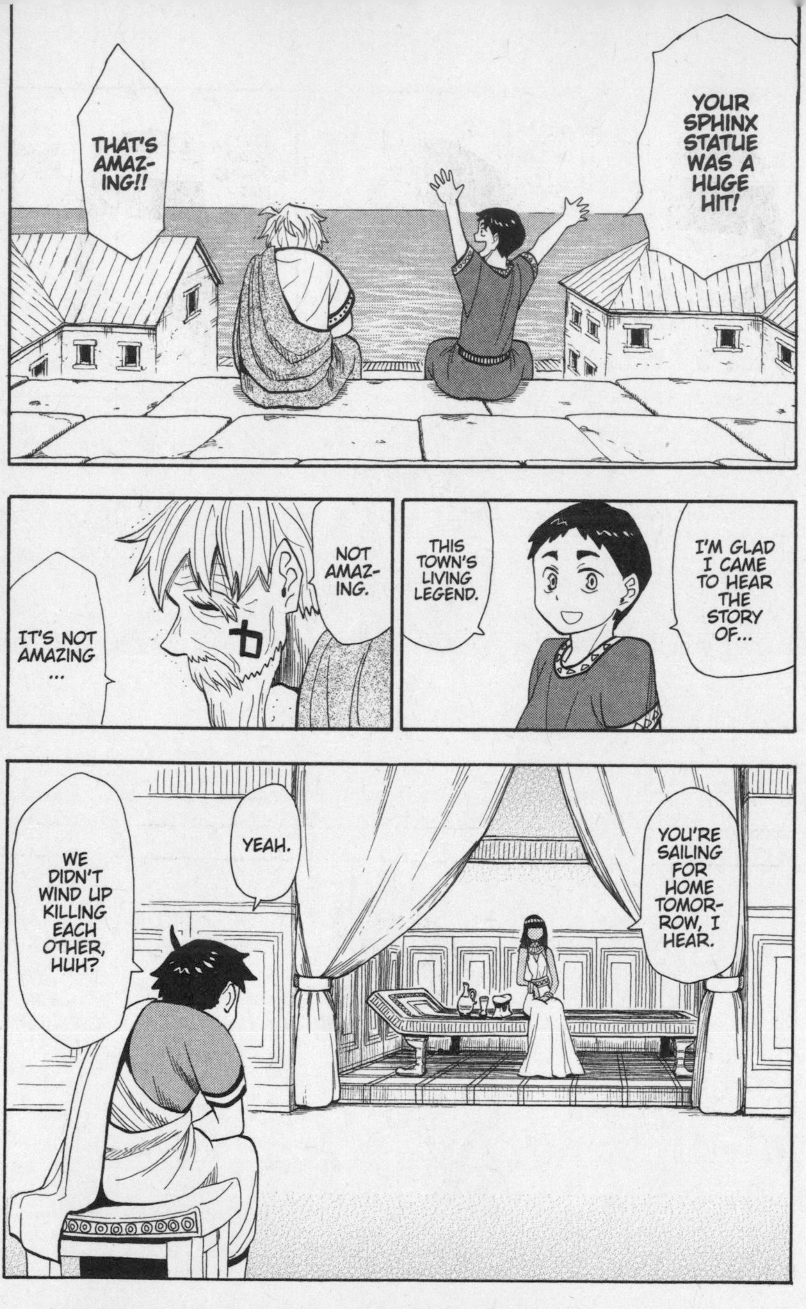
YOUR SPHINX STATUE WAS A HUGE HIT!
THAT'S AMAZ-ING!!
I'M GLAD I CAME TO HEAR THE STORY OF...
THIS TOWN'S LIVING LEGEND.
NOT AMAZ-ING.
IT'S NOT AMAZING ...
YOU'RE SAILING FOR HOME TOMOR-ROW, I HEAR.
YEAH.
WE DIDN'T WIND UP KILLING EACH OTHER, HUH?

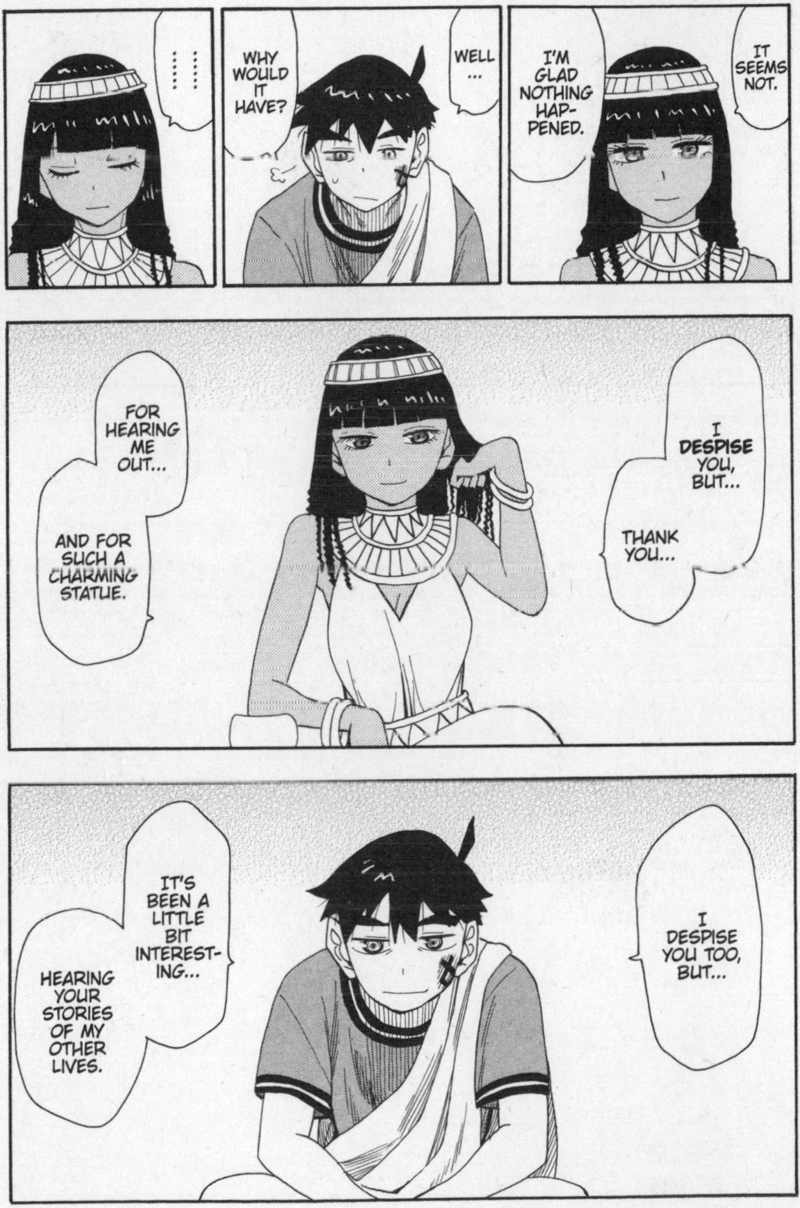
IT SEEMS NOT.
I'M GLAD NOTHING HAP-PENED.
WELL ...
WHY WOULD IT HAVE?
......
I DESPISE YOU, BUT...
THANK YOU...
FOR HEARING ME OUT...
AND FOR SUCH A CHARMING STATUE.
I DESPISE YOU TOO, BUT...
IT'S BEEN A LITTLE BIT INTEREST-ING...
HEARING YOUR STORIES OF MY OTHER LIVES.

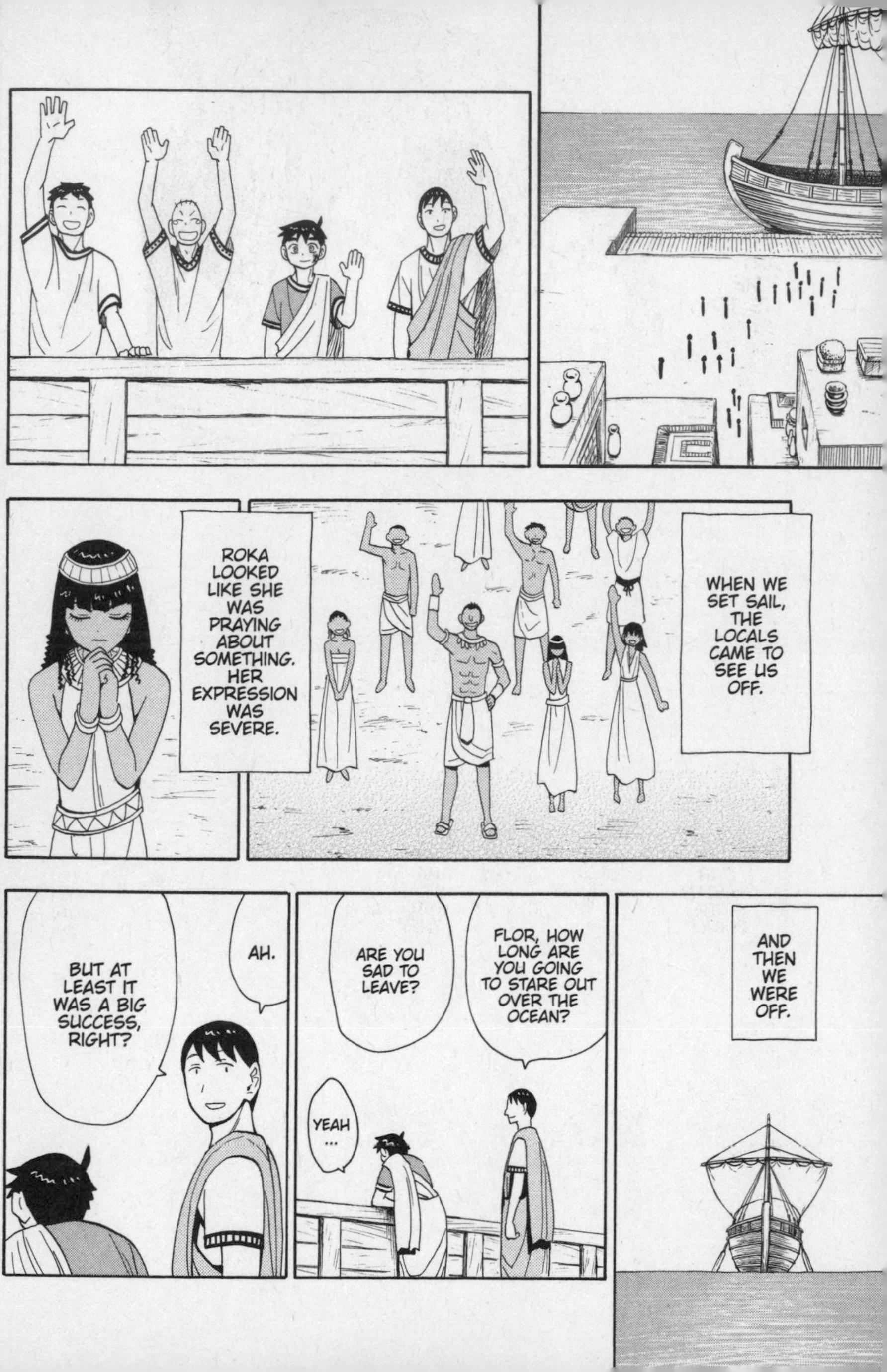
WHEN WE SET SAIL, THE LOCALS CAME TO SEE US OFF.
ROKA LOOKED LIKE SHE WAS PRAYING ABOUT SOMETHING. HER EXPRESSION WAS SEVERE.
AND THEN WE WERE OFF.
FLOR, HOW LONG ARE YOU GOING TO STARE OUT OVER THE OCEAN?
ARE YOU SAD TO LEAVE?
YEAH ...
AH.
BUT AT LEAST IT WAS A BIG SUCCESS, RIGHT?

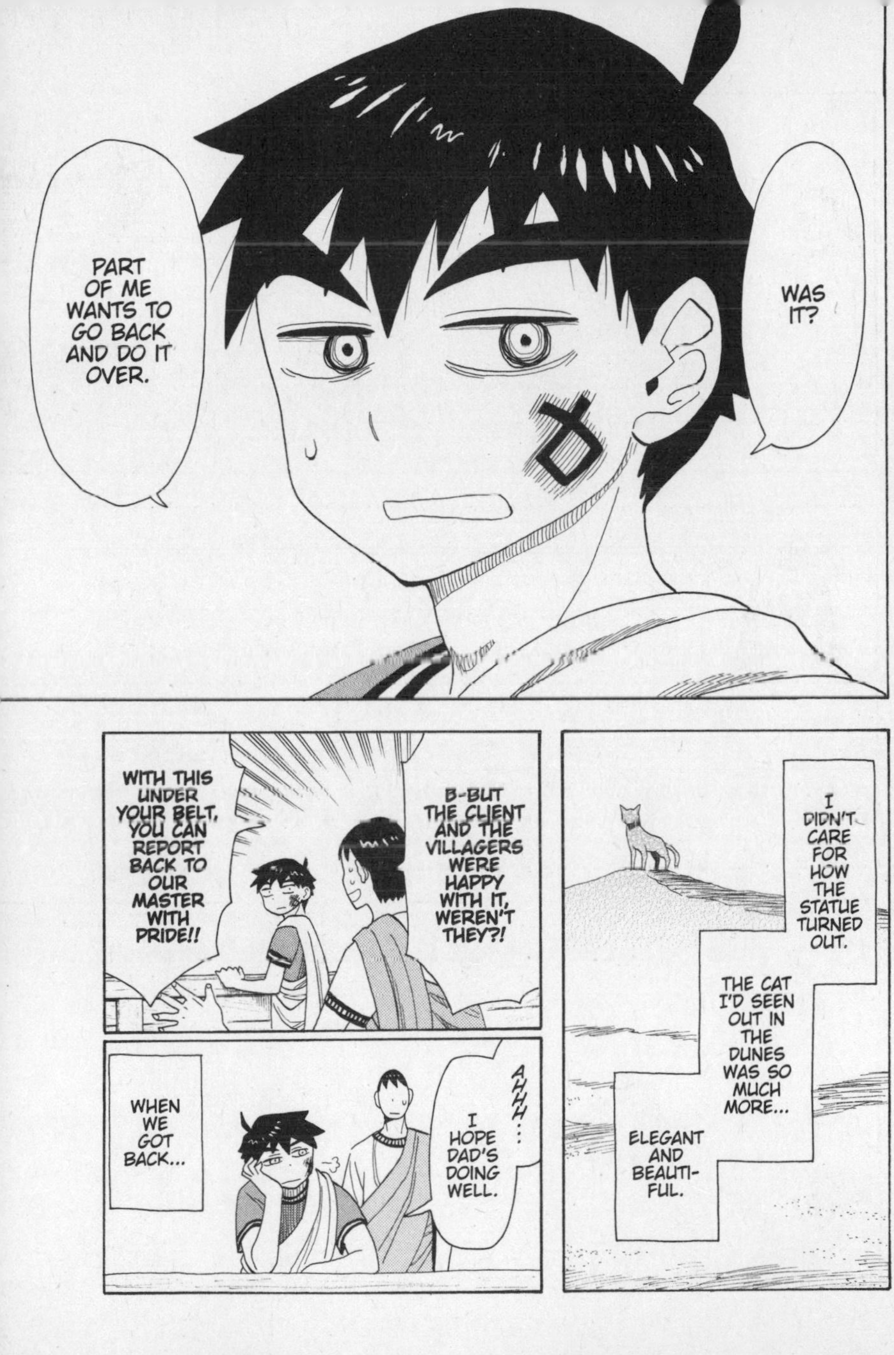
WAS IT?
PART OF ME WANTS TO GO BACK AND DO IT OVER.
I DIDN'T CARE FOR HOW THE STATUE TURNED OUT.
THE CAT I'D SEEN OUT IN THE DUNES WAS SO MUCH MORE...
ELEGANT AND BEAUTIFUL.
B-BUT THE CLIENT AND THE VILLAGERS WERE HAPPY WITH IT, WEREN'T THEY?!
WITH THIS UNDER YOUR BELT, YOU CAN REPORT BACK TO OUR MASTER WITH PRIDE!!
AHHH...
I HOPE DAD'S DOING WELL.
WHEN WE GOT BACK...

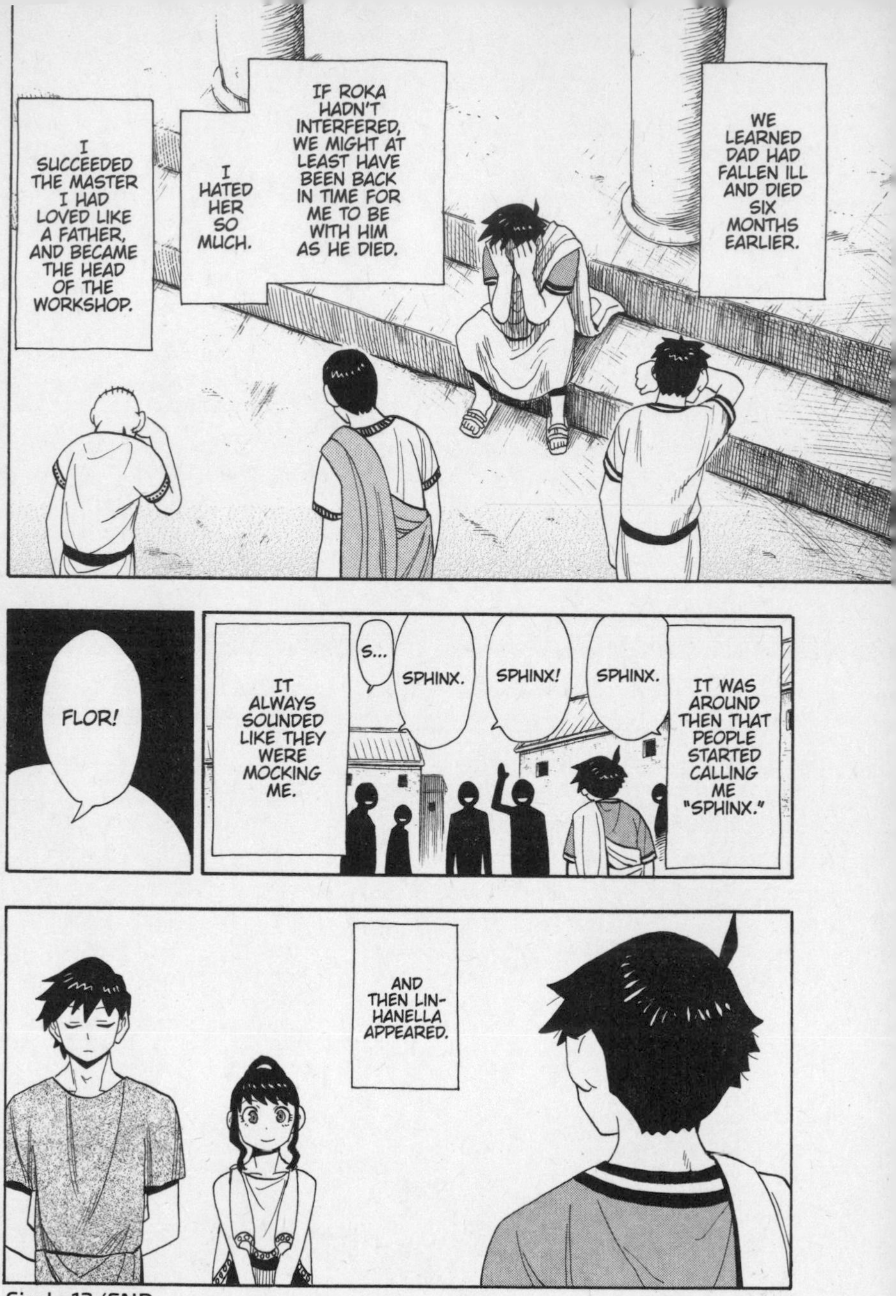
WE LEARNED DAD HAD FALLEN ILL AND DIED SIX MONTHS EARLIER.
IF ROKA HADN'T INTERFERED, WE MIGHT AT LEAST HAVE BEEN BACK IN TIME FOR ME TO BE WITH HIM AS HE DIED.
I HATED HER SO MUCH.
I SUCCEEDED THE MASTER I HAD LOVED LIKE A FATHER, AND BECAME THE HEAD OF THE WORKSHOP.
IT WAS AROUND THEN THAT PEOPLE STARTED CALLING ME "SPHINX."
SPHINX.
SPHINX!
SPHINX.
S...
IT ALWAYS SOUNDED LIKE THEY WERE MOCKING ME.
FLOR!
AND THEN LIN-HANELLA APPEARED.

Circle 12/END

Spirit Circle

Nono

Circle 13
Flor 4

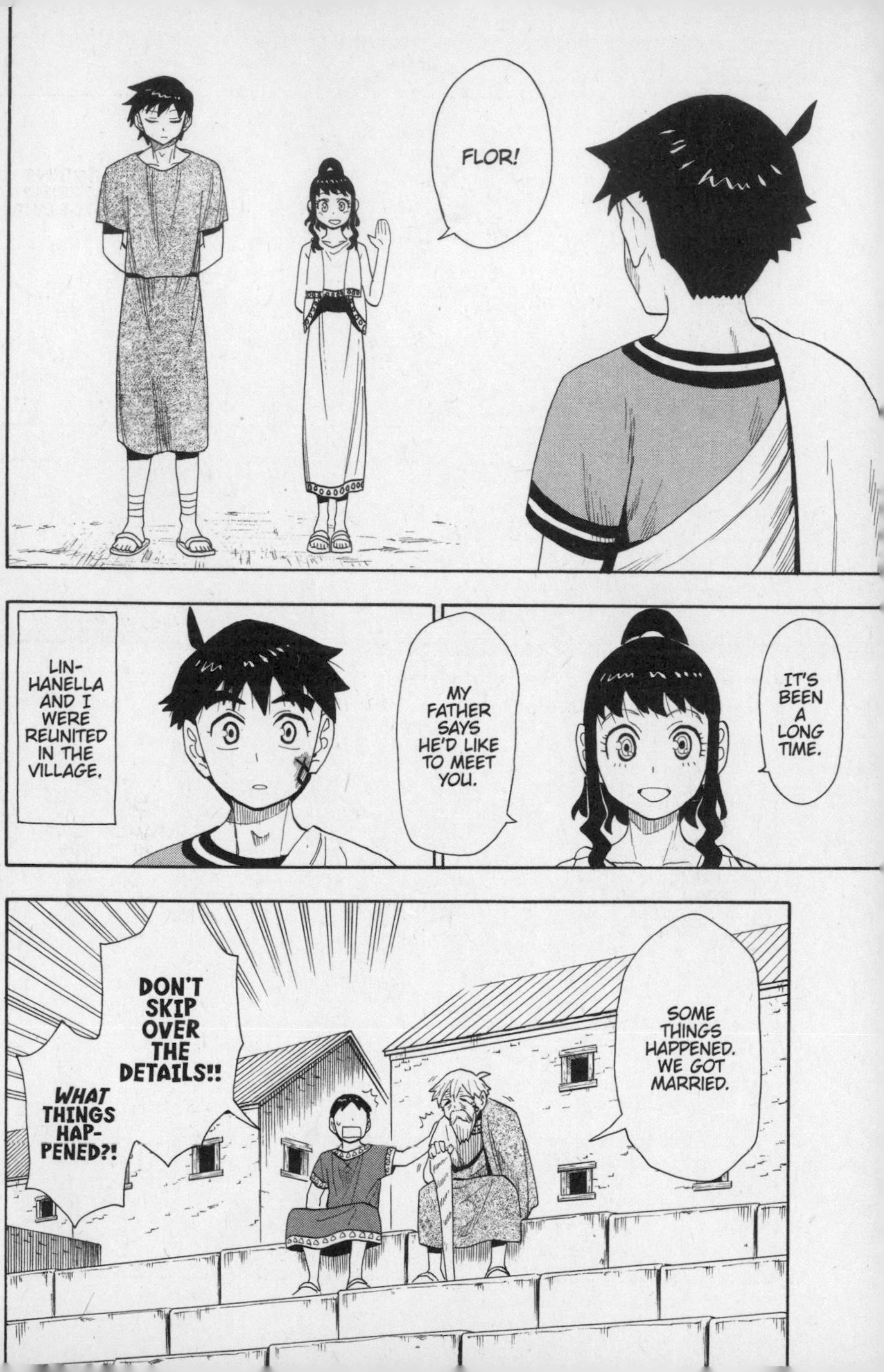
FLOR!
IT'S BEEN A LONG TIME.
MY FATHER SAYS HE'D LIKE TO MEET YOU.
LIN-HANELLA AND I WERE REUNITED IN THE VILLAGE.
SOME THINGS HAPPENED. WE GOT MARRIED.
DON'T SKIP OVER THE DETAILS!!
WHAT THINGS HAP-PENED?!

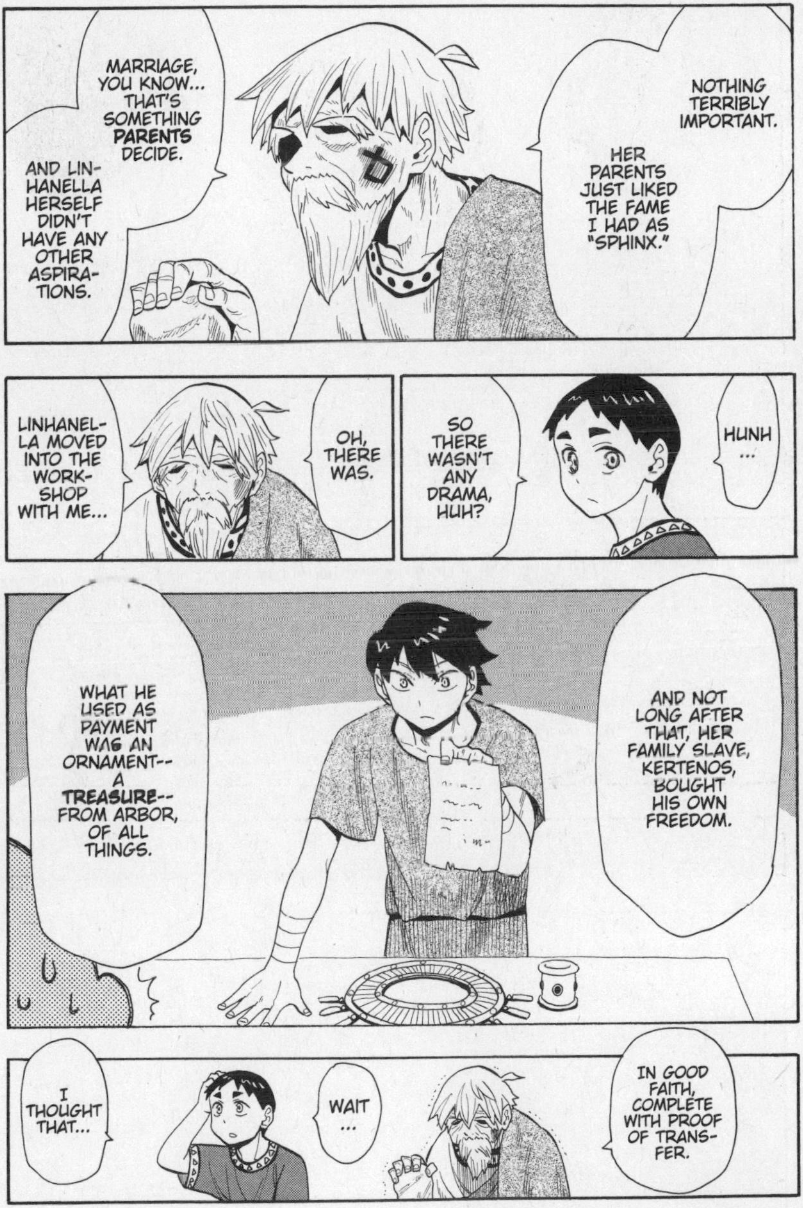
NOTHING TERRIBLY IMPORTANT.
HER PARENTS JUST LIKED THE FAME I HAD AS "SPHINX."
MARRIAGE, YOU KNOW... THAT'S SOMETHING **PARENTS** DECIDE.
AND LIN-HANELLA HERSELF DIDN'T HAVE ANY OTHER ASPIRA-TIONS.
HUNH ...
SO THERE WASN'T ANY DRAMA, HUH?
OH, THERE WAS.
LINHANEL-LA MOVED INTO THE WORK-SHOP WITH ME...
AND NOT LONG AFTER THAT, HER FAMILY SLAVE, KERTENOS, BOUGHT HIS OWN FREEDOM.
WHAT HE USED AS PAYMENT WAS AN ORNAMENT-- A **TREASURE**-- FROM ARBOR, OF ALL THINGS.
IN GOOD FAITH, COMPLETE WITH PROOF OF TRANS-FER.
WAIT ...
I THOUGHT THAT...

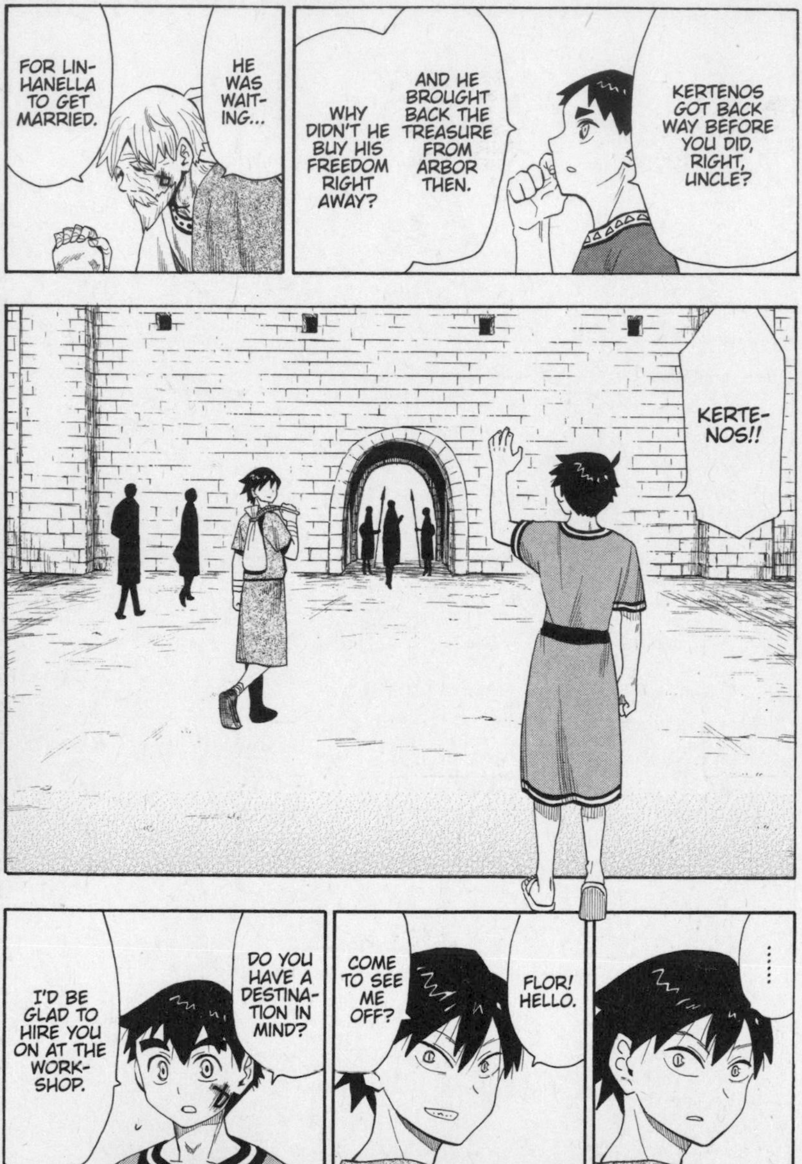
KERTENOS GOT BACK WAY BEFORE YOU DID, RIGHT, UNCLE?
AND HE BROUGHT BACK THE TREASURE FROM ARBOR THEN.
WHY DIDN'T HE BUY HIS FREEDOM RIGHT AWAY?
HE WAS WAITING...
FOR LINHANELLA TO GET MARRIED.
KERTENOS!!
......
FLOR! HELLO.
COME TO SEE ME OFF?
DO YOU HAVE A DESTINATION IN MIND?
I'D BE GLAD TO HIRE YOU ON AT THE WORKSHOP.

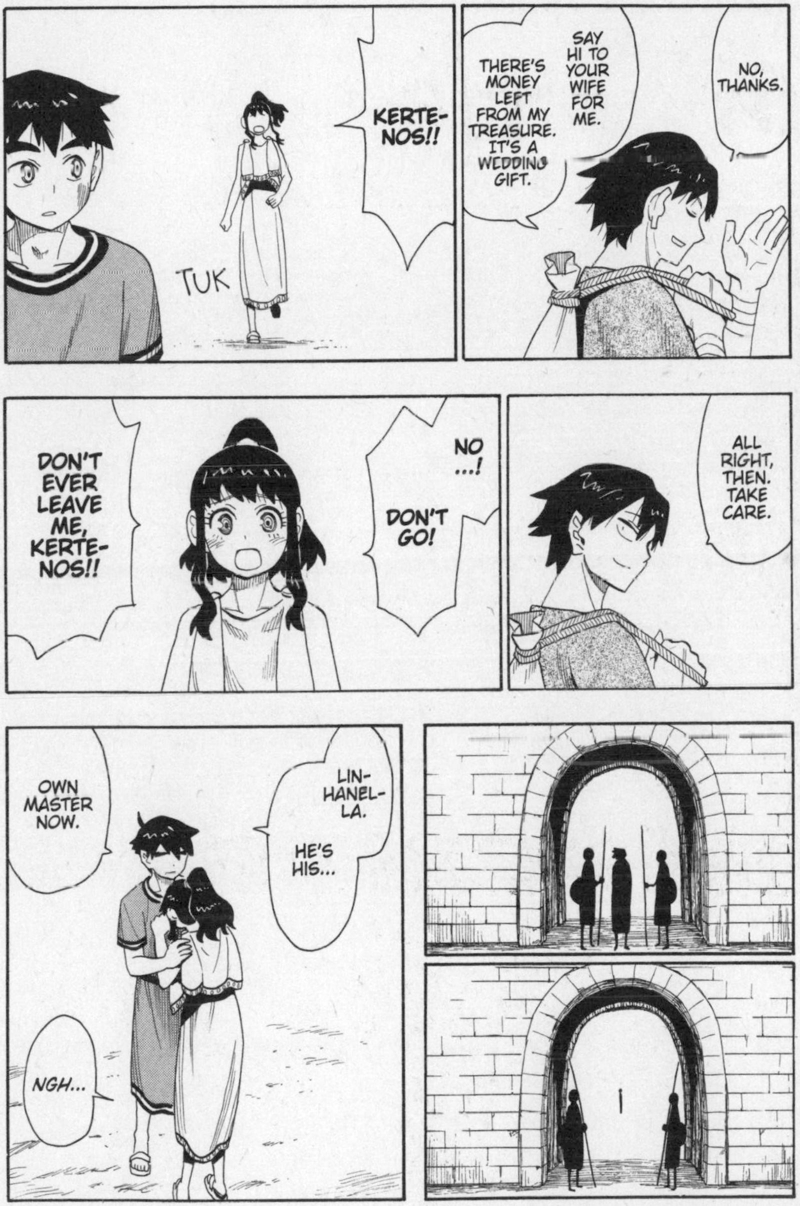
NO, THANKS.
SAY HI TO YOUR WIFE FOR ME.
THERE'S MONEY LEFT FROM MY TREASURE. IT'S A WEDDING GIFT.
KERTE-NOS!!
TUK
ALL RIGHT, THEN. TAKE CARE.
NO ...!
DON'T GO!
DON'T EVER LEAVE ME, KERTE-NOS!!
LIN-HANEL-LA.
HE'S HIS...
OWN MASTER NOW.
NGH...

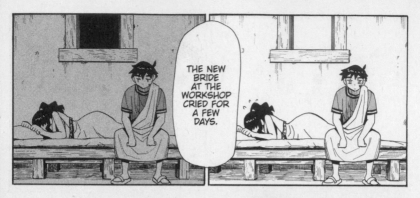

THE NEW BRIDE AT THE WORKSHOP CRIED FOR A FEW DAYS.
I WASN'T THE ONE WHO BROUGHT DRAMA TO OUR MARRIAGE.
IT WAS LIN-HANELLA AND KERTE-NOS.
BUT SHE NEVER SPOKE OF HIM AGAIN AFTER THAT.
AND I HAVE NOTHING MORE TO TELL.
WHAT DID YOU THINK THEN, UNCLE?
NOTH-ING, REALLY.
NOTH-ING?

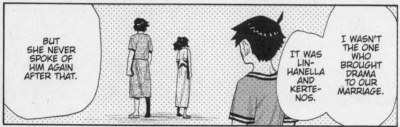

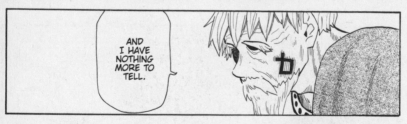

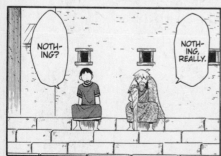

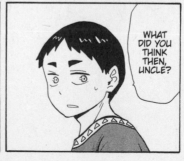

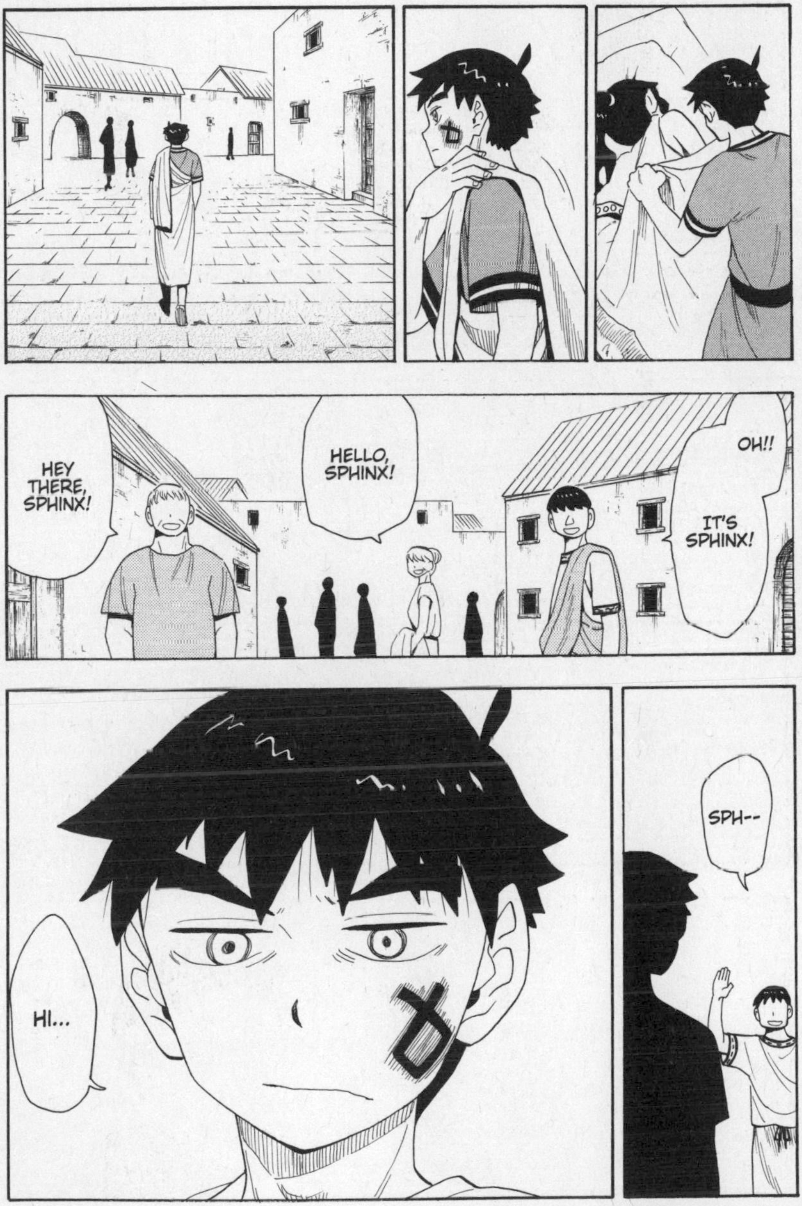
OH!!
IT'S SPHINX!
HELLO, SPHINX!
HEY THERE, SPHINX!
SPH--
HI...

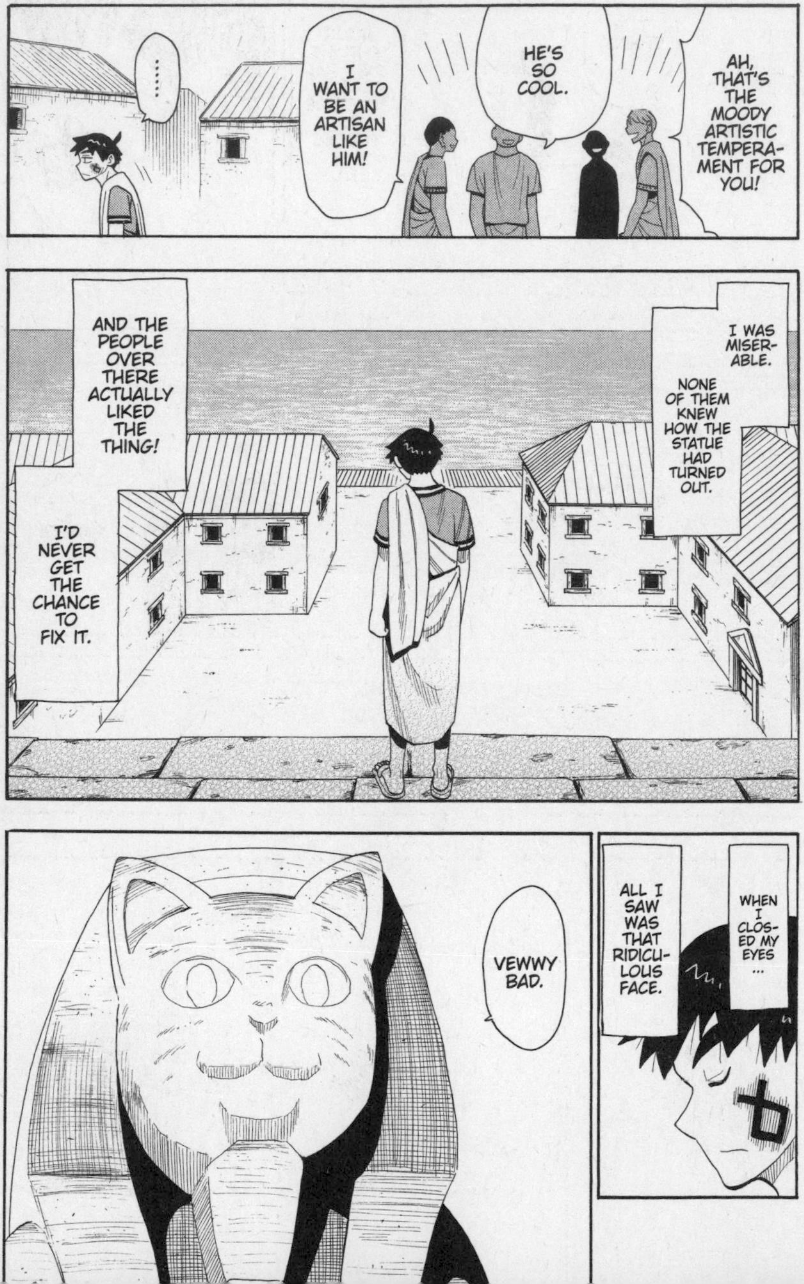
AH, THAT'S THE MOODY ARTISTIC TEMPERAMENT FOR YOU!
HE'S SO COOL.
I WANT TO BE AN ARTISAN LIKE HIM!
......
I WAS MISERABLE.
NONE OF THEM KNEW HOW THE STATUE HAD TURNED OUT.
AND THE PEOPLE OVER THERE ACTUALLY LIKED THE THING!
I'D NEVER GET THE CHANCE TO FIX IT.
WHEN I CLOSED MY EYES...
ALL I SAW WAS THAT RIDICULOUS FACE.
VEWWY BAD.

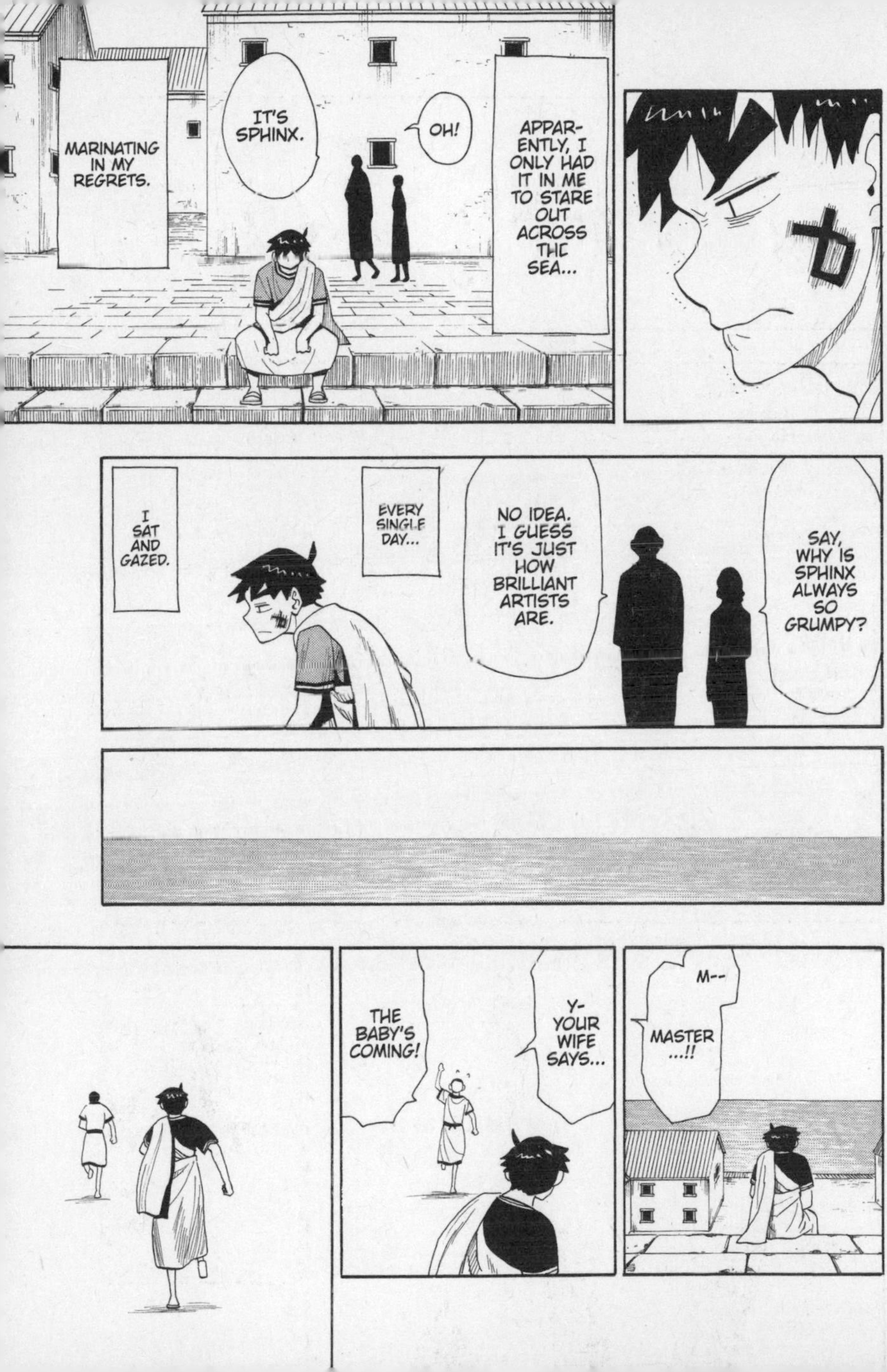
APPARENTLY, I ONLY HAD IT IN ME TO STARE OUT ACROSS THE SEA...
OH!
IT'S SPHINX.
MARINATING IN MY REGRETS.
SAY, WHY IS SPHINX ALWAYS SO GRUMPY?
NO IDEA. I GUESS IT'S JUST HOW BRILLIANT ARTISTS ARE.
EVERY SINGLE DAY...
I SAT AND GAZED.
M--
MASTER ...!!
Y-YOUR WIFE SAYS...
THE BABY'S COMING!

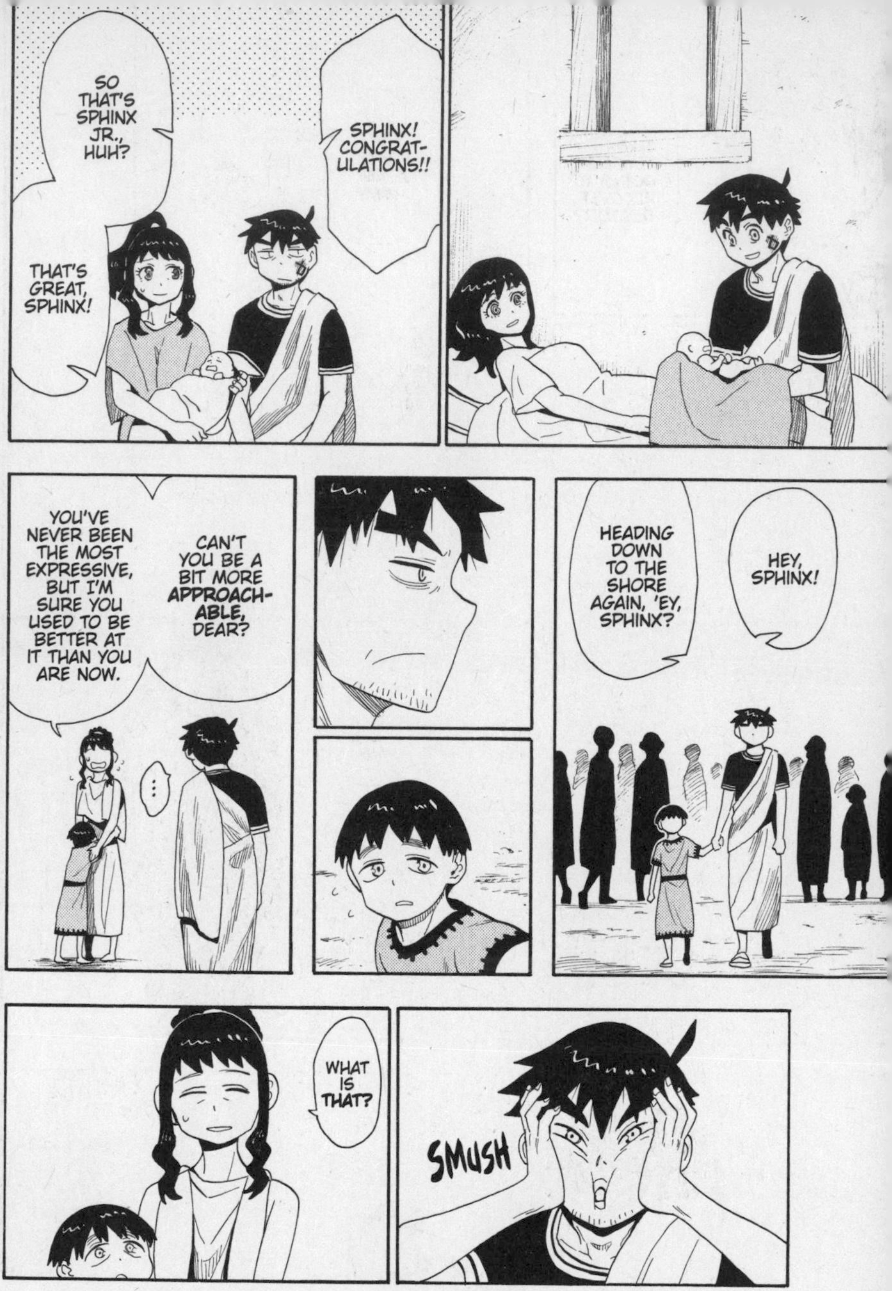
SPHINX! CONGRAT-ULATIONS!!
SO THAT'S SPHINX JR., HUH?
THAT'S GREAT, SPHINX!
HEY, SPHINX!
HEADING DOWN TO THE SHORE AGAIN, 'EY, SPHINX?
CAN'T YOU BE A BIT MORE APPROACHABLE, DEAR?
YOU'VE NEVER BEEN THE MOST EXPRESSIVE, BUT I'M SURE YOU USED TO BE BETTER AT IT THAN YOU ARE NOW.
...
SMUSH
WHAT IS THAT?

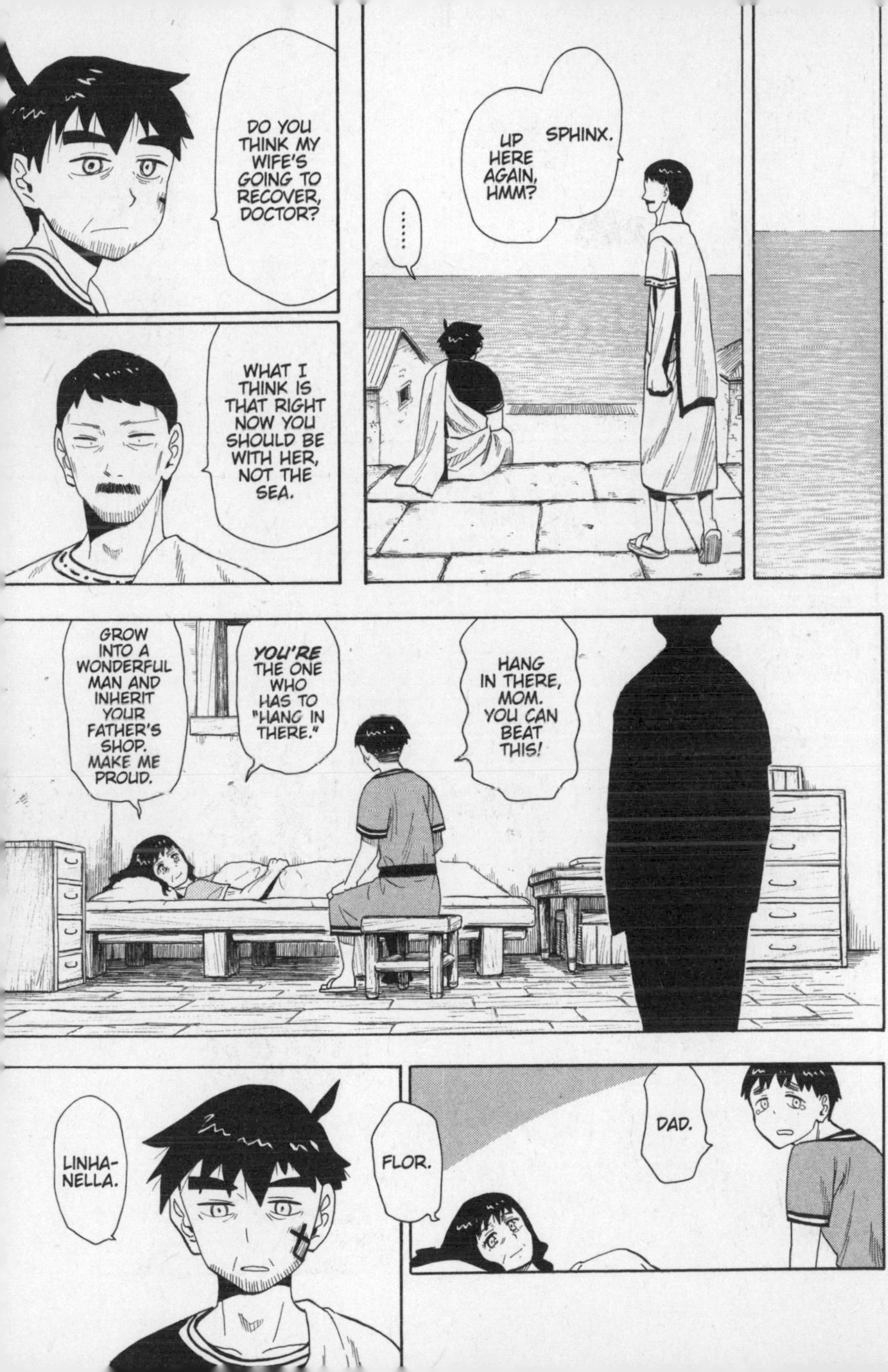
SPHINX.
UP HERE AGAIN, HMM?
......
DO YOU THINK MY WIFE'S GOING TO RECOVER, DOCTOR?
WHAT I THINK IS THAT RIGHT NOW YOU SHOULD BE WITH HER, NOT THE SEA.
HANG IN THERE, MOM. YOU CAN BEAT THIS!
YOU'RE THE ONE WHO HAS TO "HANG IN THERE."
GROW INTO A WONDERFUL MAN AND INHERIT YOUR FATHER'S SHOP. MAKE ME PROUD.
DAD.
FLOR.
LINHA-NELLA.

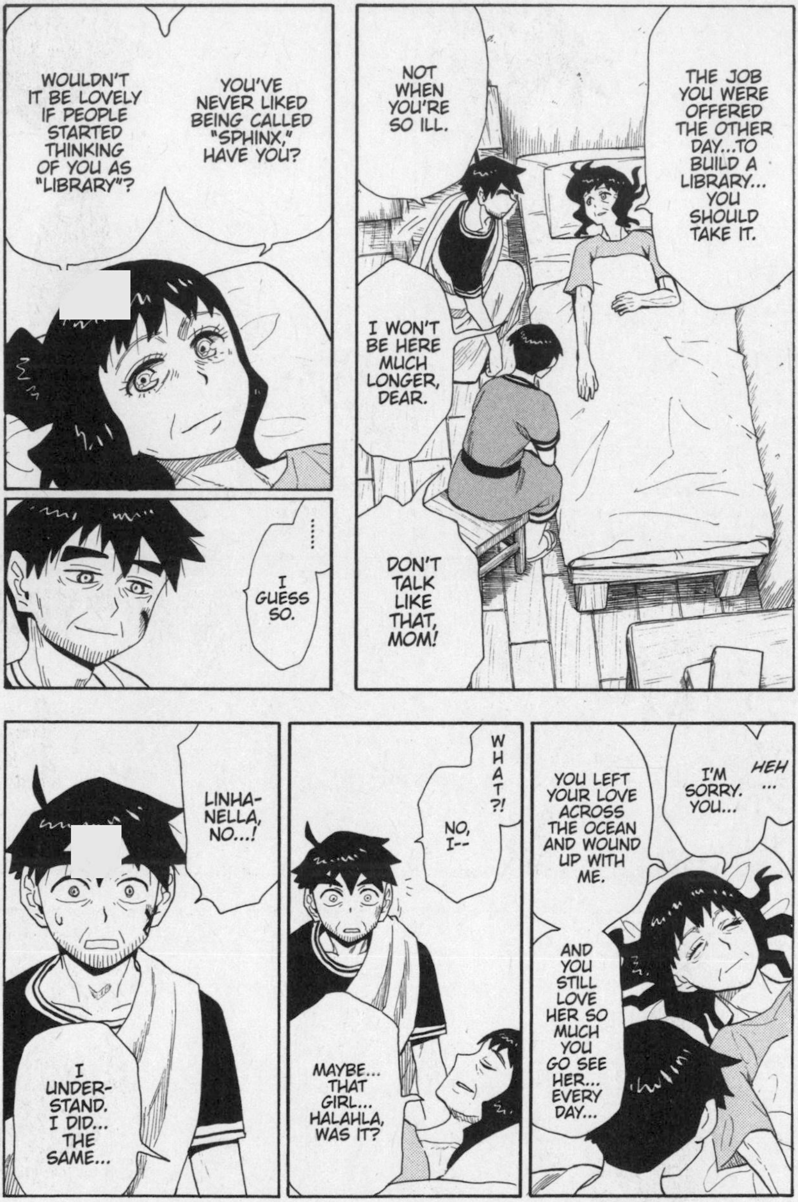
THE JOB YOU WERE OFFERED THE OTHER DAY...TO BUILD A LIBRARY... YOU SHOULD TAKE IT.
NOT WHEN YOU'RE SO ILL.
I WON'T BE HERE MUCH LONGER, DEAR.
DON'T TALK LIKE THAT, MOM!
YOU'VE NEVER LIKED BEING CALLED "SPHINX," HAVE YOU?
WOULDN'T IT BE LOVELY IF PEOPLE STARTED THINKING OF YOU AS "LIBRARY"?
......
I GUESS SO.
HEH...
I'M SORRY. YOU...
YOU LEFT YOUR LOVE ACROSS THE OCEAN AND WOUND UP WITH ME.
AND YOU STILL LOVE HER SO MUCH YOU GO SEE HER... EVERY DAY...
WHAT?!
NO, I--
MAYBE... THAT GIRL... HALAHLA, WAS IT?
LINHA-NELLA, NO...!
I UNDER-STAND. I DID... THE SAME...

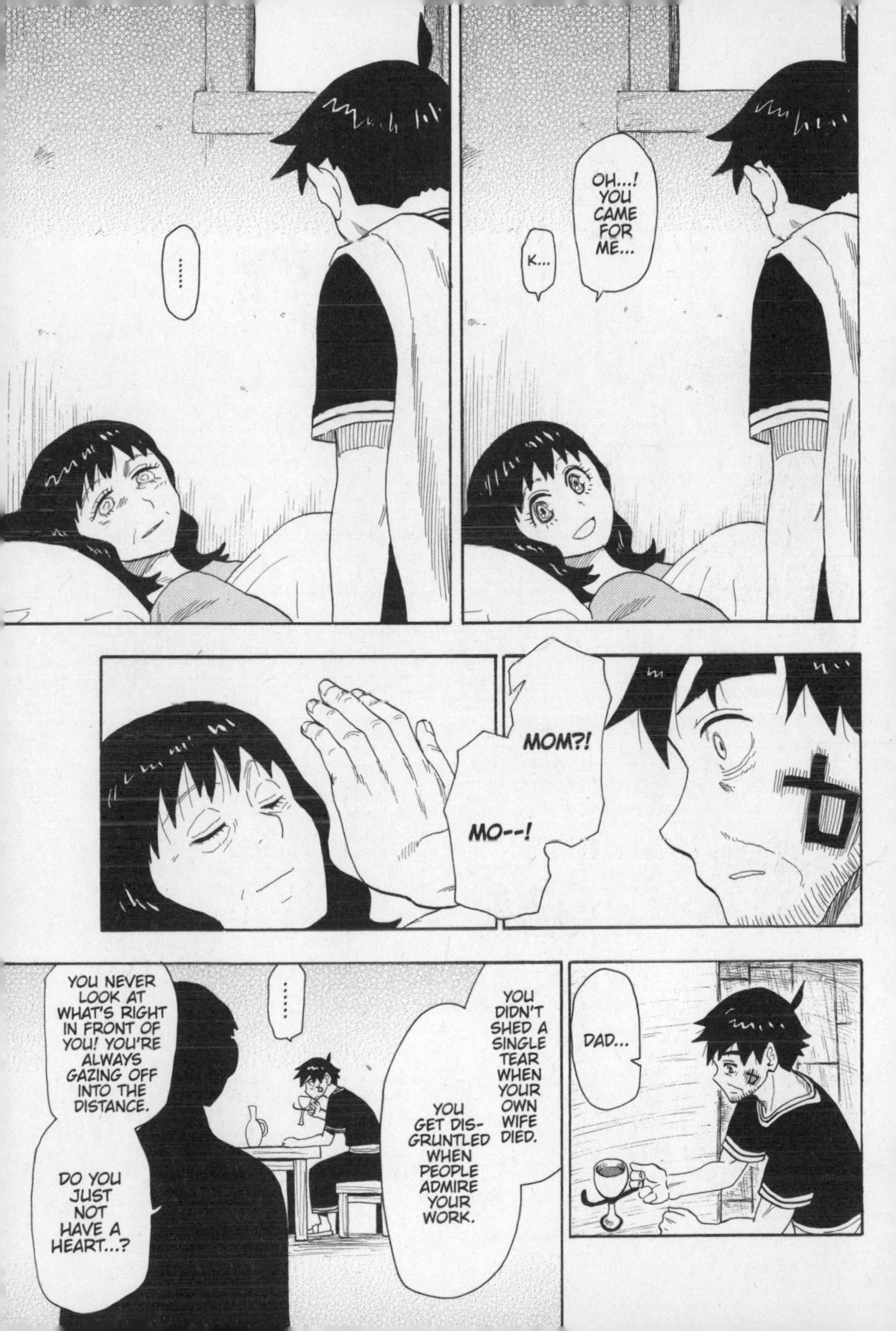
OH...! YOU CAME FOR ME...
K...
......
MOM?!
MO--!
DAD...
YOU DIDN'T SHED A SINGLE TEAR WHEN YOUR OWN WIFE DIED.
......
YOU NEVER LOOK AT WHAT'S RIGHT IN FRONT OF YOU! YOU'RE ALWAYS GAZING OFF INTO THE DISTANCE.
YOU GET DIS-GRUNTLED WHEN PEOPLE ADMIRE YOUR WORK.
DO YOU JUST NOT HAVE A HEART...?

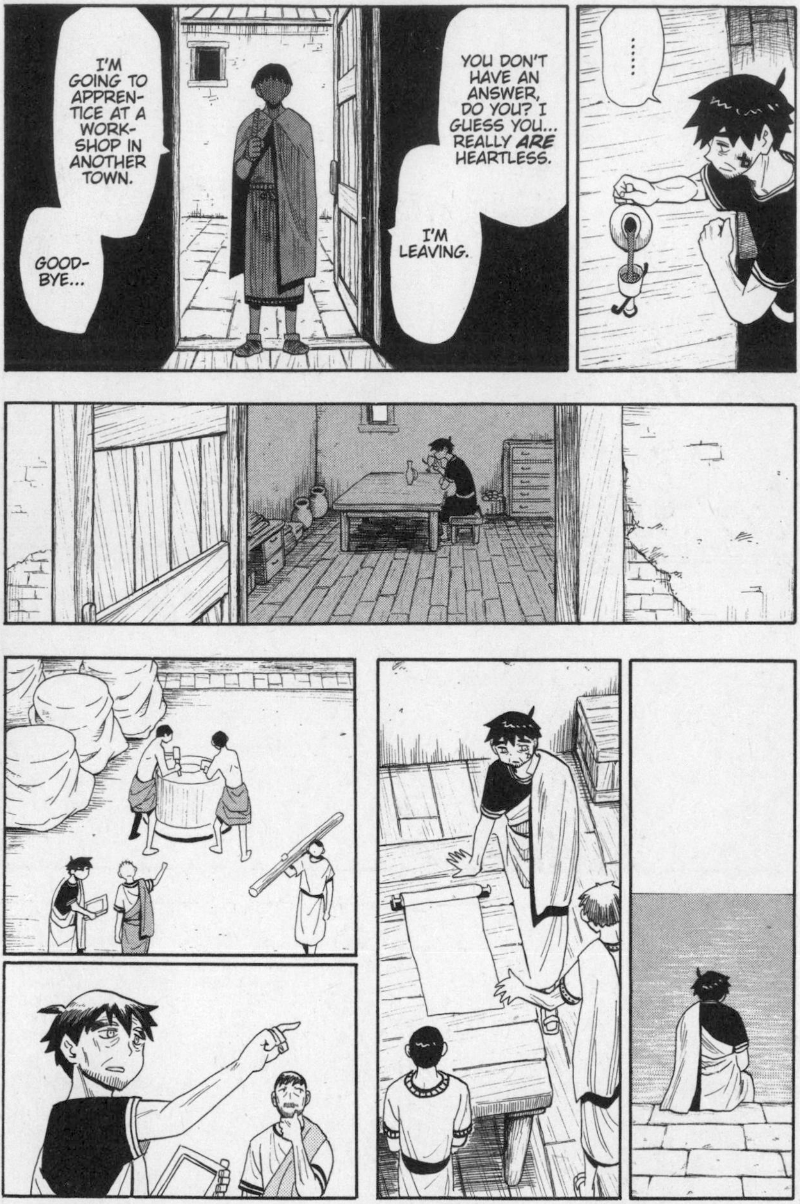

……
YOU DON'T HAVE AN ANSWER, DO YOU? I GUESS YOU... REALLY *ARE* HEARTLESS.
I'M LEAVING.
I'M GOING TO APPRENTICE AT A WORKSHOP IN ANOTHER TOWN.
GOOD-BYE...

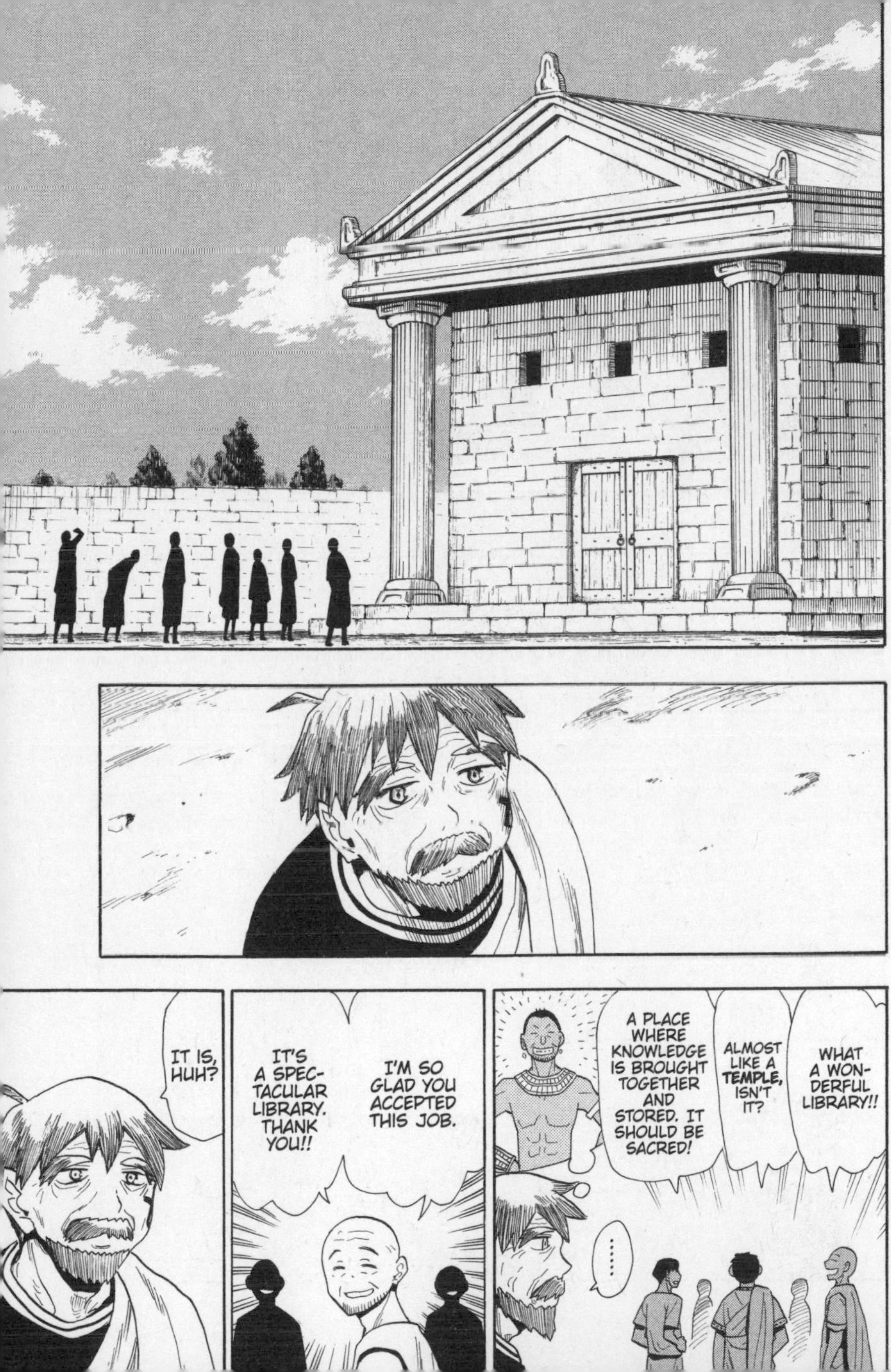
WHAT A WONDERFUL LIBRARY!!
ALMOST LIKE A TEMPLE, ISN'T IT?
A PLACE WHERE KNOWLEDGE IS BROUGHT TOGETHER AND STORED. IT SHOULD BE SACRED!
......
I'M SO GLAD YOU ACCEPTED THIS JOB.
IT'S A SPECTACULAR LIBRARY. THANK YOU!!
IT IS, HUH?

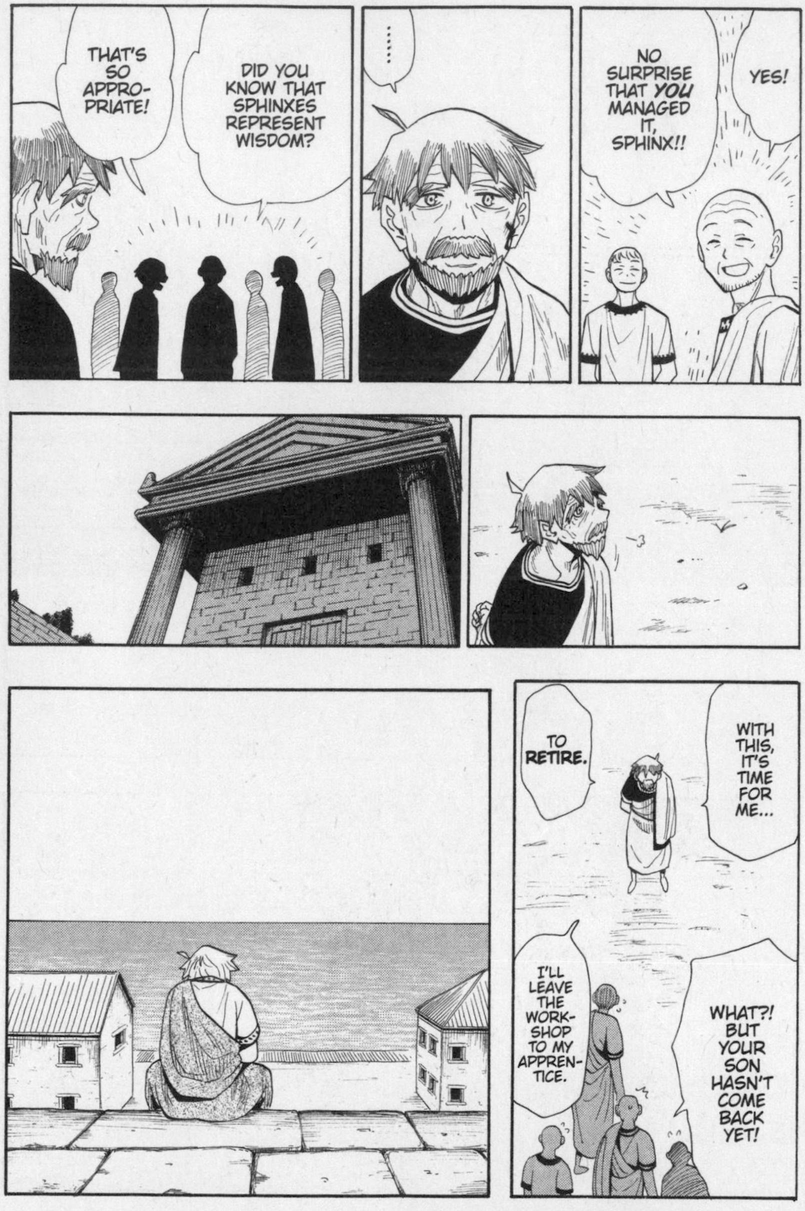
YES!
NO SURPRISE THAT *YOU* MANAGED IT, SPHINX!!
......
DID YOU KNOW THAT SPHINXES REPRESENT WISDOM?
THAT'S SO APPRO-PRIATE!
WITH THIS, IT'S TIME FOR ME...
TO **RETIRE.**
I'LL LEAVE THE WORK-SHOP TO MY APPREN-TICE.
WHAT?! BUT YOUR SON HASN'T COME BACK YET!

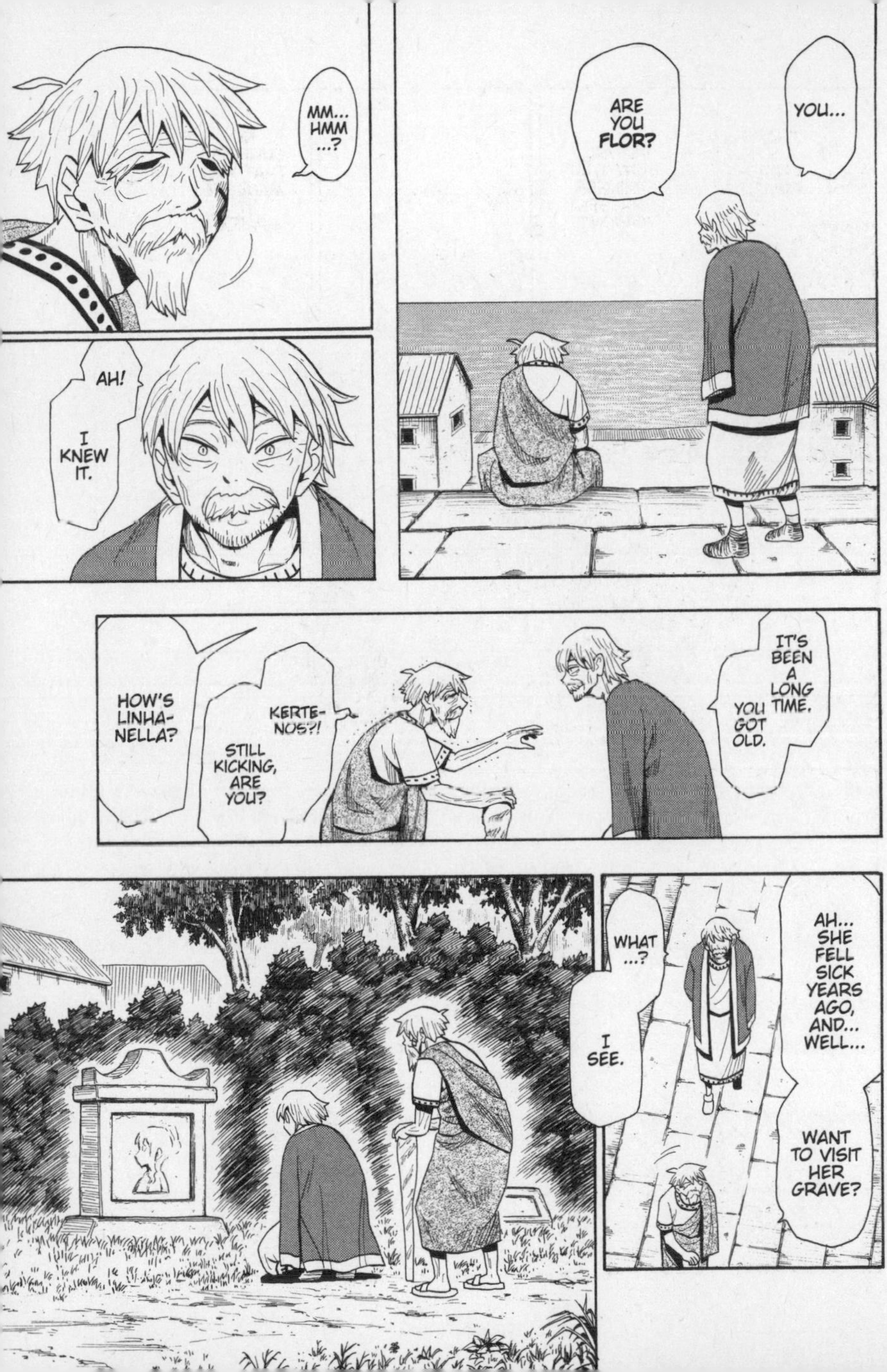
YOU...
ARE YOU FLOR?
MM... HMM ...?
AH!
I KNEW IT.
IT'S BEEN A LONG TIME.
YOU GOT OLD.
KERTE-NOS?!
STILL KICKING, ARE YOU?
HOW'S LINHA-NELLA?
AH... SHE FELL SICK YEARS AGO, AND... WELL...
WHAT ...?
I SEE.
WANT TO VISIT HER GRAVE?

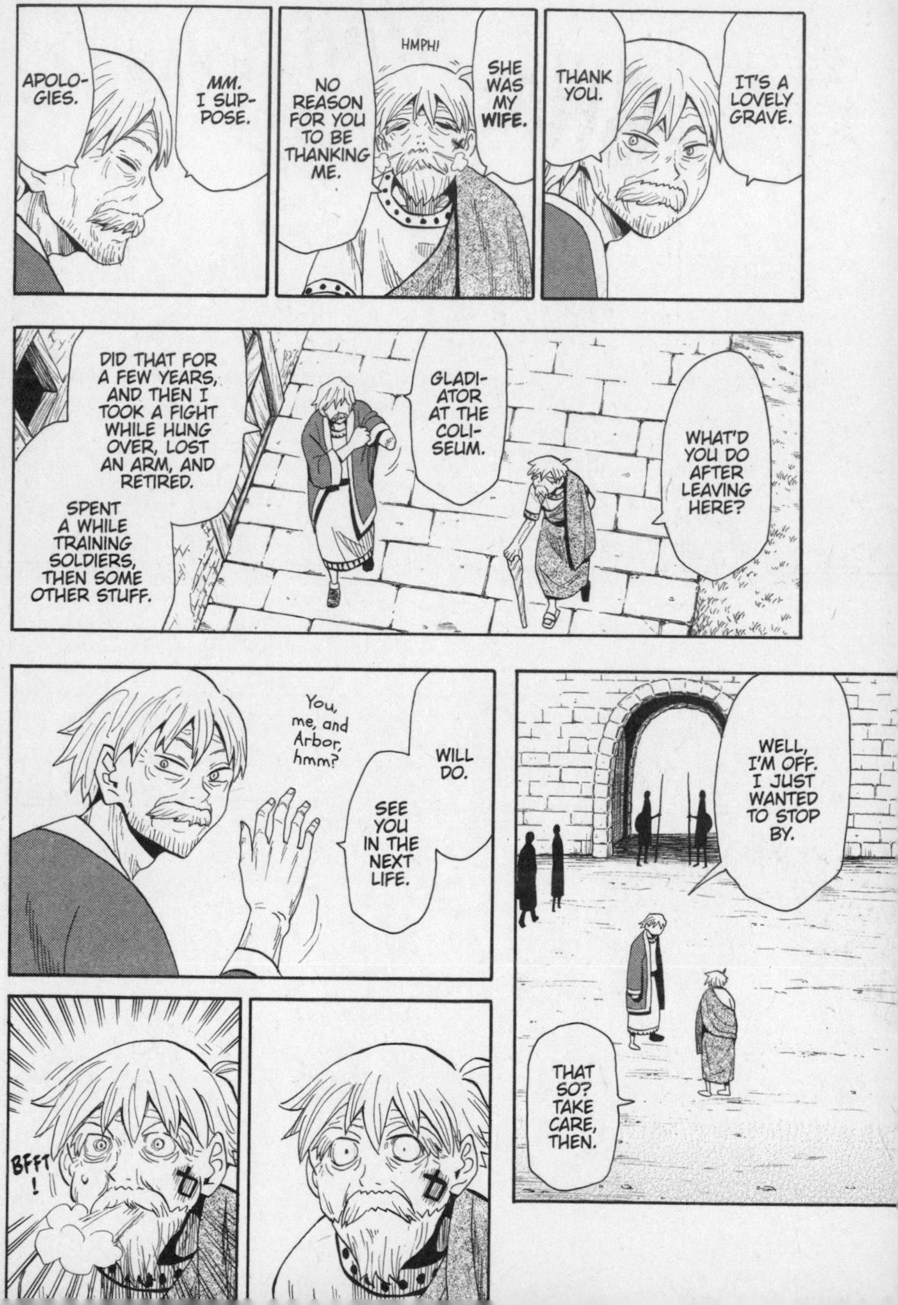
IT'S A LOVELY GRAVE.
THANK YOU.
SHE WAS MY WIFE.
HMPH!
NO REASON FOR YOU TO BE THANKING ME.
MM. I SUP-POSE.
APOLO-GIES.
WHAT'D YOU DO AFTER LEAVING HERE?
GLADI-ATOR AT THE COLI-SEUM.
DID THAT FOR A FEW YEARS, AND THEN I TOOK A FIGHT WHILE HUNG OVER, LOST AN ARM, AND RETIRED.
SPENT A WHILE TRAINING SOLDIERS, THEN SOME OTHER STUFF.
WELL, I'M OFF. I JUST WANTED TO STOP BY.
THAT SO? TAKE CARE, THEN.
WILL DO.
SEE YOU IN THE NEXT LIFE.
You, me, and Arbor, hmm?
BFFT!

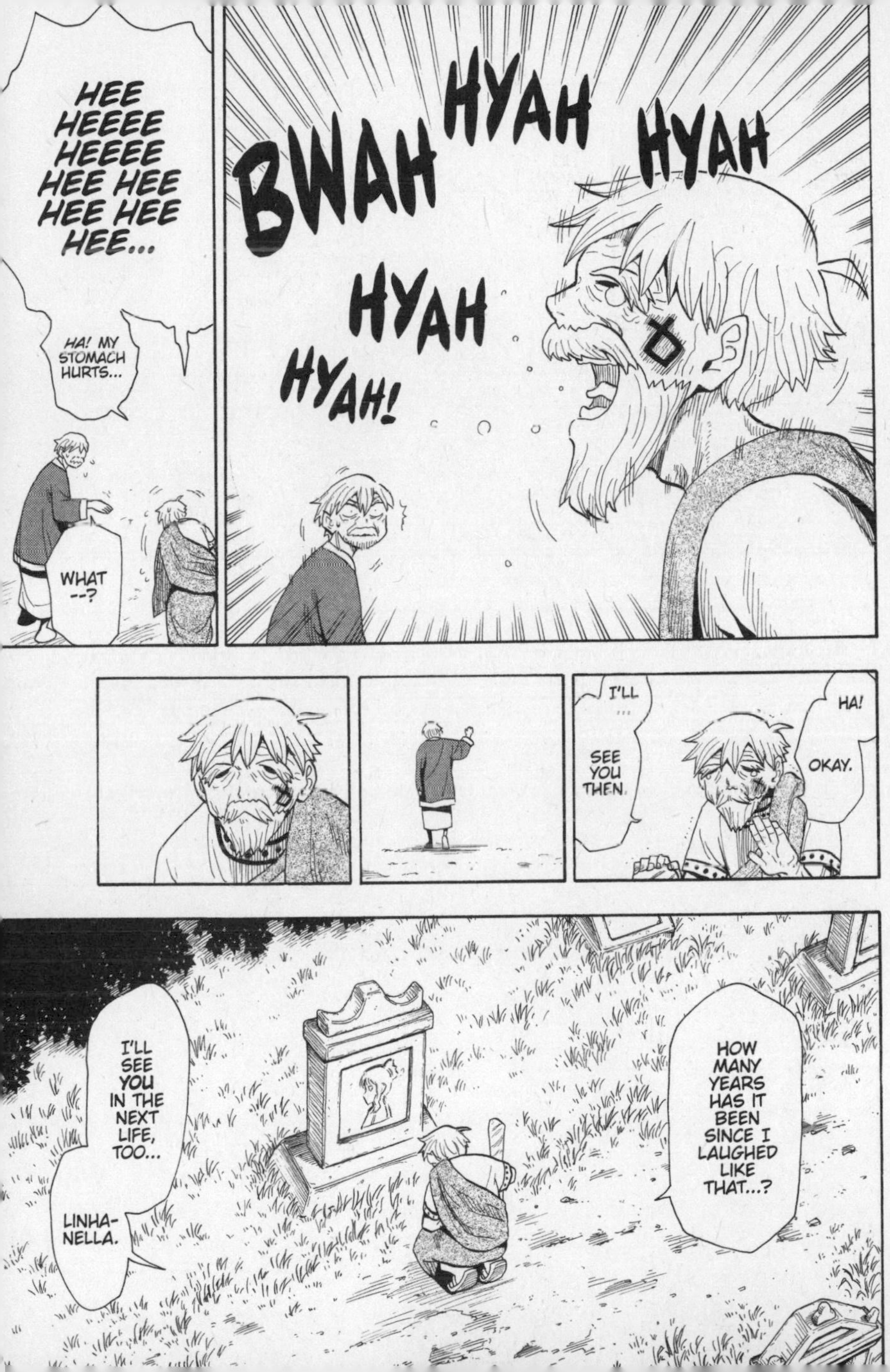
BWAH HYAH HYAH HYAH HYAH!
HEE HEEEEE HEEEEE HEE HEE HEE HEE HEE...
HA! MY STOMACH HURTS...
WHAT --?
HA!
OKAY.
I'LL ...
SEE YOU THEN.
HOW MANY YEARS HAS IT BEEN SINCE I LAUGHED LIKE THAT...?
I'LL SEE YOU IN THE NEXT LIFE, TOO...
LINHA-NELLA.

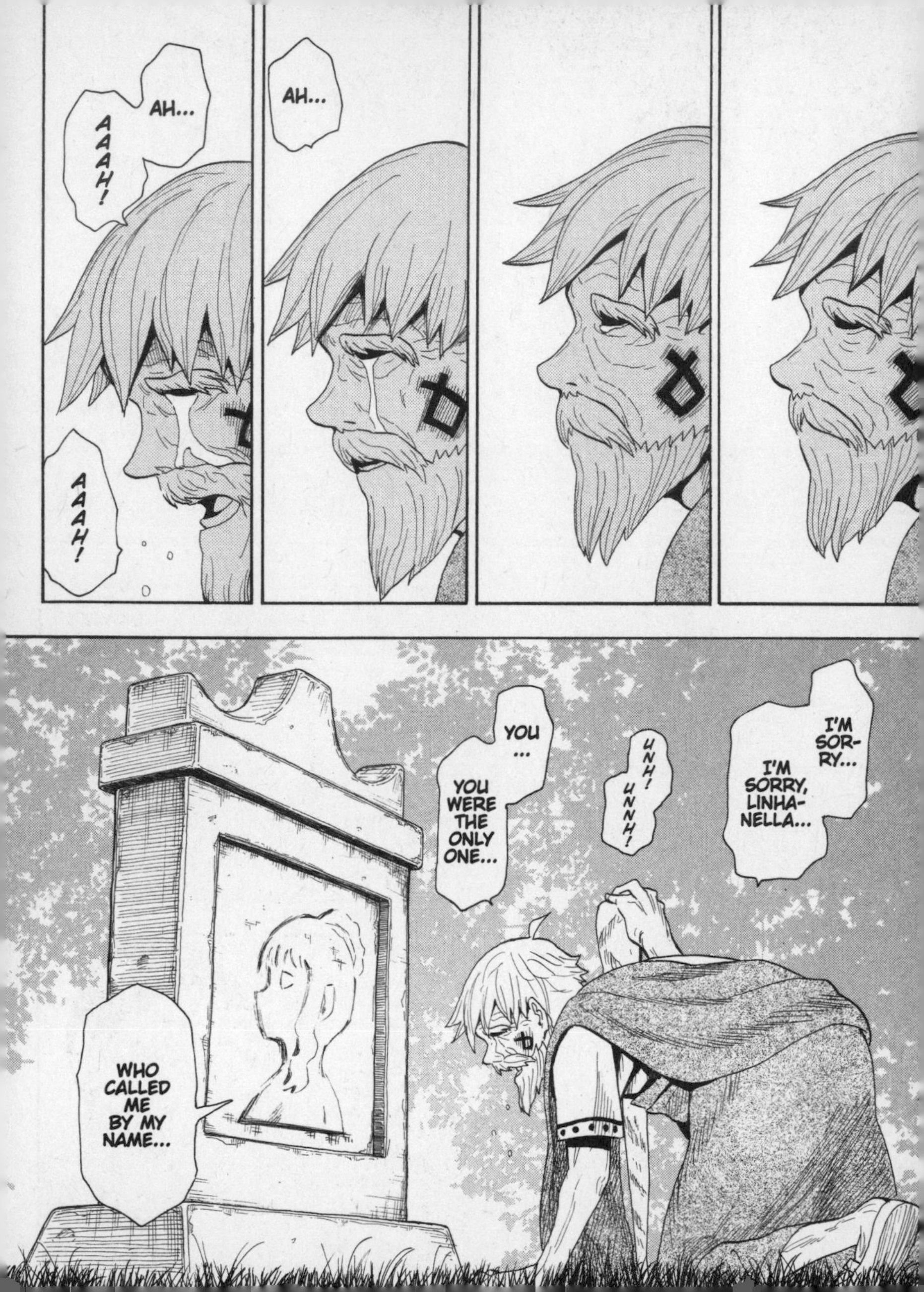
AH...
AH... AAAAH!
AAAAH!
I'M SORRY... I'M SORRY, LINHANELLA...
UNH! UNNH!
YOU... YOU WERE THE ONLY ONE...
WHO CALLED ME BY MY NAME...

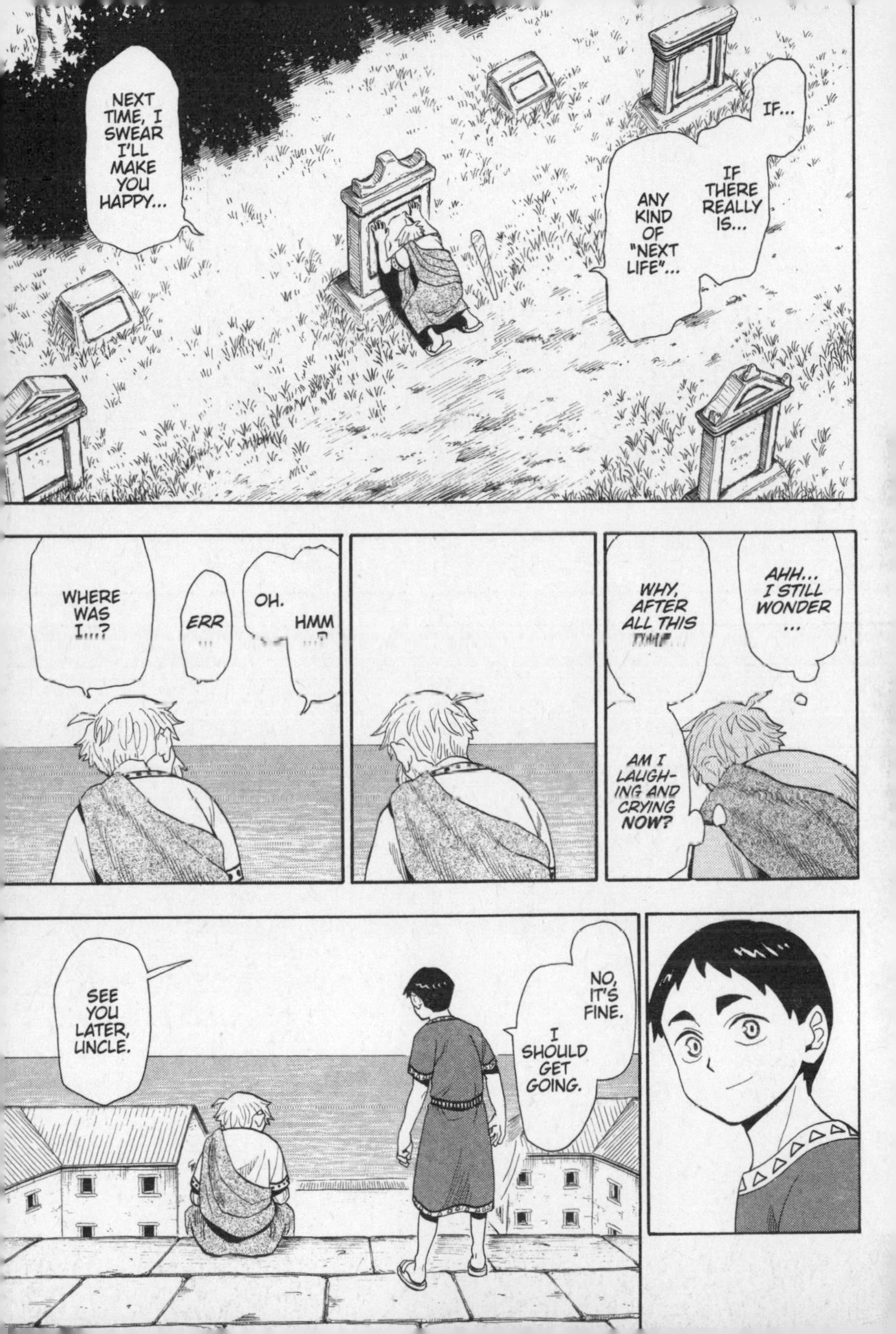
IF...
IF THERE REALLY IS...
ANY KIND OF "NEXT LIFE"...
NEXT TIME, I SWEAR I'LL MAKE YOU HAPPY...
AHH... I STILL WONDER ...
WHY, AFTER ALL THIS TIME...
AM I LAUGHING AND CRYING NOW?
OH.
HMM
ERR...
WHERE WAS I...?
NO, IT'S FINE.
I SHOULD GET GOING.
SEE YOU LATER, UNCLE.

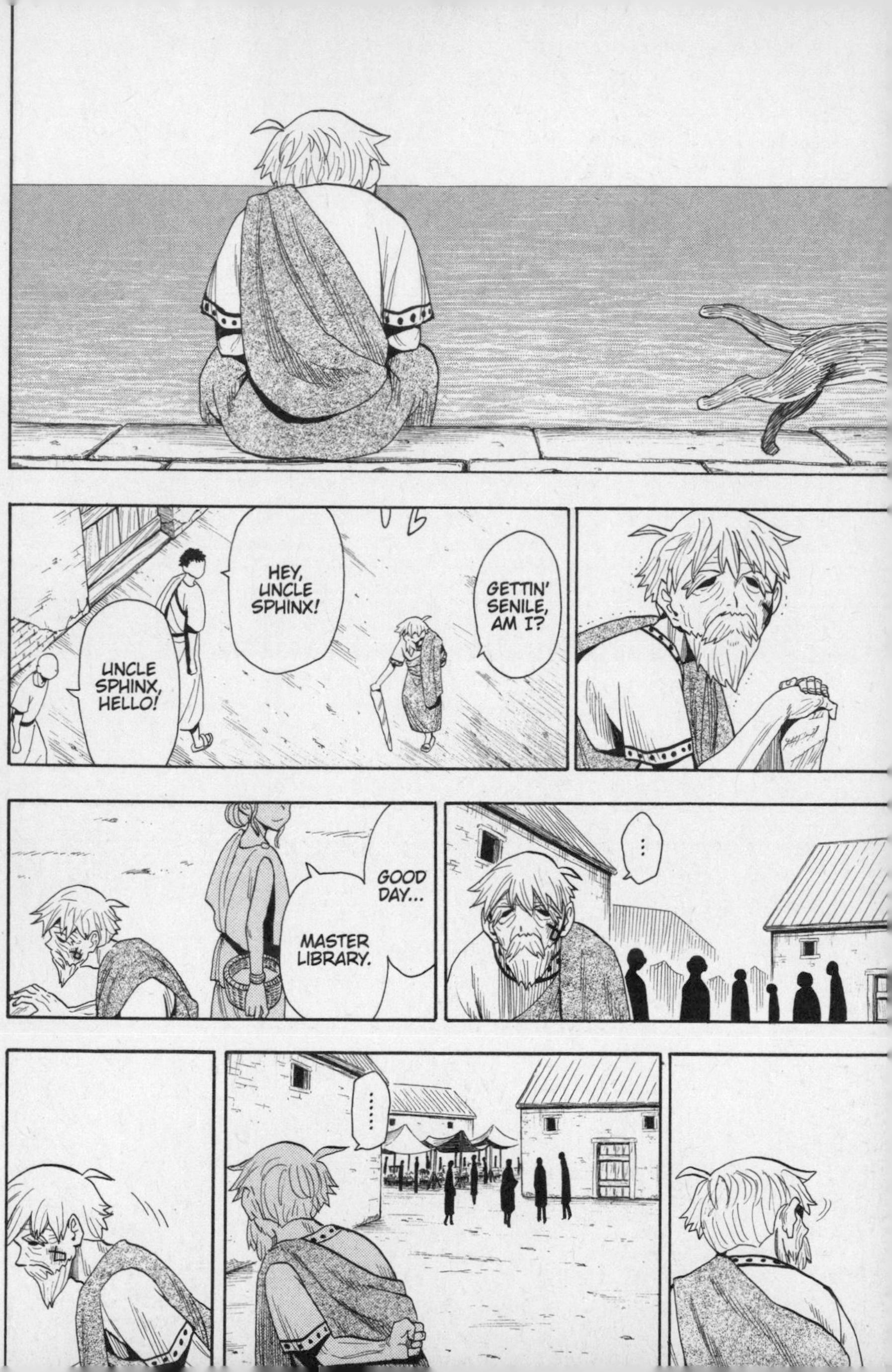
GETTIN' SENILE, AM I?
HEY, UNCLE SPHINX!
UNCLE SPHINX, HELLO!
...
GOOD DAY... MASTER LIBRARY.
......

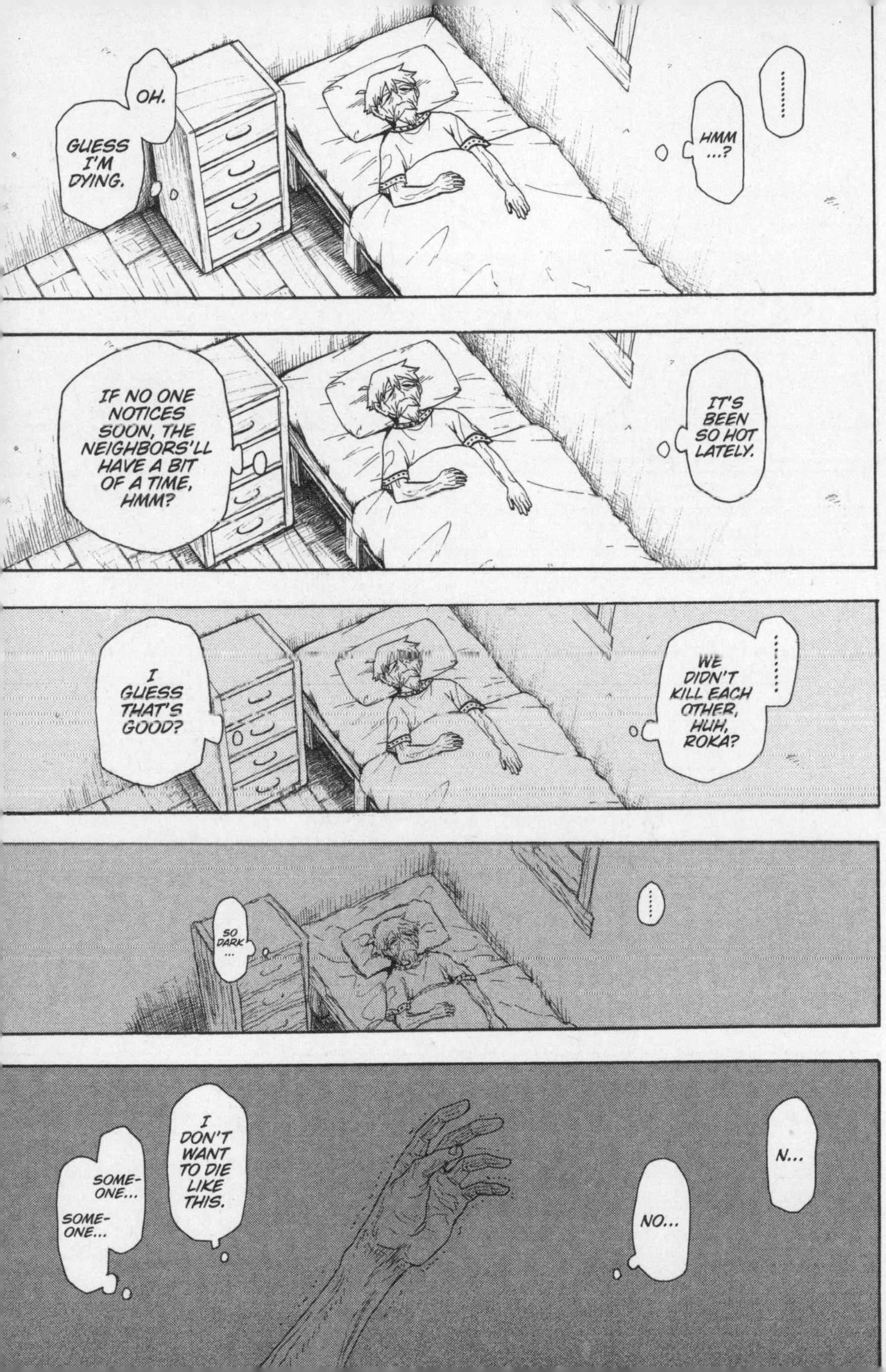

……
HMM …?
OH.
GUESS I'M DYING.
IT'S BEEN SO HOT LATELY.
IF NO ONE NOTICES SOON, THE NEIGHBORS'LL HAVE A BIT OF A TIME, HMM?
……
WE DIDN'T KILL EACH OTHER, HUH, ROKA?
I GUESS THAT'S GOOD?
……
SO DARK …
N...
NO...
I DON'T WANT TO DIE LIKE THIS.
SOME-ONE...
SOME-ONE...

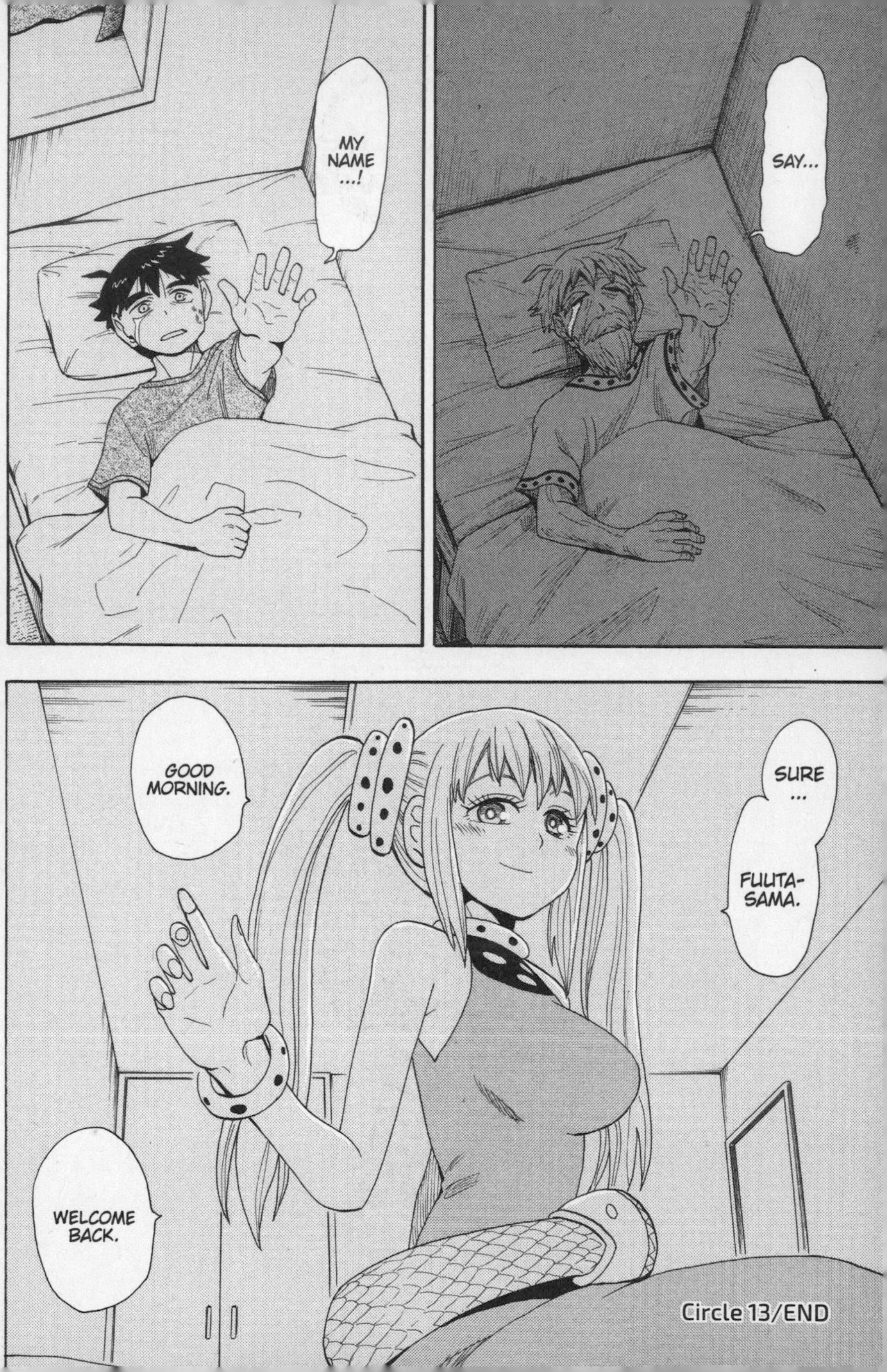
SAY...
MY NAME ...!
SURE ... FUUTA-SAMA.
GOOD MORNING.
WELCOME BACK.
Circle 13/END

Circle 14
Past-Life Hangover

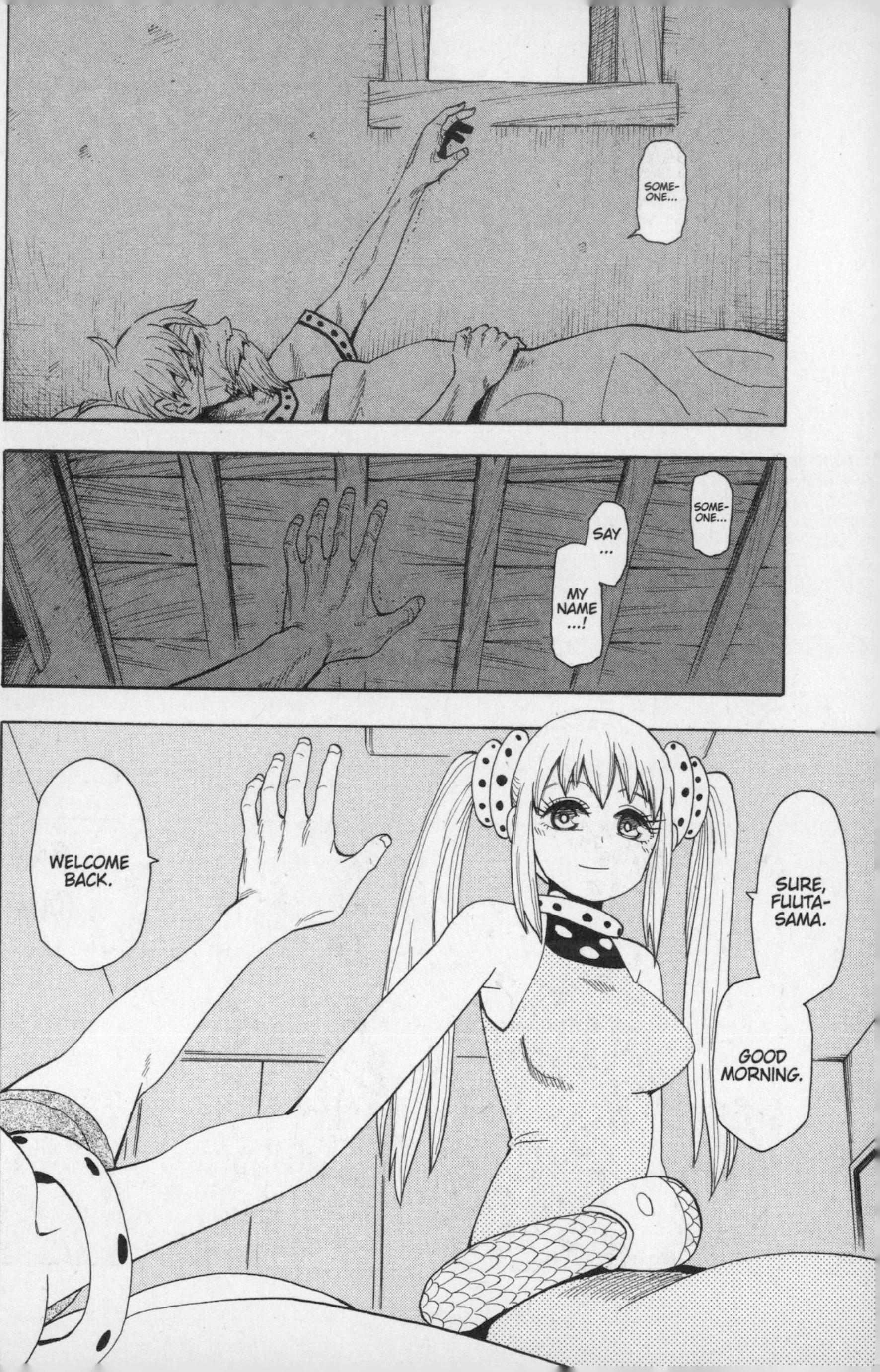
SOME-ONE...
SOME-ONE...
SAY ...
MY NAME ...!
SURE, FUUTA-SAMA.
GOOD MORNING.
WELCOME BACK.

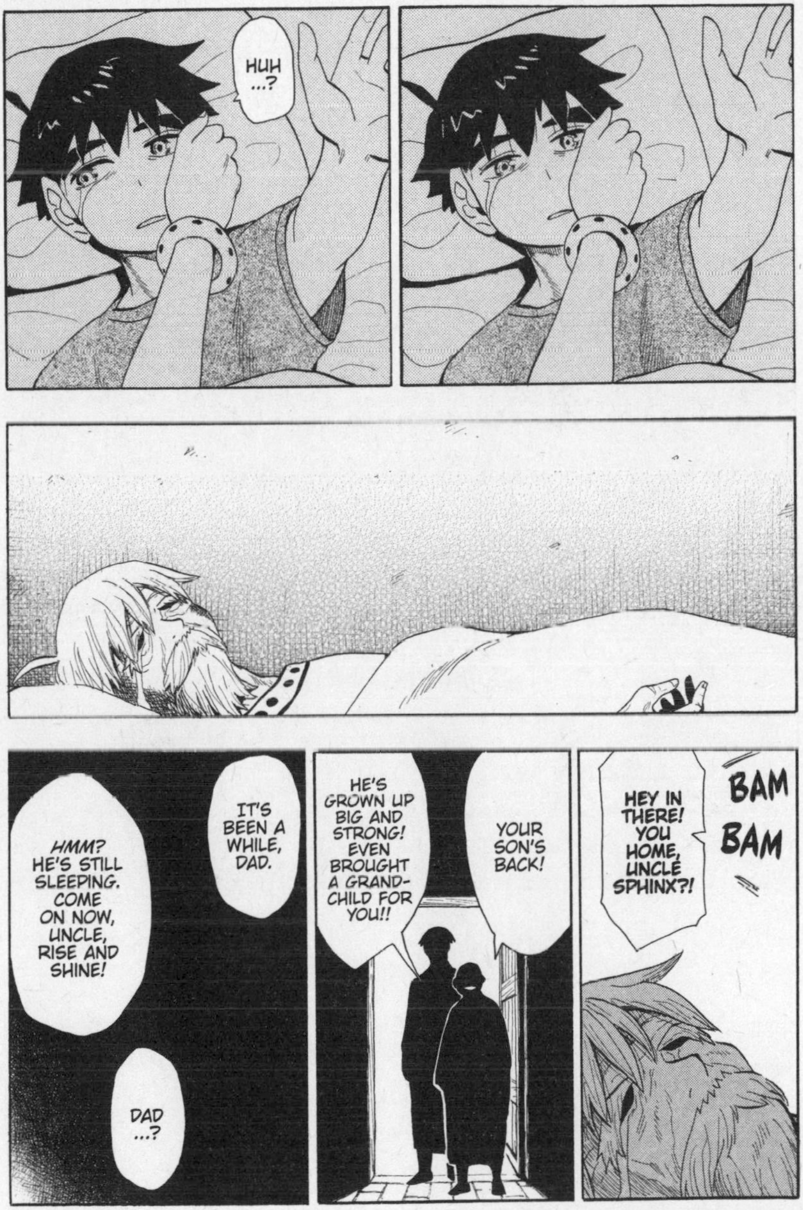
HUH ...?
BAM BAM
HEY IN THERE! YOU HOME, UNCLE SPHINX?!
YOUR SON'S BACK!
HE'S GROWN UP BIG AND STRONG! EVEN BROUGHT A GRAND-CHILD FOR YOU!!
IT'S BEEN A WHILE, DAD.
HMM? HE'S STILL SLEEPING. COME ON NOW, UNCLE, RISE AND SHINE!
DAD ...?

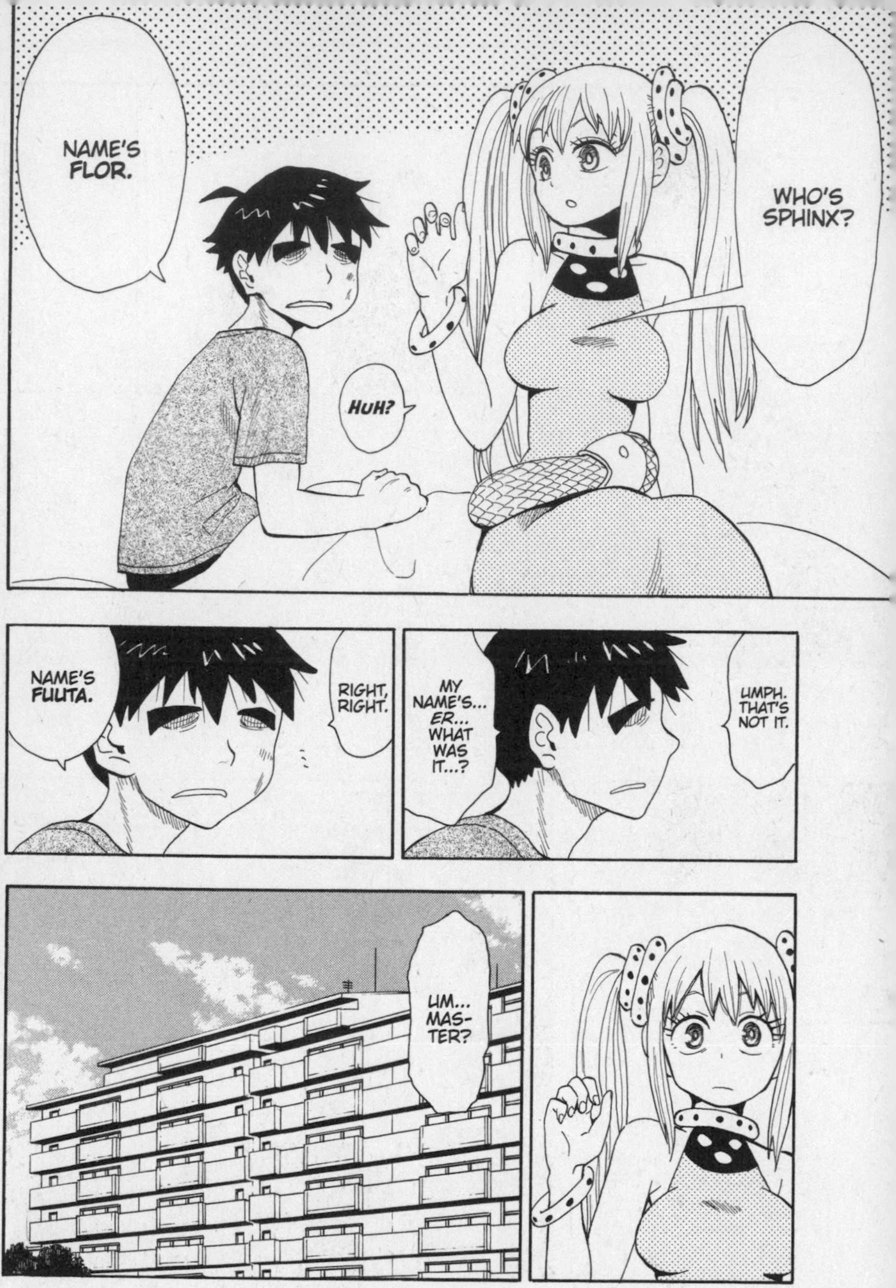
WHO'S SPHINX?
HUH?
NAME'S FLOR.
UMPH. THAT'S NOT IT.
MY NAME'S... ER... WHAT WAS IT...?
RIGHT, RIGHT.
NAME'S FUUTA.
UM... MAS-TER?

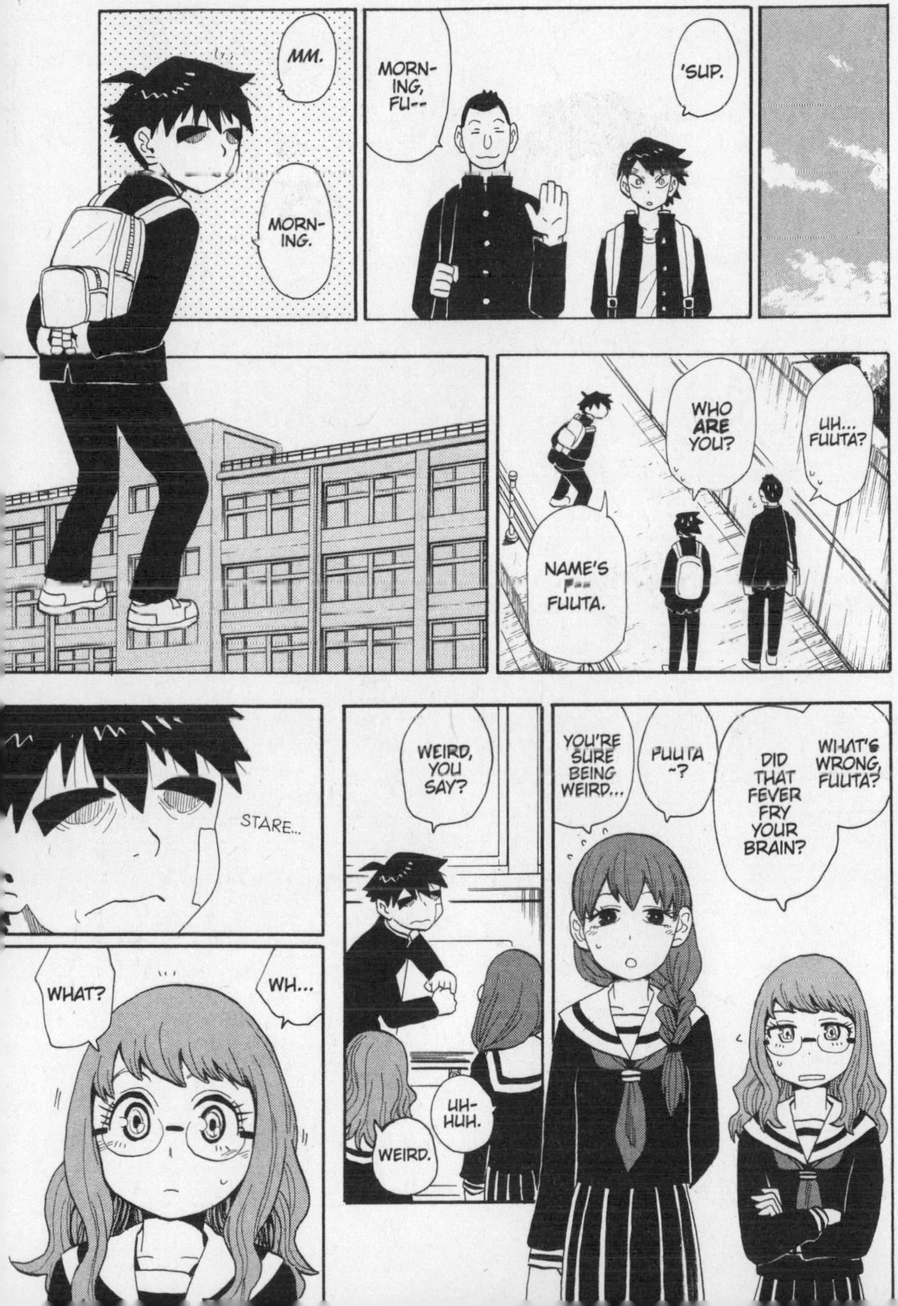
'SUP.
MORNING, FU--
MM.
MORN-ING.
UH... FUUTA?
WHO ARE YOU?
NAME'S F-- FUUTA.
WHAT'S WRONG, FUUTA?
DID THAT FEVER FRY YOUR BRAIN?
FUUTA ~?
YOU'RE SURE BEING WEIRD...
WEIRD, YOU SAY?
UH-HUH.
WEIRD.
STARE...
WH...
WHAT?

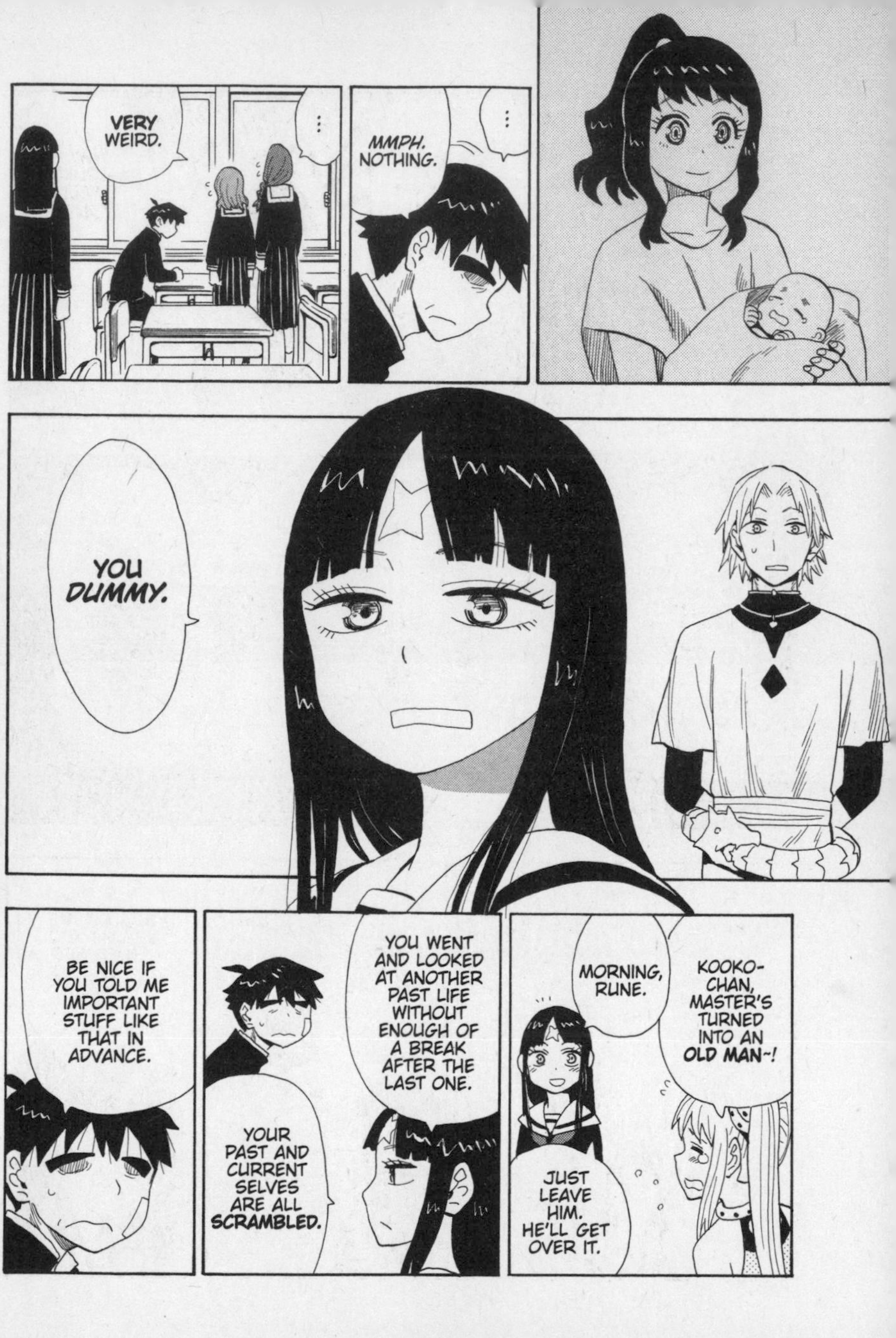
...
MMPH. NOTHING.
...
VERY WEIRD.
YOU DUMMY.
KOOKO-CHAN, MASTER'S TURNED INTO AN OLD MAN~!
MORNING, RUNE.
JUST LEAVE HIM. HE'LL GET OVER IT.
YOU WENT AND LOOKED AT ANOTHER PAST LIFE WITHOUT ENOUGH OF A BREAK AFTER THE LAST ONE.
YOUR PAST AND CURRENT SELVES ARE ALL SCRAMBLED.
BE NICE IF YOU TOLD ME IMPORTANT STUFF LIKE THAT IN ADVANCE.

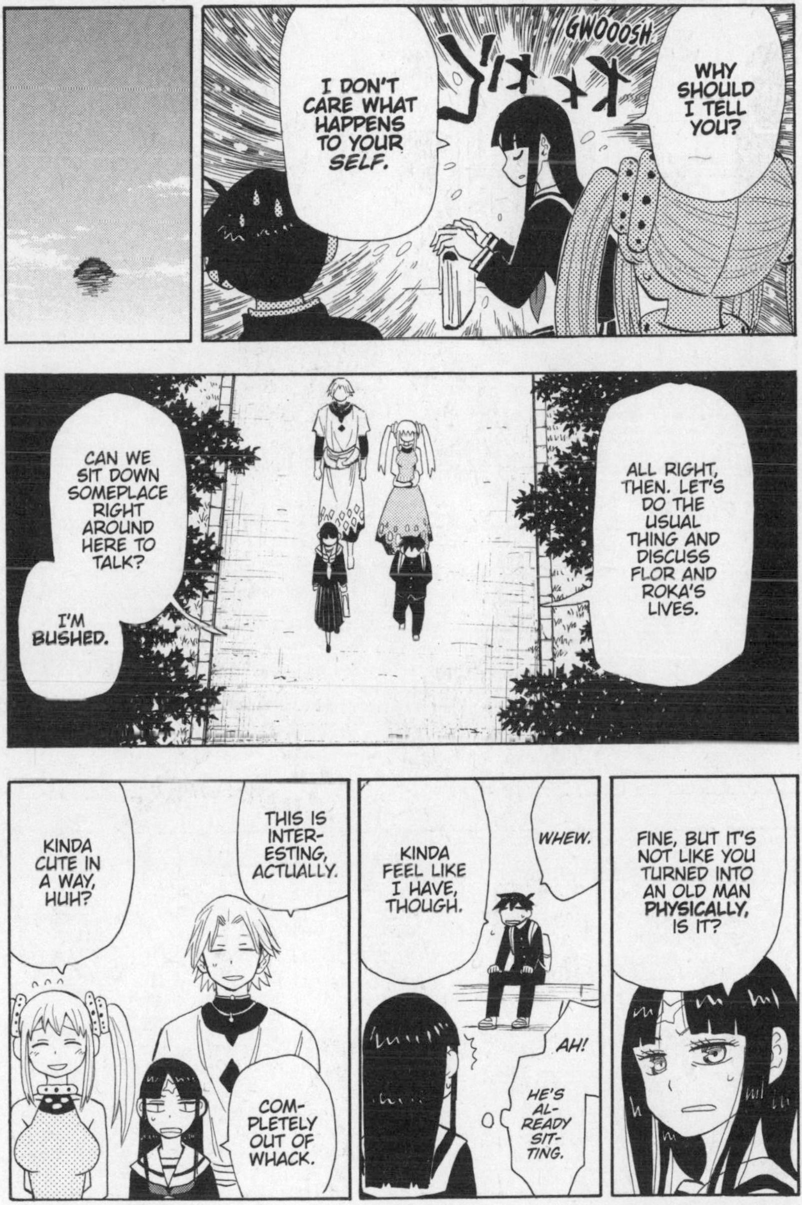
GWOOOSH
WHY SHOULD I TELL YOU?
I DON'T CARE WHAT HAPPENS TO YOUR SELF.
ALL RIGHT, THEN. LET'S DO THE USUAL THING AND DISCUSS FLOR AND ROKA'S LIVES.
CAN WE SIT DOWN SOMEPLACE RIGHT AROUND HERE TO TALK?
I'M BUSHED.
FINE, BUT IT'S NOT LIKE YOU TURNED INTO AN OLD MAN PHYSICALLY, IS IT?
WHEW.
KINDA FEEL LIKE I HAVE, THOUGH.
AH!
HE'S ALREADY SITTING.
THIS IS INTERESTING, ACTUALLY.
KINDA CUTE IN A WAY, HUH?
COMPLETELY OUT OF WHACK.

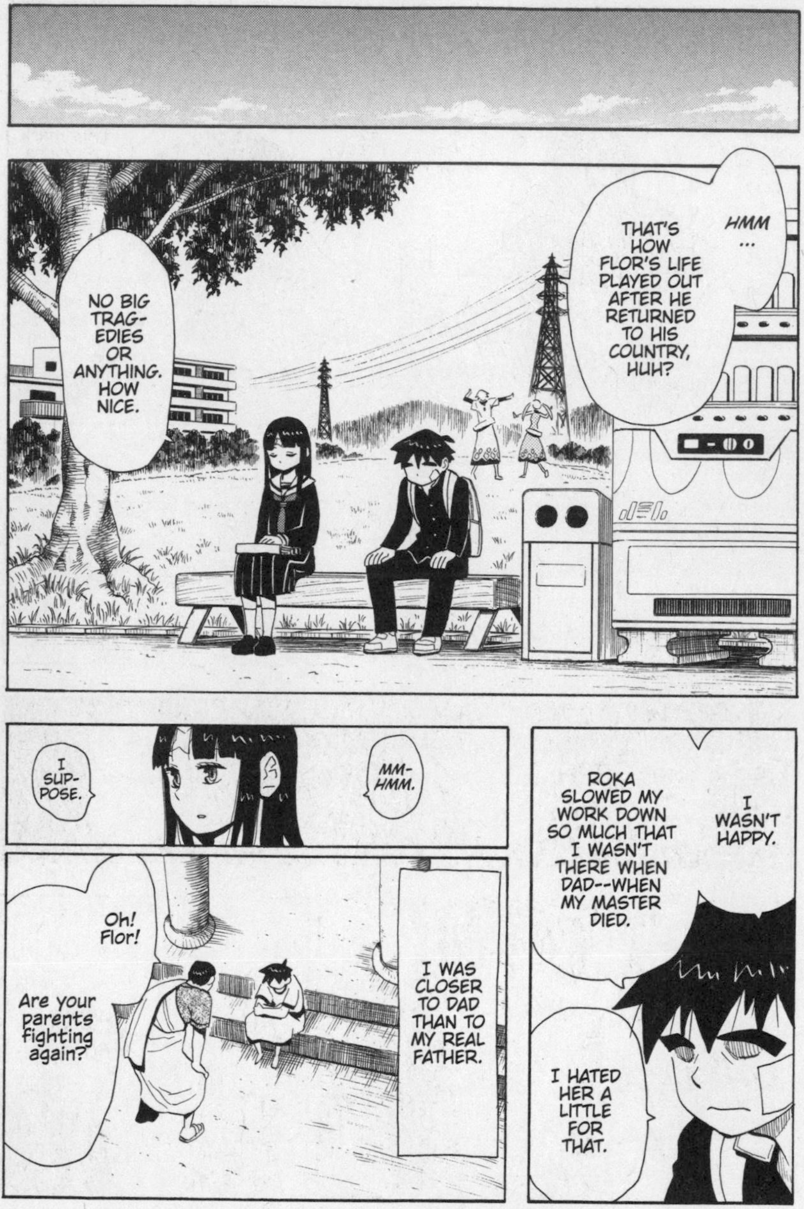
HMM ...
THAT'S HOW FLOR'S LIFE PLAYED OUT AFTER HE RETURNED TO HIS COUNTRY, HUH?
NO BIG TRAG-EDIES OR ANYTHING. HOW NICE.
I WASN'T HAPPY.
ROKA SLOWED MY WORK DOWN SO MUCH THAT I WASN'T THERE WHEN DAD--WHEN MY MASTER DIED.
I HATED HER A LITTLE FOR THAT.
MM-HMM.
I SUP-POSE.
I WAS CLOSER TO DAD THAN TO MY REAL FATHER.
Oh! Flor!
Are your parents fighting again?

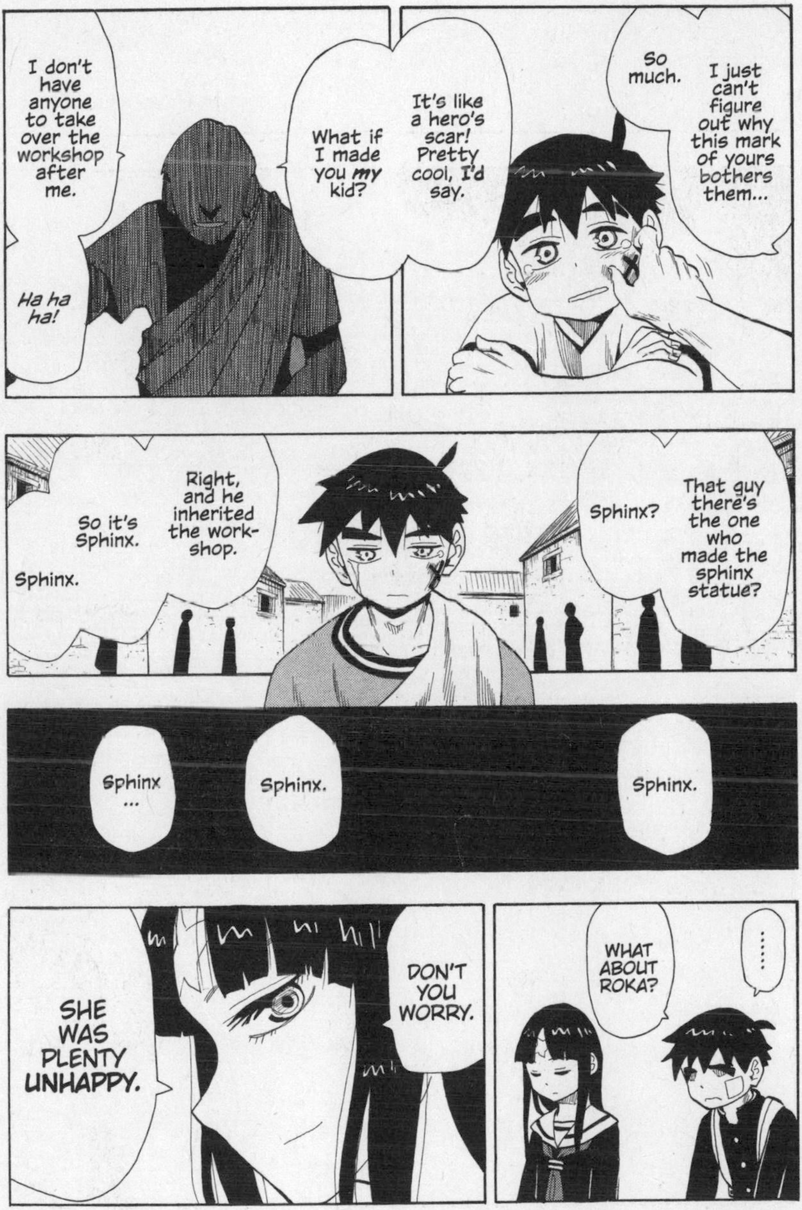
I just can't figure out why this mark of yours bothers them...
So much.
It's like a hero's scar! Pretty cool, I'd say.
What if I made you *my* kid?
I don't have anyone to take over the workshop after me.
Ha ha ha!
That guy there's the one who made the sphinx statue?
Sphinx?
Right, and he inherited the work-shop.
So it's Sphinx.
Sphinx.
Sphinx.
Sphinx.
Sphinx ...
......
WHAT ABOUT ROKA?
DON'T YOU WORRY.
SHE WAS PLENTY **UNHAPPY.**

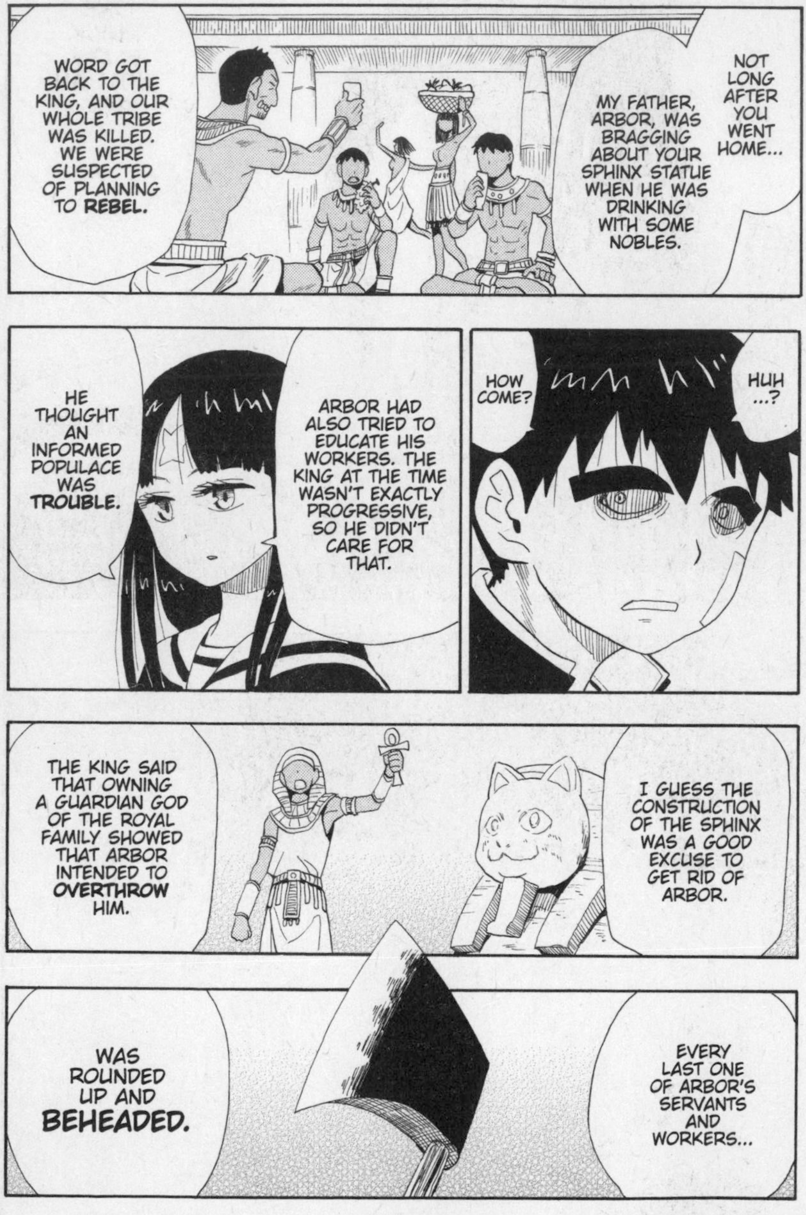
NOT LONG AFTER YOU WENT HOME...
MY FATHER, ARBOR, WAS BRAGGING ABOUT YOUR SPHINX STATUE WHEN HE WAS DRINKING WITH SOME NOBLES.
WORD GOT BACK TO THE KING, AND OUR WHOLE TRIBE WAS KILLED. WE WERE SUSPECTED OF PLANNING TO **REBEL.**
HUH ...?
HOW COME?
ARBOR HAD ALSO TRIED TO EDUCATE HIS WORKERS. THE KING AT THE TIME WASN'T EXACTLY PROGRESSIVE, SO HE DIDN'T CARE FOR THAT.
HE THOUGHT AN INFORMED POPULACE WAS **TROUBLE.**
I GUESS THE CONSTRUCTION OF THE SPHINX WAS A GOOD EXCUSE TO GET RID OF ARBOR.
THE KING SAID THAT OWNING A GUARDIAN GOD OF THE ROYAL FAMILY SHOWED THAT ARBOR INTENDED TO **OVERTHROW** HIM.
EVERY LAST ONE OF ARBOR'S SERVANTS AND WORKERS...
WAS ROUNDED UP AND **BEHEADED.**

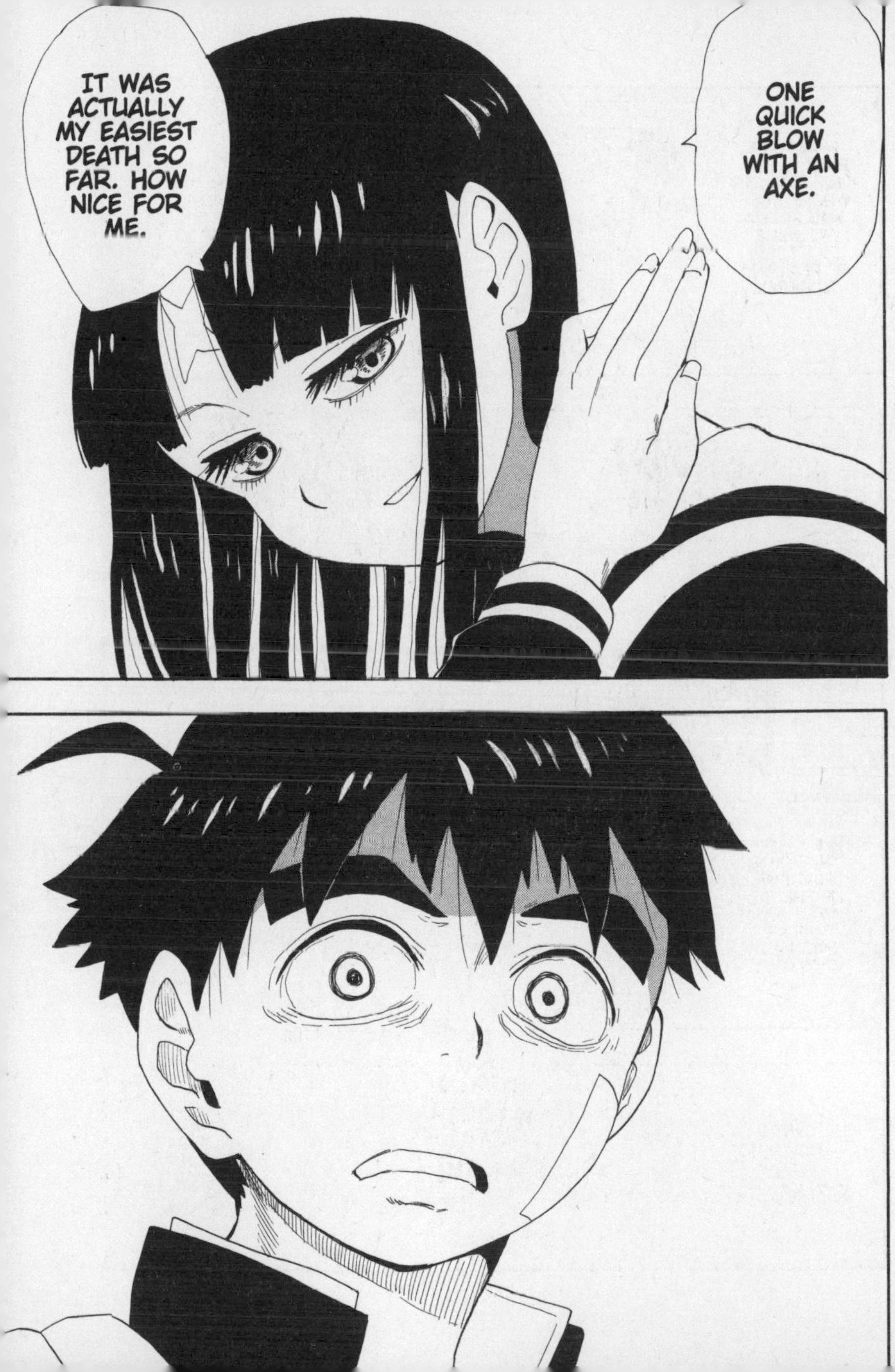
ONE QUICK BLOW WITH AN AXE.
IT WAS ACTUALLY MY EASIEST DEATH SO FAR. HOW NICE FOR ME.

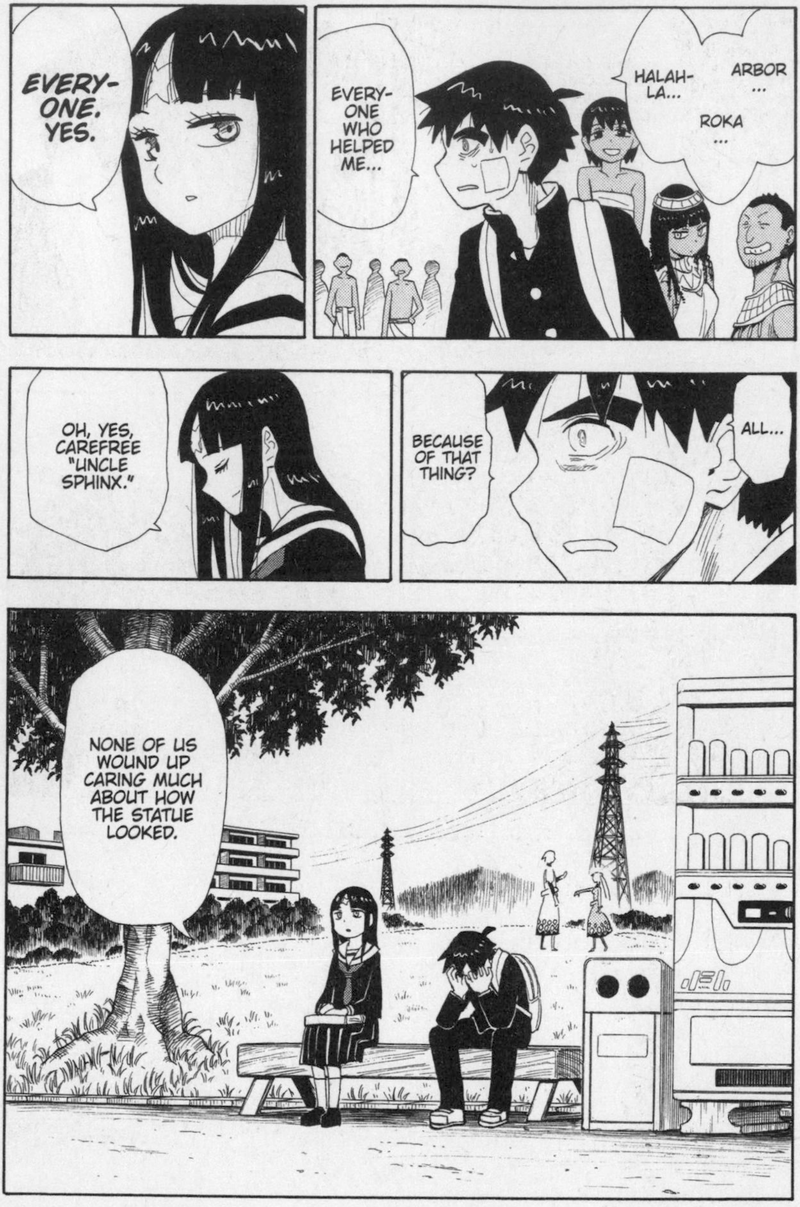
HALAH-LA... ARBOR... ROKA...
EVERY-ONE WHO HELPED ME...
EVERY-ONE. YES.
ALL...
BECAUSE OF THAT THING?
OH, YES, CAREFREE "UNCLE SPHINX."
NONE OF US WOUND UP CARING MUCH ABOUT HOW THE STATUE LOOKED.

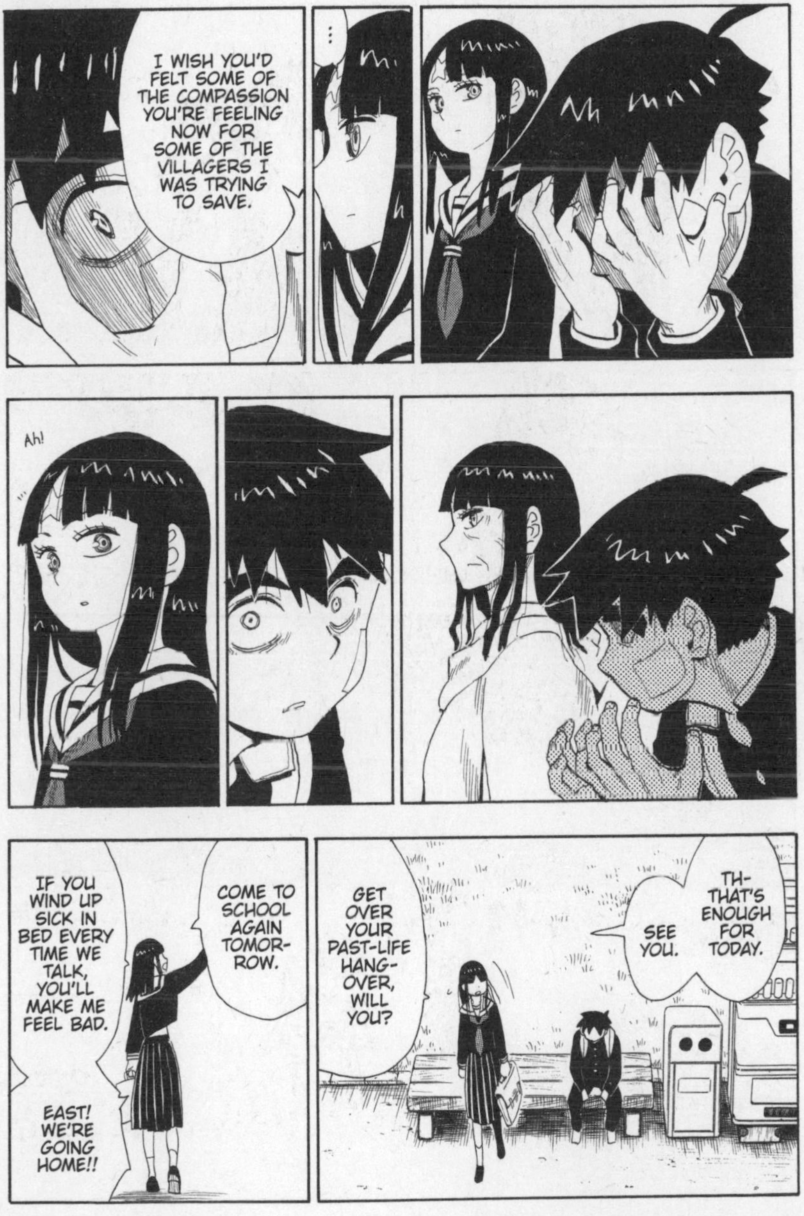
...
I WISH YOU'D FELT SOME OF THE COMPASSION YOU'RE FEELING NOW FOR SOME OF THE VILLAGERS I WAS TRYING TO SAVE.
Ah!
TH-THAT'S ENOUGH FOR TODAY.
SEE YOU.
GET OVER YOUR PAST-LIFE HANG-OVER, WILL YOU?
COME TO SCHOOL AGAIN TOMOR-ROW.
IF YOU WIND UP SICK IN BED EVERY TIME WE TALK, YOU'LL MAKE ME FEEL BAD.
EAST! WE'RE GOING HOME!!

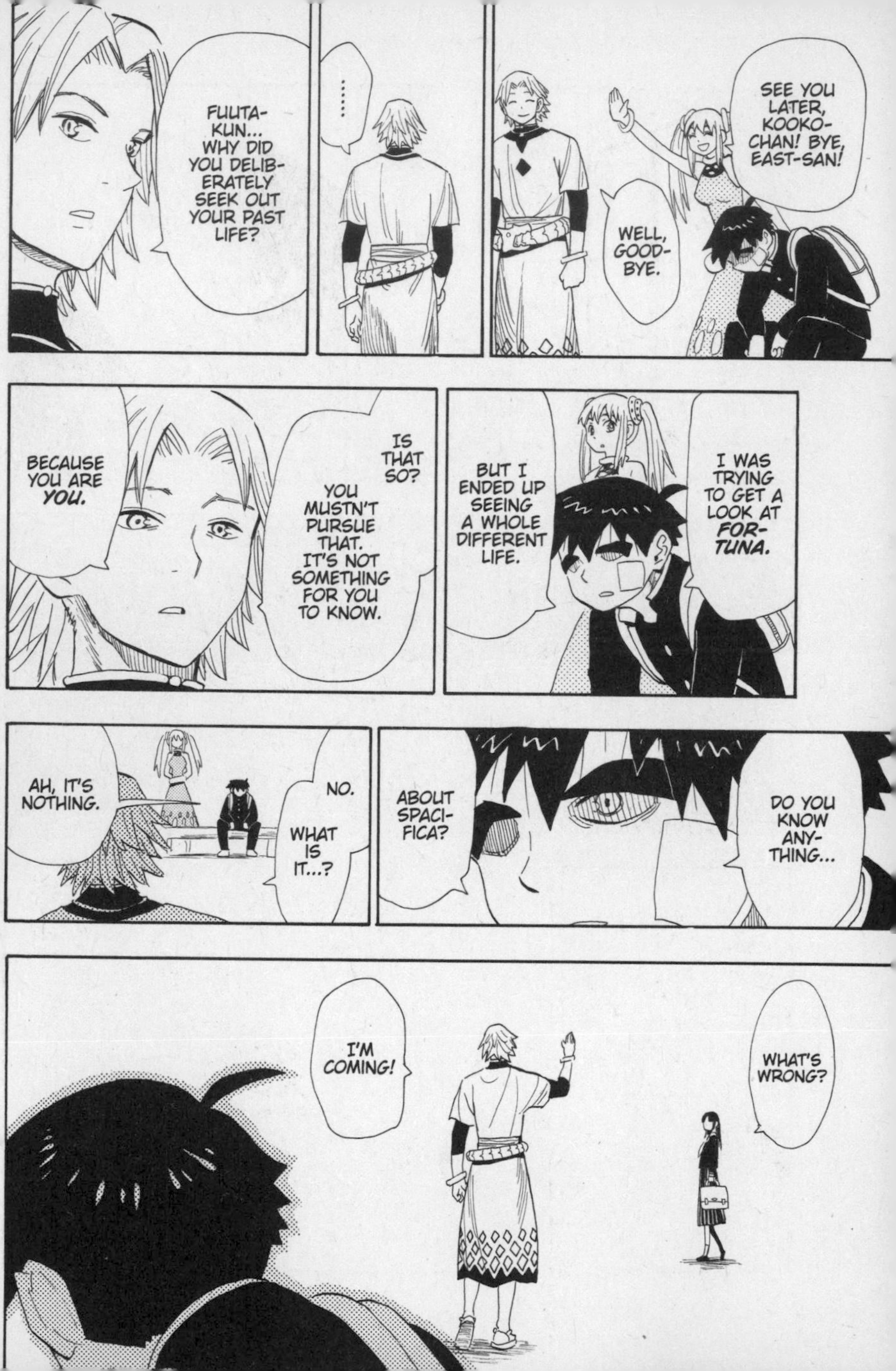
SEE YOU LATER, KOOKO-CHAN! BYE, EAST-SAN!
WELL, GOOD-BYE.
......
FUUTA-KUN... WHY DID YOU DELIBERATELY SEEK OUT YOUR PAST LIFE?
I WAS TRYING TO GET A LOOK AT *FORTUNA.*
BUT I ENDED UP SEEING A WHOLE DIFFERENT LIFE.
IS THAT SO?
YOU MUSTN'T PURSUE THAT. IT'S NOT SOMETHING FOR YOU TO KNOW.
BECAUSE YOU ARE *YOU.*
DO YOU KNOW ANYTHING...
ABOUT SPACIFICA?
NO.
WHAT IS IT...?
AH, IT'S NOTHING.
WHAT'S WRONG?
I'M COMING!

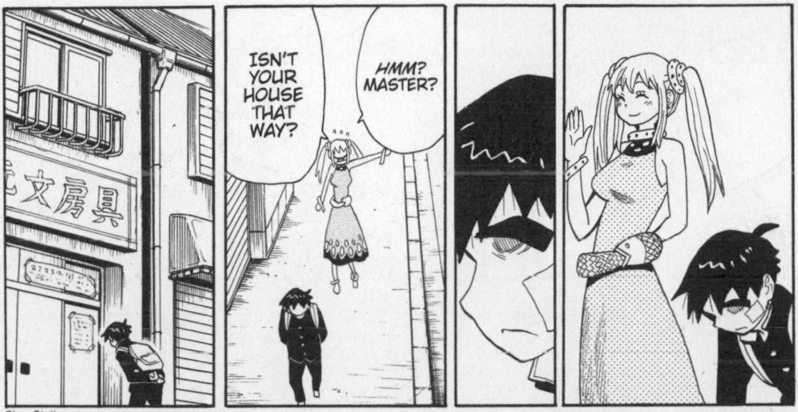
HMM? MASTER?
ISN'T YOUR HOUSE THAT WAY?

Sign: Stationery

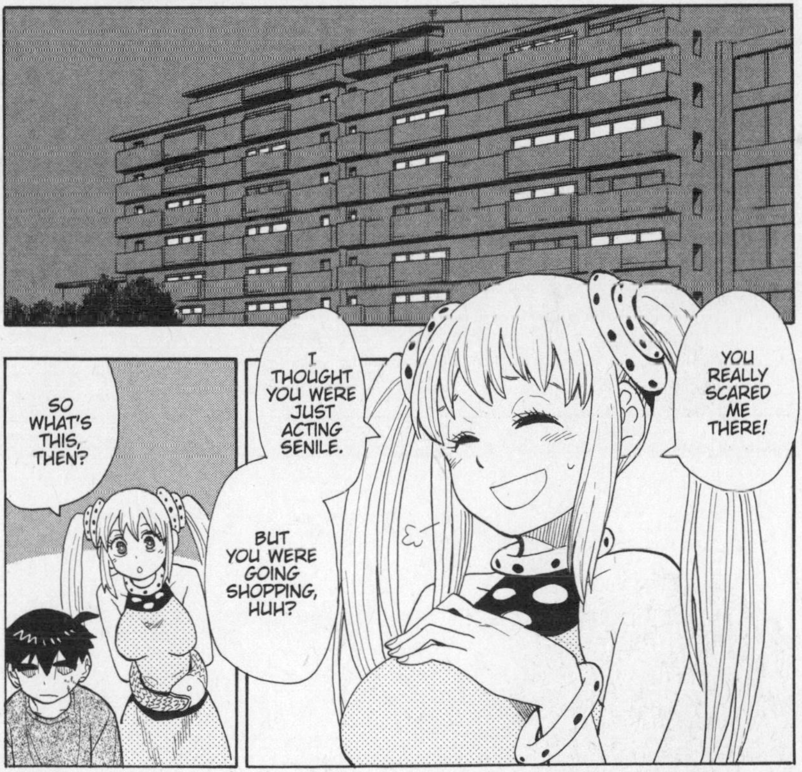
YOU REALLY SCARED ME THERE!
I THOUGHT YOU WERE JUST ACTING SENILE.
BUT YOU WERE GOING SHOPPING, HUH?
SO WHAT'S THIS, THEN?

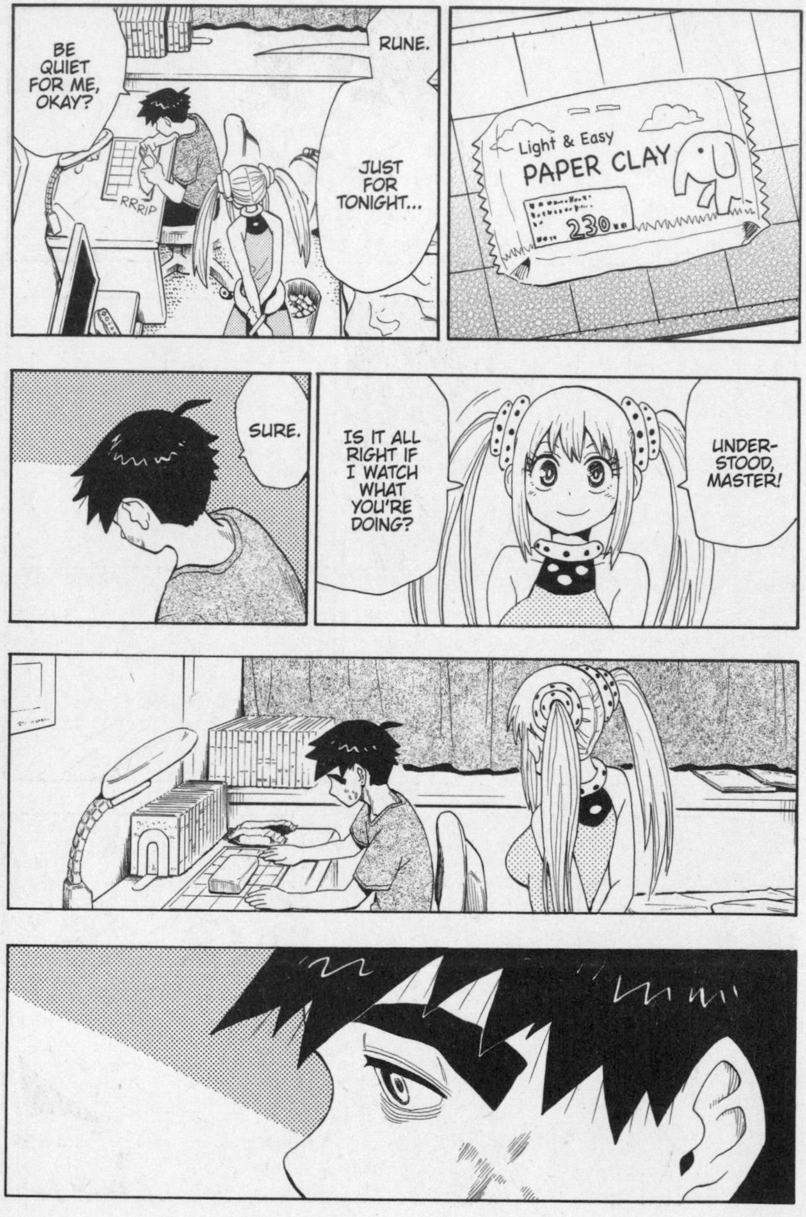
Light & Easy
PAPER CLAY
230
RUNE.
JUST FOR TONIGHT...
BE QUIET FOR ME, OKAY?
RRRIP
UNDER-STOOD, MASTER!
IS IT ALL RIGHT IF I WATCH WHAT YOU'RE DOING?
SURE.

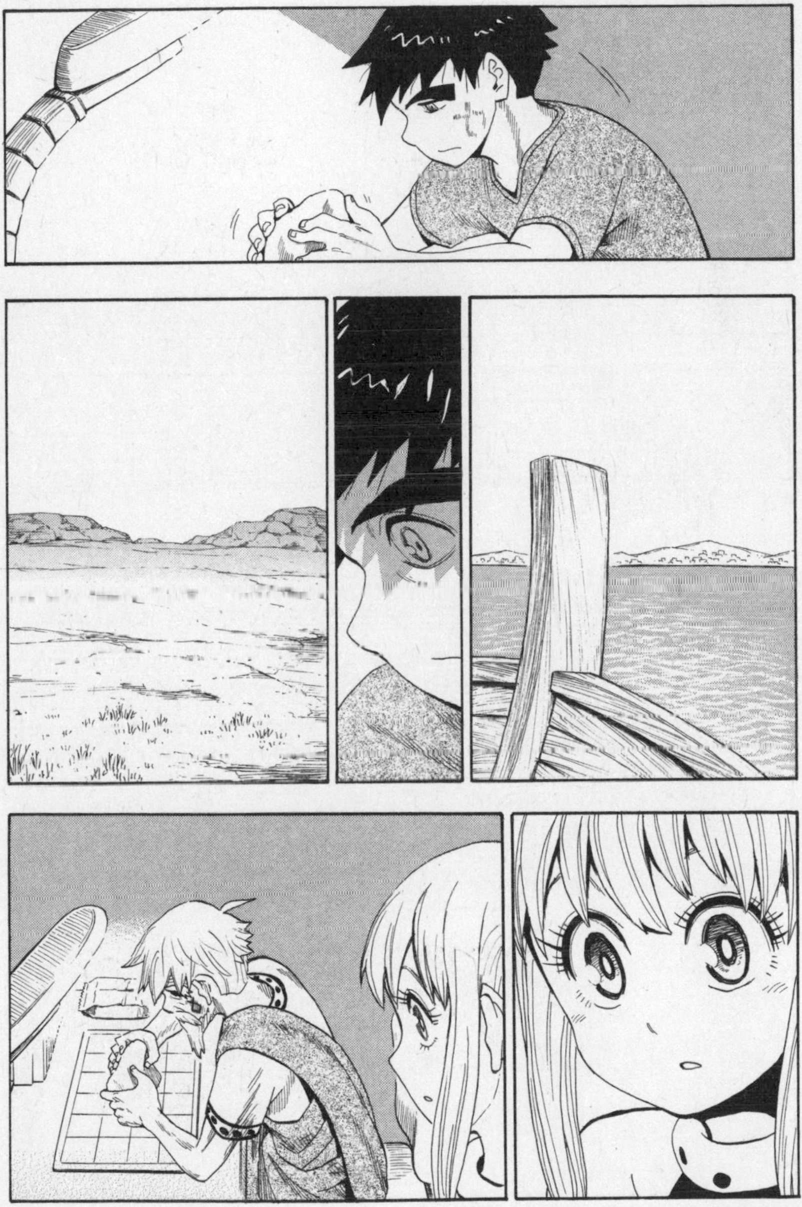

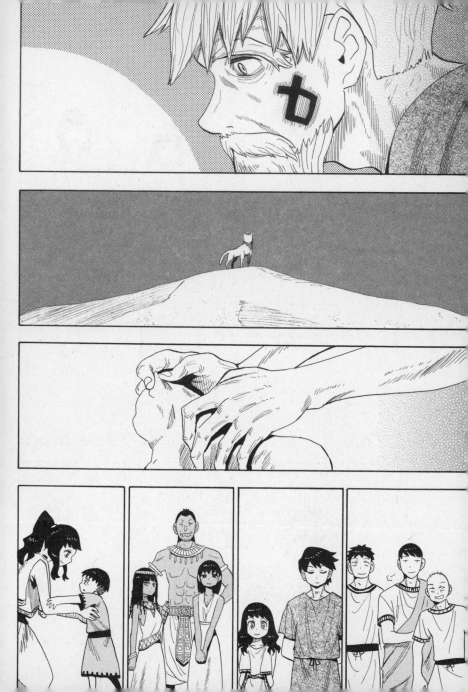

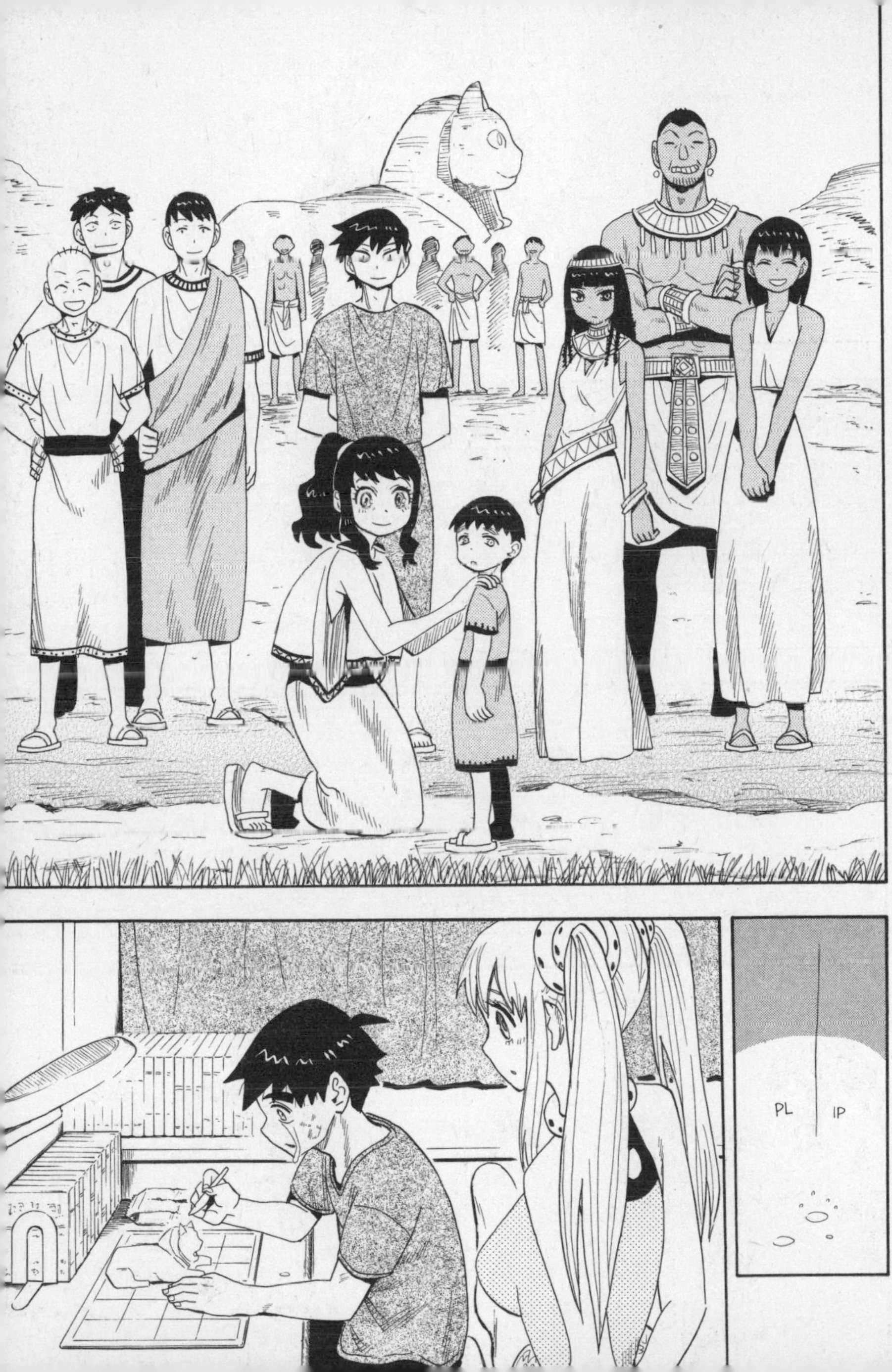
PL IP

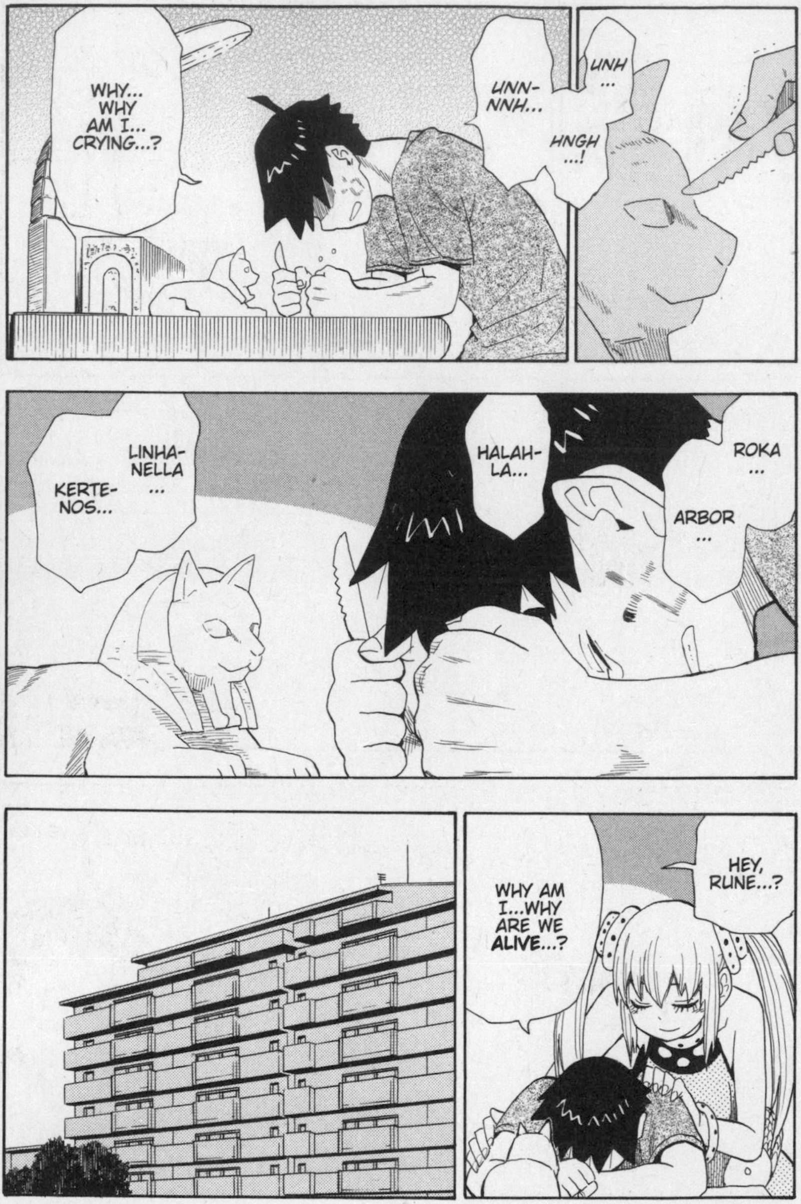
UNH...
UNN-NNH...
HNGH...!
WHY... WHY AM I... CRYING...?
ROKA...
ARBOR...
HALAH-LA...
LINHA-NELLA...
KERTE-NOS...
HEY, RUNE...?
WHY AM I...WHY ARE WE ALIVE...?

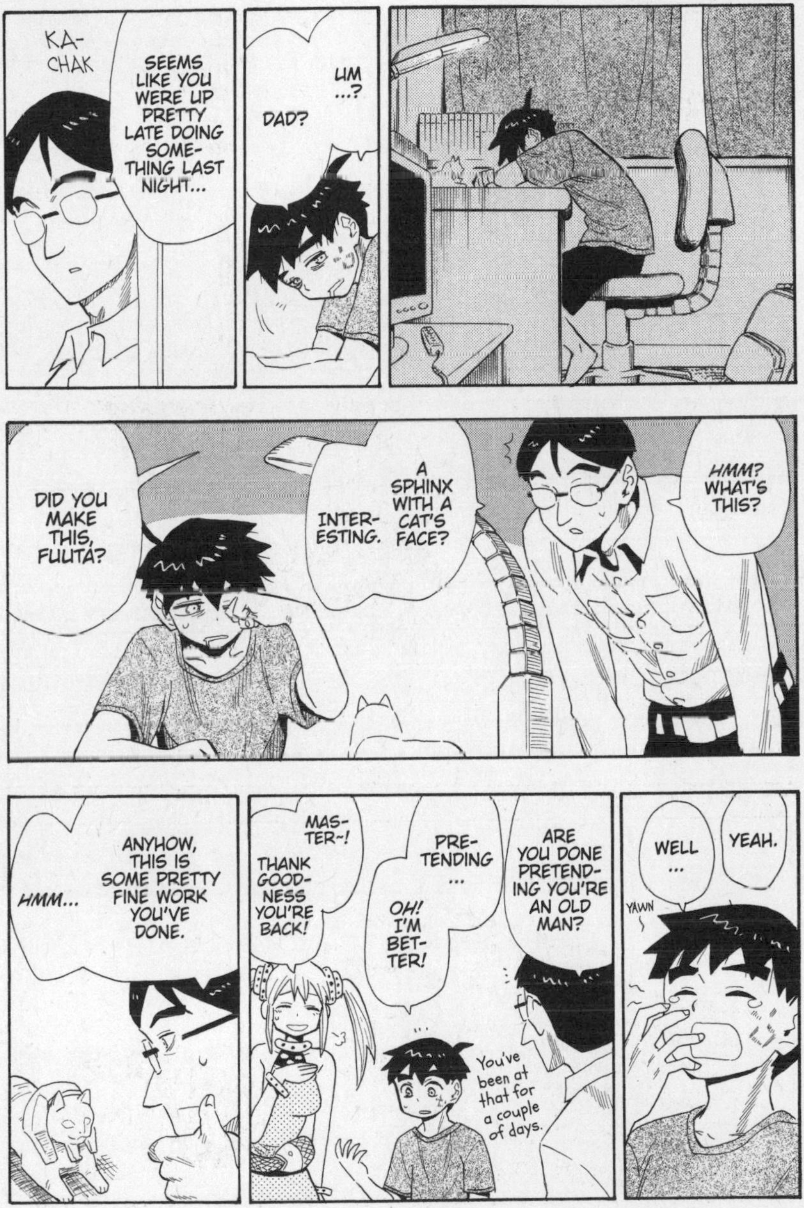
UM ...?
DAD?
KA-CHAK
SEEMS LIKE YOU WERE UP PRETTY LATE DOING SOME-THING LAST NIGHT...
HMM? WHAT'S THIS?
A SPHINX WITH A CAT'S FACE?
INTER-ESTING.
DID YOU MAKE THIS, FUUTA?
YEAH.
WELL ...
YAWN
ARE YOU DONE PRETEND-ING YOU'RE AN OLD MAN?
PRE-TENDING ...
OH! I'M BET-TER!
MAS-TER~!
THANK GOOD-NESS YOU'RE BACK!
You've been at that for a couple of days.
ANYHOW, THIS IS SOME PRETTY FINE WORK YOU'VE DONE.
HMM...

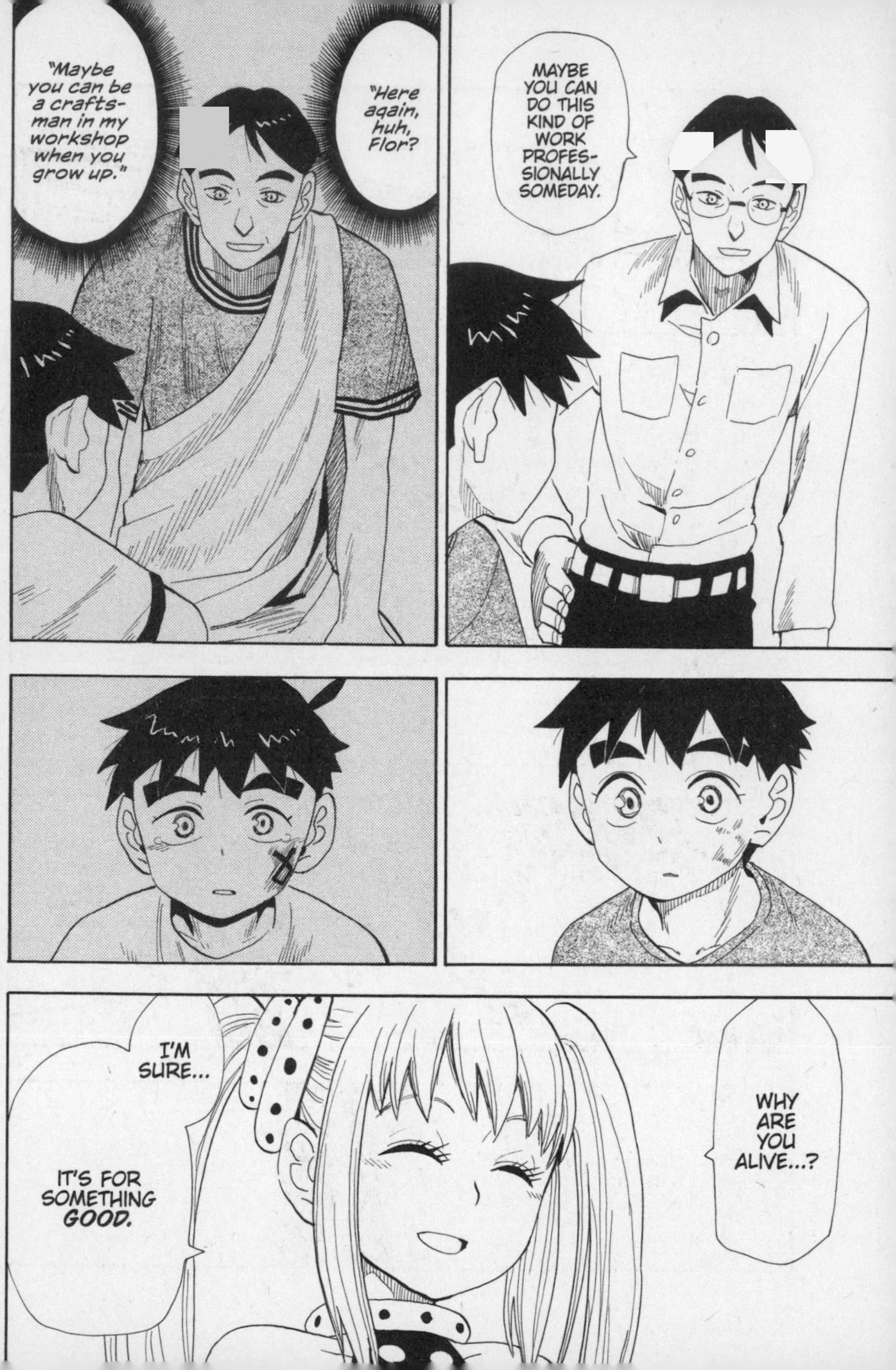
MAYBE YOU CAN DO THIS KIND OF WORK PROFES-SIONALLY SOMEDAY.
"Here again, huh, Flor?
"Maybe you can be a crafts-man in my workshop when you grow up."
WHY ARE YOU ALIVE...?
I'M SURE...
IT'S FOR SOMETHING GOOD.

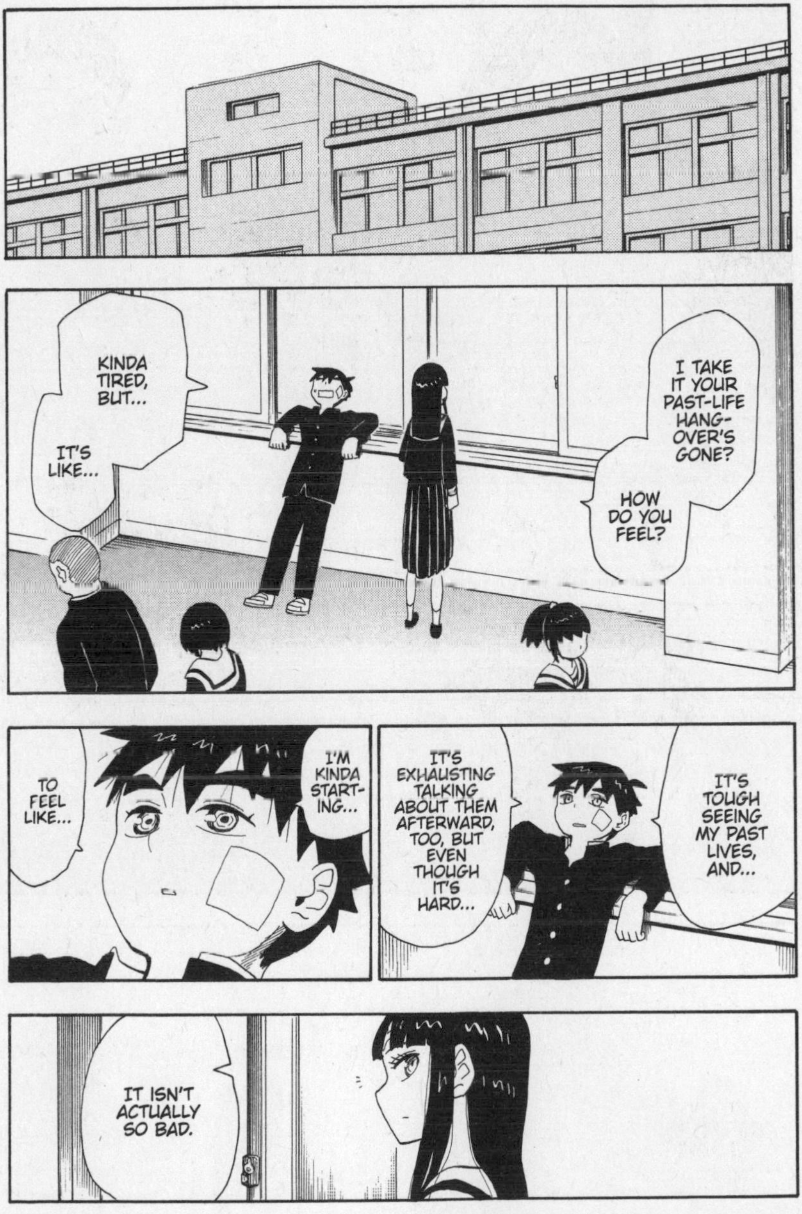
I TAKE IT YOUR PAST-LIFE HANG-OVER'S GONE?
HOW DO YOU FEEL?
KINDA TIRED, BUT...
IT'S LIKE...
IT'S TOUGH SEEING MY PAST LIVES, AND...
IT'S EXHAUSTING TALKING ABOUT THEM AFTERWARD, TOO, BUT EVEN THOUGH IT'S HARD...
I'M KINDA STARTING...
TO FEEL LIKE...
IT ISN'T ACTUALLY SO BAD.

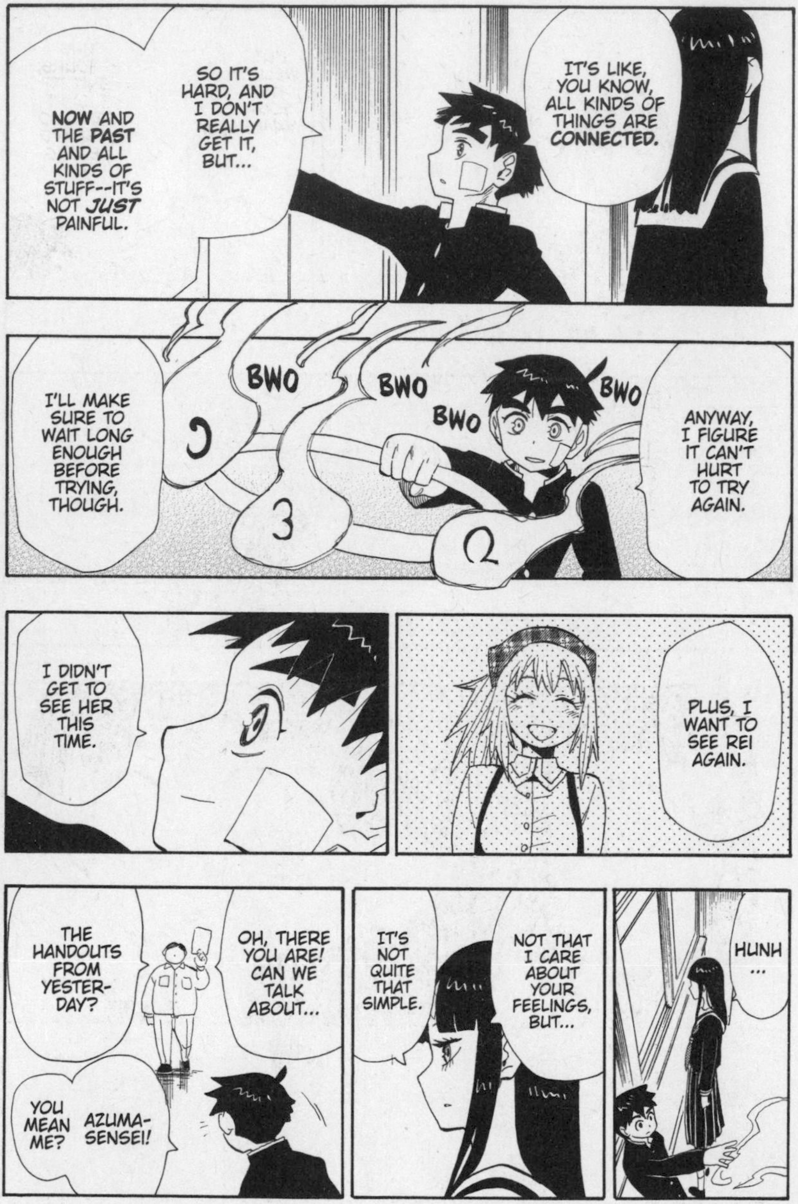
IT'S LIKE, YOU KNOW, ALL KINDS OF THINGS ARE CONNECTED.
SO IT'S HARD, AND I DON'T REALLY GET IT, BUT...
NOW AND THE PAST AND ALL KINDS OF STUFF--IT'S NOT JUST PAINFUL.
ANYWAY, I FIGURE IT CAN'T HURT TO TRY AGAIN.
BWO
BWO
BWO
BWO
I'LL MAKE SURE TO WAIT LONG ENOUGH BEFORE TRYING, THOUGH.
PLUS, I WANT TO SEE REI AGAIN.
I DIDN'T GET TO SEE HER THIS TIME.
HUNH...
NOT THAT I CARE ABOUT YOUR FEELINGS, BUT...
IT'S NOT QUITE THAT SIMPLE.
OH, THERE YOU ARE! CAN WE TALK ABOUT...
THE HANDOUTS FROM YESTER-DAY?
AZUMA-SENSEI!
YOU MEAN ME?

THIS IS YOURS, ISN'T IT? I CAN'T SEE WHO ELSE IT'D BELONG TO.
BUT, WELL... IT'S YOUR *NAME.*
WHAT DOES THIS SAY...?
OH! RIGHT! IT'S NOT FLOR.
I GOT IT WRONG. I'M VA--
VAN... NO, NOT VAN. FO--
THAT'S NOT IT...
......
THIS SAYS "FLOR," THEN?
......
...
WHAT'S THE MATTER, OKEYA-KUN?
OKE-- *OH!* RIGHT, RIGHT. OKEYA FUUTA!!
I SPACED OUT A LITTLE. *HA HA HA!*

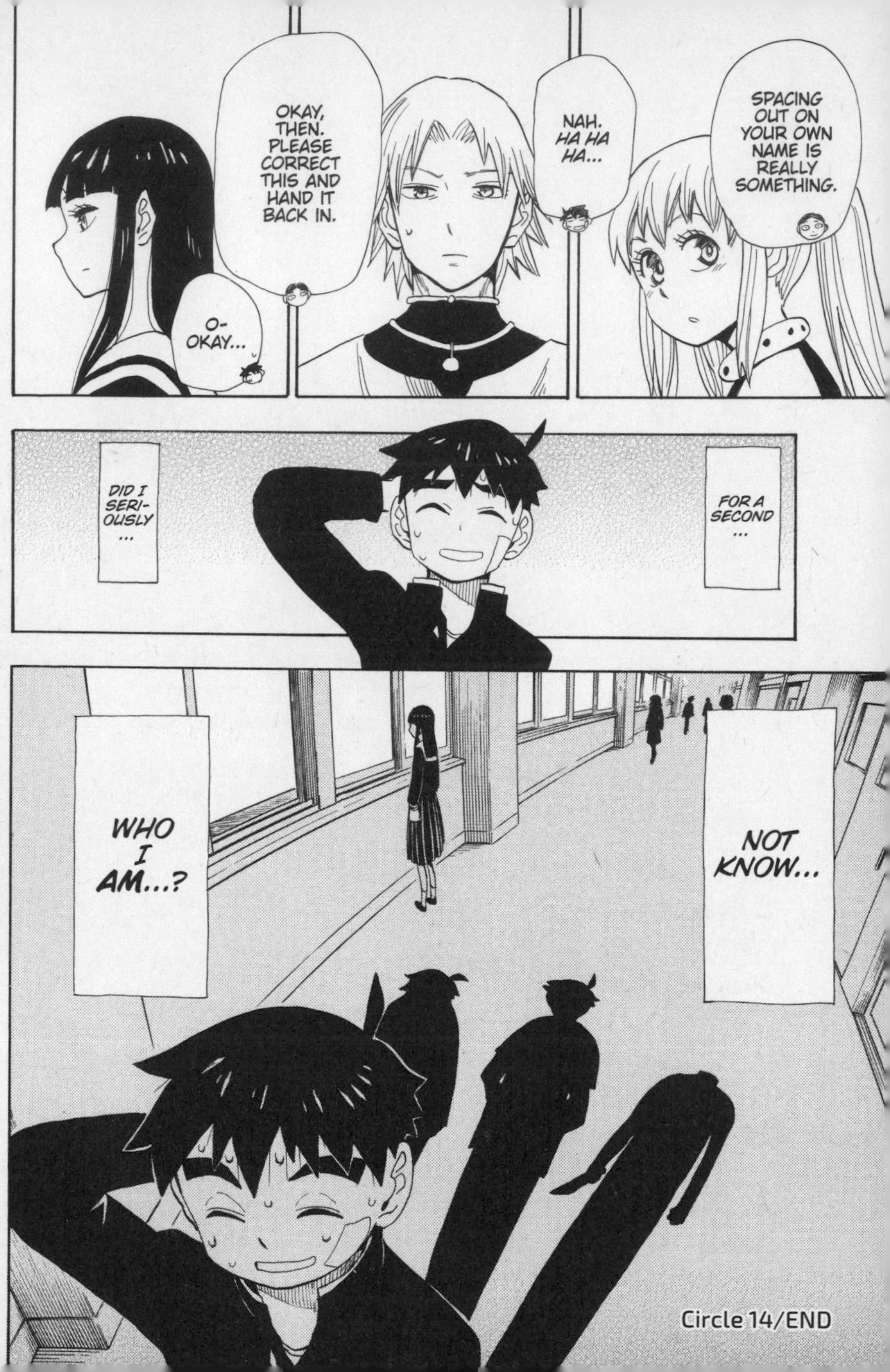
SPACING OUT ON YOUR OWN NAME IS REALLY SOMETHING.
NAH. HA HA HA...
OKAY, THEN. PLEASE CORRECT THIS AND HAND IT BACK IN.
O-OKAY...
FOR A SECOND...
DID I SERI-OUSLY...
NOT KNOW...
WHO I AM...?

Circle 14/END

Volume 2

Production staff
Jueru Choden
Hitoshi Usui
Akira Sagami

Title logo/Cover design
Eiichi Hagiwara

Supervising editor
Takehiro Sumi

VOL.2

story and art by **SATOSHI MIZUKAMI**

TRANSLATION
Jocelyne Allen

ADAPTATION
Ysabet Reinhardt MacFarlane

LETTERING AND LAYOUT
Lys Blakeslee

COVER DESIGN
Nicky Lim

PROOFREADER
Shanti Whitesides
Julia Kinsman

ASSISTANT EDITOR
Jenn Grunigen

PRODUCTION ASSISTANT
CK Russell

PRODUCTION MANAGER
Lissa Pattillo

EDITOR-IN-CHIEF
Adam Arnold

PUBLISHER
Jason DeAngelis

SPIRIT CIRCLE VOL. 2
© Satoshi Mizukami 2012
Originally published in Japan in 2015 by SHONENGAHOSHA Co., Ltd., Tokyo.
English translation rights arranged through TOHAN CORPORATION, Tokyo.

Seven Seas books may be purchased in bulk for promotional, educational, or
business use. Please contact your local bookseller or the Macmillan Corporate
and Premium Sales Department at 1-800-221-7945, extension 5442, or by
e-mail at MacmillanSpecialMarkets@macmillan.com.

Seven Seas and the Seven Seas logo are trademarks of
Seven Seas Entertainment, LLC. All rights reserved.

ISBN: 978-1-626926-80-6

Printed in Canada

First Printing: January 2018

10 9 8 7 6 5 4 3 2 1

FOLLOW US ONLINE: *www.gomanga.com*

READING DIRECTIONS

This book reads from *right to left*, Japanese style.
If this is your first time reading manga, you start
reading from the top right panel on each page and
take it from there. If you get lost, just follow the
numbered diagram here. It may seem backwards at
first, but you'll get the hang of it! Have fun!!

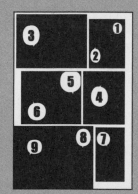